CIVIL WAR

MARCUS ANNAEUS LUCANUS (A.D. 39–65) was the nephew of the philosopher Seneca and close friend of the young emperor Nero, until a poetic rivalry and possibly political differences led to their falling out and Lucan being banned from both reciting his poetry in public and pleading in the law courts. He was a prolific and popular poet, but his only work to survive is his *Civil War*, a trenchantly anti-Caesarean epic about the fateful struggle between the rival leaders Julius Caesar and Pompey the Great, which ended in disaster for the Roman Senate at Pharsalus in 48 B.C., the battle which forms the poem's dramatic climax. In A.D. 65, after the great fire had ravaged Rome and with much discontent against Nero simmering across the empire, Lucan joined the Pisonian conspiracy to assassinate the emperor, which failed and resulted in the execution by forced suicide of many of those involved. Along with his uncle, the author Petronius, and many other prominent Romans, Lucan took his own life, reputedly dying while reciting defiant verses from his epic. Since antiquity Lucan's poem has been read as part of the classical canon, alongside the works of Virgil and Ovid. Its influence on the literary tradition from medieval to modern times is considerable, while Lucan's death created a legacy of literary-political martyrdom that fired the imagination of revolutionary thinkers from the Renaissance to the many revolutions of the eighteenth and nineteenth centuries.

MATTHEW FOX studied Classical Languages and Literature at the University of Oregon and earned his Ph.D. in Comparative Literature and Classics at Princeton. He has taught classics, anthropology, humanities, and writing at Princeton, St. Peter's College (NJ), Deep Springs College (CA), where he held the Robert B. Aird Chair in Humanities, and Rutgers University, and now teaches at Whitman College (WA). His research focuses on the classical epic tradition and ancient cultures of poetic and musical performance.

ETHAN ADAMS received his Ph.D. in Classics at the University of Washington. He has taught at his alma mater, the College of the

Holy Cross in Massachusetts, at the Intercollegiate Center for Classical Studies in Rome, and at Loyola Marymount University in Los Angeles. His research interests are Latin epic poetry, particularly Ovid, and ancient Roman topography.

LUCAN

Civil War

Translated by
MATTHEW FOX

Introduction and Notes by
MATTHEW FOX *and* ETHAN ADAMS

PENGUIN BOOKS

PENGUIN BOOKS

Published by the Penguin Group

Penguin Group (USA) Inc., 375 Hudson Street,
New York, New York 10014, U.S.A.
Penguin Group (Canada), 90 Eglinton Avenue East, Suite 700, Toronto,
Ontario, Canada M4P 2Y3 (a division of Pearson Penguin Canada Inc.)
Penguin Books Ltd, 80 Strand, London WC2R 0RL, England
Penguin Ireland, 25 St Stephen's Green, Dublin 2,
Ireland (a division of Penguin Books Ltd)
Penguin Group (Australia), 250 Camberwell Road,
Camberwell, Victoria 3124, Australia
(a division of Pearson Australia Group Pty Ltd)
Penguin Books India Pvt Ltd, 11 Community Centre,
Panchsheel Park, New Delhi - 110 017, India
Penguin Group (NZ), 67 Apollo Drive, Rosedale, Auckland 0632,
New Zealand (a division of Pearson New Zealand Ltd)
Penguin Books (South Africa) (Pty) Ltd, 24 Sturdee Avenue,
Rosebank, Johannesburg 2196, South Africa

Penguin Books Ltd, Registered Offices:
80 Strand, London WC2R 0RL, England

This translation first published in Penguin Books 2012

3 5 7 9 10 8 6 4 2

Translation copyright © Matthew Fox, 2012
Introduction and notes copyright © Matthew Fox and Ethan T. Adams, 2012
All rights reserved

Map illustration: Ancient World Mapping Center, University of North Carolina, Chapel Hill

LIBRARY OF CONGRESS CATALOGING IN PUBLICATION DATA
Lucan, 39–65.
[Pharsalia. English]
Civil war / Lucan ; translated by Matthew Fox ; introduction and notes
by Matthew Fox and Ethan Adams.
p. cm.—(Penguin classics)
Includes bibliographical references.
ISBN 978-0-14-310623-4
1. Epic poetry, Latin—Translations into English.   2. Pharsalus, Battle of, Farsala, Greece,
48 B.C.— Poetry.   3. Rome—History—Civil War, 49–45 B.C.—Poetry.   I. Fox, Matthew
(Matthew Aaron) II. Adams, Ethan. III. Title.
PA6479.E5F69 2012
873'.01—dc23   2011041074

Printed in the United States of America
Set in Sabon

LUBENS DEDICO
MERITO
R.F.

nec cinis exiguus
tantam conpescuit umbram
prosiluit busto

Contents

CIVIL WAR

Preface

This new translation of Lucan aims to bring before a wider modern audience a Latin classic that has deeply influenced the literary and historical tradition since it was written. The project has been a collaborative effort, with intensive work sessions, reviewing the text and writing or drafting notes, spread over several summers. I am largely responsible for the translation, but Ethan Adams and I vigorously reviewed Books One through Six together, a rewarding process that, unfortunately, our busy schedules prevented us from continuing for the last four books, and instead we had to fall back on e-mail exchanges. We both contributed to the notes and introduction, and Adams has translated and annotated Petronius' *Civil War* parody in the appendix.

The following people have helped along the way in some form or other and deserve thanks: T. Corey Brennan, Tom Figueira, Mark DeStephano, Bill Thayer, Andrew Smith, and Ross and Kay Peterson; Michael Millman, Lorie Napolitano, and Elda Rotor at Penguin, for patience and assistance; Ilaria Marchesi for friendship and constant encouragement. The thirty-one undergraduate students of my spring 2009 Latin Poetry course at Rutgers University kindly and eagerly test-drove the translation, and supplied five weeks of invigorating discussion of Lucan and Caesar that carried me through review and revisions. Elaine Fantham first shared Lucan with me and graciously read the first rough drafts of portions long ago. Denis Feeney and Simone Marchesi of Princeton each kindly read and offered helpful criticisms on the introduction. Beena Kamlani has read, and helped rework as necessary, the entire manuscript with diligence and great skill. The participants at the conference on the civil war in Roman history and literature, held at Amherst College in the fall of 2008, offered rich and timely food for thought. Elizabeth Robinson, Brian Turner, and Richard Talbert of the Ancient World Mapping Center at UNC–Chapel Hill courteously took on the task of preparing the handsome map. A whole phalanx of scholars, critics, and historians have also contributed through their works to the making of this book, and the Further Reading list may serve doubly to acknowledge some, but by no means all, of their worthy labors. My hearty appreciation goes also to Ethan Adams for sharing the march through Lucan's fields, for his command of Latin poetry, and for the rollicking hours spent together enjoying the solemn absurdities of Lucan's vision and trying to capture it in worthy English.

To my parents, and to Dianna Shea, for their selfless love and support over the years, a formal bow of gratitude is long overdue. And my wife, Kathleen Shea, has sacrificed much free time and sleep watching our two children in order to give me breathing space to devote to Lucan, for which I can't possibly thank her enough.

Finally, without the bountiful support and superlative example of Robert Fagles, this translation would not have seen the light of day. Among many other concrete instances of help, he found funds to pay for the retrieval of the first four books from a crashed hard drive, which foolishly I had failed to back up. This volume is dedicated, deservedly and gratefully, to his memory.

—M.F.

Ethan Adams would like to thank Stephen Hinds, Catherine Connors, and Alain Gowing for their guidance and advice. He would also like to express his gratitude to his colleagues Matthew Dillon, William Fulco, and Katerina Zacharia for their enthusiastic support over the last several years. The following have also shared advice and friendship: Wayne Rupp, Eric Dugdale, Spencer Cole, Chris Chinn, Sean Easton, Marco Zangari, John Chesley, and Chiara Sulprizio. His parents and family deserve his highest thanks for their many years of patience and help. Finally, highest praise goes to Matthew Fox for being an exemplary co-conspirator, host, reader, critic, and friend. To Matt, Kate, and the girls: Thank you.

—E.A.

Introduction

In the first century BC, the Roman Republic collapsed in spectacular violence. Few literary works have had a deeper or more lasting impact on how later generations would imagine those historic spectacles than Lucan's *Bellum Civile*. Written more than a century after the civil war battles that it narrates, it is an epic that transmutes history into myth, and historical actors into haunting literary characters. But this is a poem that also aims at direct political engagement. For this reason, *Civil War* tends to explode tidy conceptual walls between history, literature, and politics, between art and life, fiction and fact. Its rhetoric aims at what we would call regime change, and Lucan died, tragically young, backing a failed coup d'état, the botched Pisonian conspiracy against the emperor Nero in AD 65. The poem suffered too, since Lucan left it unfinished when he committed forced suicide at the age of twenty-five.

The truncated text fits, if unintentionally, the poem's fragmented aesthetics. For Lucan's is a world in shambles, crumbling physically, ravaged morally, and sifted from the wreckage of long civil disorders. Sulla, Marius, Cinna, Sertorius, Catiline, Pompey, Caesar, each left his mark in blood: Pharsalus was two generations or more in the making. Outside the poem, still to come, were Brutus and Cassius, Antony and Cleopatra, Sextus Pompey and Octavian (soon Augustus) in the forties and thirties BC. Only then came some peace and restored order under the new autocracy that Augustus forged. Like all ancient epics, *Civil War* tells a foundation story: how generations of Roman civil strife laid waste the world, but upon this rubble the foundation was laid for the peaceful—and forcibly pacified—Principate of the Caesars. This is the *literal* thrust of the disputed "praise of Nero": "the crimes, the guilt" of civil wars "are pleasing" if they were necessary "to bring forth Nero" (1.36–48). One implication: Neronian Rome is a world so corrupt that collective historical guilt has become a source of genuine pleasure. Virgil and Horace had of course praised Augustus while shedding tears of regret for civil violence; but no Augustan poet had ever so brazenly collapsed his pathos for civil wars into glorification of Augustus' peace.

Lucan is more explicit and insistent than his poetic predecessors in refusing to cast the civil wars as an aberration of history, a past evil best left unspoken (*nefas*) and, in effect, unremembered. To him, such waves of violence lie in the very order (or chaos) of things, and given the nature of the world and man they will replay over and again, a "hateful sequence" of Fortune and Fate, chance and doom. But things need not be so bleak; so long as a courageous, principled few, like a Cato or Brutus, choose to risk their lives for a higher cause than personal interest, and take a valorous stand against the tyrant for liberty and the "commonwealth" (*res publica*), there will be hope, and heroism. This tragic clash, between political principles and power gained on the battlefield, between hope and history, has become the very essence of what we mean by and expect from "epic" stories—and with no small debt to Lucan.

Suitably for a poem about civil conflict, *Civil War* is full of both dissident and dissonant voices. In the midst of battles we hear longings for peace, strains of hope for a better way, and urgent calls for moral accountability and personal virtue. But sounding beneath this idealism are tones of cynical despair, occasioned most by the (hindsight) historical inevitability of Caesar's victory, though this political despair also tends to reverberate into cosmic, existential desperation. Above all, the primary narrator's moods and voices vary in their engagements and detachments, so that the plural of the opening "we sing" (*canimus*) seems appropriate. This is not just the "royal we" of a sovereign narrator, but perhaps of some other sort of collective: an unruly mob (an arena crowd?), a political faction (Roman senators?), or just the contrary voices inhabiting an individual's fractious subjectivity. A schizophrenic narrator, divided against and at war with himself, would suit perfectly the poem's chief subject: "how a powerful people / turned on its own heart its conquering hand" (1.2–3). Civil strife comes to rest, at last, in the self, and can end only in suicide. Desperation indeed!

MARCUS ANNAEUS LUCANUS

Two Senecas and singular Lucan
eloquent Corduba speaks of.

—MARTIAL 1.61.7–8

Details of the poet's life come from two brief ancient biographies transmitted with the text (by Suetonius and an obscure Vacca), from Tacitus' account of his death in *Annals* 15, and from various other references in contemporary and later authors. We are told that he was born in Corduba, Spain, on November 3, AD 39, and brought in his first year to Rome. Corduba was the chief administrative city of Hispania Baetica, the wealthy Roman province in southern Spain that willingly sided with Caesar in the civil war of 49 BC, when Pompey's commanders were making nuisances of themselves among the provincials; in 45 BC, when Pompey's sons made Baetica their base of resistance to Caesar, Corduba was the site of a large-scale slaughter in the aftermath of Munda. But under Augustus the city saw rebuilding, expansion, and the settlement of veterans. Lucan's grandfather, Lucius Annaeus Seneca the Elder, was born ca. 55–50 BC, to a Corduban family of equestrian status that prospered under Augustus' peace, for his three sons all rose to positions of power in the imperial administration: Novatus—later L. Junius Gallio by adoption— was proconsul of Achaea ca. AD 52 (according to Acts 18:12 he dismissed charges against Paul) and later suffect consul; Annaeus Mela, Lucan's father, served as an imperial procurator but seems to have avoided politics; and L. Annaeus Seneca the Younger was the famous Stoic philosopher, playwright, and tutor to young Nero, and later as his advisor exercised extensive political influence. From a young age Lucan must have known Nero, who was just two years older. The two may well have studied together and listened to lectures from Seneca.

Lucan lived a privileged life. He moved in the most elite circles of Roman society and his education was the best available. He studied literature, rhetoric, and philosophy with the Stoic scholar Annaeus Cornutus, whose Greek handbook on etymological and allegorical interpretations of mythology survives. Lucan must have taken eagerly to study of the poets, both Greek and Latin, for his epic everywhere displays a wide familiarity with them. He also would have trained in oratorical declamation, how to compose and deliver persuasive deliberations (*suasoriae*) and model forensic speeches (*controversiae*). These rhetorical exercises were studious elaborations on well-worn themes, recycling court cases, figures, and scenarios from the Greek and Roman past. Much detail about these rhetorical schools comes from the surviving works of the elder Seneca, who wrote for his sons what he remembered about famous orators and poets (such as Ovid) from his own day. Typical *suasoriae* addressed questions like "Should Alexander the Great sail the Ocean?" or "Should Cicero beg pardon from Antony?" Many of Lucan's speeches look like classic rhetorical deliberations (for example: Should Caesar cross the Rubicon? Should Massilia admit Caesar? Should Pompey, after Pharsalus, seek aid from Parthia or Alexandria?).

It was during such rhetorical training that Lucan would have learned to relive the main events of the late Republic and to feel deeply their pathos (or, in other moods, snicker at their pathetic bathos). Persius, another of Cornutus' students whose verse satires Lucan reportedly admired, recalls how in youth he was forced to learn the "lofty words of dying Cato," much praised by his teacher, and to recite them for his father and invited friends (*Sat.* 3.44–47). Lucan probably had similar formative experiences (perhaps even with Persius—and Nero himself), and his conflicted treatment of republican heroes such as Cato, Brutus, and Pompey reveals the extent to which his personality and moral outlook were molded by such histrionic speeches that resurrected past heroes and their exemplary circumstances. Moreover, the fact that Roman ruling-class youths spent their days praising, rehearsing the lives, and mouthing the dying words of "tyrannicides" like Brutus and hard-line political martyrs like Cato is an instructive token of the contentious political culture of Julio-Claudian Rome.

Lucan was just a baby when his grandfather Seneca died, and his uncle Seneca was exiled to Corsica by Claudius on charges of adultery with the emperor's niece (AD 41). When Agrippina replaced Messalina as empress, she had Seneca recalled (AD 49) to tutor her son Domitius, whom Claudius then adopted and gave the name Tiberius Claudius Nero Caesar. In AD 54 Claudius died and Nero, not yet seventeen, became emperor. For the first five years of his reign Seneca had sweeping influence over state affairs—until Nero came of age by murdering his mother. Around this time (AD 59) Nero, we are told, summoned Lucan back from studies in Athens to join his circle of friends, and awarded him an early quaestorship (giving entry into the Senate) and a position in the priestly college of augurs. As a quaestor he helped organize and stage gladiatorial games, reportedly to popular acclaim. For his augural duties he would have learned technical and theoretical minutiae of divination, the aspect of ancient religion that comes into sharpest relief in Bellum Civile.

Lucan's poetic talents were impressive, which accorded with, but apparently soon rankled, Nero's own poetic and musical ambitions. During the Neronia, the emperor's lavish arts festival of AD 60, he delivered a praise-poem to Nero (laudes Neronis) in Pompey's theater, receiving a victory crown; at the same time, or in another venue of poetry competition, Lucan delivered a poem on Orpheus. He gave public recitations of three books (presumably the first three) of Civil War, boasting of his rivalry with Virgil. But soon after, says Suetonius, Nero turned against him, abruptly calling a Senate meeting while Lucan was reciting. In the same account, Lucan then became more brazen and offensive in criticizing Nero, even ridiculing his poetry in public restrooms: while noisily relieving his bowels he quoted a line of Nero's, "you would think it was thundering underground." Their breach widened, and Nero banned Lucan from reciting poetry and from speaking in the law courts. This ban may have come as early as AD 62, around the time that Nero broke with Seneca, in pretended amicableness, and his extravagantly wealthy advisor retreated from public life into philosophical retirement (Tacitus, *Ann.* 14.51–6). As Tacitus tells it, Nero thereafter became more tyrannical, depraved, paranoid, and ruthless in suppressing opponents, real or imagined. As competent men fell, and administration of the empire suffered, real hatred of Nero rose among the ruling class and populace alike. It was in these years (AD 62–65) that Lucan composed the remainder of his *Civil War*, along with much other poetry that has not survived. He was married to Polla Argentaria, possibly related to the Greek declaimer Argentarius often cited by Seneca the Elder. Lucan's lost works included *Letters from Campania*: if their title plays on Ovid's exile letters *Ex Ponto*, it may be that he spent some of his time in quasi exile down in the luxury villas around the bay of Naples. In 62–63, war with Parthia erupted, ending in a brokered peace; Lucan's frequent, derisive references to the Parthians may reflect their prominence in news reports from the East.

Meanwhile, Nero had begun to devote himself to performing his poetry and songs on public stages, currying popular favor by satisfying his musical ambitions. Then in the summer of AD 64, amid an atmosphere of unceasing revelry and notorious debaucheries, a conflagration ravaged Rome over six days. The fire leveled whole city districts, destroying dozens of ancient shrines, temples, and public buildings along with their archives, treasures, and artworks. While restoring the city Nero took occasion to build himself the Golden Palace (*domus aurea*) and came under suspicion of arson. To quell widespread resentment, members of the obscure religious sect of Christians were rounded up as scapegoats and ostentatiously executed. The provinces were plundered to support rebuilding, and a general state of desperate panic seems to have spread through Italy, with wide reports of ill omens and portents for Nero (cf. Tac., *Ann.* 15.33–47). Lucan's lost works included a poem on the fire, which may have given voice to the arson charge (Statius says it told of "the wicked fires of a *guilty* master," *Silvae* 2.7.61). The persistent, foreboding image in Lucan's epic, of a world torn apart at the seams, is right in tune with the general tenor of emergency that Tacitus describes for AD 64–65.

It is little surprise, then, that a plot to assassinate Nero was hatched during this crisis, and all accounts of Lucan's life and the Pisonian conspiracy name him as a ringleader. Tacitus says that Seneca was now under virtual house arrest and ate nothing but wild fruit for fear of poison. So in addition to personal grievances and political opposition, Lucan's motives may have included family solidarity. Others of republican and Stoic sympathies would also have been outraged at this flagrant instance of political repression. Suetonius calls Lucan "almost the standard-bearer" of a plot with dozens of men and women, from senatorial, equestrian, and military families, either involved, aware, or later (rightly or wrongly) implicated. Nero was to be replaced as head of state by Gaius Calpurnius Piso; whether such a change of leadership would have "restored the republic" is a point made moot by the plot's failure and suppression. Events of AD 68–69, when civil war erupted and Nero fell, suggest that monarchy was now the most feasible political regime given the structural realities of the Roman Empire. But for Nero, the failed coup was the beginning of the end. In 66 the Jews of Judea rebelled against Rome, and in the city there were more plots, arrests, and eliminations. In early 68, Nero's own governors and armies began to defect, first in Gaul, then Spain; as rebellion and mutinies flared, Nero, sensing his doom, took his own life. The Julio-Claudian dynasty ended as it began, in civil war.

But Lucan did not live to see the civil war that his poem seems to advocate and/or predict. (And in any chronology, it is almost certain that parts of the epic were written as Lucan was plotting to kill Nero.) In mid-April 65, on the eve of action, the conspirators were betrayed, and a long, sordid season of executions, suicide banquets, exiles, and property confiscations followed (Tacitus, *Ann.* 15.53–16.21 spares no grim details). Seneca received the death sentence before his nephew, and Tacitus relates the claim that some may have planned to elevate him to power instead of Piso. The historian's account is quite biased against Lucan: he is presented as a cowardly turncoat, incriminating his mother and friends in desperate hopes of salvation. Whatever the truth, he soon followed his uncle's lead into voluntary death: on April 30, 65, he cut his veins. As his limbs chilled he recalled some lines of his on the death of a soldier and, quoting them (if from *Civil*

War, possibly 3.763–73, or more defiantly, from the death of Vul-
teius in Book Five), died. He was six months short of twenty-six
years old.

To the end poetry was his first and greatest love. Suetonius
says that before opening his veins he wrote instructions to his fa-
ther to correct some of his verses. But care for publishing his works
would soon have fallen to his widow, Polla, since his father, Mela,
also fell victim to Nero the next year. It is possible that Polla re-
married a wealthy literary Epicurean of Campania named Pollius
Felix.[1] What is certain is that she long cultivated Lucan's memory
and, perhaps in AD 89, for the fiftieth anniversary of his birth,
commissioned poems from Statius (*Silvae* 2.7) and Martial, his
age peer and fellow Spaniard (7.21–23). The first two of Martial's
epigrams read:

  This is the day which conspired in a great birth
giving Lucan to the people and to you, Polla.
Ah! Nero, cruel, more hateful than any shade—
this at least should not have been allowed to you.

Apollo's poet, his great birth makes memorable
the light that returns. Mob of Muses, favor the rites!
It's earned them, since it gave the world you, Lucan,
so that Baetis might mingle in Castalia's water.

Bellum Civile was his only work to outlast the Roman Empire,
but into late antiquity Lucan's larger corpus still circulated.
Statius' "birthday poem" for Lucan gives some idea of this col-
lection's contents and possible arrangement. If Statius' summary
follows their published order (an attractive but hardly certain as-
sumption), Lucan's earlier poems, presented first, were Iliadic (on
Hector's death and Priam's ransoming of his body) and Odys-
sean (a *katachthonion*, or trip through the underworld), then his
Laudes Neronis, *Orpheus*, and his poem on the city fire. Then
came a "pleasant address" (*iucunda allocutio*) to his wife, perhaps
on a theme of consolation (one meaning of *allocutio*), and last the
civil war epic. Vacca's list includes, among others, *Letters from
Campania*, prose declamations, and an unfinished *Medea* tragedy.

Since Statius is addressing Lucan's widow, it seems likely that his list would represent the "authorized" collection of the poet's best works, the rest (on this assumption) being minor works for die-hard fans. Though we can only guess at their contents, such a reconstructed organization suggests a conscious attempt to present an organic poetic career to rival those of Virgil and Ovid, both of whose oeuvres build from lesser genres and youthful themes upward to a masterpiece of hexameter epic. (For the fate of Lucan's epic in later centuries see "Reception and Influence" below.)

THE POEM

Lucan's *Bellum Civile* is an eight-thousand-line Latin poem in ten books written in dactylic hexameters, the meter of all ancient epics from Homer's and Hesiod's to Virgil's works and Ovid's *Metamorphoses*.[2] It narrates the main events in the civil war of 49–48 BC between Julius Caesar and Pompey the Great (Gnaeus Pompeius Magnus). Its dramatic climax is Caesar's decisive victory at Pharsalus in northern Greece (Book Seven) and Pompey's murder in Egypt (Book Eight), and it breaks off with Caesar embroiled in the next stage of war in Alexandria. Had Lucan lived longer, it probably would have stretched to twelve or fifteen books, following one or the other of his dominant Latin epic models, Virgil's *Aeneid* and Ovid's *Metamorphoses* (though longer arrangements are also conceivable). Among hypothetical endpoints the most favored are the noble suicide of Cato at Utica in 46 BC or Caesar's assassination in March 44. Since Lucan's main theme is the tragic death of Roman *Libertas* and the enduring struggle against tyranny, either end would fit. As it stands, *Civil War* is a sophisticated poem that thwarts easy interpretation and engages in multivocal dialogue with its historical sources and literary predecessors. The following sections thus aim to sketch the poem's most crucial dimensions.

Civil War is the third great epic of the post-civil-war period and the last one of the Julio-Claudian dynasty. Virgil's *Aeneid* had imitated the opaque narratorial voice characteristic of Homeric

epic, and its overwhelming success served the ends of Augustus'
cultural and political revolution. Ovid's *Metamorphoses* hides
within the illusory world of myth but shoots occasional winks
and smirks at the trappings of Augustus' absolute power. Lucan's
narrative technique takes much from the engaged, ironic, satirical
approaches of Augustans like Ovid—both his epic and his elegi-
acs which inform it—and Horace of the *Satires*, *Epodes*, and
Epistles. Using all the poetic resources at his disposal, Lucan ar-
rays his verses like an engine of war against the Principate and
those texts such as the *Aeneid* that sanctioned it. In temperament
Lucan displays the somber seriousness of Virgil, but in his art-
istry, which relies on sarcasm and swagger, he is more like Ovid.
Also like Ovid before him, Lucan's epic tends toward generic hy-
bridity, mixing styles, conventions, motifs, and modes from epic,
didactic, satire, lyric, elegiac, tragedy, history, and oratory. The
result is a poem that is "very serious; it is deadly serious. But it is
also as funny, as sardonic, as a poem can be."[3] This tragicomic,
film-noir ambivalence is one key to its greatness, its lasting ap-
peal, and perhaps its relevance or resonance in a "(post-)postmod-
ern" world.

EPIC, HISTORY, CIVIL WAR

Civil War is what critics call "historical epic." The term needs
some explanation. Epic and history, as narrative genres, began
with Homer. In classical Greece, historians such as Herodotus
and Thucydides began to differentiate their works from Homeric
verse by writing in prose and by rationalizing their representa-
tions of human events, psychology, and the natural world. The
principal casualty of this new "rational" (*logikos*) outlook was
the Olympian gods, who in the poetic tradition were fully real-
ized actors but in prose history were circumscribed as currency
in human discourses (politics, rhetoric, religion) and phenomena
of human psychology (visions, dreams, omens, etc.). The narra-
tor of history aimed to assess things that everyone could touch
and see, renouncing the poet's traditional claim to privileged di-
vine knowledge. The Olympian gods now seemed little more

than fictions, part of the "many falsehoods similar to the truth" that Hesiod's Muses boasted of knowing how to spin (*Theogony* 27).

But in the Hellenistic period any such neat line between sober prose history and fanciful epic poetry was blurred, as prose writing itself diversified and epics on recent events came into vogue. Both developments tend to point toward the meteoric career of Alexander the Great, whose exploits of conquest became fodder for prose "romances" (popular histories) and panegyric poetry even during his life. After Alexander's death, his biography bloomed with all sorts of fabulous adventures, folk morality tales, and sanctioning encounters with the divine. The divine machinery of epic invaded prose history. On the other hand, in the learned environment of Alexandria, poets like Callimachus forged a leaner, smarter, enlightened aesthetic for epic and other verse genres, which included ample scope for philosophical and historical discourses.

It was this more sophisticated and hybrid literary culture of Alexandria and Hellenistic Greece that first influenced Roman literature—epic and history, verse and prose—at its inception in the third century BC. Early Latin poets such as Naevius and Ennius adapted Greek epic meter and models to national epics that narrated Roman history, both mythologizing the hallowed past and glorifying contemporary events. Naevius' *Bellum Poenicum* (written in the native Saturnian meter) included both the story of Aeneas' arrival from Troy and the First Punic War (264–241 BC), in which the poet himself had fought. Soon after, Ennius adapted Greek hexameter for his eighteen-book *Annales*, which narrated Roman history from Aeneas, through Romulus and Remus and the Etruscan kings, to the Republic, devoting more than half of it to events of recent memory and his own time, especially the wars with Hannibal and those in Greece that followed.

After Carthage had been destroyed in 146 BC, and wealthy Corinth sacked and plundered the same year, Rome was master of the Mediterranean. A century later Roman historians such as Sallust would date the beginning of Rome's decline into "disturbances, rebellions and, lastly, civil wars" to this time, when "a powerful few, to whom many had yielded to gain their goodwill, aspired to domination under the honorable names of fathers and plebs."⁴ Sallust refers to the partisan divide in Rome's ruling oligarchy between *optimates* who upheld the status quo and the *auctoritas* of the Senate, and the *populares* who supported the people's causes (or claimed to) in return for their support. From the violent deaths of the reformers Tiberius and Gaius Gracchus in 133 and 121 BC, to the full-scale civil conflicts between partisan armies of Marius and of Sulla in the 80s and 70s BC, political strife and armed violence escalated. Both sides brandished as needed the rhetoric of liberty and the restoration of traditional law and order. Crassus, Pompey, Caesar, Cicero, Cato—all the leading men who oversaw the death of Rome's "free" Republic were survivors of this bloody chaos. As a class they proved incapable of settling the many pressing problems of a growing empire except through further civil war.

Julius Caesar crossed the Rubicon River in January 49 BC, beginning a civil war against the Senate *optimates* in Rome led by Gnaeus Pompey. He had spent nine years in Gaul honing his formidable talents in war. His enemies made the grave mistake of leaving the city, heading south and eventually to Greece. Caesar was quickly able to consolidate his hold on Italy and Rome before heading west to Spain to deal with Pompey's loyal legions there. His armies spent six months laying siege to the coastal Greek city of Massilia (Marseille) lest it become a strategic base for his enemies, while Caesar was in Spain bringing Pompey's commanders roundly to heel. He was appointed dictator and then "duly elected" consul for 48 BC, before going to confront Pompey in Greece. Indecisive conflicts in western Greece were followed by a pitched battle in early August at Pharsalus in Thessaly. Though outnumbered roughly two to one, Caesar achieved a massive victory: some fifteen thousand soldiers of the Senate's allied armies fell, and Pompey fled in disgrace. Seeking to recoup his losses in Alexandria, Pompey was treacherously butchered by agents of the young king Ptolemy. When Caesar arrived in pursuit, he was delivered the head of his enemy and former son-in-law. He soon found himself tangled in the dynastic civil war between Ptolemy and his sisters Arsinoë and Cleopatra, the latter of whom seduced him into backing her claims (their child was born the next year).

These events are most authoritatively related in Caesar's own brilliant three-book commentary, *Bellum Civile*, which begins on the eve of war and breaks off suddenly in the early stages of conflict in Egypt. Lucan's *Bellum Civile* also covers the same stretch of events and ends at the exact same point. It is clearly integral to his design to follow and challenge Caesar's text, arraying the ample resources of the literary tradition of epic hexameter against Caesar's own commentary.[5] For Caesar's text was the opening salvo in a propaganda war and ideological revolution that would culminate with Augustus, who veiled a "divine" hereditary monarchy in Republican titles and rhetoric. And Lucan's project, as a poet of anti-Caesarean historical epic, is to break through the wall of consolidated power and historical destiny that Augustus had so successfully built. He had done so, following Caesar's lead, by controlling the cultural discourse, through every means available but not least through the collaborative power of poetry.

Augustus' poets were vital in shaping the cultural outlook and atmosphere that made the Pax Augusta more than a military autocracy achieved through sheer exhaustion of any concerted will to resist. Virgil and others (mainly Horace, all the others with considerably more ambivalence) had offered up an imaginative rendition of history that made Augustus' ascent to power the teleological end of eternal Fate. The myth grafted the hoary old legend of Rome's foundation by Aeneas after arrival from Troy onto the Julian clan's self-laudatory fiction of descent from Venus through Aeneas and his son Iulus/Ascanius. So framed, Caesar became the literal end of Roman history, and his heirs were destined to rule the world after he had ascended to heaven as a man-made god (*divus Iulius*). Anyone interested in deconstructing this official ideological fiction would need to attack it at the roots: the Augustan myth in such founding texts as the *Aeneid* and Caesar's own account of victory in his *Bellum Civile*.

The radical change that Lucan makes to the epic tradition is to follow the historian's lead in dispensing with the Olympian gods. This was a brilliant and necessary move in order to challenge the cultural supremacy of the *Aeneid* and the Augustan mythology that it sanctioned. Instead of the sublime, all-controlling rhetoric of the gods, we get dubious mortal rhetoric and the will to power it labors to mask. Instead of comfortably certain prophecies and oracles, we get a proliferation of ambiguous divinatory sign systems (astrology, reading entrails, necromancy, oracles of Delphi and Ammon) viewed through skeptical or mock-serious lenses. The culminating instance of such scenes, Cato at the oracle of Ammon, settles on skepticism. Urged to consult the oracle, Cato refuses in philosophical and paternalistic disdain: "its credence preserved, he made no examination / but left Ammon to the people" (9.736–37). Lucan's own rejection of traditional epic's divine apparatus forges the most distinctive marks of his poem's narrative voice. For its narrator is one who searches for answers to history's enormities, but is regularly frustrated by uncertain dead ends at the limits of human inquiry. He and his characters long for access to a higher plane of knowledge but are routinely thwarted or deluded in their attempts to access higher (or lower, infernal) truths.

Lucan's historical epic deconstructs history and epic. By rejecting epic's gods, *Civil War* reveals the *Aeneid*'s world for what it is, a poetic construct, a rhetorical fiction, a mask for the narrator and those interests served by the narration. And by using Caesar's civil war commentary, and other Roman civil war historical texts, as *materia*, raw material, for a sophisticated *verse imitation of prose history*, he is able to subject history-as-narrative to scrutiny. For Lucan's poem of civil war seems most of all to be about who gets to make and write history, and *cui bono*, in whose interest, history is written. What role do history-writing *and* epic-writing play in the making, the legitimating, of history? In other words, what kinds of events and moral actors are truly *memorabile*, worthy of memory, and why?

This dimension becomes clearest after Pharsalus and the death of Pompey, when all the strands begin to come together. The opposition between Caesar and Pompey, which had always been merely a choice between two savage masters (cf. 2.340–43, 7.800–810, 8.426–33), now resolves itself into a more fundamental choice, between the moral example of "stern" Cato or of Alexander the Great. Lucan could hardly have made this contrast more explicit: the passages to compare are 9.746–59, on Cato's moral example, and 10.18–64, on "Philip's crazy offspring," the "lucky bandit" Alexander the "Great." Alexandrian "greatness" is presented as an insane, insatiable lust for conquest, as bloody brutality in quest of power and the pursuit of endless *luxuria*, wasteful extravagance (cf. 10.131–213). Alexander, who "stormed with human slaughter and finished off all nations with a sword," was

A fatal evil on the earth, a bolt of lightning
that struck all peoples alike, an adverse star
unto the nations. (10.42–44)

By contrast, Cato's "triumphal march" through the snake-infested wastes of Libya is said to set the worthiest example to follow, and prompts this critical observation: "Who has ever deserved a *great name* for conquest, for shedding people's blood?" (9.750–51). Of course, both Caesar—also a "bolt of lightning" (cf. 1.157–72)—and Pompey the *Great* followed in the bloody footsteps of Alexander. Cato, on the other hand, stands in for a different model of virtue, one that draws both on philosophy—Stoic, but not only—and on the idealized *mos maiorum*, the old Republican virtues of hardy preservation of individual and collective liberty through simplicity of living and selfless service to the state. Cato urges his men (supposedly *voluntarii*, since he turned away the rest to desert to Caesar's side) to "train your minds on our great task, the utmost toils of virtue" (9.474–75), because "the path to law and order is hard, and so is the love of our fatherland, now falling to ruin" (9.479–80).

If, as some scholars argue, Lucan's representation of Cato is itself too absurd to be credible, this may be partly because the historicity of the model morality, the *mos maiorum* or "way of the ancestors," had ceased to be believed. Instead a caustic cynicism had set in. The historian Sallust, for instance, writing during the civil wars, had come to doubt the presence of true virtue even in the earliest stages of the Republic: "the injustices of the stronger . . . *were endemic right from the beginning*. . . . the fathers

harassed the plebs with commands fit only for slaves, made deci-
sions in a kingly fashion about execution and flogging, evicted
people from the land, and, with everyone else disenfranchised,
lived in sole command."[6] But reality's pessimism should not in-
validate the value of the unrealized ideal. Still, Lucan does not
seem deluded about the dim prospects of society in general being
crafted along the lines of true virtue. Who, after all, given the
choice, would want to live in hazard of death by snakebite in the
wastes of Africa, instead of in the lap of Alexandrian luxury and
Cleopatra's arms?

    Even supposing
it wasn't that man full ready for wicked war
and hunting for resources in the world's rubble,
put ancient leaders in, names from poverty's age,
Fabricius or grave Curius, have him lie down,
bring in that consul, dusty from Etruscan plowing—
he will pray to lead such a triumph for his country! (10.188–94)

   Caesar(ism) is bound to win out because, given human nature,
any man put in Caesar's place would act exactly the same way.
   Alexander was a notorious admirer of Homer and Achilles:
Caesar, too, is possessed by the glorious myths of Troy (9.1177–
1242). If history-as-narrative had derived from the deep stream
of Homeric epic, history-as-action was also always driven by
men who were avid readers of epic, fired by its prize of immortal
glory for heroic exploits. But it is possible these great men are
simply, but tragically, poor readers of epic, deriving from it the
wrong lessons, deluded by false notions of the heroic. After all,
Achilles' rage was "destructive" (*Iliad* 1.2) and for himself it re-
sults only in grief and the noble gesture of pity for his fallen
enemy, the fatherly king Priam. (Lucan, recall, began his career
by reworking this scene from *Iliad* 24.) Seen from this angle,
there is a kind of radical traditionalism in Lucan's engagement
with the epic tradition. Despite his refusal of its gods, the ethos
he tends to (seem to) proffer is quite in line with Homer's men of
action, who do their best in the face of a bleak world of hostile
gods and a history stacked against them.[7]

POETIC TRADITION, STYLE, THEMES

Lucan knew and drew upon a wide range of poetic predecessors, Greek and Latin, including Homer, Hesiod, Apollonius Rhodius, Ennius, Callimachus, Catullus, Lucretius, Virgil, Horace, Tibullus, Propertius, and Ovid, as well as dozens of other Greek and Latin authors of tragedy, satire, epigram, didactic and mythographic verse. Hardly a line passes that has not been shown to allude to one, often more than one, phrase or motif in an earlier poet (or prose author). While many particular links are suggested in the notes, here a few broader comments will suggest Lucan's strategies and tendencies in how he reads his predecessors and reworks them into his epic of civil war.

I. Gigantomachy

The Augustan poets make frequent explicit or implicit comparison of Rome's civil wars with the primordial war between the Olympian gods and the Giants, monstrous children of Earth. Pharsalus had in fact taken place in Thessaly, the mythical location of the gods' victory, an accident that made the comparison all the more seductive. This motif was regularly linked to another, the *recusatio* or "refusal" to write epic poetry on national themes to honor Augustus. By Ovid's time such poetic refusals to write "gigantic" epic had become cliché, and he makes great fun out of this already in his earliest poems (cf. *Amores* 2.1, *Met.* 1.151–62). Lucan takes the theme and runs with it, starting in the praise of Nero, which provides the (or one) key to interpret it: if civil-war atrocities were the Fates' way to bring forth Nero, "and eternal kingdoms cost gods dearly, nor heaven be slave to its Thunderer unless the savage Giants had lost the wars . . ." (1.36–41). So, the Caesars are the gods, the Giants the losing side(s), and world domination is the prize balanced against the great costs in death, destruction, and punishments. The theme is also metapoetic: Lucan responds to his predecessors that he, finally, *will not refuse* to take up the burden of writing a national civil-war epic. The sardonic irony is that this Gigantomachy will not give glorious praise to Caesar but expose the civil wars as the source of "crime made law" and a monstrous worldwide tyranny. In fact, Lucan takes the last logical step and interprets Caesar's victory at Pharsalia as the ultimate reversal, the defeat of the gods themselves by gigantic mountain-piling mortals (7.533–38; cf. also 3.331–36, 4.623–38, 6.99, 6.322–25, 6.455–58, 6.739, 7.172–79, 9.818–19.)

II. Fata and Fortuna

Lucan rejects the Olympian gods as epic actors on the stage of human history. He replaces them with Fata ("the Fates") and Fortuna ("Fortune"). His use of these "gods" or cosmic forces or folk-explanatory principles (or whatever) is one of the most highly charged aspects of the poem and lends it its greatest sense of cosmic, and interpretive, indeterminacy. The words for fate and fortune occur more than any other nouns in the poem.[8] Whether or not his use of these notions can be shown to possess philosophical consistency, it no doubt serves effective poetic ends. For the dark, fatal oscillation of Fortune and Fate casts a tragic mood of cosmic uncertainty and doom over his narrative of dire civil conflicts.

The Stoic doctrine of benevolent Providence, the bedrock of that school's cosmology and ethics, is one main thread of Lucan's Fata (e.g. 2.7–12 is recognizably Stoic). Cato's dictum "wherever fate leads, virtue is safe to follow" (2.304) also reflects Stoic ethical teaching regarding the benevolence and justice of the higher powers guiding human affairs. But Stoic Fata is profoundly at odds with any anti-Caesarean project, since to assert fate is to play into the Virgilian scheme of Rome's Augustan destiny: as Jupiter tells Venus in the Aeneid (1.286–96), Julius Caesar is destined to establish an endless empire, then ascend to the heavens, and Augustus will rule it in peace. Lucan undercuts this Augustan triumphalism by interpreting Roman history through a negative fatalism that is both naturalistic and hearkens to Greek epic-tragic notions of hubris. The first causes of the war are described as "Fates' hateful [invida] sequence: the mighty don't stand long. . . . Great things rush to ruin: the powers that give bounty have set this limit on increase. Not to any foreign nations

did Fortune lend her envy [*invidia*] to use against the people rul-
ing land and sea" (1.76–77, 88–91). Large size undermines itself,
since it attracts a cosmic spite or envy (*invidia*; the Greeks called
it *phthonos*) that is here connected with both the Fates and
Fortune.

For its part, *Fortuna* derives complex resonances from popular,
religious, poetic, and historiographical perspectives on the role of
chance, luck, and fortune in human events (*tyche* in Greek). Cae-
sar, for instance, had criticized the nondecisive victory of the
Pompeians at Dyrrachium by recalling that "Fortune, a force uni-
versally powerful but particularly so in war, brings about great
changes by slight adjustments of her balance" (BC 3.68), and again
soon after, "[the Pompeians] failed to remind themselves of the
everyday accidents of war [*belli casus*], how factors that are fre-
quently trifling—mistaken suspicion, or sudden alarm, or reli-
gious scruple—have caused great disasters" (BC 3.72).[9] Lucan's
Caesar is without a doubt represented as closely allied with For-
tune, from his perspective as her favorite, but from a "cosmic" or
a sovereign narratorial perspective as the mortal agent of her
invidia against a Rome grown too great to bear itself.

Caesar's destructive Fortune thus threatens a benevolent Stoic
Fata. By casting the civil wars as a contest between the forces of
Fortune and Fate(s), Lucan stages a showdown between the cos-
mological models championed by different philosophical schools.
In his *De Natura Deorum* (3.65ff.), Cicero included a strong cri-
tique of Stoic benevolent Providence, arguing that the abuses of
reason and lucky prosperity of "great" but wicked men would
suggest that gods don't care for mortal affairs: "no house or state
can be regarded as an example of reason and discipline if good
deeds go unrewarded and crimes unpunished. So, too, there can
be no divine guidance of human affairs if the gods make no dis-
tinction between good and evil." Such is the conclusion to be
drawn from the apparent good fortune of flagrant criminals. But,
he says, "I am reluctant to follow up this line of argument, as it
seems to play into the hands of the criminal. And so it would, if
virtue and vice were not deep matters of our own conscience,
quite apart from any gift of reason from the gods. If conscience
goes, everything collapses around us."[10]

Similarly in Lucan, Caesar's wicked victory challenges the very idea of a rational universe tended by benevolent gods. If Caesar and his good fortune win, the Stoics and their cosmology lose. And this conclusion plays "into the hands of the criminal"—the universe is random, aleatory, and humankind is left at the mercy of events and its own dubious moral nature: "nothing is settled and fortune wanders uncertain, twisting and turning events and chance rules mortals" (2.13–14). Infamously, on the eve of Pharsalus and the death of liberty for all time, Lucan declares atheism: "In fact there are no powers over us: blind chance ravages the centuries: we say 'Jove reigns,' we're lying" (7.524–26).

Instead of visible divine powers, Lucan shows us a world dominated by competing rhetorical projects, foregrounding the power of the spoken word to shape reality to mortal interests and partial, partisan ends. In line with this, Lucan's favorite way to end a speech is with *fatus*, "having spoken," from *fari*, "to speak, declare," the source also of *fatum/fata*: speech is action, a declarative projection of how things are to be. All these elements combine in Caesar's potent speech-act (his *alea iacta est* moment) after crossing the Rubicon: "'Fortune, I follow you. Faith can go to the winds. I put my trust in the Fates. Let war decide!'" So declaring [*fatus*], in night's darkness the rapid general drives his army . . ." (1.245–48).

III. Cosmic Conflagration

Stoic natural philosophy held that the world would eventually "burn out" (Greek *ekpyrosis*). This eschatological doctrine appears in prominent places in Lucan, providing an image of global dissolution that adds crackle to the discordant chaos of civil war (cf. 1.78–87, 2.306–9, 7.160–63, 7.943–51). In Lucan's hands it can achieve true sublimity: "a common pyre awaits the world, it will mix their bones with stars." This belief was connected to a physical theory that the heavenly bodies, composed of the element of fire, were nourished by waters from Earth, and when these waters were all consumed the parched world, too, must be destroyed by fire. (Lucan refers to the physical theory at 1.449–51 and 10.318–22.) The doctrine held that after destruction the world would "rise again in splendor" (Cicero, *De Nat. Deo.* 2.118); Lucan never offers any comforting circularity to his image of a fiery end.

IV. Crime Made Law

Civil war is symptomatic of some breakdown in normal lawful order, a paradoxical anomie where fellow citizens (*cives*) treat one another as enemies (*hostes*) against whom one wages war (*bellum*). For Lucan, either the cause or the chief symptom of the suicidal collapse of moral order is an all-pervasive *furor* ("madness, rage, violent frenzy") manifesting itself in "sheer license of steel" (1.9). Addressing his fellow Roman citizens (see "Apostrophe" below), Lucan interrogates the causes and the wicked deeds committed in this state of furor and anarchic violence.

Roman poets from Catullus on described the chaos of civil war as a confusion of right and wrong, good and bad, law and crime: "all things utterable and unutterable [*fanda nefanda*] mixed up in evil fury [*malo furore*]" (Catullus 64.405). Caesar says the same thing (about his enemies' war preparations) at the outbreak of the civil war: "all divine and human laws [*iura*] are being mixed up" (*BC* 1.6). In diagnosing the symptoms and the progress of the disease of civil war, Lucan goes beyond the idea of simple moral and legal confusion to the positive legalization of what had been criminal. This will be a main theme of the epic: "crime made law we sing" (*iusque datum sceleri canimus*, 1.2). It is the ultimate metamorphosis, criminal wrong turned into sanctioned right, and Lucan will dare to narrate this unspeakable horror (*nefas*) that unleashed the world "into contention to win a common guilt [*nefas*]" (1.6). In the aftermath of Pharsalus, we learn that common guilt equates, if perversely, to wholesale innocence (7.1012–18). A strange idea, to be sure, but what Lucan seems to mean is that the blood of civil war was spilled so widely that some measure of absolution, or forgetting, of all of it is required. This seems to strike deep at some truth, hard to express, about the social psychology of collective trauma.

When Octavian "restored" the Republic in 27 BC, he received the name Augustus, and a golden "shield of virtue" (*clupeus virtutis*) was hung up in the Senate house. It listed four virtues, qualities meant to connect with Augustus' achievements in ending civil war and stabilizing the state: *virtus*, *clementia*, *iustitia*, *pietas* (virtue/valor, clemency, justice, filial-religious dutifulness). *Civil War* investigates all these value terms (with others such as *fides*, "trust/faith," *honos*, "honor," and *pudor*, "shame/honor") and shows them to be destroyed, rendered void, or worst of all, perverted to sinister ends in the rabid conditions of civil war. For instance, Julius Caesar's willingness to pardon enemies, his signature gift for clemency, is depicted as deeply problematic to the ethos of honor cultivated by Rome's aristocrats. Its effect (to Lucan, its shrewdly calculating political aim) was to render his pardoned enemies subservient to his will; thus clemency is a particularly useful virtue for the aspiring tyrant. So too *virtus*, the manly martial valor that made and kept Rome strong and free, is shown undermining itself in civil war and serving the tyrant's ends. The prime example is Caesar's soldier Scaeva, whose exploits at Dyrrachium are hailed by his comrades, who see him as "a living image and likeness of Great Virtue." But the narrator calls him wretched, because "you gave up so much valor to get a master" (6.277, 287). Virtue has turned into vice, and bravery has been reduced to slavery.

For Lucan the war will settle the question of right (Pompey, but more so Cato) versus might (Caesar). When Caesar wins, all justice is upended, since the "better cause" has been beaten and the worse cause is both victorious and—de facto and by ideological fiat—the "just cause." Caesar tells his troops before Pharsalus, "today . . . will prove, with Fate as witness, who took up arms more justly. This engagement will render the loser guilty" (7.304–6). On his side, Pompey asserts the better cause to his men: "Our greater cause urges us to hope for favor from powers above" (7.409–10); but earlier, in private before the senators, his more pessimistic speech belies his battlefield rhetoric: "Among the gods above you've beat me, Caesar, with your hostile prayers. . . . Today . . . Pompey will be a name that's either hated or pitied by all peoples. This final cast of lots for everything will bring all evils on the vanquished. All the guilt will fall upon the victor" (7.131–32, 141–45). Pompey seems beaten in spirit before his army is defeated in battle: he is neither confident that he can win nor, even if he does, that he will be hailed as glorious victor rather than hateful tyrant. Caesar and Pompey concur on one point: the loser will become the enemy of the state. But their contradictory positions about the *victor's* postwar status merge into a single overarching perspective: the victor will be proven, by Fate's fiat, to be both "more just" *and* saddled with "all the guilt" of the war. The victor establishes (a new) justice through guilty deeds: *ius datum sceleri*, "crime made law." Such an outcome also seems to prove that the powers ruling the world (Fate, Fortune, the shadowy "gods above") have no real concern for justice among mortal affairs. Humans are on their own.[11]

V. Apostrophe

A peculiar stylistic feature of *Bellum Civile* is its frequent use of apostrophe or the "direct address" of a character, either by another character or, the more notable effect, by the primary narrator (the address to the "citizens" in 1.9 is the first of almost two hundred instances). In ancient rhetoric apostrophe was a device used when the orator "turned away from" the case at hand to address someone directly whether present or absent. It could be used to varied effect: for instance, for invective railing against a defendant, to arouse pity or sympathy in the audience and jury, or to summon up the imagined presence of absent figures, even the dead. A recent study of Lucan's uses of apostrophe argues that the poet employs it to evoke and focus the reader's emotional response to characters and their actions, while also maintaining the reader's awareness of his own presence. By making regular and repeated breaks into the narrative, the narrator seeks to disrupt the reader's complacent identification with its characters, thereby evoking reflection on its status as fiction and on the power of words to shape and interpret events into meaningful patterns that command assent.[12] By this reading, Lucan wants us to stop and think about the rhetorical powers of language, poetry, and narrative; he wants us to become good judges of history.

The use of apostrophe was also characteristic of didactic poetry (for example, Hesiod's *Works and Days*, Lucretius' *De Rerum Natura*), and Lucan's collective addressee, the citizens of Rome, may be marked out as recipients of a didactic work aimed to instruct them about the wrongs inflicted and suffered by themselves in the civil wars. Lucan's other apostrophes serve to highlight and discuss the exemplarity of events and characters, both good and bad, directing the reader toward ways to undo the grave damage done to language and meaning through their abuse in the amoral furor of civil war. In this reading, Lucan's narrator "appears not as a nihilist, but as an individual deeply interested in ethics," so that "deconstruction in the *Bellum Civile* is always employed in a search for meaning."[13] Past translators (such as Duff, 1928), failing to appreciate Lucan's strategic uses of apostrophe and deeming it empty rhetorical excess, have often translated it away into third-person expressions. The present translation instead respects and reflects each instance of apostrophe in the poem.

VI. Spectacles of Sacrifice

If apostrophe "turns away" from the events themselves to engage the reader in dialogue with the narrator and the characters, Lucan's preferred metaphorical framework to present narrative action is the public spectacle, staged in the theater, circus, and gladiatorial arena. This metaphoric code is suggested right at the start, with the opening imagery of "matched pairs of eagles," and the poet's challenge to the wisdom of "display[ing] Latin carnage to hateful nations" (1.10–11). To the epic task of vividly portraying deaths in battle, *Civil War* brings an eye trained by imperial Rome's notoriously grisly culture of blood sports, a culture that Caesar and Augustus did much to create by lavishing festival games and triumphs on the Roman public.

That preeminent imperial spectacle, the staged naval battle (*naumachia*), seems to inspire Lucan's mode of depicting naval warfare at Massilia with its "many *marvelous* forms of death upon the sea" (3.661). Here as elsewhere, men's bodies are mangled in luridly graphic detail, evoking arena entertainment where watching violent death becomes a pastime. Later, the amphithe-ater metaphor is made explicit when a raft of Caesar's men is trapped in sight of spectators from land, and they decide to prove their courage (*virtus*) through a scene of mass suicide. Their cap-tain, Vulteius, encourages them to regard their coming fate as a spectacle of virtue, set up by the gods, for the eyes of both sides; they will win glory by putting on a good show of "unconquered courage" (cf. 4.517–20). The Vulteius episode calls to mind cri-tiques of gladiatorial culture by Lucan's uncle Seneca, who re-garded the arena's staged homicides "for sport and jest" as the epitome of Rome's "wicked reversal of morals" (*perversitas morum*), which called for the most careful training to relearn "what is good and bad." A barbarian gladiator in a *naumachia* who killed himself rather than kill others is offered as a glorious example from which "men learn how much more honorable it is to die than to kill."[14] The upholding of suicide as the height of honor, in that it represents the ultimate refusal to submit to bru-tal mockeries of slavery, is a moral paradigm that could be read through both the doomed gladiator and Cato's noble end at Utica. In the fatal cage of Caesarean Rome's spectacle culture, suicide was the last bastion of individual liberty: "no one is ever forced to a willing death [*velle mori*]" (4.509).

But Pompey, too, who built the first permanent stone theater in Rome in 55 BC, had a hand in establishing the full-time enter-tainments of the late Republic. Lucan ties Pompey's character and his fate to his theater. In the city of leisure he "had unlearned leadership" and was "pleased by applause in his theater," becom-ing "a shadow of his great name" (1.144–48). On the eve of Phar-salus, Pompey dreams he is back in his theater, the Roman plebs "extolling his name to the stars with ecstatic voices" (7.12). But this is a delusion, an omen so contrary to the coming reality that he could never hope to read it correctly (cf. 7.22–28). For instead of victorious spectators of triumphal games, his armies will be-come the grim death spectacle on which Caesar will feast his eyes (7.914–28), discerning in the heaps of dead "his fortune and his gods above" (7.928). Pompey himself, in a great tragic reversal, will become the duped and mutilated victim of wrathful gods.

Throughout, the poem raises the metaphor of violent spectacle to cosmic and theological levels: the civil wars are worldwide games staged by the gods for their own satisfaction. Both armies arrive in Greece, kept "well matched" (*pares*, 5.2) by Fortune for the land of Macedon (really Thessaly), which has been preparing from time immemorial (ever since the days of the Gigantomachy) for just such a bloody global showdown (cf. 6.371–458). It's a "fate-damned land" (6.459) infested by savage witches such as Erictho, who has been plying her magic to steer the pitched battle here so that she "would enjoy the profit from the world's blood" (6.649). And the heavens themselves broadcast the once-in-a-life-time event so that "if the mind of man had read through skillful augury all the heavens' strange new signs, the whole world could have watched the spectacle at Pharsalia" (7.239–42).

And what was the main event? After Pompey flees we learn that Pharsalus became an instance of an apparently eternally re-curring contest: "Thessaly's conflict after your departure is no longer for Pompey's world-famous name nor zeal for war, but it will be the matched duel [*par*] that we always have: Liberty ver-sus Caesar" (7.806–9). One of Lucan's greatest lines, it is also a real crux of interpretation. Are we to believe that Liberty and Caesar are truly "equal"? If so, does that give hope that either side—and therefore Liberty—might win? Or is it instead an end-less stalemate? At the least, perhaps, the triumphal closure of Caesar's victory is hereby forestalled, opening Virgil's Augustan vision of "empire without end" up to history's basic and overrid-ing contingency. Instead, as T. S. Eliot wrote, "There is no end of it, the voiceless wailing, no end . . . to the drift of the sea and the drifting wreckage."

Cato's refusal to submit to Caesar after the defeat at Thapsus and his subsequent suicide were quickly interpreted as a symbol of defiance to the new order. Lucan's portrayal of him reflects the new mythology surrounding Cato and the idea of noble suicide in the early empire. In his version, Cato summons up the old mar-tial ideal of *devotio*: a general vows his own life and the opposing army to the infernal gods in return for victory, then goes down fighting in a blaze of glory (cf. 2.322–39). This Roman martial model of expiatory self-sacrifice was easily elided as metaphor into such principled philosophical suicides as Socrates and, so fused, could be a compelling model for political martyrdom in the Principate.[15] In Lucan and Seneca one sees that the straitened fate of the gladiator could also inspire sympathy as a kind of noble model for bravely facing one's end and, in the process, bearing a last glorious witness to the truth of virtue before the blood-glutted eyes of a world gone mad.

VII. Lucan's Heroines and Tragic Choruses

Ancient epic is famous for its female characters, and the space it provides to feminine voices and perspectives (as imagined, of course, by male authors) is distinctive (though tragedy shares this with epic). Homer's Helen, Andromache, Hecuba, Briseis, Nausicaa, Calypso, Circe, and Penelope had inspired Virgil to try to live up to the model, with his Creusa, Dido, the Sibyl, Lavinia (a virtual nonentity), and Amata. Ovid, more than any, had poured his imagination into the feminine side of the mythological tradition, spending large portions of his works speaking in the voice of or through the perspective of female characters. Lucan also takes seriously this aspect of the epic tradition, infusing feminine voices and perspectives into the male-dominated discourse of war and politics found in prose history (women are hardly mentioned, for instance, in Caesar's own civil-war commentary, with even Cleopatra reduced to a reference).

The climactic female figure in *Civil War* is Cleopatra, the femme-fatale Ptolemaic Helen who stoops to conquer Caesar, and then will lead Rome down a fatal path to Alexandrian decadence (10.65–213). But before this endgame, Lucan gives many other female characters and groups of women space on his epic stage. In general, Lucan's women seem closer than men to the gods, liable to be inspired with mantic frenzy (the mantic matron at 1.719–41, the Delphic Pythia in Book Five), or possessed of magical powers (Thessalian Erictho, who holds a preeminent place in this epic world). In all these instances it seems clear that Lucan proposes a metapoetic connection between potent, inspired feminine voices and the poet's own voice (for example, at

1.727–28 the mantic matron echoes the poem's opening question). As usual in epic, just as in ancient practice, women are also heard as the dominant voices of lament and public expressions of sorrow. A "sad patrol" of the city's matrons early in Book Two complain to the gods above, acting like a tragic chorus whose song drapes the rest of the epic in a dark funereal shroud. Similarly, the dead Julia, Caesar's daughter and Pompey's wife, possessed by Fury-like jealousy at his new wife, Cornelia, rises in a dream to haunt her former husband (3.9–37). Likewise, Cato's former wife, Marcia, returns to him while still mourning for her recently dead husband, Hortensius, and they reunite in a lovely (non)wedding described by detailing all the usual Roman marriage customs that it lacked (2.346–414).

But the leading female role in the epic by far is Cornelia. At the end of Book Five, Pompey sends her away to safety in Lesbos, after a touching pillow quarrel in which she pleads to be allowed to face the same hardships as him. When Pompey flees Pharsalus, he hastens to Lesbos to rescue his wife before heading south, and from here on, through Pompey's death and the flight of her ship to Cato in North Africa (9.138), much of the narrative is told through Cornelia's grief and pathos at losing Pompey. More important, her voice delivers Pompey's last will to his sons: to keep fighting the civil war, using the glory of their father's name for all it's worth, and follow Cato for the cause of liberty.

RECEPTION AND INFLUENCE

As mentioned above, Lucan's widow, Polla, likely took care to publish his poetry. During his life the civil-war epic had caused enough sensation to inspire a smart parody of the first book by Petronius in his satirical novel the *Satyricon* (for a translation of which see the appendix in this volume). Had Nero lived longer it is conceivable that efforts to suppress the epic might have occurred. As it was, Lucan's ignominious end as a conspirator against Nero sufficed to cast a radioactive cloud over his name and verses; or so one surmises from the sharply divided opinion on his epic in the next generation. His poems were popular enough to sell well, but still generated negative criticism. The epigrammatist Martial (who was Lucan's age, but lived into Trajan's reign, dying ca. AD 104) summarized Lucan's current reputation thus:

> There are some who say that I am not a poet.
> But the bookseller who sells me sure thinks so. (14.194)

Martial is apparently countering the view of certain harsh critics with the author's obvious popularity in the market. Suetonius' life of Lucan, probably written in the reign of Trajan (98–117) and generally unfavorable, ends with this comment on Lucan's dissemination: "I remember his poems being lectured on, copies made and put out for sale, not only with care and attention to detail but also poor, sloppy editions." With a touch of disdain this makes the same point as Martial: Lucan's poetry (one assumes especially his epic) had made it into the curriculum of at least some schools, and enjoyed a vigorous appeal on the street, such that upscale and down-market publishers found it worth the ink and papyrus to have their scribes make copies.

The rhetorician Quintilian (ca. 35–100, also from Spain; it is possible he met Lucan and/or Seneca) wrote a brief judgment on Lucan that both reflects the contemporary range of opinion and has greatly influenced his later reception: "Lucan is fiery and excited and most illustrious for his clever phrases [*sententiae*], and (to say what I think) should be imitated more by orators than by poets" (*Inst.* 10.1.90). This laconic sentence is frequently read as sharply dismissive, but this oversimplifies it. For Quintilian clearly grants Lucan's merits—abundant energy and skillful expression—then presents him as a model for orators, at least, if not one easily imitated by other poets. That he *is* exemplary for orators is praise in a textbook on the art of rhetoric. Still, the studied qualification seems again to reflect the opinion that Lucan is not quite a poet, or somehow does not set a good example for poets.

The weird view that Lucan was simply "not a poet" quickly worked its way into the received wisdom of late imperial grammarians. The Christian rhetorician Lactantius (ca. 240–320), the

Virgilian commentator Servius (early fifth century), and the ency-
clopedist Isidore of Seville (ca. 560–636) all reflect this view.[16]
Servius wrote: "Lucan hasn't earned a place in the number of
poets, since he seems to have composed history, not a poem"
(commentary on *Aen.* 1.382). Isidore expands, with an opinion
some scholars have attributed to Suetonius: "a poet has the duty
to take things that have actually happened and give them a dif-
ferent appearance with ambiguous/indirect images [*obliquis figu-
rationibus*], transforming them with a certain dignity. For this
reason Lucan is not put in the number of poets . . . [same as in
Servius above]." It is beside the point here that a reasonable case
can be made that Lucan fits this description of the poet's duty.
Modern critics have shown that the real issue is Lucan's refusal
to represent gods in human form, following the paradigmatic
model that looms behind this reductive definition of "poetry":
Virgil's *Aeneid*. Since epic narrative represents gods acting in
human history and Lucan's poem does not, therefore it cannot be
epic or, more sweeping, not a poem, nor its author a poet.[17]

In a way, this view did not matter much, since Lucan was none-
theless being read, commented on, and passed down: poet or not,
he had won a solid place in the selective canon of read texts. The
fruit of this focus in Roman education is two full sets of ancient
grammatical commentary transmitted with the text.[18] Yet, if for
Roman readers Lucan's nonpoem, with its anti-imperial politics,
fell short of the definitive poetic grandeur of Virgil and his full-
bodied gods, it is precisely the absence of the gods, as well as its
nontriumphal view of Rome's imperial destiny, that must have
appealed to Christian readers in late antiquity and the Middle
Ages. To them, the Greco-Roman deities were the false gods of
"pagan" religion, and Roman secular domination was excoriated
for its corrupt morality.[19] Virgil, Horace, or Ovid required some
Christianizing strategy to render their polytheism palatable to
church doctrine (usually through natural and/or moral allegory),
whereas Lucan, who grew up on Stoic allegorical theory and
wove its naturalistic pantheism into the basic texture of his po-
etic universe, needed no such reading strategy. He had already
done the theological demolition work for them. In Lucan the
gods have gone missing, their oracles fallen silent; it almost looks

like a world getting ready for the Advent of the Word—with Cato a proto-Christian prophet crying out in the Libyan wilderness.

More than four hundred complete and partial manuscripts of Lucan's nonpoem attest to its medieval popularity, the earliest dating to the ninth and tenth centuries. The earliest vernacular renditions include one in medieval Irish called *In Cath Catharda* ("The Civil Battle") from around 1100, and a twelfth- or thirteenth-century Icelandic version that, significantly, circulated with Sallust's histories as part of a collection known as *Romverja saga* ("Roman History"). Arnulf of Orleans, a twelfth-century classics professor, wrote a copious commentary on Lucan, displaying great mastery and generous appreciation of the poem; notably, Arnulf calls Lucan "not purely a poet but both poet and historian."[20] Lucan's historical poem—with Arnulf's notes—fed into thirteenth-century Roman histories in medieval French, such as the *Faits des Romains* (ca. 1213) and Jehan de Tuim's *Li Hystore de Jules Cesar* (ca. 1240).

Lucan deeply influenced the great vernacular poets of the thirteenth and fourteenth centuries, including Dante, Petrarch, and Chaucer. The latter wrote in his *House of Fame*,

Then saw I on a pillar by,
Of iron wrought full sternely,
The greate poet, Dan Lucan,
That on his shoulders bare up than,
As high as that I might it see,
The fame of Julius and Pompey;

Dante's poetic rivalry with Lucan is often conspicuous and allusions to *Civil War* abound in the *Commedia*. Not only is Lucan's "holy Cato" cast as a proto-Christian saint who with his stern Stoic virtue guards the gates of Purgatory. Dante has the Lucanesque effrontery and genius to have Virgil's soul claim that, in fact, just after death he had been summoned by the witch Erictho to bring back a soul from the lowest depths of Hell (cf. *Inf.* 9.22–27). Meanwhile Petrarch's attempt, with his unfinished *Africa*, to revive Latin historical epic owes much in inspiration and design to the difficult model set by *Bellum Civile*.

The first print edition (*editio princeps*) came out in Rome in 1469 (the same year as Virgil's), with several critical editions following in the sixteenth and seventeenth centuries. Renaissance poets, Continental and British, avidly read and emulated Lucan as a classical model alongside and in counterpoint to Virgil and Ovid. Shakespeare's awareness of *Civil War* is visible in likely and unlikely places. Among the former are the Roman histories (*Julius Caesar* and *Antony and Cleopatra*); among the latter is the prologue to *Romeo and Juliet* ("Where civil blood makes civil hands unclean" owes an undeniable debt to Lucan). Christopher Marlowe's line-for-line translation of the first book (published posthumously in 1600) is a paragon of Elizabethan classicizing blank verse; its influence is felt in his *Tamburlaine*. Less well known is Samuel Daniel's fascinating historical epic *The Civile Wars between the houses of Lancaster and York*, published between 1595 and 1609 and treating the dynastic wars of the previous century. Daniel's use of Lucan as a model is apt and sophisticated, often simply lifting the Latin and rendering it in English. The beginning stanzas will prove the point:

> I sing the civill Warres, tumultuous Broyles,
> And bloody factions of a mightie Land:
> Whose people hautie, proud with forraine spoyles,
> Upon themselves turn-backe their conquering hand;
> Whil'st Kin their Kin, Brother the Brother soyles;
> Like Ensignes all against like Ensignes band;
> Bowes against Bowes, the Crowne against the Crowne;
> Whil'st all pretending right, all right's throwne downe.
>
> What furie, o what madnes held thee so,
> Deare *England* (too prodigall of blood)
> To waste so much, and warre without a foe,
> Whilst *Fraunce*, to see thy spoyles, at pleasure stood!
> How much might'st thou have purchast with lesse woe. . . .
>
> Yet now what reason have we to complaine?
> Since hereby came the calme we did inioy;

The blisse of thee *Eliza*; happie gaine
For all our losse: when-as no other way
The Heavens could finde, but to unite againe
the fatall sev-red Families, that they
Might bring foorth thee: that in thy peace might growe
That glorie, which few Times could ever showe.

    Come sacred *Virtue*: I no *Muse*, but thee,
Invoke, in this great labour I intend. . . .

The transposition of Elizabeth for Nero certainly raises eyebrows, and the eschewing of any Muse but Virtue is a great twist on Lucan's own dismissal of help from the Muses (while France replacing Parthia as foreign enemy is the coup de grâce).

In 1614 Sir Arthur Gorges published the first complete English translation of Lucan into octosyllabic couplets, which was followed in 1627 by Thomas May's more satisfactory translation in heroic couplets. May was quite possessed by Lucan, and wrote three tragedies, *Cleopatra*, *Antigone*, and *Julia Agrippina*, that display his influence. By 1630 he had finished a seven-book English continuation of Lucan, bringing the narrative down to the assassination of Caesar, which he then translated into Latin and had published at Leiden in 1640 (the *Supplementum Lucani*, later printed in at least two editions of Lucan's text). May's fascination with Lucan had a timely political dimension, with civil war between Crown and Parliament first erupting in England in 1642, resulting in the execution of Charles I and the establishment of the Commonwealth in 1649, the year before May's death. May wrote parliamentarian pamphlets and his *History of the Parliament*, which liberally quotes Lucan and depicts a history of decline into strife and war since Elizabeth. On the other side, May's younger contemporary Abraham Cowley, a Royalist partisan, wrote his own *Civil War* poem in three books, which also exhibits much influence of Lucan. He left the poem unfinished and unpublished because of the Royalist defeat, and a version of just the first book was published in 1679, twelve years after his death.[21] In Marvell's *Horatian Ode, Upon Cromwell's Return from Ireland*, Cromwell is endowed, à la Lucan, with Caesar's lightning force, which, reversing the identifications, blasts the "Caesar" of Charles I.[22]

Continental authors, enmeshed in currents of republicanism, Protestantism, and overseas wars of conquest and rival imperial projects, found in Lucan poetic strategies for treating painful histories of rearguard resistance, tragic violence, and noble failure. Ercilla's Spanish epic *La Araucana*, on the bitter conquest of Chilean natives, and d'Aubigné's *Les Tragiques*, an apocalyptic poem on Huguenot resistance, mined Lucan for ways to narrate stories of liberty's valiant struggle against ever-triumphing tyranny.[23]

With the English monarchy restored in 1660, aspiring republicans were now more prone to identify with Cato, Brutus, and Lucan himself. Addison's tragedy *Cato* (1713) turned the noble suicide at Utica into a stage sensation that helped fire the American Revolution. Addison's contemporary Nicholas Rowe (1674–1718) was Lucan's next ardent English admirer. His expansive Augustan translation, on par with Dryden's Virgil and Pope's Homer, appeared posthumously in 1719. It was reissued throughout the eighteenth and nineteenth centuries and is readily available in libraries today.[24]

Romantics found that Lucan's passionate subjectivity and taste for the outlandish macabre fed their gothic sensibilities. Goethe opens the "Classical Walpurgisnacht" of *Faust Part II*, Act II (written in 1830), on Pharsalia's bloody field with a literarily self-conscious Erictho summing up *Civil War*:

"How often it has been repeated! And it must
recur eternally. Each wants to rule alone
and, holding power gained through power, neither yields
it to the other.—Those not competent to rule
their own unruly selves, with eager arrogance
seek to impose their will upon their neighbor's will.—
Here a battle was fought that grandly illustrates
how power always meets some power greater still,
how fragile is the many-flowered wreath of freedom,
how the stiff laurel, on the tyrant's head, is pliant.

Great Pompey, here, had dreams of burgeoning hopes fulfilled,
there wakeful Caesar watched each movement of fate's scales!
They are well matched—who wins, the world already knows."

(Translated by Stuart Atkins, Princeton, 1984)

Victor Hugo's sprawling episodic epic of world history, *La Lé-
gende des siècles* (published in the 1880s), quotes Lucan's appari-
tion of the fatherland rebuking Caesar in its introductory vision
of the cosmic wall of time:

All was found there: matter, spirit, filth and sunrays,
all the towns—Thebes and Athens—all the layers
of Romes above the heaps of Carthages and Tyres,
all the rivers, the Scheldt, the Rhine, the Nile, the Arle,
the Rubicon telling whomever may be Caesar:
"If you're still a citizen, you are only one
as far as me."

In 1912 the sculptor (and Confederate Civil War veteran) Moses
Ezekiel was commissioned to create the Confederate Memorial
for Arlington National Cemetery in Washington, D.C. One side
of the statue reads, "To our Dead Heroes by the United Daugh-
ters of the Confederacy Victrix Causa Diis Placuit Sed Victa
Catoni." Ezekiel's choice of *Bellum Civile* 1.128 (1.141 in the
translation), perhaps Lucan's most infamous *sententia*, to sum
up the historical complexities of the American Civil War and the
touchy nature of North-South reconciliation is, at the very least,
thought-provoking.

This quick survey of Lucan's rich reception history should suf-
fice to show his deep impact on Western literature and politics.
On one hand, his controversial topic and technique made his
poem loom large in debate about the nature of, and proper limits
between, poetry and history. On the other, he has played a unique
role among classical poets in stimulating and sanctioning mod-
ern republican political ideals and their critiques of entrenched
monarchy and absolute power. The work itself ensures its longev-
ity and its shaping power, for wherever Caesar and Pompey

appear together, sundered by the firm and principled voice of Cato, there will be Lucan—with his plea for liberty and resistance to tyranny. His bold stance may not have won him many admirers in his own time, but as a prism on the many forces that tore apart the Roman people, it has few peers. As such, it has undoubtedly helped shape the political and ideological landscape of the modern world.

Lucan's fortunes ebbed in the nineteenth and twentieth centuries, as *Civil War* fell under the dominance of hostile literary critics and ungenerous philologists (it bears noting that Ovid suffered the same fate). It was the age of the dreary prose translation: H. T. Riley published a literal, copiously annotated version in 1853; Duff's prose gloss appeared alongside the Latin text in his Loeb edition (1928); and no less a figure than Robert Graves rendered up his strange paraphrase in 1957 (the predecessor to this volume, but long out of print). Graves detested Lucan, openly despising his poem in his introduction (with many factual errors); one gets an impression that it was a by-product of research for his historical novels. For his part, Duff wrote in his introduction, "No reasonable judgment can rank Lucan among the world's great epic poets. He does not tell his story well: the successive episodes are neither skillfully connected nor well apportioned [etc.]." He then predictably trots out Quintilian against him and concludes, "The truth is, that Lucan is not a poet in the sense in which Lucretius and Virgil are poets." And so on. Still, it was in the century from 1850 to 1950 that Lucan's text was put on a solid footing through painstaking professional philology. Haskins's school text with English notes came out in 1887. Usener and Endt published the two sets of ancient scholia in this period. And the poet and eminent classicist A. E. Housman published his edition of the text in 1926. It has been the basis of most subsequent scholarship (while his caustic judgments on his predecessors have given scandalous delight to later classicists).

Even in the doldrums of this downturn Lucan had his rearguard defenders. In 1939 Antony Snell wrote a brief but spirited defense of Lucan against the tyrannous tide of present tastes. His thesis was simple: "The object of this article is to plead that

Lucan is an underrated poet, and well worth reading at length."²⁵
Since the 1960s and '70s, scholarly and literary tastes have swung
decidedly in Lucan's favor, until today, when every year sees an-
other fresh crop of insightful studies on Lucan. Very much part
and product of this ongoing reappraisal, the present translation is
intended to contribute to the continuing appreciation and enjoy-
ment of Lucan's unique and fiery historical "nonpoem" among
modern readers.

MATTHEW FOX
ETHAN ADAMS

NOTES

1. For the evidence and arguments see Nisbet, "Felicitas at Surrentum
   (Statius *Silvae* II.2)," *Journal of Roman Studies* 1978, pp. 1–11.
2. The title *Pharsalia*, by which Lucan's epic has also been known in
   recent centuries, has no authority in antiquity or the manuscript
   tradition, which referred to it as either *Bellum Civile* or *De Bello
   Civili*.
3. Johnson, *Momentary Monsters: Lucan and His Heroes* (Ithaca,
   1987), p. 46.
4. Sallust, *Histories*, frag. 12, trans. Woodman (Penguin, 2007),
   p. 144.
5. On these grounds some critics have argued that Lucan intended to
   end the poem where it does; but the most we can say for certain is
   that he brought his ending into alignment with Caesar's text be-
   fore he very suddenly died, not that he intended to leave it this way
   (which cannot be proven either way).
6. Sallust, *Histories*, frag. 11, pp. 143–44.
7. This reading of Lucan responds to Sklenar (2003), who in turn cri-
   tiques his key interpretive model, Johnson 1987. In a world with-
   out gods, goodness may be futile, but such an (epic) vision does
   not of itself extricae humankind from the mortal coils of exis-
   tence: even nihilism must give way to practical—moral—choices
   of how to live (even if one choice is *not to live*, to die, an option
   rehearsed again and again in *Bellum Civile*).
8. *Fortuna* occurs 146 times, forms of *felix* ("lucky, favored by for-
   tune") 45 times, and forms of *fatum* (singular, "fate, doom,
   death") and *fata* (plural, "fate, the Fates") 258 times.

9. Trans. Carter (Oxford, 2008), pp. 113, 115.

10. Cicero, *De Natura Deorum* 3.85, trans. McGregor (Penguin, 1972), p. 230.

11. On such grounds critics such as Sklenar (2003) interpret Lucan as a nihilist.

12. These and the following remarks draw upon D'Alessandro Behr's *Feeling History: Lucan, Stoicism, and the Poetics of Passion* (Columbus, OH, 2007).

13. Ibid., pp. 7, 181.

14. Seneca, *Moral Epistles*, 95.33–35, 70.25–26; discussed in M. Leigh, *Lucan, Spectacle and Engagement* (Oxford, 1997), pp. 259ff.

15. For a full and intelligent study of Roman suicide see T. Hill, *Ambitiosa Mors: Suicide and Self in Roman Thought and Literature* (New York, 2004), with a long chapter on Lucan.

16. See discussion in Feeney, *The Gods in Epic* (Oxford, 1991), pp. 263–64.

17. The critical afterlife of this notion has been torturous, often leading to rather ridiculous absurdities: for instance, Morford obligingly retraces the tired question only to reach the conclusion, "Yet Lucan's *Bellum Civile* is a poem; it is not a speech (or a series of declamations) or, by any stretch of the imagination, could it be called history. It is epic, but epic that has changed its terms" (*The Poet Lucan* [New York, 1967], p. 87). It is worth recalling, however, that *history* is exactly what the carping ancient critics called it.

18. These are the *Commenta Bernensia* and the less full *Adnotationes super Lucanum*, which give typical grammatical and stylistic notes, historical and cultural explanations, and constant cross-references to Virgil.

19. Augustine was familiar enough with Lucan to quote him several times, even for casual purposes, in *City of God*, where he tends, very much like Lucan, to read Roman history and even Virgil's *Aeneid* in the scathingly harsh light of Sallust's historical works.

20. Arnulf's work is known as the *Glosule super Lucanum*.

21. The whole poem was discovered, in manuscript among private papers, by Allan Pritchard and published only in 1973 (*Abraham Cowley: The Civil War*, Toronto).

22. Among the several scholars of early modern England tracing Lucan's influence, D. Norbrook and A. Shifflett deserve special mention (see Suggestions for Further Reading). Their works have helped trace the fertile impact of Lucan on authors such as May,

Jonson, Marvell, and Milton, especially in regard to notions of po-
litical engagement.

23. See Quint, *Epic and Empire* (Princeton, 1993), and Nicolopulos, *Poetics of Empire in the Indies* (University Park, PA, 2000).

24. Also, Brown and Martindale have published an excellent edition of Rowe's Lucan (London, 1998).

25. A. Snell, "Lucan," in *Greece & Rome* (1939), pp. 83–91.

Suggestions for Further Reading

The following works include studies devoted to Lucan, the reception history of *Civil War*, and some general works relating to Latin literature and culture germane to the study of Lucan's poem, its literary tradition, and its historical context. Any of the focused studies on Lucan will provide the interested reader with sufficient entry into the much more extensive bibliography on the poem.

Ahl, F., *Lucan, An Introduction* (Ithaca: 1976).

Bartsch, S., *Ideology in Cold Blood: A Reading of Lucan's Civil War* (Cambridge, MA: 1998).

Boyle, A. J. (ed.), *Roman Epic* (London: 1993).

Braund, S., and G. W. Most (eds.), *Ancient Anger: Perspectives from Homer to Galen* (Cambridge: 2003).

Brunt, P. A., *The Fall of the Roman Republic and Related Essays* (Oxford: 1988). (Especially the title essay and chapter 6, "*Libertas* in the Roman Republic.")

Connolly, J., *The State of Speech: Rhetoric and Political Thought in Ancient Rome* (Princeton: 2007).

D'Alessandro Behr, F., *Feeling History: Lucan, Stoicism, and the Poetics of Passion* (Columbus, OH: 2007).

Dominik, W. (ed.), *Roman Eloquence: Rhetoric in Society and Literature* (London: 1997). (Especially chapter 8, J. Farrell, "Towards a Rhetoric of (Roman?) Epic.")

Fantham, E., "The Angry Poet and the Angry Gods: Problems of Theodicy in Lucan's Epic of Defeat," pp. 229–49 in Braund and Most (eds.), 2003.

———, *Roman Literary Culture: From Cicero to Apuleius* (Baltimore: 1999).

Feeney, D. C., *The Gods in Epic* (Oxford: 1991).

Gelzer, M., *Caesar: Politician and Statesman* (Cambridge, MA: 1968).

Gowing, A., *Empire and Memory* (Cambridge: 2005).

Griffin, M., "Philosophy, Cato, and Roman Suicide," 2 parts, *Greece & Rome* (1986), pp. 64–77, 192–202.

Hardy, P., *The Epic Successors of Virgil* (Cambridge: 1993).

Henderson, J., "Lucan / The Word at War," *Ramus* (1987), pp. 122–64.

Hill, T. D., *Ambitiosa Mors: Suicide and Self in Roman Thought and Literature* (New York: 2004).

Johnson, W. R., *Momentary Monsters: Lucan and His Heroes* (Ithaca: 1987).

Keith, A., "Lament in Lucan's *Bellum Civile*," in A. Suter (ed.), *Lament: Studies in the Ancient Mediterranean and Beyond* (Oxford: 2008), pp. 233–57.

Leigh, M., *Spectacle and Engagement* (Oxford: 1997).

Martindale, C., *Redeeming the Text: Latin Poetry and the Hermeneutics of Reception* (Cambridge: 1993).

Masters, J., *Poetry and Civil War in Lucan's* Bellum Civile (Cambridge: 1992).

McDonnell, M., *Roman Manliness: Virtus and the Roman Republic* (Cambridge: 2006).

Morford, M. P. O., *The Poet Lucan: Studies in Rhetorical Epic* (New York: 1967).

Norbrook, D., *Writing the English Republic: Poetry, Rhetoric, and Politics 1627–1660* (Cambridge: 2000).

O'Hara, J., *Inconsistency in Roman Epic* (Cambridge: 2007).

Phang, S. E., *Roman Military Service: Ideologies of Discipline in the Late Republic and Early Principate* (Cambridge: 2008).

Quint, D., *Epic and Empire* (Princeton: 1993).

Rudich, V., *Dissidence and Literature under Nero: The Price of Rhetoricization* (London: 1997).

Shifflett, A., *Stoicism, Politics, and Literature in the Age of Milton: War and Peace Reconciled* (Cambridge: 1998).

Sklenar, R., *A Taste for Nothingness: A Study of Virtus and Related Themes in Lucan's* Bellum Civile (Ann Arbor: 2003).

Sowerby, R., *The Augustan Art of Poetry: Augustan Transla-tions of the Classics* (Oxford: 2006), especially the section "Rowe's Lucan" (pp. 174–208).

Tucker, R. A., "Lucan and the French Revolution: The *Bellum Civile* as a Political Mirror," *Classical Philology* 66 (1971), pp. 6–16.

Notes on the Text and Translation

The Latin dactylic hexameter is a six-foot line of quantitative verse, ranging in length from twelve to seventeen syllables (twelve almost never, generally fourteen or fifteen), in which the last foot is always a spondee (two longs) and the other five feet can be spondees or dactyls (long, short, short). Most lines have a noticeable caesura, or "cutting," somewhere toward the middle, where in recitation there is a slight but effective pause between half-lines. Latin, with its grammatical inflections and lack of articles, is notorious for its compression. Monosyllabic nouns and verbs, plentiful in English, are rare in Latin, which also has fewer long consonant clusters than English and none of our silent letters. All this adds to the density of the Latin line even though metrically it can be half again as long as the iambic pentameter that is so ingrained to the English ear. The proem, showing the six long stressed syllables and the caesura, will exemplify Lucan's verses:

Bélla per Émathiós // plus quám ciuília cámpos	15
iúsque datúm scelerí canimús, // populúmque poténtem	17
ín sua uíctricí // conuérsum uíscera déxtra	14
cógnatásque aciés, // et rúpto foédere régni	14
cértatúm totís // concússi uíribus órbis	13
ín commúne nefás, // inféstisque óbuia sígnis	15
sígna, parés aquilás // et píla minántia pílis.	16
104 syllables	

The translation is "free verse": most lines have five or six beats (only occasionally four or seven) and most also have the suggestion

of a caesura, which may, as in the first line, hinge between two
stressed syllables and beckon a slight pause while reading:

Of cívil wárs and wórse // wáged on Emáthian fíelds,	14
of críme made láw we síng, // how a pówerful péople	13
túrned on íts own héart // its cónquering hánd,	10
of ránks of rélatíves, // and a bróken páct of rúle	14
that drágged a sháken wórld // with áll its stréngth	10
ínto conténtion // to wín a cómmon gúilt,	11
of stándards ópposite hóstile stándards,	10
pártisan éagles // and spéars sháking at spéars.	11

93 syllables

The main aim was to find phrases and clauses to match those
in the original, allowing as much as possible for words and ideas
to unfold in the same order as in the Latin. The inevitable creep
of extra lines is already evident, the seven Latin lines spilling over
into eight in English (elsewhere, alas, the ratio is more like 4:5 or
even 2:3). Other stats: 93 syllables to the original 104 (an encour-
aging economy); 65 words to 47 in Latin (the encouragement
wanes); 41 stressed syllables to the 42 stressed beats in Latin (a
satisfying point of concord). Latin verse teaches one to conserve
resources, challenging one to find ways in prosy English to say
more in less: the definite article, for example, is reserved for strict
necessity ("the" first occurs only at line 16).

So much for sheer numbers. Lucan's verse is full of wordplay,
soundplay, and conceptual play, which summons creative cour-
age from the translator but which often ends in compromise (if
not near defeat). For example, "civil wars and worse" is a pale
rendition of Lucan's *bella plus quam civilia* "wars more than
civil," a strange phrase even in Latin, which exploits ambiguity
to achieve a surplus of interpretive potential (see note on 1.1–8).
The single word "guilt" fails to capture the Latin *nefas*—which
means, approximately, a misdeed so outrageous that even its
mention is enough to offend gods and men—unless one allows
the full legal and moral strength of "guilt" to sound forth there
at line's end, like a judge declaring a death sentence to the single
crushing blow of his gavel. Lucan is quite fond of alliteration,

and the translation uses it freely to bind together phrases and lines into a sonic texture to match syntactic and conceptual units: for example, in Latin, *civilia campos*, *populumque potentem*, *victrici conversum viscera*, *rupto regni*, *certatum concussi commune*; so in English, "wars and worse waged," "powerful people," "heart/hand," "ranks of relatives . . . rule," "shaken . . . strength," "contention . . . common."

Lucan likes to manipulate the placement of words for unique effects, which once in a while one is able to approximate. So, for example, describing the pivotal geographical location of Delphi, he writes (5.75–76):

> Hesperio tantum quantum summotus Eoo
> cardine Parnasos gemino petit aethera colle

—the whole point of the first line being to stretch west and east out to opposite ends of the line and provide a word picture of the distant ends of the earth. So, in English,

> Sunset is just as far removed from Dawn
> at Parnassus; its twin peak hinges up to the sky

This sort of thing is very common in Lucan, and one can hardly replicate it all without seriously straining the sense and syntax of the English (and probably exhausting the reader). And where some line seems to torture grammar or normal word order, it is safe to assume that some poetic effect in the original is the motivating cause.

As noted in the introduction, several key terms in Lucan recur again and again, playing like leitmotifs in a symphony, and thus some care has gone into rendering them consistently with single English words. The most important of these: *fortuna* is always "fortune," and *fata/fatum* is "fate(s)" (capitalized or not depending on context), except a couple times *fatum* is "doom"; *virtus* is always either "virtue" or "valor" depending on context; *libertas* is "liberty" (except once, at 8.447–48, *libertate fugae* is rendered as "freedom for retreat"); *natura* is always (or almost always) "nature"; *civile bellum* and *civilia bella* (plural) are always "civil war(s)," and the many variations on this crucial idea (such as *civilia arma*) are always recognizable by the use of "civil." The very common word *dux*, which is a poetic fill-in for real-life but more prosaic terms such as *imperator*, *consul*, and *praetor*, is rendered variously, for metrical and poetic purposes, as "general," "leader," "chief," and "commander."

In general, explanatory material is not added into the translation, but is reserved for the notes, so that the reader can be reasonably confident the translation reflects what is found in the Latin. There are just a couple of notable exceptions to this rule. First, Lucan likes to call the sun god "Titan," which is rendered as "the Titan Sun" and even just "the Sun." So, too, Lucan uses the Latin—and Greek—names of the winds, which were meaningful in Latin, indicating the wind direction, but which mean nothing to modern readers. While sometimes the names appear in the translation as they stand, at other times they are translated as "north wind" (for Boreas), and so on, or even added alongside the proper name is a reference to the wind direction. A list of wind names and their directions will be found just before the notes.

We have mainly followed the text of A. E. Housman's 1927 (corrected) edition. But comparison with Giovanni Viansino's text (Milan: Mondadori, 1995), which tends to follow the manuscript tradition over emendations, conjectures, and line transpositions in Housman and Shackleton Bailey (Teubner 1988), has led to the adoption of other readings at times (listed below). His copious literary notes have also been indispensable. Similarly, Duff's prose gloss in his Loeb edition (1928) has been a constant aid, especially where Lucan's Latin is opaque or difficult (as it often is). Innumerable times we mulled the Latin, and what Duff made of it, then consulted commentaries as well as what other translators had done: we are proud to say that on several occasions we feel that we have been able to correct or improve Duff's by now standard interpretations of hard passages. (By the same token, wherever doubts remained, we hope we have made intelligent choices and not introduced too many new mistakes.)

TEXTUAL VARIANTS FROM
HOUSMAN'S OXFORD EDITION

Book One: 16 *oris*; 74–75 included; 1.227 *fatis*; 1.234 *seu*;
1.282 included; 1.432 *Mosa* (see note at 1.468); 1.615
nigrum; 1.641 *moventibus* (translation also reflects Hous-
man's reasoning for *sequentibus*).

Book Two: 106 *praecipitasse*; 292 *compressas*; 2.387 *huic
maximus*; 2.406 *iunctus Apise Pisaurus*; 2.425 *Vescinis*;
2.473 *Luceriae*; 2.554 *qua . . . hostis*; 2.673 *ausus*; 2.703a
omitted (added by Housman); 2.710 *quae*.

Book Three: 101 *fausta*; 132 *exhaustae*; 149 *nil iam*; 328
rerum; 286 *Xerxes*.

Book Four: 171 included; 4.719 *metuens incauto*.

Book Five: 443 *rigente*; 535a omitted (added by Housman);
549 *nota*; 650b–51a included; 651 *Chaoniae*; 804–5
vadis . . . fugis.

Book Six: 27 *rabido*; 187 omitted; 207 omitted; 408 *antra*;
556 omitted; 782 *alii*.

Book Seven: 20 *venturis* (but borrowing Housman's *mens* as
subject); 154 omitted; 161 included; 180 *dementibus*; 257–
58 omitted; 387 *non expleat*; 388 included; 462 *tempus*;
464 *parentes*; 514–20 in order (in Housman, after 488); 658
voluitque; 677 *te praesente*; 746b–49a omitted.

Book Eight: 51 *sed*; 157 *nimis*; 195 *quas Psyriae* (see note at
8.232); 294 *regnandi*; 321 *redit*; 345 *extolletque*; 716 *Idalio*.

Book Nine: 38 *Creta*; 160 included; 241 *quem*; 427 *quorum*;
494 omitted; 592 *certare*; 627 *suco* (a tough choice); 632–33
in order (inverted in Housman); 674a omitted (added by
Housman); 808 *perfundere . . . tignis*; 954 *natatum*.

Book Ten: 43 *qua*; 107 *duci*; 117 *Meroitica*; 10.122a omitted
(added by Housman); 123 *quorum*; 322 *invictis*; 472a omit-
ted (added by Housman); 10.518 included.

Chronology of
Roman Historical Events

753 BC	Traditional date for founding of Rome by Romulus and Remus
509 BC	End of monarchy and beginning of Republic in Rome, L. Junius Brutus first consul
387 BC	Gauls invade Italy and sack Rome
218–201 BC	Rome's Second Punic War against Carthage and Hannibal
133 BC	The tribune Tiberius Gracchus and supporters killed in political strife in Rome
121 BC	Gaius Gracchus commits suicide, supporters executed by Senate in Rome
107 BC	First consulship of Marius, opens military recruitment to landless poor citizens
106 BC	Birth of Gnaeus Pompeius (Pompey); birth of Marcus Tullius Cicero
104–100 BC	Marius elected consul five times in succession
100 BC	Birth of Gaius Julius Caesar; birth of Metellus Scipio (approx.)
95 BC	Birth of Marcus Porcius Cato the Younger
91–88 BC	Social War between Rome and Italian allies
88 BC	Sulla elected consul, marches legions on Rome; Marius driven into exile
86 BC	Seventh consulship and death of Marius
85 BC	Birth of Marcus Junius Brutus
83 BC	Birth of Marcus Antonius (Mark Antony)
83–81 BC	Sulla returns from the East, defeats Marians in the city, appointed dictator (81)

80 BC   Sulla is consul; Pompey defeats Marians in Africa,
               triumphs and is named Magnus ("the Great")

79 BC   Sulla retires from politics, dies the following year

77–71 BC   Pompey campaigns against Sertorius in Spain, receives
               second triumph (71)

73–71 BC   Spartacus slave revolt, suppressed by Lucullus, Crassus,
               and Pompey

ca. 73 BC   Birth of Cornelia, daughter of Metellus Scipio

70 BC   Pompey is consul

67–61 BC   Pompey suppresses pirates, campaigns in the East;
               third triumph (61)

59 BC   Triumvirate of Crassus, Pompey, and Caesar; Pompey
               marries Julia; Caesar is consul

58–50 BC   Caesar's legions conquer Gaul

54 BC   Death of Julia and her child in childbirth

53 BC   Death of Crassus and his son in battle at Carrhae;
               Pompey marries Cornelia (52)

50 BC   Pompey and Senate refuse to allow Caesar to stand for
               consul in absentia

49 BC   Civil war begins: Caesar crosses Rubicon, Pompey and
               Senate leave Rome (Jan.); surrender of Corfinium,
               Pompey leaves Brundisium (Feb.–Mar.); Caesar holds
               Senate in Rome (Apr.); siege of Massilia, Caesar defeats
               legions in Spain (Apr.–Oct.); Curio defeated in Africa,
               Gaius Antonius defeated in Illyria (Aug.–Oct.); Caesar
               appointed dictator in Rome (Dec.)

48 BC   Caesar is elected consul, crosses to Illyria (Jan.); fight-
               ing in Dyrrachium (Jan.–July); Caesar defeats Pompey
               and Senate at Pharsalus (Aug. 9); Pompey flees to Egypt
               and is killed (Sept. 28); Caesar in Alexandria with
               Cleopatra (Oct.–Dec.)

47 BC   Caesar declared dictator; Caesar concludes war in
               Egypt (Mar.), wins war in Pontus (Aug.), returns to
               Rome (Sept.), and departs for Africa (Dec.)

46 BC   Caesar consul, and dictator for ten years; Pompeians
               defeated at Thapsus, Cato commits suicide at Utica
               (Apr.); Caesar returns to Rome, celebrates quadruple
               triumph (July–Sept.)

45 BC	Caesar consul, dictator for life; sons of Pompey defeated at Munda in Spain (Mar.); Caesar celebrates Spanish triumph (Oct.)
44 BC	Senatorial conspirators murder Caesar (Mar. 15); Caesar's nephew Octavian is his heir
43 BC	Octavian defeats Antony at Mutina (Apr.); Octavian, Antony, and Lepidus form Second Triumvirate and enact proscriptions of enemies (Oct.); Cicero is killed (Dec.)
42 BC	Julius Caesar is declared divine; defeat of Brutus and Cassius at Philippi (Oct.)
36 BC	Octavian's admiral Agrippa defeats Sextus Pompey in Sicily
31 BC	Octavian defeats Antony and Cleopatra at Actium (Sept. 2)
30 BC	Antony and Cleopatra commit suicide in Alexandria
27 BC	Octavian receives the honorary titles Augustus and Princeps
AD 14	Death of Augustus (Aug. 19); his stepson Tiberius inherits imperial power, establishing the Julio-Claudian dynasty
AD 37	Death of Tiberius; Caligula becomes emperor; birth of Nero
AD 39	Birth of Lucan in Spain (Nov. 3)
AD 41	Caligula murdered by praetorian guards conspiring with senators
AD 41–54	Claudius is emperor; possibly poisoned by his wife, Agrippina, mother of Nero
AD 54	Nero becomes emperor at seventeen
AD 65	Pisonian conspiracy against Nero; death of Lucan, Seneca, and others
AD 66–70	Great Jewish revolt in Judaea; Vespasian and son Titus suppress it, sack Jerusalem
AD 68	Provincial governors revolt; Nero flees Rome, commits suicide (June 9)
AD 69	Civil war in Roman Empire; four emperors in a year; Vespasian becomes emperor

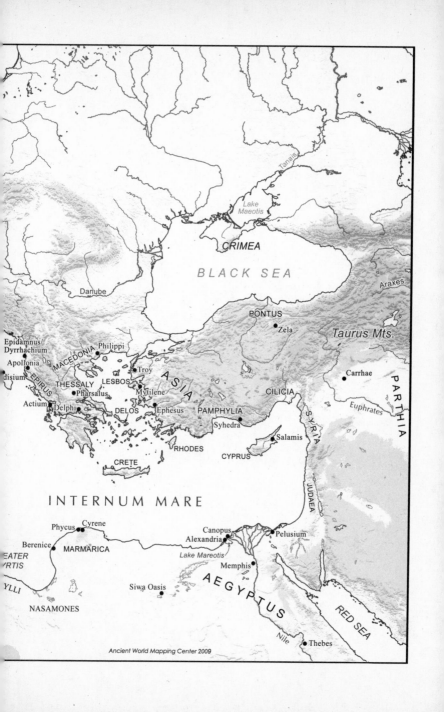

Epidamnus/
Dyrrhachium
Apollonia
Actium
EPIRUS
MACEDONIA
Philippi
THESSALY
LESBOS
Pharsalus
Delphi
Troy
Mytilene
DELOS
Ephesus
ASIA
PAMPHYLIA
Syhedra
RHODES
CRETE
CILICIA
SYRIA
IUDAEA
CYPRUS
Salamis
Carrhae
PARTHIA
Euphrates
Taurus Mts.
Araxes
PONTUS
Zela
CRIMEA
BLACK SEA
Tanais
Lake
Maeotis
Danube

INTERNUM MARE

Phycus
Cyrene
Berenice
MARMARICA
EATER
YRTIS
YLLI
NASAMONES
Siwa Oasis
Canopus
Alexandria
Lake Mareotis
Memphis
Pelusium
AEGYPTUS
Nile
Thebes
RED SEA

Ancient World Mapping Center 2009

Civil War

BOOK ONE

Proem announces the theme of civil war, invokes the emperor Nero as muse for this civil-war epic, and sketches the various causes for the war (1–199). Caesar crosses the Rubicon after facing down an indignant apparition of the fatherland (200–251), and takes the town of Ariminum, whose citizens quietly lament their fate (252–85). The tribunes, driven out of Rome by the Senate, meet up with Caesar, and Gaius Scribonius Curio urges Caesar to defend his interests: the stakes are all or none (286–321). Caesar musters and addresses his troops, laying out his case for armed defense of his and their rights against pretenders to tyranny in the city (322–81). The centurion Laelius strongly seconds his speech, silencing murmurs of hesitation among the men (382–424). Catalogue of Caesar's troops, which come from all corners of the provincial Gallic frontier and leave the empire exposed to the sundry foreign tribes of the north (425–98). Terror, panic, and flight throughout Italy accompany the rumors of Caesar's approach, and the city is abandoned by the Senate and Pompey (499–560). Catalogue of dreadful omens and portents reported upon Caesar's coming, including sightings of the ghosts of Sulla and Marius (561–625). The Etruscan diviner Arruns is summoned to interpret and to oversee expiatory rites, which entails a catalogue of Roman religious practices (626–73); Arruns prophesies "things worse than we fear" (674–83). Nigidius Figulus, erudite senator and Pythagorean astrologer, interprets the coming threats from the positions of the stars and constellations (684–718). A Roman matron, inspired by Phoebus, foretells battles to come in Thessaly, Egypt, Africa, and Spain, a headless trunk in the Nile's sands, an end to war in the middle of the Senate, and still more conflicts closing with a "second Philippi" (719–41).

BOOK ONE

PROEM AND PRAISE OF NERO

Of civil wars and worse waged on Emathian fields,
of crime made law we sing, how a powerful people
turned on its own heart its conquering hand,
of ranks of relatives, and a broken pact of rule
that dragged a shaken world with all its strength
into contention to win a common guilt,
of standards opposite hostile standards,
partisan eagles and spears shaking at spears.

What *fury*, citizens, what anarchy of iron?
Did it seem good to display Latin carnage   10
before hateful nations—when proud Babylon
should have been spoiled of its Italian trophies
and Crassus' ghost still wandered unavenged—
good to wage wars that held no hope for triumphs?
Oh, how much of earth and sea might have been gained
with all the blood our citizens' hands have drained—
where the Sun dawns, where night conceals the stars,
where midday boils and seethes on blazing shores,
and where stiff winter, never relaxed by spring,
binds the cold Black Sea in a Scythian freeze.   20
We might have yoked the Chinese, the wild Araxes,
or whatever tribe knows where the Nile rises.
Then, Rome, if you love wicked war so much,

[handwritten marginal note: Much carnage]

[handwritten marginal note: What Rome United could have accomplished]

3

once you have subjected all the world to Latin laws,
then attack yourself. You've not lacked yet for foes.

But now that walls are teetering under roofs half ruined
in Italy's cities, and from crumbled structures
massive stones lie idle, homes are left untended,
and the rare resident wanders through ancient cities,
now that Hesperia's thorny and year after year   30
lies fallow, and plowlands lack the hands they call for,
you're not to blame, fierce Pyrrhus, nor can Hannibal
be called responsible for so much damage—
to plunge so deep takes more than any sword:
such gaping wounds belong to civic hands.

But if the Fates could find, to bring forth Nero,
no other way, and eternal kingdoms cost
gods dearly, nor heaven be slave to its Thunderer
unless the savage Giants had lost the wars—
by god, we don't complain; those crimes, the guilt,   40
are pleasing at this price; let Pharsalia's fields
swell with curses, Hannibal's shade glut on blood—
let fatal Munda's final battles begin!
To these fates, Caesar, add Perusia's famine,
the labors of Mutina and those fleets that sank
at cruel Leucas, the slave wars under fiery Etna;
still Rome owes a lot to her civil war armies—
for it was done for *you.*
                              When your watch is through
and you seek the stars at last, your chosen court
of heaven will welcome you, delighting the pole.   50
You could hold the scepter, or you may like to mount
Phoebus' flame-bearing chariot, range the earth—
unfazed by the change of sun—with roving fire;
whatever you please: each god will cede to you,
and nature will relinquish her right to you
to be what god you will, install your world throne.

But do not choose your seat in Arctic regions,
nor in warm skies inclined to adverse south winds:
from these your gaze on Rome would be aslant.
If you weigh on any one part of boundless space   60
the axle will feel the load. Keep your weight
to the middle: balance heaven. May the sky
be clear, serene there, no clouds obstructing Caesar.
Then may humankind put arms aside, consult
its own good, may each nation love each other,
and may peace, dispatched throughout the world,
chain tight the gates of belligerent Janus.
But you're a god to me *now*: and if as seer
my heart is seized by you, I'd have no need
to rouse the god who stirs up Delphi's secrets   70
or to bother Bacchus to abandon Nysa—
you are enough to empower Roman poems.

THE CAUSES OF WAR

I've in mind to reveal the causes of great matters,
and the deed is immense: to expose what drove
a people to arms, raving, what struck peace
from the globe. Fates' hateful sequence: the mighty
don't stand long. A grave downfall, excessive weight:
Rome couldn't bear herself. So when, with seams torn,
the world's last hour will draw all time to a point,
reverting to primal chaos, all cosmic signs   80
will flow into one mass mixture, flaming stars
will fall in the sea, lands refuse to spread their shores
shaking off the waves; Phoebe will turn against
the sun her brother, unwilling to drive her team
across its own warped course, and claim that day is hers.
The whole contraption of the world ripped apart
shall riot, confounding its treaties in discord.

Great things rush to ruin: the powers that give bounty
have set this limit on increase. Not to any foreign
nations did Fortune lend her envy to use   90
against the people ruling on land and sea.
Made slaves of three masters, *you* caused the damage,
Rome, with fatal bonds of tyranny never before
loosed against the crowd. Foul concord! Blinded
by depths of greed! What use to unite your strength
to hold the world in common? As long as earth
shall light on sea and air on earth, and labors
keep the Sun revolving, night following day
through the same sum of signs, no pledge to reign
as peers will hold. All power is impatient of equals.   100

Don't search the *foreign* nations for examples
to prove that this is fate. A brother's blood
soaked Rome's first walls. Nor were land and sea
the prize then for such fury: a measly asylum
united its lords in a strife that divided them.

Their discordant concord held out for a time—
peace in spite of the chiefs. The only delay
on certain war was Crassus in the middle.
Just as Corinth's isthmus cuts the waves, and keeps
the twin Greek seas apart, not allowed to meet,   110
but take that stretch away and the Ionian
would pummel the Aegean; so, too, the savage
arms of chiefs that Crassus parted, when he met
his miserable doom—he poured his Latin blood
out in Carrhae, staining that Assyrian land—
the Parthian defeat unleashed Roman furies.
(So your ranks achieved more than you believed,
Arsacides: you gave those you beat a civil war.)

Iron divided the kingdom. The fortune
of a people—so powerful they possessed   120
both lands and sea, the whole entire world—
just wasn't big enough for two. The marriage vows,

the torches made funereal by a dire omen,
were null and void when Julia joined the shades,   *Death of*
cut off by the cruel hand of the Fates. Because   *Julia*
if they had let you linger longer in the light,   *a Cause*
you alone might have held in check your father
and your raging husband, joined their hands—though armed,
their swords put down—as when the Sabine women
stood in between and joined fathers to sons-in-law.   130
Your death broke the faith; the chiefs could start the war.

Pompey(?)   Their rivalry in valor gave them motives:
Magnus, you fear your former triumphs might be dimmed
by novel exploits, that your laurels for the pirates
might give way before the conquered Gauls. And you
are being roused by skill, your series of spoils,
and a fortune that cannot stand to be second place.
Caesar could bear none better, Pompey no equal.
Which one took up arms more justly? Knowing that
is not allowed—a high judge acquits each one: 140
Gods favored the victor, but Cato the lost cause.

Nor were the rivals peers. One verged on old age,
was calmer, more sedate from wearing the toga;
in peace he'd unlearned leadership, now seeking
popular fame through benefactions, moved by   *Pompey*
shifting fashions, pleased by applause in his theater.
Trusting bygone fortune, he never recruited
any fresh forces. He stands in his great name's shadow.
Like a mighty oak in a bountiful field,
weighed down with a people's old war spoils   150
and gifts devoted by leaders, its strong roots
no longer holding it, just its sheer fixed mass,
spreading its naked branches through the air,
its trunk and not its boughs now casting shadow.
And though it nods, about to fall in the breeze,
and many strong young trees rise up around it,
it alone is honored.
                    Whereas with Caesar,   *(Julius)*

no mere name and leader's fame was his, but valor
that could not stay in place, and not to conquer
in war was his only shame; sharp, intractable,   160
responsive to his prospects and his rages,
never afraid a drawn sword might be reckless;
he followed up successes, pressed the favor
of his star, shoved hard obstructions to his goal—
making his way with ruin was his joy.
As when, pressed through the clouds by winds, a lightning
bolt—the sky struck, world shaking with thunder—
flashes, cracks the day, and people shudder in
terror, their eyes dazzled by snaking flame;
raging against its precincts, no matter can   170
forbid its passage; it strikes, spreads wide its great
mayhem, turns back, regroups its scattered fires.

These were the leaders' reasons. But underneath
were public seeds of war, which always sink
a powerful people. For when Fortune imported
excessive resources from a world brought low,
and morals took a backseat to prosperous times
and enemy plunder made luxury persuasive,
with no end to gold or houses, former foods
famished the craving. Men stole and wore apparel   180
barely fit for their sons' young wives. The nurse of men,
Poverty, fled. Summoned from round the world
came each clan's special plague. They bought up giant
tracts of land—those once furrowed by Camillus'
hardy plowshare, that felt old Curius' shovel—
for vast estates now worked by foreign tenants.

This wasn't a people who tranquil peace could please,
who could let arms lie, let their liberty feed them;
so anger flared up easily, and driven by indigence,
crime came cheap. By steel one could gain great honor   190
and overpower his fatherland. The measure of right
was might. Laws won popular votes by coercion,
just order was disturbed by consuls and tribunes.

The rods of office were bought, and the people
auctioned off their favor, and the fatal polling   *corrupt*
around the city brought back year after year   *Rome*
the Campus Martius to the auction block.
Usury ran rampant and interest, greedy for payments,
rose, and trust shattered: many found profit in war.

War mongering

CAESAR CROSSES THE RUBICON RIVER

Now the cold Alps were past on Caesar's course,   200
and in his mind the great revolts and coming war
had been conceived. At the waters of narrow Rubicon
the leader saw the mighty image of his fatherland
full of sorrow, trembling clearly in night's darkness,
white hair disheveled on her head crowned with towers,
locks shorn and arms laid bare she stood before them;
choked by sobs she spoke: "How far will you go?
Where do you bear my standards, men? If you come
as lawful citizens, you must stop here." Cold dread
seized their leader's limbs. His hair stood high on end,   210
and faintness checked his footsteps at the river's edge.

Soon he spoke: "You who overlook the city's walls
from Tarpeia's rock, Thunderer, you Phrygian housegods
of Iulus' clan, and secrets of Quirinus who disappeared,
and residing on high Alba, Jupiter of Latium,
and Vestal fires and you, O godly apparition,
Rome—favor my endeavors. No furious arms   *Caesar*
attack you. See me, victor on land and sea,   *believes*
Caesar, always and even now your soldier.   *he's the*
He will be guilty who made me your enemy."   *good*
                                                   guy   220

So he broke all that held war back, and across
the swollen stream straightway he led the standards.
As in the wild fields of heat-blistering Libya
a lion sees his foe close at hand and doubts,

crouching down while he gathers up his rage;
but then, once he's lashed himself with his savage tail,
bristled his mane and let forth a mighty roar
from his massive jaws, then, should an agile Moor
twist a lance that strikes, or a spear pierce his wide
chest, heedless of such wounds it runs him out and through.   230

From a modest spring, urged by scanty waves, falls
the mud-red Rubicon when parched by summer heat;
winding through low valleys it fixes the sure border
that divides Gallic fields from Ausonia's farmers.
But winter gave it strength and swelled its waves:
three times Cynthia's horn had risen heavy with rain,
and moist winds had also melted Alpine snows.
The cavalry moved first, lining the stream's course
to obstruct its flow. Then the whole throng forces
an easy ford across the now-broken river's waves.   240

Caesar, once he has touched the opposite bank
of the river he has subjected, speaks out
where he stands in Hesperia's forbidden fields:
"Here, right here, I shed peace and our defiled laws.
Fortune, I follow you. Faith can go to the winds—
I've put my trust in the Fates. Let war decide!"

So declaring, in night's darkness the rapid general
drives his army, like stones from Balearic slings;
swifter than a retreating Parthian shooting arrows,
he swoops to invade nearby Ariminum, while   250
stars flee the sun's flame, leaving the morning star.

THE AFTERMATH AT ARIMINUM

And now the day that would see the first tumults
of war dawned. Either gods willed it, or south winds

drove them, but storm clouds cast a gloomy light.
As ordered, his soldiers lay down their standards
in the captured forum, when a trumpet blast, a blare
of raucous brass and horns sound impious war.
The people's rest is shattered, and up from their beds
young men jump and grab down arms fastened to shrines
of household gods—arms that long peace gave them.
They take up shields with frames laid bare and drooping,
spears with crooked points, rough and rust-bit swords.
They see the eagles shining from Roman standards
and high in the midst of his ranks regard Caesar—
they go numb with fear, cold dread seizes their limbs,
and tacit in their chests they turn mute protests:
"Damn these walls, built so close to the Gauls!
Doomed by our poor location!"

                              "Deep peace everywhere,
people resting, tranquil—but us, we're first prey,
first camp for these madmen."

                              "Fortune, far better
if you'd placed us under eastern, or cold north skies
and made us nomads, than to guard Latium's gates."

"First we saw Senones, then the raiding Cimbri,
and Libya's Mars, and the furious advance
of Teutons. Whenever Fortune harasses Rome,
our home is her warpath."

                         Each man groaned in secret,
none dared to fear in public. No voice is trusted
to misery, but just as silent as in the country
when all is calm and winter stills the bird flocks
and mid-sea quits its roaring, so great was their quiet.
Light had dissolved night's chilly shadows when,
behold, torches of war are sparked in Caesar's mind
full of doubts, urging him to battles, and Fate
breaks all bonds of shame. Fortune works it so
the leader's revolts are just. She finds causes for arms. . . .

(Handwritten margin notes: "town", "militia", "dilapidated" 260, "unready"; "unhappy occupation" 280)

(Line numbers in margin: 260, 270, 280)

CURIO URGES CAESAR TO WAR

control rome to control the world

The Curia, deserting what's right, had expelled
from the factious city controversial tribunes,
warning them with reminders of the Gracchi.
These now sought Caesar's approaching standards,
bold Curio with them and his venal tongue,   290
once the people's voice; to guard their liberty
he rashly embroiled the plebs with armed powers-that-be.
When he spied the leader turning many cares
over in his chest he said:
                                    "While my voice could
aid your interests, Caesar, though the Senate opposed me,
I prolonged your command, as long as law
allowed me to mount the Rostrum and to draw
indecisive citizens over to your side.
But now the force of war has silenced laws
and we are driven out from gods and country,   300
to suffer a willing exile. Your victory
will make us citizens again. So while
the factions are bewildered, with no firm resolve,
act fast—delay is always harmful if you're ready.
The game and risks are the same, but the stakes are greater:
Gaul kept you campaigning for two five-year terms—
but what a small plot of ground! Wage a few easy battles
and Rome will have subjugated all the world for *you*.
But right now, no long triumphal pomp awaits
to welcome your return, nor is the Capitol   310
requesting sacred laurels. Gnawing envy
denies you all, and you will hardly escape
penalty for all your annexed nations. No,
your son-in-law has plans to oust his own
father-in-law from power. You cannot have
a world divided—but you can own the whole."

So he spoke, and though hell-bent on war already,
the speech adds rage and ignites the leader, as much
as clamor aids the Olympic stallion—though pent in
behind starting bars, he's straining over the gates   320
and now leans hard to burst free from the bolts.

all or nothing

CAESAR ADDRESSES HIS TROOPS

He musters his companies to arms and standards
and calls to order with his gaze the loud confusion
of the crowd, bids them silent with a hand, and says:
"Comrades in arms, a thousand perils of Mars
have proven you and I, in ten years of victory now—
is this what your bloodshed in northern fields deserves,
your wounds, your deaths, for winters passed in the Alps?
Rome is sounding her loud alarms for conflict
as if Punic Hannibal himself had crossed the Alps!   330
Cohorts are filling up, full-strength with raw recruits,
whole forests fall for fleets. What are their orders?   *Sucessful*
Pursue *Caesar* on land and sea!   *Campaign*
                                                             before,
                        "But what
if my standards fell, subdued by hostile Mars,
and at our backs rushed in the savage tribes of Gauls?
And *now*—when Fortune drives me with successful
undertakings, when gods summon me to the pinnacles—   *betrayed*
they attack me!   *now*

                        "Bring on their lazy, peacetime leader
with his upstart armies, his war partners in their togas—
Marcellus, full of words, and the empty names of Catos!   340
Indeed, shall Pompey's hired foreign clients
keep on glutting him with endless power?
Should he have triumphed before the age permitted?
Will he never let go of honors he stole in the first place?
Am I to protest *now* that he harnessed the countryside

and world hunger served his ends? Who doesn't know
of the camp pitched in the frightened Forum, the swords
surrounding the troubled law courts grimly flashing
and how the soldier dared to break through the law
when Pompey's standards concluded Milo's trial?   350
Now, too, to escape weary old age in private life,
he plans wicked wars; he's used to civil warfare—
Sulla's student in crime vies to surpass his master.

  "Like wild tigers that never lose their fury
while in Hyrcanian woods they follow their mother
to her dens and feast on thick blood of slaughtered cattle,
so, once so used to licking Sulla's sword blade,
Magnus' thirst endures. And blood, once swallowed,
never permits the throat it pollutes to be tamed.
What end will be found for such enormous power?   360
Where's the limit of crime?

                            "Descend your throne already,
foul man! At least let your Sulla teach you *that*!
First it was Cilician pirates, then the Pontic wars
with a tired king, killed at last with barbaric poison—
shall Pompey now win Caesar as his final province
because when ordered to lay down victorious eagles
I disobeyed? But if my own work's wages are seized,
at least let *these* men get paid, without their leader,
for their long wars. This troop should march in triumph,
whoever is their captain!

                            "Where will you retire   370
for bloodless old age after the wars? Your veteran years,
where will you spend them? What fields will they give
to you, my worthy men, so you may till them?
What walls for your weary bones?

                            "Or is it better
that your pirates, Magnus, become colonial farmers?
Raise high the standards victorious so long now!
We must use the strength that we have made!
Arms will get you all the just deserts refused you!
The gods will not fail us—for I am not after

plunder or a kingdom. We go to drag masters   380
out of a city now prepared to serve them!"

So he spoke, but the doubtful crowd grumbled
hushed and unsure murmurs. However fierce their minds
and spirits swelling for slaughter, their fathers'
household gods, and piety, break them. But grim
love of steel and fear of their leader recall them.

For high-ranking Laelius, wearing his oak leaves,
badge of honor for saving a comrade's life, shouts out:
"If I may, O greatest governor of the Roman name,
and if it is right to confess true words—that you   390
have held in check your strength with long endurance
is *our* complaint. Have you lost your trust in us?
As long as warm blood moves our breathing bodies
and strength of arm remains to spin these long spears,
will you suffer the toga's disgrace and the Senate to reign?

"And is it really so dreadful to win a civil war?
Lead me across the Scythian nations, down the shores
of inhospitable Syrtes, through the hot and thirsty
sands of Libya—these hands tamed the tumid waves
of Ocean with the oar, to leave a conquered world   400
behind us, and broke the foaming Rhine's north currents—
to follow your lead takes equal strength and will.
Whomever your trumpets call me against, Caesar,
is not my fellow citizen. I swear by your standards
lucky in ten campaigns, and by your triumphs,
whoever the enemy be, if you order me
to bury my sword in my brother's chest
or my parents' throats, or deep in the belly
of my wife, large with my growing offspring,
though my hand be unwilling, I will do it all!   410
Or to plunder the gods, set fire to their temples—
flames will melt their statues into army coinage.
If you say 'Pitch camp beside the Tuscan Tiber,'
I'll boldly go mark its lines in Hesperia's fields.

Whatever walls you wish to throw down, level flat,
these arms will drive the ram to strew their stones.
You just name the city and I will utterly raze it,
even if it is Rome."

        All at once the cohorts
gave their assent and made known with high hands
their pledge to take part in any war he charged them.   420
Their clamor struck high heaven, as loud as when
Thracian Boreas bears down on the pine-clad crags
of Ossa, and the sound of strong tree trunks hard-pressed
and swaying, rebounding back, rings out through the sky.

CATALOGUE OF NORTHERN TRIBES
FREED FROM CAESAR'S LEGIONS

When Caesar sees how bent his army is on war,
how fate is with him, he does not delay his fortune
with any idleness, but recalls the scattered cohorts
posted throughout Gaul and, with his standards gathered,
heads for Rome.

        The tents pitched by Lake Leman,
and forts perched high in Vosegus, by a winding bank,   430
holding in check Lingones warriors' painted arms,
are all deserted. They leave the fords of Isara,
which leads its own waves a long way before it falls
into a better-known stream, thus losing its name
before it reaches the sea. The blond Ruteni
are freed from long occupation. The gentle Atax
is pleased to be rid of the weight of Latin ships,
as is the Var (now Italy's extended border).

And also where the sea pounds the hollow cliffs
of Hercules' sacred harbor—neither west nor   440
northwest winds can touch it, but only Circius'
breezes blow along its shores, keeping Monoecus
a safe haven for anchors.

And that uncertain coastline
which land and sea by turns lay claim to, whenever
Ocean surges inland, or removes his tides receding.
Whether a deep-sea wind churns up the waves
and drops them there, or the second heavenly body
moves the restless waves of Tethys, and lunar phases
set them seething, or the flame-bearing Titan,
to drink those wholesome waters, raises the ocean,   450
drawing its swells to the stars—I leave it to those
who ponder the world's workings: but you, whatever
causes such constant motions, may hide forever,
just as the gods have willed.
                Then left the men who held
the fields of the Nemetes, and the Atyrus' banks—
sloped gently down to a sea the Tarbelli enclose.
Standards and enemy withdrawn, Santoni rejoice,
and Bituriges, and nimble Suessones with their long spears;
the Leuci and Remi, experts at hurling the javelin,
Sequani, the best tribe at reining their steeds on the curve,   460
and skillful Belgian drivers of the chariot they've borrowed;
Arverni, who dare to imagine themselves the brothers
of Latins, with Trojan blood, and the too-rebellious
Nervii, stained with Cotta's death and their broken treaty;
Vangiones, who imitate the Sarmatians' dress
with their loose breeches, and untamed Batavi,
sharpened for war by blares of curved bronze horns.
So, too, where the Mosa River winds, where the Rhône
picks up the Arar's rapid course, bearing it seaward,
and where, high on mountaintops, that tribe lives   470
by the jutting white-capped crags of the Cebennes.

You Treviri were happy that battles had changed course,
and the now-shorn Liguri—once their fair hair flowing
down their necks was the finest of all the long-haired folk—
and those whose altars appease with grisly bloodshed
bitter Teutates and fierce, awfully worshipped Esus
and Taranis, whose cult is harsher than Scythian Diana's.

You, too, the poet-seers who send off with praises
the strong-hearted and war-slain into eternity,
you Bards, now safe, poured out a flood of songs.   480

And you Druids, laying down your arms, renewed
your old barbaric rites and sinister sacraments.
Only you know gods and heavenly powers, or else
you alone do not know: deep in the forest apart
you dwell in sacred woods; your authors teach
that shades do not seek the silent seat of Erebus
or the pallid realm of Dis below, but one spirit
rules the same limbs in another world. If you sing
what you know, death is the middle of a long life.
Surely these people on whom the Bear looks down   490
are happy in their error, for the greatest of terrors
does not oppress them—the fear of death. The minds
of their men make them eager to rush on the sword,
their hearts receptive to death—they count it cowardice
to be sparing of life that returns.
                                   You cohorts, too,
posted to keep the Belgae safe from long-haired Cayci,
headed for Rome and deserted the Rhine's wild banks,
leaving the world exposed to every tribe.

RUMORS OF WAR

When Caesar's massive buildup of manpower
gave him confidence to hazard greater things,   500
he occupies all Italy and fills up nearby walls.
Empty rumors, also, multiply sensible fears
and invade the people's courage and convince
of coming doom, and quick reports of sudden war
free countless tongues to broadcast false accounts:

"They say that where Mevania's bull pastures spread
bold squads of cavalry are charging, bearing conflict,
and where the river Nar glides to meet the Tiber
the barbarous troops of savage Caesar are roving."

"He himself is marching all his eagles and standards   510
gathered in mass formation and in crowded camps."
They seem not to recall him as he was: he's bigger
to their minds, a monster fiercer than foes he conquered.

"They say that those who live between the Rhine and Elbe,
torn from their northern homes and native fatherlands,
follow behind him, with orders to cruelly sack the city
with Romans looking on."
                              So does each with fear
lend force to rumors of evils that have no substance.
They fear what they imagine.
                              Nor was it only the masses
stricken by empty terrors: in the Senate house also   520
the fathers themselves leap down from their seats,
and as they flee, the Senate commissions the consuls
to issue the hateful decree of war. Then, uncertain
of what refuge to seek, where to escape what they fear,
each makes a mad dash for wherever, and harries
the headlong populace—stuck in long lines together
they break out in mass confusion.
                              You would believe
that wicked torches had seized the rooftops, or now
their shaken homes were hanging, swaying for a fall.
So the mad mob storms headlong through the city.   530
As if their only hope in this distress was to escape
their fathers' walls, they rush out without thinking.

As when the stormy south wind drives the deep sea
off the Libyan Syrtes shoals, and the broken weight
of the mast with its sails crashes down with a boom,
and the pilot abandons ship, dives in the sea swell
with his sailors, each man grabs a plank for safety

even before the ship's seams have been ruptured.
So was the city abandoned—each flees into war.

  No parent, weary in age, was able to call back   540
a son, nor any wife her husband with her tears,
nor did the gods of the family hearth detain
anyone while they framed a prayer for safety.
No one lingered at their doorways, so maybe
their last view of their beloved city might fill
their eyes as they fled—an irrecoverable mob.
How easily the gods grant men the highest,
and how difficult to sustain it! The city packed
with conquered peoples and nations and able
to hold, if gathered together, the whole human race,   550
was left by coward hands an easy prey for Caesar.
When a Roman soldier, pressed by the enemy,
finds himself besieged on foreign shores,
he evades the nightly perils in a narrow trench—
he hastily builds a mound of sod for defense
that proves secure as he sleeps sound in his tent.
But if you so much as hear the word "war," Rome,
you're deserted. Your walls can't be trusted a single night.
Yet so much panic has to be given mercy:
they got scared when they saw Pompey in flight.   *Pompey*   560
                                                          flees
                                                          Rome

OMENS, PRODIGIES, AND
PORTENTS OF WAR

  Then, lest a single ray of hope for the future
ease their trembling minds, clear promises of worse
fates to come were added: the menacing gods
flooded the earth and sky and sea with prodigies.
The dark nights saw new, unknown stellar bodies,
heaven's vault in flames, and torches flying across
the void of space, and the hair of the dreadful star,

the comet, which means a change of kings on earth.
Sheet lightning flashed in a sky deceptively clear,
and fire in the heavy air took on various shapes—
now long like a lance, now flecked like a lamp's glow.   570
A silent bolt of thunder lit the cloudless sky
and, gathering its fire from northern regions, struck
the peak of Latin Alba, and the lesser stars
that usually run their course in night's vacuum
appeared at midday; and with her horns united
when Phoebe reflects her brother's entire orb,
suddenly she dimmed, hidden by Earth's shadow.
The Titan Sun himself, with his head mid-heaven,
hid his dazzling chariot in dead black darkness,   580
shrouding the world in gloom he forced the nations
to despair of daylight—as dark as the night when the sun
turned back east, away from Thyestes' Mycenae.

    Brutal Mulciber let loose the mouths of Etna
on Sicily, nor did the flames fly skyward, but
showering wide, its fires fell down on Hesperia.
Black Charybdis churned up blood from sea depths.
The bark of Scylla's dogs cowered to a whimper.
The flame from the Vestal altars was defiled,
and the fire that marks the close of the Latin Games   590
split into factions, and surged up into twin peaks
like the two Theban pyres. The earth stood poised
on her axis, the Alps shook off their age-old snows
with a nod of their necks, and Tethys flooded out
western Calpe and the highest summits of Atlas.
They say the native gods wept, and the Lares'
sweat bore witness to the city's labors, and gifts
fell down in their temples, and birds of bad omen
defiled day, and wild beasts dared to wander from
forests by night and nested in the middle of Rome.   600

    Then human speech flowed from the tongues of cattle
and monstrous human babes were born, deformed or with
too many limbs—mothers terrified by their own infants.

Gossip spread the Cumaean Sibyl's dire verses
through the populace. Then with their lacerated arms
those who placate fierce Bellona sang of the gods,
and whirling their bloody heads of hair the Galli,
lamenting, wailed dismal tidings to the people.
Bones laid to rest in urns were heard to groan.
The clash of arms and booming voices in untrodden   610
forest groves were heard, and ghosts in close combat.
Farmers whose fields were by the outside walls
turned tail and ran, because a mighty Fury encircled
the city, shaking before her a pine tree, its crown on fire,
and tossing her hissing hair—like the one that possessed
Agave of Thebes, or the Fury that hurled the daggers
of mad Lycurgus, or Megaera who, bid by unjust Juno,
made Hercules shudder in dread, though he'd seen Dis already.
Trumpets pealed, and a clamor as loud as cohorts
colliding in battle was produced on a pitch-black night   620
when not a wind was stirring.
                            Out of the middle
of the Campus, Sulla's shade was seen to rise up
and chant dreadful oracles. Farmers saw Marius
raise his head up from the Anio's cold waters,
breaking out of his tomb there—and they fled.

ARRUNS, THE ETRUSCAN SEER

   Thus it was agreed that, according to ancient custom,
Etruscan seers ought to be summoned. Of these, Arruns
was the oldest, and dwelt in the walls of deserted Luca.
Learned in the lore of lightning strikes and of veins
still warm in the vitals, the warnings of wings straying
   on air,   630
first thing he said was that the monsters—which nature,
in discord, produced without seed—must be captured
and with the odious offspring of sterile wombs

be burned on unholy flames. Next he told the anxious   *burn*
citizens to circle the city, those priests whose power it is   *abominations*
to purge the walls with holy water, moving around
the long and hallowed encircling boundary space.   *holy water*

     Then followed the band of minor Gabine priests
and the Vestal choir led by their ribboned priestess,
the only one allowed to see the Trojan Minerva.   640
Then those who keep the wills of gods and secret songs
and who recall Cybele from her bath in little Almo,
and augurs, learned in watching left-hand birds,
the Seven Men for holy feasts, the Titian Guildsmen,
the Salii parading the shields that fell from heaven,
and with his pointed cap, the well-born Flamen.

     While this procession winds around the widespread city
with long revolvings, Arruns collects the scattered
fires of the lightning bolt, buries these in the earth
with gloomy murmurs, and nods to mark the spot as sacred.   650

     Then he leads to sacred altars the choice neck of a bull.
When he began to pour wine and sprinkle meal along
his slant knife blade, the victim for this unpropitious
sacrifice struggled long against it. But then, when
the girt-up attendants pressed down his fearsome horns,
he fell to his knees and offered his neck for the slaughter.

     No normal blood flowed, but from the gaping wound—
instead of red blood—poured forth black slime.
Stunned by these deadly offerings, Arruns pales   *bull*
and inspects the entrails for the anger of the gods.   *sacrifice*   660
Their very color shocked the seer: the white guts   *full of*
were tinged with foul spots, corrupt with chilly gore, *ichor*
and speckled all over with splotches of livid ichor.
He discerns the liver, moist with decay, and sees   *seer shocked*
menacing veins on the hostile side. The lung tissue
is missing. The film dividing the vital organs is thin.
The heart lies wasted, and pus discharges from gaping

lesions in the viscera, the large omentum betraying
their hiding places.
                              And there!—this never appears
in entrails except to condemn some crime—he sees   670
the fibrous mass of an extra lobe growing on the liver.
One part hangs sick and flabby, the other's malignant:
the veins throb and pound too quickly. In these he reads
the great and evil fates, and cries out:
                                          "Gods above,
it is hardly my right to reveal what you set in motion,
for my sacrifice has not been found acceptable
to Jupiter on high, but into the slaughtered bull's chest
infernal gods have entered. We fear the unspeakable—
but more than we fear is coming. May the gods soften
what we have seen, the intestines prove untrustworthy,   680
or let our art's founder, Tages, be found an imposter!"
So the Etruscan sang, winding adaptable omens
up in shrouds of many ambiguous phrases.

NIGIDIUS FIGULUS READS THE STARS

   But Figulus was devoted to knowing the gods
and heaven's secrets—not even Egyptian Memphis
could match his knowledge of astral counts and motions:
"Either this world wanders endlessly without law,"
he said, "and the planets drift on random paths,
or else, if fate moves them, the times are ripe
for catastrophe in the city and all humanity.   690
"Will the earth crack open and swallow cities whole?
Or scorching air ravage our mild climate?
Will the earth deceive us, deny us crops of wheat?
Or waters everywhere be spoiled with poisons?
What brand of disaster, O gods, what plague for your rage
are you preparing?
                    "The time fixed for the death of many

converges on one day—if Saturn's cold noxious star
were kindling now in mid-heaven his dark fires,
Aquarius would have dumped showers as on Deucalion,
and waters, far and wide, would hide the whole earth.   700
If Phoebus' rays were now vexing the Nemean Lion,
then his chariot would set fire to the sky
and bathe the world in global conflagration.
"These stars are not active. But you, who ignite
perilous Scorpio's fiery tail, and inflame his claws,
what scheme are you plotting now, you Pursuer Mars?
For mild Jupiter sets deep in the west, and Venus,
her healthful star is faint, and quick Mercury lingers—
Mars alone holds heaven. Why have the zodiac signs
deserted their paths and affect the world darkly,   710
and the side of sword-bearing Orion shines too brightly?

    "The madness of war is upon us, the power of iron,
the fist, will confound all justice, and wicked crimes
will be called virtue—and this fury will continue
for many years. What use to beg the gods for an end of it?
Peace comes with a tyrant.
                        "Drag out, Rome,
your chain of endless pains and loss for a long time—
you're free now only as long as there is civil war!"

A MATRON, INSPIRED, PROPHESIES WARS

    These forecasts were enough to panic the people.
But more pressed on. For as from the peaks of Pindus   720
a Bacchant full of Theban Lyaeus storms down,
so a matron rushes through the bewildered city,
revealing in words what Phoebus urged in her breast:

    "Where do you take me, O Paean? Rapt across the sky,
what land do you set me down in? I see Pangaea's heights,

white with snow, and under Haemus' crags, wide Philippi.
What fury—Phoebus, teach me—is this that opposes
ranks of Roman hands and weapons, a war without a foe?

"And now where? First you lead me toward the dawn,
where the sea is dyed by the currents of Lagus' Nile.   730
I recognize the one whose headless trunk
lies on the river sands.
                         "Across the sea, the shifting Syrtes
and arid Libya, where gruesome Enyo has transferred
Emathian ranks. Now over the cloud-capped Alps
I'm dragged, and the Pyrenees that rise to the sky . . .
I return to my native city, where an impious end
to war is found—in the middle of the Senate.
The factions clash again, and around the world
I go again. Phoebus, let me see a new shore
and a different land—I've already seen Philippi."   740

So the passion left her, spent, and down she fell.

BOOK TWO

Amid the many omens of divine wrath, the poet asks whether the
world is ruled by an eternal order of fatality or by random chance
and fortune, then prays that the gods will not give omens of the
future to terrorize mortal minds (1–17). The scene continues its
focus on Rome and its funeral-like sorrows (18–247): the matrons
placate the gods and voice their sadness (31–46); the men going to
war complain that they were not born in an earlier age nor given
a chance to fight a foreign enemy (46–70); the elders recall as om-
inous precedent the civil wars of their youth between Marius and
Sulla (70–247). Marcus Junius Brutus visits his uncle and fa-
ther-in-law, Marcus Porcius Cato, by night, seeking his counsel in
the troubled state of affairs (248–345). Near morning, Marcia ar-
rives from the pyre of her husband, Hortensius, to ask Cato to
take her back as wife, which he does but without ceremony (346–
414). Pompey's retreat to Capua occasions a geographical de-
scription of Italy focusing on the Apennine Mountains (415–61).
Caesar's advance southward is described in general terms as rag-
ing, bloodthirsty, and like a storm (462–86). The hasty flight of
other generals, Libo, Thermus, Sulla, Varus, Lentulus Spinther,
and Scipio (487–505), lends distinction to the opposition to Cae-
sar of Lucius Domitius Ahenobarbus at Corfinium, who is be-
trayed by his own soldiers and shamed by the clemency of Caesar's
pardon (506–54). Pompey addresses his troops, associating Caesar
with the likes of Catiline, Marius, Cinna, and Sertorius, and ar-
guing that this is not a true and proper war but a mere vindication
of the fatherland, then sings at length his own praises (555–629).
His men give no applause, and Pompey abandons Italy to Caesar
and withdraws his army to Brundisium (630–45), which is then de-
scribed (646–63). Pompey sends his son Gnaeus to seek allies in the
East and the consuls to rally support in Greece (664–86). Caesar

catches up with Pompey and attempts an ambitious naval block-
ade, which the poet likens to Xerxes' bridging of the Hellespont
(687–718), but Pompey finally escapes with his fleet by night
(719–43). Caesar takes Brundisium, capturing two of the enemy's
ships, and Pompey departs for exile from which he will not return
(744–79).

BOOK TWO

FATE AND/OR FORTUNE

   Now gods' wraths were manifest; the signs of war
the world gave were clear: nature's laws for things
that bind them were upset by monstrous turmoil—
foreboding signs she gives of pending evil. Why,
Ruler of Olympus, did you add these cares
to anxious mortals, to know future disasters
through dire omens? Either the creator of things,
when first flame abated and he obtained the reign
over rude and formless matter, fixed the causes
eternally—by which he holds all in order,   *10*
obeying the law himself—then partitioned
the world into ages, set limits for the fates;
or nothing is settled and fortune wanders uncertain,
twisting and turning events, and chance rules mortals.
May it be sudden, whatever you devise. Let
the minds of men be blind to future fate.
Leave them free to hope within their fears.

CITY IN MOURNING

   So when they had conceived what great disasters
the steadfast powers above had resolved to levy

on the world, all city business ceased as for a funeral.   20
Signs of honor were cloaked in plebeian dress,
and no lictors' rods went accompanied by purple.
They stifled their laments, but sorrow deep
and speechless drifted everywhere.
                                    Just as death
first strikes a house with silence, before the corpse
is laid out and mourned, or the mother, hair unbound,
has ordered her handmaids to madly beat their breasts—
but when she clutches his body, stiff from vanished life,
his face devoid of soul, his eyes menacing in death,
it is not yet grief, but fear has left her. Mindless   30
she broods, and wonders at the loss.
                                    The matrons put off
their former dress, and attend the shrines in sad patrols.
Some bathe the gods in tears, others beat hard
their breasts upon the floor and, frantic, tear their hair
and scatter it over the sacred threshold, assail
with teeming wails ears more used to hearing prayers.
Not all lay prone in the lofty Thunderer's temple.
They distributed the gods so that no altar lacked
a mother displaying hostility.
                                    One whose cheeks
were torn and wet, her arms black and blue from blows,   40
said:
          "O mothers of misery, bruise your breasts now—
now mangle your hair! Do not hold back your anguish
for the final disasters! We have the power to weep now
while fortune still wavers—when one of the leaders wins
we will have to rejoice." So she prods and goads,
spurring on their grief.
                                    Nor did the men heading off
to war and to opposite camps hold back a flood
of just complaints to the cruel wills of the gods:
"What a pitiful lot to not be born in the times
of the Punic Wars, to fight at Cannae and Trebia!"   50

"Gods, we don't want peace—enrage foreigners!
Excite some savage cities! Let the world conspire
in arms, squads of Medes stream down from Susa
of the Achaemenids, the Scythian Danube not hinder
the Massagetae, or for blond Suebi to be poured out
by the Elbe and untamed headwaters of the Rhine
in northern extremes—"

                   "Make us the enemies
of each and every people—just turn away *civil* war!"

"May Dacians and Getae press us on each side—
let one leader attack the Spaniards, and let the other   60
turn his standards against the arrows of the East—
no hand would be free to strike at Rome."

                             "Or, if it please
the gods for Hesperia's name to perish, let the whole sky
settle it—gather fire and strike the earth with lightning.
Cruel father, strike both parties and leaders at once,
while neither yet deserves it!"

                        "Do they have to produce
such a crop of new crimes, to see who will rule the city?
Hardly worth the price of civil wars, if neither
one should win."

                    Such were the complaints aroused
by piety that was dying.

ELDERS RECALL MARIUS AND SULLA

                    Sad parents had their own troubles: 70
they detest the heavy fate of persisting old age
and their years, saving them for second civil wars.
So one seeks out examples for his great fear, and speaks:

"This is like the upheavals the Fates contrived
when the Teutons' conqueror, after his Libyan triumphs,

in exile Marius hid his head in swampy reeds.
Stagnant quicksand and wide marshlands concealed
your hopeless property, Fortune. And later, iron shackles
wore down the old man, dirty from long imprisonment—
he would die, a happy consul, in the city he'd ruined,   80
and was paying for his crimes in advance—even death
often fled from him. In vain was the power granted
to an enemy to take his hated life, who with sword in hand
for bloodshed, froze and dropped it, going numb . . .
He saw a bright light in the prison full of shadows,
and terrible gods of crime, and Marius' future,
and shuddering he heard:
                              'You have no right to touch
that neck! Before he dies, he must keep eternal decrees
and bring death to many. Lay down your empty fury!
If you want to avenge the death of your wiped-out people,   90
Cimbrian, just spare this one old man.'
                                          "No,
not divine favor but the great wrath of gods above
protected that fierce man, useful to Fate, who desired
Rome's destruction.
                        "Then hauled over an adverse sea
to a hostile land, chased through vacant shanties,
he hid in Jugurtha's realms he'd ravaged for his triumph,
and laid in Punic ashes. Carthage and Marius
both took solace in fate: although cast down,
they pardoned the gods. There he acquired the wrath   100
native to Libya. As soon as his fortune returned,
he set free droves of slaves, and chain gangs broke
their iron bonds and raised up savage hands. The leader
let no man bear his standards who wasn't used to crime
or had no guilt to offer to the camp.
                                        "Ah, Fate!
that day when Marius the victor stormed the walls—
Grim Death raced that day with mighty strides!
Nobles died with plebs, the sword swept wide,
and no heart was given any reprieve from steel.

Gore pooled in temples, and road stones soaked
slippery red with blood. Age didn't matter—   110
they'd hasten without remorse the final day of elders
whose years were waning, or would cut the fate
of poor nursing infants still on life's first threshold.
What crime made little ones deserve to be slaughtered?
It was enough that they were able to die.
Furious passion impelled them, and whoever looked
for guilt was considered too slow. Many died
simply to round off a number. The bloodthirsty conqueror
picked up a head chopped off of who knows who,
ashamed to walk with empty hands. One's only hope   120
for safety was trembling kisses on that filthy hand.
Let a thousand blades follow death's new signals,
degenerate people! No decent way for men to earn
centuries of life, let alone the brief time gained—
until Sulla returned.

                    "Who had time to weep
for mobs of dead? Or for Baebius, his guts scattered,
ringed by countless hands that ripped him limb from limb;
or for Antonius, who presaged these evils—a soldier
swung your head by its mangled white hair and threw it
dripping onto a banquet table. Fimbria butchered   130
the Crassi's corpses. Cruel stakes were soaked
with putrid flesh of tribunes. And Scaevola also,
ignored by dishonored Vesta—they offered your body
to her eternal flames, before her inmost shrine—
your worn-out old throat shed so little blood
her fires burned on.

                    "All *that* was right before
his seventh year holding the fasces. That was the measure
of life for Marius—all that bad fortune can dish out
he suffered, and every gift of good fortune enjoyed:
he traveled the distance that the Fates spread out for man."   140

    "Think of all those cadavers fallen at Sacriportus,
and the Colline Gate covered with downed battalions

when the seat of the head power of world affairs
nearly changed location, and the Samnites hoped
to inflict worse wounds on Rome than at the Caudine Forks!"

   "Then came Sulla, as avenger of vast manslaughter.
He drained what little blood remained in the city;
and while he forcefully excised the rotting limbs—
his remedy was too much, his hand went too far
pursuing the disease. Sure, the guilty perished,   150
but, by then, only the guilty had survived!
Vendettas were given liberty, and wrath rioted
when freed from the reins of law. It was not all
done for one cause; each man committed offenses
that served himself. The conqueror issued one order:
'Anything goes.' Servants drove wicked steel
through their masters' bowels; sons were drenched
in paternal blood—they even fought over who
would get to behead their parent; and, for the reward,
brothers fell upon brothers. Fugitives crowded tombs,   160
living bodies mixed confused with those buried there.
Caves of beasts could not contain all the people.
One man slipped a noose on his neck and broke it,
another leapt down headlong and dashed himself
hard on the ground—they stole their deaths away
from the bloody conqueror. One man piled high
wood for his own pyre, and while he still had blood
and freedom, dove into the fire, embraced the flames.
Leaders' heads were borne on pikes throughout
the troubled city, then heaped in the heart of the Forum.   170
Anybody slain anywhere could be identified there.
Thrace never saw so much crime, hung up in
the Bistonian tyrant's stables, nor did Libya
in the doorways of Antaeus, nor Greece in sorrow
weep for so many limbs mangled in Pisa's halls.
Then, already decaying and losing their identities
as time wore on, disconsolate parents gathered
the heads they knew and fearfully stole them away.

"I myself remember the disfigured features
of my brother they killed, how I wanted to place him   180
onto the flames of a pyre that they were refusing,
how I witnessed all the corpses of Sulla's peace,
through all those truncated bodies I searched for a neck
to match his head.

                          "Why mention the blood that appeased
Catulus' ghost? The victim, a Marius, paid
grim offerings to a shade which perhaps refused them,
unspeakable atonements for the ravenous tomb.
We saw his mangled limbs with as many wounds,
and though his whole body was gashed and bleeding
no blow was lethal . . . we saw the heinous conduct   190
of unspeakable cruelty—they spared the dying from death.
His severed hand fell down, his tongue, cut out,
throbbed without a sound and beat the empty air.
They pruned his ears, and lopped off his fine long nose.
And finally, after he'd watched his own limbs dismembered,
they dug in the hollow sockets and gouged out his eyeballs.
You'll hardly believe so brutal a crime, that one person
could take so much punishment—just like how limbs
are broken by the tremendous weight of fallen rubble . . .
bodies that drift to shore are no more deformed,   200
of men who died mid-sea. Why did it please them
to mutilate Marius' face as if it were worthless,
and destroy their advantage? For, to please Sulla
with their bloody misdeed, he'd have to have been
still recognizable.

                          "Fortuna of Praeneste saw
all her colony farmers put to the sword at once—
a community perished in the time it takes one man.
The flower of Hesperia, Latium's last young men
were cut down, staining the sheepfold of poor Rome.
Often famine, or the sea's fury, or a sudden collapse   210
of a building, or a pestilence or plague or havoc of war
has caused so many violent deaths at one time—
but never before had punishment! So thick the crowd

of troops of men, turning white as death came over them,
their conquerors could hardly move their arms.
And the slain could hardly fall down in the slaughter
but slumped and bobbed their necks. The heavy carnage
weighed on them, and the corpses took part in the killing,
for the bulk of cadavers crushed anyone still alive.

"Unmoved and free of cares *he* sat on high,   220
a spectator of his great crime. So fearlessly
he condemned poor crowds of thousands to death.

"The Tiber's stream received all of the heaps
of Sulla's corpses. At first they fell in the river,
but then on other bodies. Sea-bound ships stuck fast,
the bloody massacre dammed up the river's course;
in front of it flowed seaward, but behind it the waters
gathered high in a mass. And soon the mounting pressure
of blood forced a passage and flooded the whole plain,
rushing wildly down to the Tiber River's channels,   230
adding to the dammed-up waters. The bed and banks
could not contain the surge, and bodies littered the plain.
At last it struggled hard into the Tyrrhenian Sea
parting the deep blue waves with a torrent of blood.

"For *this* did Sulla deserve to be called 'Blessed'
and 'Savior'? His tomb raised in the middle of Mars' Field?
These things we will suffer again, this cycle of war
is coming. This will be the result of civil conflicts.
And yet, fear sees graver ends, and much of humanity
is gathering for battles with far greater losses.   240
The most that Marius' exiles fought to regain
was Rome; and Sulla's victories fulfilled no more
than the utter destruction of his hated rivals.
But these men, long in power, who now rush together—
Fortune, you call them elsewhere. If Sulla's end were enough,
neither would be inciting civil wars."
                                        So elders sadly wept,
mindful of the past, and so, fearing for the future.

BRUTUS VISITS CATO BY NIGHT

But no terror had stricken the heart of Brutus,
a lofty soul, and in the great turbulence of dread
he had stood apart from the popular sorrows.   250
By night, the world asleep, while Helice
of Arcady revolves on her slanted axles,
he calls at the humble halls of his kinsman Cato.
He finds him sleepless, turning public cares,
the fates of men, the city's fall, afraid for all—
except for himself. With these words he greets him:

"Expelled from every land and longtime fugitive,
Virtue's last refuge is you, who are not shaken
by any storm of Fortune. Please guide my mind,
it wavers. Brace my doubts with your firm strength.   260
Others can follow Magnus, or Caesar's arms—
Brutus' only leader shall be Cato.
                              "Will you keep peace
and hold your steps unmoved in a wavering world?
Or have you resolved to join the leaders in crime,
the raving people's ruin—to absolve the civil war?
Each man's own ends drag him into wicked battles:
a home in scandal and laws to be feared in peacetime,
to drive off hunger with steel, or confound credit
and debts in world collapse. Fury drove none to arms:
they head to camp won over by hefty bribes. You alone   270
choose war for its own sake?
                              "What profit the years
of endurance, free from the corrupt morals of our age?
This will be the sole reward for your long virtue:
while others are already, these wars will *make* you guilty.
Gods above, just do not let those hands
be moved to deadly arms! Any spear *you* cast
will not fly blind amidst the cloud of missiles.
Lest so much virtue go to waste, the whole fortune

of war will thrust itself on you. Who will not want
to die by your sword, though already reeling with wounds,   280
and make it your crime?

       "Better for you to live apart
from arms, tranquil, alone, at ease. Like the celestial
bodies that roll forever, unshaken by their driftings.
The earth's atmosphere is inflamed by lightning,
and lowlands welcome winds and flashing tracks
of fire. But out beyond the clouds stands Olympus.
By divine law, small things are troubled by discord
while the great remain at peace.

       "How pleased Caesar's
ears would be to hear that so great a citizen
had joined the conflict! Nor would he be pained   290
that you preferred the camp of his rival, Magnus.
For Cato's consent to civil war is more than enough
of consent to Caesar himself. A Senate majority,
the consul and other nobles following a civilian
into battle, stirring up troubles. Now add Cato
under Pompey's yoke, and the only free man left
in the world will be Caesar.

       "But if you are pleased
to take up arms to guard our laws and fatherland
and to preserve our liberty—then in Brutus
you see an enemy of neither Pompey nor Caesar,   300
but of the postwar victor."

       So he spoke. But Cato
from his heart's veiled depths delivered these holy words:

"Brutus, I consider civil war the highest crime.
But wherever fate leads, virtue is safe to follow.
I fault the gods above who will make me guilty.
Who would wish to watch the stars and world falling
and feel no fear himself? Who, when high heaven rushes
to ruin, the earth shakes and disorder wrecks the universe,
would sit with folded hands? When unknown nations
are joining Italy's fury and come to Roman wars—   310

even kings across the sea, under other stars—
am I to live 'alone, at ease'?
                              "Keep far off that fury,
O gods above, that I should be carefree as Rome falls!—
A disaster that would move even the Dahae and Getae.

    "Just as when death leaves a father bereft of sons,
grief itself bids him to lead the long funeral train
to the pyres—he is pleased to put his own hand
in the dark fires, and himself holds smoking torches
to the heaped grave mounds—so I will not be torn
away before I embrace your lifeless body, Rome. And I   320
shall follow Liberty's name, even her empty shade!

"So be it: let the stern gods demand full atonement
from Rome, nor ought we defraud war of any blood.
Would that the heavenly gods and Erebus allowed
this head to be doomed, to pay the penalty in full!
As enemy ranks overcame Decius self-sacrificed,
may both armies stab me, let barbarous hordes
aim at me their Rhineland lances, may I be pierced
by every spear and, standing in the middle, take
the blows of the entire war. May this blood redeem   330
whole peoples, and this sacrifice make good in kind
whatever debt hangs over Romans and their ways.
Why should a people submissive to the yoke,
and willing to suffer brutal tyranny, perish?
Drive the steel in me alone, who guards in vain
our empty rights and laws.
                              "This, this throat will give
peace and an end of evils to Hesperia's peoples.
When I am gone, whoever wills to hold power
will not need war.
                              "Why *not* follow the public standards
with Pompey in the lead? But, if fortune favors   340
him too, he'll claim all right to be given the world—
of that I am certain. So, *with* me may he conquer,
lest he think he conquers for himself."

                                    His words
are sharp incentives for anger in the younger man
and boil his blood with too much love of civil war.

MARCIA REMARRIES CATO

Meanwhile Phoebus scattered chilly darkness,
and knocks sound at the door. In rushes pure Marcia
in mourning, just come from the grave of Hortensius.
As a maiden she had shared a better husband's bed.
But as soon as her third child had paid the price   350
and earned the prize of the marriage contract,
her fruitful womb was given to enrich another home
and to join both houses through her mother-blood.
But after she had sealed his last ashes in their urn
she hurried here in misery, her hair let down and torn,
her breast bruised with many blows, covered with ashes
from the tomb. How else might she persuade her man?
Sadly she declares:
                        "While there was still blood in me
and the power to be a mother, I did your bidding,
Cato, and bore the children of two different husbands.   360
Now my womb is spent, and tired of childbirth, I
return—not to be passed to yet another man.
Renew the unbroken bonds of our former bed!
Allow at least the empty name of legal marriage.
Let them inscribe on my tombstone 'CATO'S MARCIA.'
Don't let it be in doubt forever after, whether
being offered I remarried—or was thrown out!
You won't have me as companion for happy times
and prosperous days. I come to be a partner for
your trials and concerns. Let me follow the camp.   370
Why should I be left behind in safety
and Cornelia be closer to civil war?"

Her words sway her man, and though the times
are strange for marriage, with fate calling for war,
they agree on simple vows, without the empty pomp,
and call the gods as witnesses for the sacred rite.

    The threshold was not crowned with festive garlands,
no white wool ribbons twined round both the doorposts.
            No customary torches, no ivory steps by which
to mount the bed, with gold embroidered blankets.   380
        The matron wears on her brow no towering crown
nor avoids touching the threshold as she passes.
        No bright saffron veil, to lightly conceal the bride's
blush of timid shame, hid her down-turned gaze.
                No jeweled girdle bound a flowing toga,
nor any lovely necklace, nor narrow linen bands
hung from her shoulders, circling her bare arms.

    Just as she was, she kept her clothes of mourning,
and as she would her sons, she hugs her husband.
Her purple was concealed, covered by funeral wool.   390
None of the usual jokes were played; the sober groom
took none of the standard Sabine festive mockery.
No relatives, no neighbors gather to share their union.
They unite in silence, and Brutus stands in as augur.

    He did not shave from his reverend face his bristling
beard, and he let no joy crack his hard appearance.
For since the time he first saw fatal arms raised up
his white hair went uncut, flowed down his steadfast brow,
and he let a grisly beard grow out on his cheeks.
He was the only one, free from zeal and hatred,   400
also free to mourn the human race.
                        Their old bed
is not tried again. His strength even stands against
wedded love. It was his custom, the unwavering
habit of tough Cato, to be moderate and observe
the limit, to follow nature, to risk his life for his country.
He believed he was born not for himself but the world.

To conquer hunger was a feast to him. A great house
was one that kept the rain out. Expensive clothes
meant the rough toga on his back, the normal dress
of Roman Quirites. His greatest use for Venus: 410
procreation. He was his city's father and husband.
He venerated Justice, was resolutely upright,
all for the common good. In none of Cato's actions
did selfish pleasure steal in and take a portion.

POMPEY BEGINS HIS LONG
RETREAT FROM ITALY

Meanwhile heading down with rapid march, Magnus
holds the walls a Dardan founded in Campania.
He makes his war base here, with this aim in mind:
oppose his enemy's movement, spread wide his troops
where with their shady hills rise the Apennines
halving Italy—and no other peak on earth   420
mounts higher and climbs nearer to Olympus.
A range that stretches between the twin waves
of the Lower and Upper Seas; its hills stretch from
where Tyrrhenian waves break on Pisa's shoals,
east to Ancona, exposed to Dalmatian breakers.
Its abundant springs feed into countless streams,
and rivers fork and flow down into both the seas.

Descending on the eastern side are the swift Metaurus
and rapid Crustumium, the Apis and Pisaurus, joined,
the Sena and Aufidus, which strikes Adriatic waves.   430
And no land empties itself into a greater river
than Eridanus, who rolls fallen timbers to the sea
and drains Hesperia of water.
                              There is a legend
that his banks were the first a crown of poplars shaded,
and that day when Phaethon drove hell-bent off course

and deeply scorched the earth and ravished all her streams,
his waves were a match for the fires of Phoebus.
No smaller than the Nile, if the Nile didn't flood
on the flat plain of Egypt or pool on Libyan sands.
No smaller than the Hister, did the Hister not pick up,   440
as it wanders the globe, creeks that would meet the sea
elsewhere, then run to Scythian beaches not alone.

   The waters heading down the western slopes
form the Tiber and deep Rutuba. Here is the source
of quick Vulturnus and, exhaling nightly vapors,
the Sarnus, and the Liris, driven by Vescine waters
through the shady realms of Marica, and the Siler,
scouring Salernum's wild tracts, and the Macra:
no ships travel its shallow bed, it runs to sea
at nearby Luna.

                    Where their straightened spine rises   450
higher in the sky, they look out on Gallic fields
and face the lower Alpine slopes. They are fertile
for Umbrians and Marsians, tamed by Sabellan plows,
and every native Latin people is embraced
by their pine-clad cliffs, which do not abandon Italy
until they are closed off by the surf of Scylla.
But their rocks stretch all the way to Lacinia's temple
and, once, beyond Italy—before the sea eroded
the connecting overhang and water beat back the land.
After the double depths knocked out the land between,   460
the hills' last stretch gave way to Sicily's Pelorus.

CAESAR HEADS SOUTH

   Caesar, raving for battle, enjoys no way of passage
unless blood is shed. That Hesperia's territories
through which he treads are not lacking in enemies
and that the fields he storms through are not vacant,

that the journey itself is not a waste—these please him.
He wages war upon war.
                              He doesn't like open gates
so much as crashing through them. He'd rather plunder
fields with fire and steel than pass through with permission
from the farmer. He feels shame to make his way   470
with consent and so to seem like a civilian.

   Now the Latin cities are in doubt, their favor
split two ways. And though in war's first rush of terror
they will surrender, still they shore their walls
with tight-packed ramparts, and ring them on all sides
with steep bulwark defenses, and equip the top turrets
of their walls with heaps of boulders and of weapons
to drop upon their enemies or shoot them from afar.

   The people lean toward Magnus, but their faith
fights with the threats of fear. As when the south wind   480
owns the sea with its howling blasts, the whole ocean
follows it. Even if Aeolus strikes his trident on
the land and looses on the tumid waves the east wind,
although a new blast blows, the former wind still holds
the sea. The sky may cede to the cloudy east wind,
but the waves uphold the south. But fear turns minds
with ease. Fortune carried away their wavering faith.

   The Etruscans were exposed by Libo's anxious flight,
and Umbria lost her rights with the rout of Thermus.
Sulla did not wage civil war despite his family name,   490
but turned back when he heard the name of Caesar.
Varus, when the ranks moved in and struck Auximon,
rushed out the other gates left unguarded at the back
and fled through woods and rocks. Out of the fortress
of Asculum, Lentulus was dislodged. The conqueror
pursued them as they went and split their ranks.
Of all of that great army, only the leader escaped
along with his standards, no cohorts behind them.

You, too, deserted the post entrusted to you, Scipio,
leaving without defense the stronghold of Luceria,   500
even though the tough young men were camped there
who, a while back, were recalled from Caesar's army
because of the Parthian threat. Until he should call them
to war himself, Magnus had loaned his father-in-law
the use of Roman blood, to replace his losses in Gaul.

DOMITIUS AT CORFINIUM

  But you, aggressive Domitius, are posted inside
the strong walls of Corfinium. Your trumpets are heard
by recruits who once stood against dishonored Milo.
When he saw far off a huge cloud surge from the plain
and the flash of troops whose weapons, struck by sunlight,   510
gleamed, he said:
                "Comrades, race to the riverbanks
and sink that bridge!—

                          "And pour forth your whole flood now
from your mountain springs, O river, draw out all your waters
to churn and dash the bridge joints and carry it away!—

"This war must stop here! Let our foe waste his time
pacing these banks here! Curb their reckless leader!
The victory is ours as soon as Caesar stops short here!"

He said no more, but hurried a force down from the walls,
in vain. For from the field Caesar spies them loosing
the bridge to break his march, and before they could finish   520
he cries out, hot with rage:
                          "It's not enough that you hide.
shivering behind walls? You have to obstruct the fields,
and now, planning to keep me away with rivers? Cowards!
The Ganges' tumid swell could not drive *me* back—

Caesar will not stand still at any river again
after the Rubicon!
                    "Dispatch squads of cavalry—
send foot soldiers with them—hold that bridge they're cutting!"

He spoke and horsemen gave full rein and galloped
down the plain, and thick as any storm cloud,
strong arms hurled javelins over the riverbank.   530
Caesar dislodges the guard and takes the river,
driving his enemy back to the safety of the tower.
Now he builds machines to launch massive boulders,
and shielded soldiers creep to the walls between them.

And suddenly a war crime—through unbolted gates
a band drags out their leader, captive. He stands at the feet
of his arrogant fellow citizen. But standing straight and tall
with threats in his gaze, his blue blood demands death by sword.
Caesar can see he wants punishment and dreads clemency,
and says, "Live on against your will. Consider this day   540
my gift to you. Give your side something to hope for
when they're conquered, an example of my character.
Or retake your arms if it suits you, and if you win
I make no bargain for myself based on this pardon."
This said, he orders his men to free his hands from bonds.

But how much better if he had been slain right there—
Fortune could have saved the Roman sense of shame!
The worst punishment of a citizen following the camp
of his country and the whole Senate with Magnus leading
is to be pardoned. Undaunted, the man swallows his wrath   550
and thinks:
                    "How return to Rome, retire in peace?
Disgraceful! Why don't I charge into the middle of war
and die straightaway in its raging? Rush resolutely, stop
all clinging to life—escape this gift of Caesar!"

POMPEY ADDRESSES HIS TROOPS

Unaware the general was captured, Magnus meanwhile
marshaled his troops, to steady his party with united forces.
He meant to sound his battle call on the following day,
and determined to test beforehand the army's fervor,
he addresses the hushed cohorts with honorable words:

"Avengers of crime, followers of better standards;   560
true Roman hands—called to arms by the Senate,
not a private citizen—declare your will for battle!
Hesperia's fields blaze with savage devastation.
Gallic madness pours out over the frozen Alps.
Blood has already defiled Caesar's swords.
Better, by god, that we've suffered war's first losses.
He has instigated crime. Right now I'm Rome's shield,
and she must make him kneel and pay! Do not call this
a lawful campaign, but the wrath of our country's vengeance.
This is no more a war than when Catiline kindled torches   570
to burn our houses down, with his friends in fury,
Lentulus and the mad fist of Cethegus' naked arms.

"What pitiful madness in a chief, when fate was willing
to make Caesar as great as Camillus or Metellus,
for him to join Cinna and Marius. But we shall lay him low,
like Catulus did Lepidus, just as my own axes
laid Carbo in his Sicilian grave. So, too, in exile
Sertorius died, having raised up fierce Spanish rebels.

"But trust me when I say I resent comparing these men
with you, Caesar, *and* that Rome has set my hands   580
against yours as you rage. I wish instead that Crassus
after victory in the Parthian wars had returned unharmed
from the land of Scythia, so that just like Spartacus, you
would meet an enemy's downfall. But if the gods above
decree that you shall be added to my titles of honor—

behold, *this* right arm has strength to hurl the spear!
My heart again is warm and eager blood flows through it.
You'll learn that those who are able to hold the peace
do not also run away from war. Let him call me
worn-out, finished—so long as my age doesn't alarm *you*.   590
In this camp the chief may be oldest; in his it's the soldiers.

"I have risen as high as a free people can raise
one citizen. Above me nothing but kingship remains.
It's no private matter if you, or anyone, seeks to surpass
Pompey in the city of Rome. Both consuls are *here*
to make a stand, along with whole ranks of leaders.
Will Caesar conquer the Senate? O Fortune, you do not
drag all things so blindly, you can't be so shameless.

"Is it his several tours against rebellious Gaul
and a life spent in labor that make his spirit so bold?   600
That he fled the Rhine's cold current and called a pond
of inconstant depth the 'Ocean'? That he turned his back,
terrified of Britons whom he'd gone to investigate?
Or have his empty threats swelled because the rumors
of his fury have expelled from their fathers' homes
the city, up in arms?
                        "He is out of his mind!
They do not all flee *him*—they follow *my* lead!
When I led my gleaming standards over the sea,
before Cynthia could twice fill her orb and wane,
the pirates quit the sea, afraid of every inlet,   610
and pleaded for narrow plots of land to homestead.
I also chased the obstinate king—an obstacle
to Roman fates—across the Scythian Bosporus, and
more fortunate than Sulla, I forced him into death.
No part of the world is free from me. Every land
that lies beneath the sun is occupied by my trophies.
Up north I am victor to the cold waters of Phasis.
I am also known in the hot and tropic zones,
in Egypt and in Syene that casts no shadows.
Out west they fear my authority, where the Baetis,   620

the river farthest west, strikes the tides of Tethys.
The Arabs know me as their lord, and the Heniochi,
ferocious in war, and the Colchians, who are known
for the fleece stolen from them. The Cappadocians, too,
are afraid of my standards, as Judaea is also,
where they worship a cryptic god, and the Sophene,
a soft people. I have subdued the Armenians,
the savage Cilicians, and the Taurus mountain range.
What else have I left my father-in-law *but* a civil war?"

The leader's words are followed by no clamor,   630
nor do his men quickly demand the trumpets
for promised battles. Magnus sensed their fear
and decided to recall the standards. He would not send
into such a critical contest an army already
defeated by tales of a Caesar yet to be seen.

When a bull in his first challenge is driven from the herd,
he seeks out lonely groves and throughout barren fields
he tests his horns on trunks of fallen trees; an exile
he does not return to pasture until he is pleased
with his neck's new-grown strength. But once he returns   640
victorious he leads his band of bull companions
into whatever mountain meadows he wants to
against the cowherd's will.
                                    So to his stronger rival
Magnus surrendered Hesperia. He fled through Apulian fields
and retired to safety in Brundisium's citadel.

POMPEY IN BRUNDISIUM

Long ago the city was founded by Cretan colonists
who sailed away from home across the sea on ships
of Athens; their sails falsely said Theseus was dead.
This side of Italy gathers into a slender strip

and juts out in the sea a narrow tongue of land   650
that keeps Adriatic waves within curving horns.
Yet the water through this narrow pass would be
no harbor, if a rocky isle did not block the violent
northwest winds and pour back the weary waves.
Here and there nature has placed huge cliff peaks
opposing the open sea, which suppress the gales
so that ships can sit restrained by a quivering cable.
From here the whole bay lies open far and wide
whether sails haul into your ports, Corcyra, or turn
left to Illyrian Epidamnos, toward the Ionian Sea.   660
Sailors shelter here when the Adriatic lets loose
full strength, when clouds cloak Ceraunia, and when
Sason off Calabria is sprayed with froth and foam.

    So then, with no trust in the affairs he leaves behind,
unable to transfer the war to rugged Iberia
because of the massive intervening tract of Alps,
he appeals to the eldest of his great offspring:

    "I call on you to scour the corners of the world.
Arouse the Euphrates and Nile, wherever my name
has become famous, every city where Rome is known   670
because of my leadership. Restore the sea to Cilicians,
now farmers scattered in fields. Rile up Egypt's kings
and Tigranes, whom I made. And don't neglect to arm
Pharnaces and both of Armenia's nomad peoples,
the savage tribes who line the Black Sea's shores,
Riphaean hordes and those that Lake Maeotis holds
on its frozen surface, which supports Scythian wagons,
and—why delay you longer? Carry my call to war
through all the East and all the cities the world over
that I have humbled. Rouse them all and make   680
the subjects of my triumphs come and join my camp.

    "But you two, whose names mark the Latin year,
ride the first north wind to Epirus. There acquire

fresh forces from the fields of Greece and Macedon,
while winter grants us a time of peace."

                                        So he spoke,
and all obeyed, launching off their hollow ships from shore.

CAESAR BESIEGES THE COASTLINE

   But never patient with peace and lengthy rests
from warfare, lest some twist of fate take place,
Caesar hunts and tracks his son-in-law's trail.
To sack so many walls on the first advance,   690
to take so many towers and drive out the enemy,
to make Rome herself, the capital of the world
and greatest prize of war, an easy prey to conquest,
might satisfy others.

                          But Caesar, reckless in everything,
thinks nothing is done if anything's left to be done.
Relentless, he pursues him, and though he possesses
all of Italy, it pains him that he still must share
that edge of coast with Magnus. But also unwilling
to let his enemies wander the open sea, he bars
the strait with jetties and casts rocks in the wide waves.   700

   But his labor is a huge waste. The greedy deep
swallows all the stones, sinks mountains in the sand.
As if lofty Eryx were thrown down in the middle
of the Aeolian Sea, no peaks would still rise up
out of the water, or if the summit of Gaurus were
torn off and sunk to the depths of Avernus' pool.

   Thus, when no mass of rock held on the seabed,
he decided to cut down trees and bind them together
to harness a bridge of oak logs with long cables.
Like the road fame sings, that pompous Xerxes built   710
over the waters, so daring to yoke with bridges

Europe with Asia, bring Sestos to Abydos, and
he walked across the strait of the swift Hellespont.
Then, to escape the threats of east and west winds,
he cut a channel and sailed his ships through Athos.

So is the face of the deep clogged by the fall
of forests. Then with rubble heaps still higher
the work rises: steep towers tremble over the sea.

Pompey sees how the mouth of the deep is shut
with new land, and gnawing cares strangle his mind—   720
how to unlock the sea and scatter war on the waters.
Often his ships, halyards taut with south wind, drove
through the sea barrier, sheering off slopes of the dirt
into the salt sea, and so making room for their keels.
And in the dark of night strong arms wind catapults
that hurl blazing branches.
                          When, at last, he chose
a time to steal away in flight, he directs his comrades
that no noise on the decks should alarm the shore,
no horn should sound the hours of the watches,
nor trumpet warn the sailors, call them to the ships.   730

The very last of Virgo was rising, who precedes
the Claws that would carry Phoebus with them,
when silently they launched the fleet. No voices call
"Haul anchor!" when the hook is pulled from deep beach sands.
As they bend the yards and raise the tall mast straight
the ships' captains shiver and are silent.
Sailors hang and fall with unfurling sails
but do not shake the strong ropes lest they whistle.

Their leader even prays to you, O Fortune,
since you do not allow him to keep hold of it,   740
at least to let him abandon Italy.
                          Fate permits it, barely.
For the sea, struck by their prows, crashes and roars,
and waves swell with the furrows of so many keels.

Therefore the foe is received into the gates and walls—
the city had lost faith and changed sides with the fates—
and rushes headlong through the winding harbor piers,
seeking the port mouth, pained that the fleet got to sea.

For shame that Magnus' flight is too small a victory!
The ships escaped to sea through a narrow channel,
smaller than the Euboean strait that buffets Chalcis.   750
Here two ships ran aground where they were taken
by a force prepared to intercept the fleet. On that shore
Nereus first turned red with the blood of civil war.
The other ships got through, but their rearguard was lost.

As when Pagasae's vessel sought the river Phasis,
earth dropped in the sea the jagged Cyanean boulders,
the *Argo* lost her stern and came out a little shorter.
The Clashing Rocks struck the empty sea in vain,
then came back and stood in place.

                               Now the sky's color
changes in the east, warning that Phoebus is rising.   760
The light is not yet white but blushing; it steals
the flames from nearer stars.

                               Now the Pleiades dim,
now Boötes' wheeling wagon is becoming faint
and recedes into the face of pure blue heaven.
The major stars are hidden.

                               Then Venus herself
flees before the warming day.

                               Now Magnus,
you hold the sea. But it's not the same fate for you
as when you chased the pirates out of every sea lane.
Tired of your triumphs, Fortune has withdrawn.
Expelled with wife and sons, dragging into war   770
all of your household gods, you go away
still great, with a retinue of peoples, into exile.

A faraway stage is sought for your ignoble fall.
Not because gods wish to deprive you of a tomb

in your country are you doomed to a sandy grave
on Pharian shores, but rather to spare Hesperia.
Far away in a remote land let Fortune hide
this crime; may Roman earth be ever preserved
from the pollution of the blood of her Magnus.

BOOK THREE

From his ship Magnus gazes back on Italy until it fades from sight, then sleeps and dreams of his dead wife, Julia, who warns of many deaths, chastises Pompey for his new, unlucky wife, Cornelia, and vows to haunt him to the end (1–49). Caesar consolidates his hold on Italy, sends Curio to Sicily and others to Sardinia, to secure the grain supply (50–75), then heads to Rome, first addressing it from the Alban hills, then entering the terrified city (76–108). He presides alone over a remnant Senate without magistrates present, and Rome is compliant to his will (108–19). Liberty opposes him in the figure of the tribune Lucius Caecilius Metellus, who attempts to stop Caesar from taking public funds from the temple of Saturn (120–51); but Lucius Aurelius Cotta urges him to give in and so preserve a semblance of freedom (152–60). Caesar plunders the treasury, full of spoils from Rome's past wars (161–77). A massive catalogue of Pompey's Greek, Eastern, and African allies (178–313). Caesar marches toward Spain and, encountering principled resistance from the Massilians (314–73), decides to besiege the city (374–415). Caesar deforests the environs, cutting down an ancient sacred grove (416–72). Caesar leaves for Spain while the siege goes on, until the Massilians win an offensive by setting fire to the Roman battlements (473–530). A massive bloody sea battle ensues, led and finally won by Caesar's admiral Decimus Junius Brutus (531–789).

BOOK THREE

POMPEY IN FLIGHT DREAMS OF JULIA

As the south wind leaned into the yielding sails
and drove the fleet, the ships moved out mid-sea,
and every sailor looked out over Ionian waves.
Only Magnus never turned his eyes away
from the land of Hesperia, while his country's harbors,
while the shores he would never return to see again
were visible, and the summits draped in clouds
and the mountaintops grew faint then disappeared.
The leader's weary body then gave way
to deep dream sleep—

                    he saw a dreadful, dire image,   10
Julia's sorrowful head rose up from gaping ground
like a Fury standing on her grave in flames:

"From Elysian fields expelled, from plains of the pious
to Stygian darkness, the place for guilty spirits,
I am torn after civil war. I myself have seen
the Eumenides with firebrands goading both your armies.
The boatman of scorched Acheron is preparing
countless rafts. Tartarus expands for more punishments.
The three sisters can hardly keep up with their work,
their hands go nonstop, and the Parcae are getting tired   20
of breaking threads of fate.

                    "When I was your wife
you led and celebrated joyful triumphs, Magnus.

57

But with your marriage your fortune also changed.
Your mistress Cornelia, who is condemned by fate
to drag down into ruin all her powerful husbands,
married into my place while my pyre was still warm.
Let her hang on your standards in wars, on waters,
as long as I may interrupt the soundness of your sleep
and no time is left free for love between you.
Caesar will own your days and Julia your nights.   30

   "Not even the oblivion brought on at Lethe's banks
has made me forget you, husband. Those who rule
the silent dead allow me to haunt you. I'll come to you
in the thick of battle when you wage war. Magnus,
my shades, my ghosts, will never allow you not to be
his son-in-law. You hack away our wedding vows
with the sword in vain. Civil war shall make you mine."

   The shade had spoken and fled, dissolving through
the embrace of her troubled husband.
                              Although threatened now
with disaster by gods and ghosts, with his mind made certain   40
of misfortune, he rushed more eagerly into warfare.
"Why am I terrified by the sight of an empty image?
Either the departed soul senses nothing after death—
or death itself is nothing."
                         Now the Titan was diving
underwater, with as much of his fiery orb submerged
as the moon lacks when she is just about to be full,
or has just been full.
                    Then a land offers a haven,
an easy approach for the ships. They furl the sails
and stow the mast, and seek the shore with oars.

CAESAR PLANS TO SECURE
THE GRAIN SUPPLIES

Caesar, when the winds snatched up the ships   50
that he'd let slip, and the sea concealed the fleet,
the leader stood alone on the shore of Hesperia;
the glory of expelling Magnus did not please him.
It upset him that the sea had saved his enemies' skins.
No good fortune was good enough for the hell-bent man.
Not even victory was worth the cost of delaying war.

Then he drove concerns for war out of his chest
and intensely busied himself with peace: what ruse
would best arouse the people's capricious favor . . .
he is well aware that the main cause of anger or praise   60
is the annual grain supply. Only hunger frees cities.
Respect is bought when men in power feed
the lazy mob. Starving masses know no fear.

He orders Curio to cross over to cities in Sicily
by that course where sudden waves buried the land
or divided it, making the land between into coastline.
The sea is very strong there and labors forever
to keep the broken mountains from restoring old ties.
This battle is also extended to Sardinian shores.
Both these islands are known for their fruitful fields.   70
Italy was supplied with foreign harvest by no other
lands before these, and none fill Rome's granaries more.
Libya is hardly more fertile, even when south winds relax
and the north wind gathers in clouds to the torrid zone
that pour down rains to produce a good year's crop.

CAESAR HEADS TO ROME

Having seen to these preparations, the conqueror
leads his troops unarmed and in the guise of peace
toward the homes of his fatherland.
                              If only he had returned
having subdued only Gauls and the northern folk,
what a long parade of achievements could have escorted him,   80
what spectacles of war! What chains he could have shackled
on the Rhine and Ocean, Gallic princes and blond Britons
following behind him, high on his chariot seat.
How great a triumph he lost by conquering more!
No cities thronged in joy as he marched by.
They watch him, silent with fear. Nowhere do crowds
stand to meet the chief. Yet he enjoys their fear
and would not have preferred to have the people's love.

And now he had surmounted the steep fortress of Anxur
and the wet road that cuts through the Pomptine Marshes.   90
He passed the lofty grove that Scythian Diana rules
and the path the Latin consuls take to Alba's heights.
From high on a hill he views from afar the city
he had not seen throughout the time of his northern wars.
He marvels as he addresses the walls of Rome:

"Home of gods, did men desert you uncompelled
by any war? What city then *will* men fight for?
It's good, by god, that the furious East is not looming
in on Latium's borders right *now*—quick Sarmatians
allied with Pannonians, Getae mixed with Dacians!   100
Fortune was kind to you, Rome—having a leader
so timid—that right now there is only *civil* war."

So he descends to a city thunderstruck by terror.
For they believe he will torch the walls of Rome,
scorch it like a captured city, scattering her gods.

This was the extent of their dread: they think his will
is equal to his power. No one has time to invent
good omens, or to feign a shout of acclamation,
let alone dissent.
                        A mob of patricians
packs the Palatine temple of Phoebus, and a Senate—   110
convened without authority—is brought out of hiding.

    No sacred benches shine with consul's luster,
and the praetors, next in lawful power, are absent,
their empty ivory chairs are moved from their places.
Everything was Caesar. The Senate assembles as witness
to one man's private interests. The fathers were prepared
to sit and vote, should he seek monarchy, or a temple,
or even the throats and exile of the Senate.
                                        Good thing
he blushed at demanding more than Rome would endure.

METELLUS RESISTS CAESAR
AT THE TREASURY

    But Liberty goes out raging: she tests through one man   120
whether right can resist might. Metellus, a real fighter,
when he sees them battering open Saturn's temple
he quickens his step and breaks through Caesar's line
and stands his ground before the yet unopened doors.
(Always and everywhere only love of gold knows
no fear of death by sword. It didn't matter at all
when our laws were lost and perished. But money,
the most worthless thing there is, incited a conflict.)
Holding back the conqueror from his plunder,
the tribune makes it known in a voice loud and clear: 130

"This temple won't suffer your blows but through my body,
and you'll get no money, you thief, unless it's splattered

with my sacred blood! Violence to this my office
is certain to reach the gods. The tribune's curses
of grueling battles hounded Crassus into war.
Draw your sword! There's no crowd here to dread
gawking at your crimes—we stand in a city deserted.
Your criminal soldiers won't get their pay from us!
Go cast down other peoples, commandeer their walls.
Poverty doesn't force you to spoil our worn-out peace.   140
War is yours, Caesar."

His words kindled the conqueror's
mighty wrath: "You hope in vain for a death of honor!
I would not even dirty my hand on your throat, Metellus!
No public office makes you worthy of Caesar's anger.
Has liberty's safety been entrusted to your protection?
Surely high and low are not so confused these days
that the laws would rather be saved by the word of Metellus
than repealed by Caesar!"

So he spoke,
and when the tribune still held out at the doors
his rage sharpened, he looked around for savage swords,   150
forgetting to feign the manners of the toga.

COTTA REMOVES HIM,
THE TREASURY IS PLUNDERED

But Cotta compelled Metellus to quit his too-bold design:
"The people's liberty, when tyranny constrains it,
perishes through liberty. But you preserve her shadow
if you willingly do what you're ordered. Being conquered,
we've submitted to so much unfairness. Our only excuse
for disgrace and baseborn fear is that we could not resist.
Just let him pilfer quickly the evil seeds of dreadful war.
Such losses affect peoples who still maintain their rights.
Poverty falls heaviest not on slaves but on their masters."   160

Metellus brushed aside, the temple was opened.
The Tarpeian rock resounds as it bears witness
to the doors unbolted with a creaking groan.
Then what is hidden deep in the temple is brought
out into the light, untouched now for many years,
the wealth of the Roman people.

                           Spoils of the Punic Wars,
spoil from Perses, and plunder from conquered Philip.
What Gauls left behind when retreating from you, Rome,
and gold for which Fabricius did not sell you to Pyrrhus.
Whatever our grandfathers' frugal habits saved up,   *170*
the wealth that Asian peoples had sent as tribute,
and what Minoan Crete had given Metellus her conqueror.
What Cato had hauled overseas from faraway Cyprus.
Last of all, the riches of captured kings of the East,
royal treasures Pompey had shown off in his triumphs—
all is carted off.

                    A tragic robbery emptied the temple,
and, for the first time, Rome was poorer than Caesar.

POMPEY'S ALLIES GATHER

  Meanwhile the fortune of Magnus stirred up cities
around the world—that would fall with him in battle.
Neighboring Greece gives troops for the nearby war.   *180*
Amphissa of Phocis sent men, and rocky Cirrha
and both the peaks of Parnassus were left deserted.
Boeotian chiefs assembled where Cadmean Dirce flows
and tireless Cephisos with its oracular waters;
and Pisa's men from the Alpheos, which sends its waters
undersea to Sicily's peoples. Arcadians leave
Maenalus, and Trachis' squads leave Hercules' Oeta.
Thesprotians and Dryopes rushed, and the ancient
Selloi left their oaks, now silent, on Chaonia's peak.

And though the war levy emptied all of Athens,   190
few of her ships call at Apollo's dockyards—
only three keels lend credence to the Battle of Salamis.
Then to arms came Crete, dear to Jove of old,
land of a hundred peoples: Knossos, skilled with the bow,
and Gortyn, no worse than Easterners with their arrows.
Then those who dwell at Dardan Oricos, and the wanderers
scattered high in Athamas' woods, and the Encheliae,
whose old name attests to the death and change of Cadmus.
Colchian Absyrtos comes, out in Adriatic foam,
and the farmers of the Peneus, and those by whose toil   200
Thessalian plows turn the soil of Haemonian Iolcos.

From here the sea was first outraged. The crude *Argo*
transgressed the shore and mingled strangers together
when she matched mortals with the winds and raging waves
of the sea for the first time, and on account of that boat
a new kind of death was added to the first.
                                        Then Mount Haemus
of Thrace is forsaken, with Pholoë, home of the fabled Centaurs.
Strymon is deserted, from where the Bistonian cranes
migrate to the warmer Nile. Also barbarian Conë,
where one fork of the branching Danube loses its fresh   210
Sarmatic waters and washes Peucë with salty waves.

Mysia, too, and the land of Ida, bathed by the cold
stream of Caicus, and Arisbe, whose soil is too thin.
The farmers of Pitane come, and those of Celaenae
who mourn your gift, O Pallas, since Phoebus punished them
when he won the contest—here the rapid Marsyas
descends in straight banks, then joins the wandering
Maeander and, once joined, begins to wind and wend.
Here also earth allows the Pactolus to emerge
from gold-rich mines, and Hermus, also rich,   220
cuts through furrowed fields. The men of Ilium
heeded the call to camp; their presence is an omen
that those standards were doomed. The myth of Troy
did not deter them, nor Caesar's claim of descent

from Phrygian Iulus.

The peoples of Syria join up,
deserting the Orontes and Ninos, famed for prosperity,
windy Damascus and Gaza, Idume rich in plantations
of date palms, unsteady Tyre and Sidon, valued for purple.
They sailed straight to war, led by the Dog's Tail polestar,
which is not better known by any other sailors' ships.   230
Further, the Phoenicians, if hearsay is believed,
were the first to dare to mark words in clumsy figures
to make the voice endure; Memphis had yet to learn
to bind her river's reeds together, and only birds
and wild beasts inscribed on stones preserved
their magic utterances.

The groves of Taurus are abandoned,
and Tarsos where Perseus landed, and the Corycian caves
vast with hollowed crags. Mallos and far-off Aegae
are noisy round their dockyards, and the Cilicians
put to sea in legitimate, no longer pirate, ships.   240

Rumors of war even roused the distant East
where they farm by the Ganges, only river in the world
that dares to debouch against the rising of Phoebus
and drives its course into the adverse east wind.
Here Pella's commander halted before the flat expanse
of Tethys, admitting defeat before the world's greatness.
And by the Indus also, whose swift divided stream
is so vast it does not notice when the Hydaspes joins it.
Those come who suck sweet juice from tender cane,
and those who paint their hair with saffron dye   250
and gird their flowing robes with colorful gemstones;
those, too, who build their own pyres and while alive
mount the blazing flames.

How glorious for a people
to take fate in their own hands and, when weary of life,
to devote the rest to the gods!

The savage Cappadocians
and the people who cannot farm on rugged Mount Amanus
came to war, and Armenians who inhabit Niphates,

hills of rolling stones. The Choatrae left their forests
that touch the sky.
                    You Arabs came to lands unknown
and marveled that tree shadows did not fall southward.   260
Then the Roman madness aroused the distant Orestae,
and Carmania's chiefs, whose sky turns toward the south,
and they still see the Bear though a bit submerged,
and Boötes there is quick to set and shines but briefly.
Ethiopia was roused, the only land not covered
by part of the zodiac, except where kneeling Taurus
bends his knee and stretches one front hoof.

  Also where the great Euphrates with the rapid Tigris—
whose founts rise close together in Persia—flows,
and who knows which name it would take if the land   270
mixed up the rivers. But the fertile Euphrates waters
the fields just as the Nile's flooding does. The Tigris
is suddenly swallowed by the earth and follows
a hidden course and then, reborn from a new source,
its current does not refuse to wed the sea's waves.

  Belligerent Parthians held their allegiance in doubt
between Caesar's ranks and the standards against him.
They were content to have reduced the sides to two.

  The nomad Scythian tribes, who are enclosed by
the cold Bactros stream and vast Hyrcanian forests,   280
dipped their arrows in poison.
                            The Heniochi come,
a tribe keen with the reins, of Lacedaemon stock,
and the Sarmatians, neighbors to the savage Moschi.
Colchis sends men from her rich fields cut by the Phasis,
as does the Halys, fatal to Croesus when he crossed it,
and the Don, which descends from the peaks of Riphaeus,
whose two banks give the names to different worlds,
for it forms the border dividing Asia from Europe,
and where it turns it enlarges now one, now the other.
They come from the raging strait where the Black Sea   290

takes in Lake Maeotis, a place that steals glory
from the Pillars of Hercules, because they deny
that access to the Ocean is had only at Gades.
The clans of Issedonia come, and the Arimaspi,
who tie their hair up with gold. The strong Arian comes
and the Massagetes, who break their long food fasts
after wars with Sarmatians by eating the horses
they've fled on. And the Geloni come, fleet as birds.

   Not when Cyrus led the forces from Memnon's kingdoms,
nor when Persian Xerxes came west with an army counted   *300*
by the numbers of spears thrown, nor when the avenger
of his brother's lost love cut the sea with mighty fleets,
did so many kings follow one leader, or so many
men of diverse dress gather, such a great confusion
of tongues and people.
                      Fortune had called all these troops
together to send as companions into colossal downfall,
a funeral train worthy of the death of Magnus.
Troops were also dispatched by horned Ammon
straightaway from Marmarica for the battle—
whoever lives in dry Libya, from western Moors   *310*
to the Paraetonian Syrtes out on the eastern shores.
So that Caesar with his luck might take all at once,
to conquer in one shot, Pharsalia put up the world.

CAESAR'S SIEGE OF MASSILIA

   So when he had left the walls of trembling Rome
he rushed his troops and flew over the cloudy Alps,
and though other peoples shook in fear at the report,
the Phocaean men, in dangers, dared to persevere—
not like fickle Greeks—in faith to rights and duties,
and to follow a cause instead of fate.
                      But first they try

to turn aside the man's invincible fury and hard mind,   320
with talk of peace they entreat their nearing enemy,
displaying Pallas Athena's olive branch before them:

"The course of fate bears witness that Massilia
has always sided with your people in foreign wars—
just look under any year within your Latin annals.
And now, if you seek a triumph in an unknown land
take our right hands, devoted to battle down foreigners.
But if you are preparing deadly contests of civil strife
and dreadful battles, we offer our tears for civil wars
and stand aside. No hand can treat accursed wounds.   330
If fury drove to arms the gods who dwell in heaven,
or if the earthborn Giants were attempting the stars,
human piety would still not dare to side with Jove
with arms or prayers, and the race of mortals below
would not know the lot of gods except through lightning,
which shows the Thunderer still reigns alone in heaven.

"Countless nations are racing together from every side—
the world is not so cowardly, dreading crime's contagion,
that your civil wars will need to conscript swords.
Better indeed if all had a mind to refuse your fate,   340
that no foreign soldier carried out these conflicts.

"Whose sword hand will not fail on seeing his father?
How will brothers cast spears across the divide of battle?
The matter will soon be over if you enlist no other forces
than what is right. This is all we ask for ourselves:
put down your eagles of terror and hostile standards
far from our city. Be willing to entrust yourself in our walls.
Permit us to welcome in Caesar and lock war out.
Let this be a place free from crime, Magnus and you
both safe here, so if fate cares for your unconquered city   350
and terms are agreed to, you both can meet here unarmed.

"But why interrupt your rapid march when Spain
calls you for crucial reasons of war? We have no weight,

no force in this campaign. We've never been lucky in war.
Exiles from the first homes of our fathers,
after Phocaea burned and her towers were taken,
small low walls on foreign shores are our safety
and loyalty is our only glory.

                              "If you intend
to blockade our walls and shatter our gates by force,
we are ready to suffer the shower of torches and missiles   360
down on our rooftops. Or if you divert our water supplies
we'll dig and find a drink, we'll lick the earth in thirst,
and if our grain runs dry, then we will dirty our mouths
with foods horrid to look at and foul to handle.
Our people are not afraid to suffer for liberty's sake
what Saguntum endured when besieged by Carthage.
Torn from their mothers' arms still clutching in vain
at breasts dry from hunger, babes will be thrown into fires.
Wives will implore their dear husbands to kill them.
Brothers will stab each other, preferring when forced   370
to wage this sort of civil war."

                              So the Greek delegate
ended; the leader's troubled face already betrayed
his wrath, and his voice at last proved his grievance:

   "These Greeks trust in vain the haste of my course!
For though we are in a hurry to get out west,
there's time to destroy Massilia. Be glad, my cohorts!
Fate offers us spoils of wars along the way.
As a wind loses power—unless it runs up against
strong dense forests, it dissipates into empty space—
and as a great fire dies down when nothing obstructs it,   380
so not having enemies harms me. I think it a waste
of armed force if those I can conquer don't fight back.

   "'If only I come alone, unmanned of my army,' they say,
then they'll open their homes to me. But they don't want
to keep anything out so much as to shut me in!
'Drive out the dread contagion of war' you say—
you'll pay the price for pursuing peace from me!

And learn also that none are safe while I live
who do not follow me to war!"
                              With these words
he redirects his march toward the city that did not fear him,   390,
where he sees walls shut and fenced round thick with warriors.

   Not far from the walls rise the heights of a hill
that on its top spreads out in a small plateau.
This mount seemed perfect to Caesar for a safe camp,
one ready to furnish with a long ring of defenses.
The nearest part of town sits on top of a citadel
as high as the hill. Between are valleys and fields.

   Then he adopted a plan that would cost great labor:
to unite the divided hills with massive earthworks.
But first, to blockade all the city that faced inland,   400
Caesar built a long barricade from his camps above
down to the sea, cutting off with a trench the pastures
and fountains. It was built up with thick sod wings
and heaped all round with arms of rough piled dirt.

   This was enough for the Greek city to be remembered
with undying fame—that it was not pushed over or laid low
by fear itself but held its ground and stopped the headlong
rush of war blazing over all, that Caesar, quick to plunder all,
stalled to conquer one. How great that fate was hindered,
that Fortune, who rushed to impose her man on the world,   410
lost those days!
                 All the forests wide are felled
and woods despoiled of trees to build a frame along
the sides, to press together the light earth and tree limbs
amassed in the middle, so that when all was done
the rampart might sustain the weight of turrets.

CAESAR CLEARS A SACRED GROVE

There was a sacred grove, inviolate for ages.
The air was dark beneath its canopy of branches
weaving chilly shadows; the sun was kept far off.
There were no rustic Pans, no powers of the forest—
Nymphs or a Silvanus—dwelt there, but savage rites   420
of gods whose altars were piled with dire sacrifices,
and every tree was bathed in human gore.
If the past that marveled at gods deserves belief,
birds were scared to roost on those tree boughs
and beasts made no dens there. No wind ever whipped
through that wood, nor lightning out of black clouds
struck it. Those trees rustle their leaves by themselves
without wind shaking. From numerous dark fountains
water falls there, and grim images of gods stand,
tree trunks felled and carved, rough and without art.   430
The site itself and the rotting timbers are enough
to make one shiver.
                        When worshipped in common forms
forces are not so feared—it adds to the terror greatly
to *not* know the gods they revere.
                        Rumor had it also
that often hollow caverns quaked and bellowed like a bull,
that yews would fall and then rise up again,
the wood would blaze, on fire without burning,
and serpents twined and wound around the trunks.
The people did not frequent it for close devotions
but left it to the gods. When Phoebus is mid-heaven   440
or dark night holds the sky, even the priest is afraid
to approach, lest he catch by surprise the lord of the grove.

Caesar sends in the axes to chop down this wood
because it is in his way. It stood there dense with timber
intact through prior wars, among other hills stripped bare.

But his men's strong hands trembled, and overwhelmed
by the awesome grandeur of the place, they believed
that if they struck those sacred trees, their axes were sure
to rebound back on their own limbs. When Caesar saw
his cohorts confused and paralyzed, he dared to be   450
the first to heave and raise a double-bladed axe
and pierce a lofty oak with steel; driving deep the blade
into the trunk now violated, he proclaims:

"Now none of you should balk at clearing this grove.
Just credit me with the guilt."
                                Then all obeyed his orders,
not because he assured them, removing their fears;
Caesar's wrath outweighed the wrath of gods.

Ash trees are cut down, knotty holm oaks fall
with Dodona's sacred oaks, and alders, fit to float,
and the cypress, reminder of no common grief.   460
They lost their locks for the first time, and lacking leaves
they let the daylight in. The wood was so dense
that falling, it propped itself back up. The Gauls
who saw it groaned, but the men locked inside the walls
are thrilled, for who would think that one can injure
gods and get away with it?
                                But Fortune saves
many guilty men, and nature's divine powers
can only vent their wrath on unlucky wretches.

When enough timber was cut, they hunt for carts
throughout the country to carry it, and farmers   470
weep to see their oxen stolen, their lands untilled
by hooked plowshares, their whole year's harvest lost.

CAESAR LEAVES FOR SPAIN,
THE SIEGE GOES ON

But the general could not stand that Mars stood still
before the walls, so turning to the forces in Spain
out at the ends of the world, he left his commands
for waging the war.

                    A rampart is built, its planks
crisscrossed, with twin turrets as high as the walls.
These were not fixed to the earth with any stakes
but crept along on tracks, the mechanism hidden.
Whenever its great weight shifted, the men, amazed   480
their walls still stood, believed that underground hollows
had been shaken by a wind blast trying to break forth.
Shots from these hit the city's highest strongholds.
But the Greeks' iron pierced Roman flesh with greater force
for their lances were not just hurled with arm power
but were twisted tightly into catapults and slung,
and did not rest until they'd passed through more than one
body, cleaving armor, bone, and straight through on their way,
leaving death behind them. They wounded and flew on.

And every boulder unleashed from a cord wound tight—   490
like rocks sheered off a cliff by the passage of time
and a sudden gust of wind—breaks everything it falls on,
and drives not only life from the body but wholly crushes
the limbs and splatters the blood.

                        But when they hide their valor,
steal up to the enemy walls packed tight in shell formation—
every soldier's shield interlocked with that behind him,
and shields overhead reinforce the helmet's protection—
then the missiles that once harmed from such long range
shoot over their heads.

                Nor is it an easy task
for the Greeks to adjust the aim of weapons equipped   500
for long distances, and they struggle to change the range.

So they start instead to roll boulders down by hand,
using the weight alone. As long as the series of shields
held out below, it repelled every weapon as if it were
hail that beats down, noisy but harmless, on rooftops.
But when the valor of the men began to waver,
and the soldiers grew weary, they broke formation,
and each shield alone was breached by constant pounding.

Next a siege shed approaches, layered with dirt;
concealed beneath the defensive roof of the screen,   510
the men try now to batter and demolish the walls
with steel. Now the ram, stronger with each swing,
attempts to knock loose the mortar in the wall's tight joints
and break one stone out from under stones above it.
But from above rains fire and massive jagged rocks
and storms of stakes and blows from blazing torches
that break their screen, and the soldiers, exhausted,
weary with wasted effort, head back to their tents.

Just to save their walls was all the Greeks had prayed for,
but now they prepare a force to mount a counterassault.   520
By night they concealed flashing torches in their shields
and the bold young men rushed out. They had no spears,
no deadly bows. Their weapon was fire, and wind soon swept
a conflagration racing over the Roman siege works.
And though it has to struggle with still-green wood,
the fire is strong and doesn't take long to leap from
every torch; rolling with thick black plumes of smoke
it devoured not only wood but massive stones,
and rugged boulders dissolved to crumbling dust.
The earthworks fell, and looked even larger in ruins.   530

MASSILIA ATTACKED BY SEA

Despairing of a land victory, they decided to try
their fortune on the sea. Their ships were not adorned
with painted planks or flashy patron figureheads,
but raw timbers, just as they lay in the mountains,
were joined to form a stable ground for naval battles.
By now the fleet with Brutus' turreted warship,
having reached the churning mouth of the Rhône,
lay anchored off the Stoechas isles.

                              The Greeks
did not want to send all their strength off to meet their fate,
so they armed old-timers along with teenage boys.   540
They manned their fleet, not only those in port,
but also retired ships found around the dockyards.

When Phoebus had cast his morning rays upon the waves
of water, which shatter them, and the air was free of clouds,
the north wind was at rest, the south winds held their peace,
the sea stood ready for war.

                              Every ship struck out
from its station: Caesar's ships from one side,
and from the other the fleet rowed by the Greeks,
matching their strength of arm.

                              The keels shook from oar strokes,
and constant blows convulsed the high sterns forward.   550

The wings of the Roman fleet had strong triremes,
and ships built with four rising tiers of oarsmen,
and vessels with more levels that plied the sea
with still more oars; all these formed in a ring
against the open sea. Liburnian galleys fall back—
content with just two tiers—in crescent formation.
Then high above them all, Brutus holds command
over the massive flagship, propelled by six full tiers

of oars across the deep; the topmost row
stretches long and far to reach down to the water.   560

   When both the fleets were just one forceful oar stroke
apart from one another, countless voices mingle
in the empty air, the crash of oars is smothered by
the clamor of cries, and no war trumpets can be heard.
They sweep the blue, fall forward in their benches,
then haul their oars back hard into their chests.

   But then as soon as beak slams into beak
the ships back row astern and missiles are fired
that fill the air and fall in the sea between them.
And now they spread out the horns of their fleet   570
and allow enemy ships to sail into their circle.

   As when the tide makes war with east and west winds,
and waves and sea run counter to each other,
so, too, ships plowed the deep with furrowed swells
and ocean was tossed back and forth by their oars.

   The Greek craft were good for both attacking
and beating retreat. They could wheel around with ease
and were not at all slow to respond to turns of the rudder.
But the Roman ship, fitted out with a sturdy hull,
was steadier, with a landlike platform for fighting.   580

   Then Brutus said to his helmsman who sat astern
where the standards flashed:
                    "Will you allow our ranks
to drift aimless on the deep, trying to match
their naval expertise? Engage them in battle!
Expose our ship broadside to the Phocaean beaks."

   He obeyed and offered the ship's side to the foe.
Then every ship that tried Brutus' wooden wall
was beaten by its own blow and clung, a captive,
to the ship it struck. Others were caught and bound

with grappling hooks and chain lengths thrown with skill,   590
entangling oars.
                    A land war rages on covered sea.
Spears are no longer hurled with a twist of the arm,
no wounds are inflicted by steel flying from afar—
combat is hand-to-hand. In this naval battle
swords are the chief weapon. Each man leans out
from within his ship to swipe at his enemies
and no one falls down dead on his own deck.

   Gore foams deep in the waves, and the current is thick,
coated with congealed blood. The mass of dead bodies
hinders the ships that were snared with iron chains   600
from being hauled up near the boats that snared them.
Some sank half-dead into the bottomless deep
and drank seawater mixed with their own blood.
Some still drawing breath and fighting off slow death
died suddenly when their ships wrecked and went down.
Missed shots complete their carnage on choppy seas
and every iron weight that seems to fall in vain
finds its man and wounds him in the midst of waves.

   A Roman vessel, walled in by Phocaean keels,
divided its crew to protect both port and starboard   610
with equal forces. From the upper deck fights Catus,
who boldly holds a Greek ship's painted sternpost
when from both sides two spears pierce his chest and back—
deep inside his body the steel meets and clashes,
and the blood is unsure from which wound to flow
until a mighty surge of blood casts both spears out
and divvies up his soul between the deadly wounds.

   Poor Telo steered his craft into this mess as well.
Ships on wild seas complied with no right hand
more than his, and no one knew tomorrow's weather   620
better than he, from watching the sun and lunar cycles.
He always readied the canvas for winds to come.
He would have rammed and broken the Latin planks

but a javelin struck his chest and trembled there,
and the helmsman's dying hand turned aside his ship.
Then Gyareus tries to crawl into his comrade's boat
but a shaft is loosed and catches him in the groin—
pinned to the ship by a stubborn dart he dangles.

There were twin brothers, a fertile mother's glory,
born from the same womb for different fates.   630
Cruel death parted the men, and their poor parents
no longer mistook them but recognized the one
who had survived—a cause of endless tears.
Ever after he caused them pain and moaning
because he looked like his lost brother.
                                        That one had dared
to grab hold of a Roman ship from his Greek deck
when the oars of both were tangled like a comb,
but from above a heavy blow cut off his hand,
yet it clung where he grabbed, on account of his grip,
and stiffened there, holding on, the sinews tense in death.   640
His virtue surged in misfortune. His wrath grows heroic
now that he is maimed. He renews the fight with his left hand
and leans down to the water to snatch up his right hand—
this hand, too, with the whole arm is sheared off.
Now without sword or shield he does not hide
down in the ship, but stands there and bares his breast
to become his brother's armor, he endures the points
of many weapons that would have killed many others,
and though long since earning death, he still holds on.
Then, with his life escaping through numerous wounds,   650
he gathers what's left in his limbs and strains with all his blood
to jump on the enemy ship—but the sap in his nerves is gone
and only his body's dead weight is left to do damage.

That ship, piled high with the blood and gore of men,
took blows to her broadside fast and furious;
and when the sea rushed in through her shattered seams
she filled to her upper decks and sank in the waves,
rolling water all round her into a whirling vortex—

the surface parts and the sinking ship went under
as the sea washed back in place.
                                    That day offered   660
many marvelous forms of death upon the sea.
An iron claw swings quickly up onto a ship
and hooks Lycidas. He would have sunk in the deep,
but his comrades grab and hold him by the shins.
He is ripped to pieces, and his blood does not flow slowly
as from a wound, but floods everywhere from open veins,
and his soul that circulated through his various limbs
is absorbed by water. Nobody's life has ever fled
through so large a passageway. His bottom half
took to death the limbs that had no seat of life.   670
But where the heaving lungs lay and the guts glistened,
there his fate was stalled; this half of the man
struggled a long time, till finally death got him all.

    The crew of one ship is way too eager for battle:
they all go to one side and leave the other empty,
since no enemy is there. Their combined weight
capsized the ship, which covered sea and sailors.
They couldn't get free to swim to open waters,
so locked in the sea they died.
                                    A unique form
of dreadful death was seen—a soldier was swimming   680
and two ships by chance transfixed him on their beaks.
His chest is torn in two by such weighty blows,
his body does not at all silence the crashing prows
that crush his bones. Blood and gore come up
and out of his mouth because his belly has burst.
When the ships back water and remove their beaks
the dislodged body with a gaping hole in its chest
took water into its wounds and sank in the sea.

    Most of another shipwrecked crew thrash their arms
against death. They dash to a comrade ship for help   690
but clutch too high on the ship whose crew denied them,
for the ship would tip if it rescued all those people,

and the impious crew above chops off their arms.
Leaving their arms still hanging on the Greek ship
they fall away from their hands.
                                    The waves could no longer
sustain the weight of corpses floating on their surface.

  By now every soldier had hurled all his weapons.
But fury invents new arms. One man throws his oar
at the enemy. Others propel a whole stern pole.
Others drive out their rowers and tear up the benches   700
and launch them. They shatter their ships to fight with.
They grab dead bodies sinking down and spoil
cadavers of their swords. Many who were helpless
without a weapon yanked the deadly javelin
out of their own wound and held their vitals in
with their left hand so their blood would hold out
long enough to throw it back and deal the enemy
a heavy blow.
                    But nothing wreaked more havoc
on that sea than the pest most contrary to water.
For oily torches, flaring with smeared sulfur, scattered fire   710
and the ships proved easy fuel; the blaze caught first
the pitch and then it liquefied the wax, nor did the waves
conquer the flames but fire spread fierce on the sea
and claimed for itself the drifting wreckage of ships.
Here a ship bails *in* water to extinguish the flames,
there men clutch burning timbers lest they drown.

  Among the thousand ways to die, only one is feared—
the one you're about to die of.
                                    But valor can't be shipwrecked—
men gather weapons that have landed in the sea
and hand them up to the ships, or continue to brawl   720
hand to tiring hand, out in the uncertain waves.
When the weapon supply runs thin they use the sea:
cruel foes grapple in struggle and glory to die
with limbs entwined, as long as each drowns the other.

In that fight was Phoceus, best at holding his breath
underwater and searching the bay for things in the sand,
or when an anchor would not respond to the rope pull
he could go down and dislodge the hook stuck in too tight.
He had grabbed an enemy and pulled him deep down under
and was coming to the surface, safe and sound, the victor.   730
He thought he was coming up in an open stretch of surf
but he hits the hull of a ship—and sinks again for good.

Some men grabbed the oars of enemy ships
to keep them from getting away. The greatest concern
was not to waste one's death. Many clung to the stern
of their ship to dampen the blow of an enemy beak
with their dying wounded bodies.

                                        Tyrrhenus was standing
tall on the high point of his ship's bow when Lygdamus,
who wields a Balearic sling, wound up and slung
a small lead ball that slammed his hollow temples.   740
His eyes explode and blood bursts the bonds of sight;
he stands there stunned and blinded, thinking this is
the darkness of death. But when he feels the vigor
still coursing through his limbs he calls out:

                                        "Comrades,
turn me around and aim me as you would a catapult!
Let every hazard of war exhaust your spirit, Tyrrhenus!
This body, for the most part dead already, still
has fighting power left. It will take a live man's place."
So he spoke and let fly a missile at the foe,
blind but not in vain—it hits a boy of noble blood,   750
Argus, right where the belly joins up with the groin;
he doubles over, driving the steel deeper.

At the other end of the ship, already conquered,
stood Argus' unlucky father—when in his prime
no other Phocaean soldier was better than he in war,
but age had sapped his strength. No longer a soldier,
the tired old-timer still served as a model.
Seeing his son fall, he makes his way down the ship,

stumbling through the benches, all the way to the stern,
and finds his son still breathing. He sheds no tears   760
nor pounds his chest, but spreads his arms and faints—
night falls for him and deep darkness shrouds his eyes;
he can no longer make out poor Argus before him.

The boy lifts up his shaky head and drooping neck
to see his father, but his throat can voice no words.
Only a silent gaze that asks for one last kiss
and for his father's hand to close his eyes to light.
As the old man recovered and deep grief for bloodshed
began to seize him, he said: "I will not waste this moment
given by cruel gods—I'll rend this old man's throat!   770
Argus, forgive your miserable father if I refuse
your last embrace, your kiss. Your blood and warmth
have not yet all flowed from your wound—you're half-alive
and there is still time for you to outlive your father."

So he spoke, and though he had stained his sword
up to the hilt in his gut, he still dove overboard
into the deep blue; to hurry and die before his son did,
he could not trust his life to just one kind of death.

The leaders' fates were turning, the gamble of war
could no longer go either way. Most of the Greek fleet   780
had sunk. Some ships now were rowed and sailed
by a crew of the victors. A few made headlong flight
back to the dockyards.
                          Oh, how parents wept
back in the city! Loud laments of mothers on the shore!
Many wives embraced a Roman soldier's corpse,
mistaking the face defaced by the force of the sea.
Over burning pyres miserable fathers fought
over headless bodies.
                          But Brutus, victor at sea,
conferred on Caesar's army its first naval glory.

BOOK FOUR

Caesar besieges the Pompeian legions in Spain, commanded by
Afranius and Petreius, outside of Ilerda at the confluence of the
Sicoris, Cinga, and Hiberus (1–52). The battle is rained out by
prodigiously torrential spring storms and flooding (53–100) caus-
ing famine and price inflation (101–5). The deep flood prompts
the poet to pray the gods to deluge Spain and rescue it from civil
war (106–30). The flood abates, Caesar's men ford the waters on
rafts (131–54), and when Petreius abandons Ilerda, Caesar pur-
sues him into a tight rocky gorge (154–79). Opposing camps are
pitched close by each other and fraternizing breaks out between
them (180–201); the poet prays for world harmony and holy uni-
versal love, and further describes the men's reconciliations (202–
21). Petreius forcefully imposes discipline on his men, haranguing
them with liberty over peace, and drives them to murder the Cae-
sarians in their camp (222–70)—cruelty that holds great propa-
ganda value for Caesar (270–76). The Pompeians flee but Caesar's
cavalry pursues and traps them; refusing battle, he wears them
down with drought and thirst until they surrender (276–356).
Afranius submits to Caesar, pleading an absence of partisan ran-
cor, and Caesar graciously pardons his troops (357–86). The
happy fate of these men released from duty is contrasted with
those who still must fight the civil war (387–423).

The scene shifts: in the Adriatic, Gaius Antonius is trapped and
starving on an island off Illyria; his men try to cross to the main-
land on rafts, but Marcus Octavius, patrolling the coast for Pom-
pey, snags the last raft on a drag line, traps Antonius' forces, and
gives them battle (424–95). Night falls and the captain Vulteius
compels his men to commit mutual suicide rather than surrender,
which they do, a shining example of liberty or death, or liberty
through death (496–611).

Another scene shift: Curio reaches Libya, where a local tells him the tale of Hercules wrestling the monster Antaeus (611–92). Curio thinks the tale bodes well for his confrontation with the combined forces of Publius Attius Varus and King Juba, who has a personal score to settle with Curio (693–728). Unsure of his troops' loyalty, Curio hastens into battle, beating Varus (729–51), but then, lured into ambush by Juba's armies, his own lines are massacred (752–827). The angry shades of Carthage feast on Roman blood (828–33) and Curio dies, receiving a sarcastic eulogy from the poet for being, if nothing else, a successful instigator of civil war (834–66).

BOOK FOUR

SIEGE OF ILERDA IN SPAIN

But Caesar was far off at the ends of the earth,
waging a savage war not guilty of much bloodshed,
but one on which the leaders' fates would hinge.

Afranius and Petreius held joint command
over the Roman forts. They shared their power
by equal turns and harmony ruled. The rampart's guard,
ever awake and careful, obeyed the password
of either man. On top of Latin troops there were
hardworking Asturians and nimble Vettones
and, Gallic immigrants of long ago, the Celts   10
whose name by now was followed by Iberian.

On a modest hill with gentle slopes spreads out
a fertile land; Ilerda stands proud there, a city
established long ago. The peaceful waters of
the Sicoris, not least among the Western streams,
glide through it. A stone bridge joins its banks, its arch
large enough to bear the winter floods.

                             Nearby,
high on a crag, stands Magnus' bivouac. No less
a hill holds Caesar's camps. A torrent divides their tents.

The land was one of rolling, sweeping plains,   20
distances hard to measure by eye, plains confined

by the rushing Cinga, whose course is not allowed
to reach the shores of Ocean, for it is only
a tributary of Hiberus and loses its name to it,
a river that gives its name to the entire land.

Bloody Mars did not attend the first day of battle.
It was a day to display the leaders' numerous forces
arrayed behind their standards. They loathed the crime.
Shame restrained their furious arms, and they grant
a one-day reprieve for their homeland's broken laws.   30
But as the vault of Olympus edged into nightfall,
Caesar quickly surrounded his forces with a trench,
deceiving the enemy by stationing troops in front of it,
concealing his fortifications with armed lines of men.

At first light he rushed his army to storm a hill
dividing Pompey's fort from the safety of Ilerda.
But fear of disgrace drove his enemy there also,
and they arrived first and occupied the high ground.
Caesar hoped with valor and steel to take
the place his foes now held.
                   Loaded down, the soldiers   40
strain to mount the slope, with their heads crooked back
they cleave to the mountain, the shield of the man behind
keeps each man from stumbling. No man was free
to lob a spear—they used them as walking sticks
to brace their steps from falling. They clutch at rocks
and roots of trees. Forgetting the enemy, they draw
their swords to hack a path.
                  Caesar sees his men
about to slip to disaster, so he sends up cavalry
to take the brunt of battle, left flank forward
to shield the infantry, who easily withdraw   50
without pursuit; the winner had done nothing—
battle denied them, victory hung in the air.

SPRING STORMS, FLOOD, AND FAMINE

So much for the verdict of weapons. The campaign's fate
was sealed now by swift and sudden changes of weather.
Winter's sluggish chill and dry north winds had kept
the rains pent up inside the cloudy sky.
Snowfall blanched the mountains, and the plains
below would frost, then melt as soon as sunlight shone.
All ground that had exposure to the waning light
of sundown stayed hard and dry in wintry calm.   60

But when the warmer Sun, in spring, has caught up with
the Ram—which had carried then dropped Helle—
and now it looks back at the other signs,
and times are balanced again in Libra's impartial scales
as daylight prevails, then Cynthia has left
the sun behind and lit her slender crescent, which
in waxing checked the north wind, as her flames
fanned up the southeast winds. These whirled every cloud
they found in their land, on gusts from Nabataea,
westward—along with winds the Arabs feel   70
and all those clouds of vapor from the Ganges,
as much as the sun since dawn could gather up and carry,
whatever the northwest wind that darkens the eastern sky
drove onward, with all the clouds that shade the Indians.

It was sunny and hot in the orient without the clouds,
nor could they dump their weight in the middle zone
but hauled their storms in flight. The north and south
were clear, no showers. The humid air streamed in
and halted at Gibraltar.
                            Here, where the Zephyrs rise
and the lowest corner of the Olympian vault   80
dips into Tethys, the clouds could go no farther
and rolled tight into balls. The air turned black, so thick
that the space between earth and sky could hardly hold it.

Now, pressed at the pole, the clouds condensed huge storms
that flowed and slowly rolled as constant lightning flashed,
although the flame and thunder were muted by the gloom.
Then a rainbow arced, encircling half the sky,
though with little light its colors hardly varied;
it drank the ocean, piped a stream to the clouds
returning water to heaven from which it poured.   90

   Then Pyrenees glaciers, ones the Sun had never been able
to melt before, began to break up, wet the rocks,
and flow into a stream. Waters no longer take
their usual routes, for every riverbed is full
and spilling over its banks.
                 Shipwrecked on the field,
Caesar's army swims. Their camps wash out and sink
into the flood. Rivers overflow into their trenchworks.
They have a hard time rustling cattle. The flooded furrows
will bear no fodder. The scavengers for food get lost
and wander buried fields to find the sunken roads.   100

   And that faithful companion of all great disasters,
cruel famine, arrived. Not even besieged by the foe,
the men go hungry. Frugal men spend their savings
for a mere crust of bread.
               Oh profit, that sickly corruption!
Sellers come forward starving—when offered *gold*.

   Now every hill and rise is hidden, and all the rivers
are one big lake, sunk in a vast abysmal waste.
Rock outcrops are swallowed and dens of beasts
and the beasts themselves consumed in swift whirlpools
of roaring waters rolling, seething stronger than Ocean.   110
Night enshrouds the sky and remains unconscious
all through the sunrise. Heaven's disfigured face—
blackness back to back—blurs nature's distinctions.

   It's like the Antarctic, lowest point in the world,
the zone of snow and perpetual winters. Its sky

sees no planets. It's frigid, sterile, births no thing
but ice, which tempers the constellations' fires;
so make it here, supreme father of the world,
and you, Neptune, governor with the trident
of the waterworld (you drew the second lot)—   120
the first, hang endless storm clouds in the air;
the second, forbid the floods to reach the sea.
Deny the streams a sloping course to the seashores
but beat them back with tides, earth quake
and widen river channels, let Rhine and Rhône
inundate these Spanish fields, the world's rivers,
turn your springs this way, snows of the Riphaeus,
melt and flow here, ponds and pools and lakes stand here,
and every swamp and marshland bog pour here,
and rescue this miserable land from civil war!   130

   But content with giving just a minor scare, Fortune
returned to her man in full force, and the gods
seconded her actions with extraordinary sanction
that earned them forgiveness.
                              At last the skies cleared
as Phoebus matched the moisture and combed out
the dense clouds into fleeces, and once again the nights
would crimson with dawn light. The order of things returned:
the waters overcasting the stars head back to lowlands;
forests raise their boughs, from swamps the hills
emerge and day appears, to firm and dry the valleys.   140

   But when the Sicoris held its banks and left the plains,
white willow stalks were soaked and woven
into small rafts, then lined with oxhide strips.
These could ferry passengers over the swollen stream.
So do Venetians on Po's wide swamps, so do Britons
navigate wide Ocean, so when the Nile holds all
they build in Memphis barges from porous papyrus.
Ferried over on these boats his troops speed to work,
cutting and rolling trees on both sides of the wild river,
and in fear of its flood they do not put the logs   150

right at the banks' edge, but extend the bridge
back up into the fields. And lest the Sicoris ever dare
renew its flood, its channel is cut and scattered in furrows
to punish its haughty waters.

PETREIUS ATTEMPTS ESCAPE

When he sees how all
is going with Caesar's fates, Petreius deserts
lofty Ilerda; distrusting the known world's manpower,
he seeks unconquered peoples always fierce for battle
and in love with death; he heads for the world's ends.

Seeing hills stripped bare and deserted camps,
Caesar calls his men to take up their arms   160
and surmount the river neither by bridge nor by ford
but with hard arm strokes. Obedient they rush in
to take a path that a fleeing soldier would fear.
Soon rearmed, they warm their drying limbs
and revive their bodies cold from crossing the torrent,
while shadows decline and day advances to noon.
At last his cavalry seizes the foe's rear flanks,
which are thrown into doubt whether to fight or flee.

Up from the plain rise twin rocky ridges,
a hollow vale between. From here a steep terrain   170
links up high hills among which safe pathways
lie hidden in dark windings. If his enemy
could just reach those gullies, Caesar sees the war
slipping away to forlorn lands and savage tribes.

"Go!" he says, "break ranks and turn back the war
stolen by flight! Fighting faces forward! Menacing gazes!
Don't let those cowards go down to lazy deaths!

Make those fugitives turn and face our steel head-on!"
He spoke, and prevented his enemy reaching the mountains.

FRATERNIZING BETWEEN ENEMY CAMPS

There, with just a small rampart between,   *180*
they pitch their camps. Not obscured by distance,
eyes on both sides behold well-known faces,
they see brothers, their own sons, and fathers—
the unspeakable civil crime is now unmasked.

For a while they're silent in fear, saluting those
they know only with nods and gesturing swords.
But soon, when burning with greater goads
love breaks the rules, a soldier dares to cross
the palisade, and opens his arms for embraces.
One calls a friend by name, one greets a relative,   *190*
others recall youth shared in childhood pursuits.
Any who did not know a foe, was not a Roman.
Weapons run with tears, kisses break into sobs,
and though not stained with blood one soldier fears
what he could have done.
                                              Why beat your breasts?
Why cry, you madman? Why pour tears in vain?
Why not admit you freely submit to crime?
Do you so fear the man whom you make fearsome?
Let him sound the war trumpet—ignore its savage song!
Let him bear the standards, you fall back! Right here and now   *200*
the Fury of civil war will be thrown down,
Caesar would retire and love his son-in-law.
Come now, Concord, unite all in an eternal bond
of embrace, this diverse universe's salve
unto wholeness, along with holy World Love.
It's here, now, our age can make a difference on the future.

So many pretexts for crime have vanished, the guilty men
have no excuse—they have seen and known their foes.
Oh Fate, you are a sinister power! That brief respite
only making the slaughter worse. There was peace.   210
The soldiers wandered through both the camps now one.
They sat and shared their meals together on hard ground,
mixing and pouring libations with their wine.
Fires burned on hearths of sod, and bedrolls joined
to wile the sleepless night with tales of warfare:
memories of first battles, with what strength of hand
they threw their spears. But while they exaggerate their feats
(and conveniently forget to mention others),
exactly what Fate wanted happened—those luckless men
renewed their bonds of trust. And for all their love,   220
the coming horror grew.
                              For when Petreius finds them
pledging peace and sees his camp has sold itself—
betrayed him—he arms his slaves and sends them off
charged with an ugly deed. They mob the unarmed foes
and kick them out of camp, sever with steel
friends embracing, and break up the peace with bloodshed.
Feral with rage, Petreius adds words that spur on the fight:
"Mindless of your country, forgetting your standards,
can't you stand up for the Senate's cause and free
yourselves from Caesar, conquer him and go home?   230
The least you could do is be conquered! You still have steel
and fate is uncertain. While you still have blood
to flow from many wounds, will you bow to a tyrant
and carry the very standards you once condemned?
What do you hope from Caesar? To be treated like his slaves?
Have you also asked that your leaders' lives be spared?
I'd never buy my safety with such foul treason!
We are not waging civil war to stay *alive*!
The name of peace is luring us to our doom.
The nations would not mine iron from pits whose depths   240
plunge ever deeper, nor ring their towns with walls,
nor mount bold stallions for war, nor flood the sea
with fleets of ships riding high with turrets,

if it were *ever* good to trade liberty for peace!
"I guess my foes have kept the oaths of crime
they swore inviolate. But you hold your own faith cheap—
you hope to be pardoned for defending a just cause!
Honor has died, and sadly! Ignorant of your fate,
Magnus, *you're* raising forces throughout the world right now,
pleading with kings who reign at the ends of the earth—   250
while *we're* here settling 'peace' that may grant you safety."

He spoke and struck their minds, restoring their love for crimes.
As when beasts are denatured, taken from the forest
and caged, they grow tame and cease to look so grim,
learning to endure mankind. But just a drop of blood
drips on their thirsty tongues, and their rabid fury returns,
the taste of blood reminds their salivating mouths;
anger boils and scarcely spares their frightened trainer.

They fall to every guilt, in loyalty committing
atrocities that Fortune, in all her divine malice,   260
could have carried out in a blind night of battles.
Hearts which they, just lately, had warmly cherished
in embraces round table and couch, they stab.
At first they groan to draw the steel, but once they strike,
and right hands clench the blades that dissuade justice,
they hate their friends, and their own wavering hearts
are made bold by the blows. The camp is in hot tumult,
and as if crime unnoticed would be wasted
they heap up each offense before their leaders' faces.
They revel in their evils.
                          Caesar, though you lost   270
a number of fine men, you see the gods in this.
For neither upon Emathian fields nor on the waves
round Phocian Massilia was Fortune with you more,
nor was the deed on Pharian shores so great,
since by this one crime of civil war you will
become the leader of the better cause.

TRAPPED AND THIRSTY,
THE POMPEIANS SURRENDER

                            Polluted
with blood of wicked slaughter, the generals didn't dare
to camp their army near Caesar's. They turn in retreat
back to the walls of high Ilerda, but Caesar's cavalry
blocks their way, driving them off the plains,   280
locking the enemy up in the parched foothills.
Caesar then is eager to ring them with a trench
and cut them off from water, make them helpless
to camp near any riverbanks or post defenses
round any abundant springs.
                            When they see their path
is doomed, fear turns into reckless rage.
Thinking them useless while under siege, they slaughtered
their horses, and forced at last to despair of flight,
they're driven to fall on their foes, and kill while dying.
When Caesar saw them run down at full speed,   290
devoted to certain death, he called:
                            "Hold weapons, men,
for now! Hold off your swords when they rush at you.
Let this war not cost *me* any bloodshed.
Victory isn't free when the foe offers up his neck.
See how they hate the light and hold life cheap—
ready to die and cause me damage. They'll toss themselves
on blades, numb to blows, pleased to bleed and die.
Let their minds cool down, their mindless frenzy tire.
Let them lose their death wish."
                            So their menace cindered,
wasted by battle evaded; he let them languish   300
while the sun sank and night's light took its place.
When no chance came for them to die in droves,
their wild rage receded and, little by little, minds cooled.

A fighter has more spirit right when he's injured,
while the fresh wound still stabs him with its pain,
while his blood is warm and muscles can still move
before the skin contracts upon the bones. But if
the victor knows his sword blow has been fatal
and stays his hand, then shivering seizes his joints,
numbness will pervade his soul and sap his strength,   310
when the blood begins to scab and crack dry on the wounds.

Now in need of water, first they drill the ground
in search of hidden springs and secret rivers.
They dig the earth with picks and shovels, then add
to these their swords, deepening wells in the hillside
all the way down to the irrigated floodplain.
Not even the pale prospectors of Asturian gold
will descend so deep, or be so far from daylight.
But they heard no sound of aquifers underground,
no new fountains sprang forth from broken pumice,   320
no damp, perspiring caves dripped—not a drop—
no vein of water trickled up through sifted gravel.

Extracted from the pit, the men are drenched in sweat,
exhausted from heavy mining in the flint rock.
Their quest for water has made them even less able
to tolerate the thirst and heat. Food does no good
to renovate their strength. Disgusted by eating,
hunger brings relief. Where the soil looks wet
they fill both fists with dirt and squeeze out oily drops
over their mouths. Wherever stagnant filth   330
puddles black and slimy, all fall on it struggling
to slurp a putrid mouthful. Men who are dying
gulp water they wouldn't think of were they winning.
Like beasts they drain milk cows' swollen udders dry
and when rich milk is gone they swallow filthy blood.
They grind down grass and leaves and shake the dew
from branches, pound green tree shoots and tender
pulp for any juice or sap that they can squeeze.

How lucky are men whom a barbarous foe in flight
has laid low in the fields after poisoning the springs!   340
Caesar, you could have openly dumped diseased
and rotting beasts in these rivers, or pale aconite
that grows on rocks on Crete—the Roman troops
would drink it anyway. Fire scorches their guts,
their dry mouths crack, their tongues are rough and scaly.
They're losing pulse, and airflow through parched windpipes
rasps and wheezes through heavy respirations,
hard breathing, which is pain on peeling palates,
but still they grasp with gaping jaws for air that hurts.
They wait for rain, some downpour like what recently   350
had everything swimming. They stare at bone-dry clouds.
And what really breaks those wretches in that drought—
they aren't beyond desert Meroë, under Cancer's claw,
where naked Garamantes plow, but caught between
the overflowing Sicoris and the quick Hiberus!
The men can see both streams—yet die of thirst!

At last the commanders yield, defeated. Afranius
proposes they sue for peace. He leads a half-dead squadron
into the enemy camp and pleads the case
of his doomed army at the feet of his victor.   360
Unbroken by disaster, he maintains his dignity
throughout the appeal—just as he had through it all,
from his former fortunes to this recent downfall.
A true leader, he calmly, firmly asks for mercy:

"If fate had trampled me under an ignoble foe,
my own right arm would have already seized its death.
The only reason I pray for your pardon now
is that I deem you worthy to grant it, Caesar.
We aren't driven by factious zeal. We did not arm
in opposition to your measures. Civil war   370
found us generals already. While we could,
we faithfully defended the former cause.
We won't delay fate. We cede the West to you

and open up the East. Rest assured, you can leave
this part of the world behind you without a care.
You flooded no fields with blood to finish this war,
no arms gone slack from steel. Forgive your foes one thing—
that you have conquered us. We ask no more.
Give rest to the weary, all the men of your amnesty
to live out their lives unarmed. Consider our forces   380
as good as slain on the field, for captives ought not join
your own lucky crew. Captives deserve no share
in your triumph. This band has served their time.
We beg you—don't force conquered men to conquer with you."

    He spoke, and Caesar is easily swayed; with mild
gaze, he dismisses them from service and penalty.

    Once fair terms of peace have been approved,
the soldiers scurry down to unguarded streams,
lie down on the banks and muddy the rivers now in reach.
Many gasp for air as they pour endless draughts   390
of water down their throats; they choke and pant for breath.
But still they thirst, the plague does not abate.
Sick from lack, they fill their bellies yet beg for more.
But soon their nerve and manly strength return.

    Wasteful luxury, never content with a little!
Your ambitious belly canvassing land and sea
for food; you glory in praise of your table spread!
Learn how little it takes to sustain a life
and how much nature requires. What heals disease
is not fine wine, vintage of some unknown consul's year,   400
drunk from gold or fluorspar goblets—but crystal-clear
water gives life. Man can live on water and Ceres' grain.
Pity the men who still wage war. These men disarmed,
forfeit to their victor, then were safe and harmless;
free from cares they disbanded to their hometowns.
Given the gift of peace, how each regrets
he ever held a sword or lobbed a spear,

or suffered thirst or prayed the gods in vain
to win a war.
        The remnant ranks must follow
Mars through countless doubtful battles, many labors   410
around the world. Fortune may never waver
or fail them in successes—still, they'll have to conquer
again and again, drenching every land in blood,
and follow Caesar through every twist of fate.
Those who know, as the world nods to ruin,
their place in life are lucky folks. No battles
call to wear them down; no trumpets disrupt them
sleeping soundly. They return to wives and newborns
under humble roofs in their own lands,
not as drafted colonists. Fortune also leaves   420
their minds free from the trouble of courting favor.
Pompey had been their leader; Caesar granted them life.
The lucky few, impartial spectators of the civil wars.

ANTONIUS TRAPPED—AN AMBUSH
AND DESPERATE SUICIDES

  The fortune of war was not equal worldwide.
She dared to attack one of Caesar's contingents
where Adriatic waves strike Salonae's headland
and warm Iader faces the mild west winds.
Having trusted the warrior tribe of Curictae,
who tend an island in the Adriatic Sea,
Antonius was now backed up to the shoreline, trapped.   430
He was prepared for an onslaught, if only he could
keep famine, that stormer of garrisons, safely at bay.
The land gave no horse fodder, it grew no golden grain.
His troops had spoiled the field of grass and cropped
the stubble with their miserable teeth, and now
they plucked dry roots from sod that lined their trenchworks.

When they saw, on an opposite shore, comrades
under Basilus, they planned a new way to escape
across the strait unnoticed. They did not extend
the usual keels, nor build ships with high sterns.   440
They lashed together, in an unusual pattern,
planks strong enough to carry heavy loads.
Hollow casks below these buoyed up the rafts,
laid out in two long rows and chained together
then overlaid with slats, crosswise in a lattice.
The oars did not face outward, exposed to missile fire;
they rowed those waves that timbers had fenced in.
Their silent motion was a sight to see, since
it bore no sails nor visibly splashed the waves.

They watch the sea and wait, as the surf ebbs,   450
for barren beaches and downward-sloping waves.
Then, just as the tide turns and begins to surge back in,
they launch one raft, and it glides down on the deep,
then two more follow. High over each a turret totters
with menacing decks, lined with rickety parapets.

Octavius, stationed to guard the Illyrian coast,
spotted one raft but held his swift ships back
to see what else would follow and increase the catch.
By leaving the sea lane clear, he lured them to repeat
their reckless course.
                            Before a herd of deer has been   460
scared by the blind of bright and reeking feathers
into the ambush, the hunter, until he has raised
his netline up on hooks, will muzzle and leash
his quick and noisy Molossian, Spartan, and Cretan hounds.
He trusts no dog to the woods, but the pointer now nuzzles
the scent of the deer tracks. When he's marked the prey,
he knows not to bark but just tugs on the leash
to show the hunter where the deer lie hidden.

The men hasten on board, filling up the barges,
and strike out from the island without delay.   470

Already the twilight barely stalled night's darkness.
Pompey's Cilicians, remembering their old tricks,
set a trap mid-sea. The strait looked clear,
but just beneath were ropes dangling in the water,
bound at either end to rocks on Illyrian outcrops.
The first raft was not stopped, nor that which followed,
but the third barge was snagged on the towline and dragged
into rocky shoals, where a bluff arched out over the surf—
how it hangs there, ever about to fall, is amazing—
and woods above threw shadows onto the water.   480
Here the sea hauls in ships wrecked by the north wind,
and often hides drowned corpses in secret caverns.
This grotto holds all the sea's spoils. When high tides
vomit out of the caves, its whirling vortex of waves
surpasses Charybdis' froth that boils off Tauromenium.

   The raft caught here, freighted with Opitergium's farmers.
The fleet casts out and soon surrounds the raft;
the cliffs on the shore are covered with backup forces.
Vulteius, the raft's captain, detects the undersea trap
and struggles in vain to cut it, then offers battle,   490
but it is hopeless—he isn't sure which way
to retreat or advance. But valor did what it could
in such a situation, caught off-guard, outmanned.
That cohort, which barely had full numbers, fought
the many thousands pouring round their raft—
but not for long. Night enveloped the shadows
and darkness brought a truce.
                              The captured cohort
is shaken and shocked by thoughts of pending doom.
Vulteius instructs them with a high-minded speech:
"Men, we're free for no more than one short night.   500
Consider, in this brief span, the outcome of this crisis.
No life is too short while any time remains for a man
to seek out his own death. Nor is the glory dimmed, boys,
to greet your fate when it is forced upon you.
What lies ahead in life is uncertain for all.
The soul earns equal praise by abandoning hoped-for years,

and cutting short one's last moments of light
so long as you summon doom with your own hand.
No one is ever forced to a willing death.
No escape lies open; our countrymen surround us,   510
intent on having our throats. Resolve to die
and all fear will dissolve. Desire what you can't avoid.

"We shall not fall in a blind cloud of warfare,
our ranks overshadowed and confused by weapons.
When corpses litter the field, each and every death
becomes as one, valor dies and is buried.
But the gods have posted us here, on this boat,
in sight of comrades and enemies. The sea will bear witness,
also the lands, and that island's rocky summits;
from opposite shores both parties will be watching.   520

"I do not know what example you're planning, Fortune,
by our great and memorable fates. But in all of history,
whatever annals record as monuments to loyalty
in service to the sword, of military duty,
our company would surpass them. For we know, Caesar,
falling on our swords for you is not enough.
But nothing greater remains, hard-pressed as we are,
than for us to offer great pledges of devotion.
Envious Fortune has cut off much of our glory,
since we are not captives with our sons and fathers.   530

"Let our enemies know that we will not be conquered!
Let them fear the raging courage of men
whose spirits take death lightly! Make them happy
no *more* ships struck their trap! They'll try to tempt us
with pledges; they'll want to bribe us with shameful life.
If only our singular death might gain more fame—
let them promise pardon, and bid us to hope for safety,
so when they see us mine our vitals with warm steel,
they don't suppose we did it from despair!
It takes heroic valor to make Caesar declare   540
the loss of a few of his men, out of so many thousands,

a true disaster. Fate can withdraw and free me,
I still would not be willing to avoid the present moment.

"I have deserted life, my comrades, and wholly live
by my impulse for coming death! It is a frenzy!
Only those who are touched by the nearness of death
are permitted to realize what a blessing it is—
the gods hide this from survivors, to keep them alive."

His zeal fired the wavering minds of his whole crew.
Before their captain's speech, the men with watery eyes   550
had watched the stars in heaven, trembling as the beam
of the Great Bear wheeled around. After his exhortation
had buoyed up their hearts with strength, they waited,
praying for dawn.
             And heaven's axle was not slow
to edge the stars in the deep, for the sun was in Gemini,
Leda's twins—at its solstice—and nearing Cancer.
A short night, then, drove Thessalian Sagittarius.

Dawn discloses day and standing on the cliffs
Histrian warriors, and Liburni at sea with the Greeks.
First they tried to stall the battle, to win through terms: 560
postpone death—maybe life to the captives would sweeten.
But the men stood devoted; they had damned the light.
Stern and ready to fight, since the end was promised
by their own hands, no rumble of war could batter
the minds of men fully prepared for the utmost.
Those few sustained attack by innumerable hands
on land and sea, so strong was their fatal pact,
and when it seemed that enough blood had flowed in battle,
they turned their rage from their foe.
             First the ship's captain,
Vulteius, bares his neck and begs to meet fate: 570
"Is there any at all whose right hand is worthy
to spill my blood? Who will attest his faith,
seal his vow to die by stabbing me?"

He can say no more, for right then many a sword
drives his vitals through. **Praising** them all, he bestows
his grateful dying blow **on the one** who stabbed him first.

They fall on one and all, a single faction
committing every unspeakable act of war.
As from Cadmus' seed sprang up the Dircean cohort,
who then slew their fellows: grim omen of Theban brothers.   580
And on Phasis' banks, from the sleepless dragon's teeth,
the Earthborn, spurred to wrath by magic spells,
filled many a furrow with their kinsmen's blood.
Medea herself shuddered to learn the horrible
power that her untested herbs could wield.

So the young men fall, sworn to share one fate,
and amid such manly deaths, to die takes little valor.
At once they cut and are cut down by lethal wounds.
No right hand—even as it was dying—failed.
No wound required the thrust of someone's blade: 590
hearts run onto steel, throats sink to the hilt.
When bloody chance drove brother to slaughter brother
and sons to slay their fathers, no hand faltered but buried
its blade's full weight in its mark. The greatest sign
of familial love was to finish it with one stroke.

Now the half-dead drag their sprawling guts across
the deck and flood the sea with bloody gore;
ecstatic with the sight of the light they've spurned,
they behold their victors with proud faces
as death comes down.

                              The raft displays its heap   600
of gruesome slaughter. The victors free the bodies
on funeral pyres, as the leaders admire
that men so loved their captain. No boat's fame
ever spread so loudly round the whole wide world.
But cowardly nations will still not understand
these men's example: how a simple feat of bravery
frees you from slavery. Instead, kings use iron

to terrify, liberty is branded by savage armies,
to keep us ignorant that swords are for setting free!
Death, why not force cowards to stay in life,   610
and come to only those with valor?

CURIO IN LIBYA—THE STORY OF
HERCULES AND ANTAEUS

                    Mars raged no less
down south, where he blazed through Libya's fields.
For Curio the bold hauled anchor off Lilybaeum
when a north wind, not too strong, filled his fleet of sails,
and between the rubbled towers of mighty Carthage
and Clipea he dropped anchor off a famous beach.
He first camps at some distance from the white surf
where the slow Bagradas plows dry sands in furrows.
Then he seeks the rocky cliffs, hollowed out all round,
which tradition, for good reason, calls Antaeus' realm.   620
Wanting to know the reason for the ancient name,
he learned from a local native what his fathers had taught.

    "Giving birth to the Giants did not tire Earth.
After them she bore a dreadful babe in Libya's caves.
Yes, sir, more than for Typhon or Tityos or wild
Briareus, Earth could justly be proud of *that*.
She was kind to heaven, too, when she didn't send Antaeus
to Phlegra's fields. And she topped her child's vast strength
with this gift: whenever his limbs grew weary,
if he touched his mother they'd surge with renewed vigor.   630
He lived in *that* cave there. They say he hid under the cliff
and carried off lions for dinner. He never slept
on animal hides or on soft tree limbs, no sir,
he'd lie on the naked earth and regain his strength.
He killed the farmers who tilled Libya's fields.
He'd kill any sailors who put in at this shore.

For long stretches his valor spurned to fall to Earth
and use the power she gave. Nothing could overcome him,
even when he stayed standing.

                           "At last the widespread rumors
of bloody evil roused Hercules, that great soul,   640
while he was relieving lands and sea of monsters,
to stop by Libyan shores to rid this land of ours.
He threw down the Nemean lion's hide. Antaeus
threw off one of Libya. The foreigner, in the custom
of Olympian wrestlers, oiled his limbs for the fight.
The other, not trusting just to touch his feet to his mother,
for extra strength poured warm sand on his body.
They locked hands and arms in a number of holds.
Each tried the other's neck with a long, heavy choke hold—
in vain. Each stood his ground; neither backed down.   650
Each marveled to have met his match. At first,
Alcides did not want to unleash his full force.
He wore his opponent down; he could tell by his heavy panting
and the cold sweat on his tiring frame. Soon his neck
grew weary and shook, then chest was pinned to chest,
then a punch to the knee from the side, and down he fell.
The victor binds his opponent's back, gone limp,
grabs him around the groin and locks his hands behind,
his feet between his thighs to keep them apart,
he holds his contender sprawled out full on the ground.   660

    "But the dry earth drinks his sweat; warm blood swells his veins.
His muscles flexed, his limbs grew taut and he fought
as if with new body; he untied Hercules' holds.
Alcides stood dumbstruck by such great strength.
Not even in Inachus' waves, before he'd honed his skills,
had he so feared the Hydra, whose lopped-off heads grew back.
The equals clash again, one with the might of Earth,
the other with his own. His cruel stepmother never
had more reason to hope: she sees his weary limbs drip
with sweat—the neck that stayed dry even hoisting Olympus. 670
And as he throws his arms around his tiring foe once more,
Antaeus falls down on purpose, not waiting for the blow,

and gets back up refreshed, stronger than before.
All the spirit in the earth rushed into his flagging form
and Earth struggled to support her wrestling son.
Then Alcides perceived how his mother's touch gave aid:
'Stand up!' he cried. 'I'm not going to let you lie
down on the dusty earth again, Antaeus.
If you fall, it'll be on my chest. I'll hold you up.'
He lifted the youth, struggling, high off the ground.   680
Earth could convey no vigor to her dying son,
for Alcides clutched him round the middle, his torso
already constricting, cold with sluggish torpor,
and for a long time he kept his foe up off the ground.

"So that's the way antiquity—who guards old tales
and is a marvel to herself—says this land was named.
But a greater name was given to *those* hills,
named for a man who got his Punic foe recalled
away from Latin strongholds. Scipio's base was there
when he took possession of the land of Libya.   690
Right *there* you see the traces of his old rampart.
The Roman conqueror first held these very fields."

Curio was elated, as if the place's fortune
would wage this war for him, as if the fates
of former leaders here would also keep him safe.
Pitching his star-crossed tents on that lucky spot,
complaisant with the camp, he abused the hills' good omen;
harassing a fierce foe, he found himself outmatched.

CURIO AGAINST VARUS AND KING JUBA

All of Africa annexed by Roman standards
was then under Varus' rule, mostly maintained by   700
Latin forces, but he also called on King Juba
with Libyan tribes from all corners of the world

who accompanied his standards. No warlord's realm
was more extensive. At its widest, his kingdom
stretched west to Atlas, neighbor of Gades,
and east to Ammon, gateway to the Syrtes.
The vast tract of his hot domain ranges inland
from the ocean to the scorching torrid zone.
His regions teem with peoples, countless follow his camp:
Autolols, nomad Numidians and Gaetuli   710
always ready on unsaddled stallions; Moors,
the color of Indians; Nasamones, a poor tribe;
swift Marmarides mixed with dark Garamantes;
the Mazax, who can twist a quivering missile
to match in speed the arrows of the Medes;
Massylian tribes who rest on bareback steeds
that have never known reins, a simple crop will turn them,
and African hunters who wander with flimsy tents;
they do not rely at all on iron weapons,
but with flowing robes ambush irate lions.   720

　　Not solely from civil-war zeal did Juba arm:
he had private ends, a personal score to settle.
Curio, that year he defiled both gods and mankind,
had tried, by a tribune's bill, to oust the king
from his ancestral throne, deposing Libya's tyrant
while making you a monarchy, Rome. Recalling this insult,
Juba considered this war the fruit of his salvaged scepter.
Therefore report of the king startled Curio also.
Further, his troops had never vowed to die for Caesar,
they had not been made soldiers in the Rhine's current,   730
but captured at Corfinium. Doubtful of former—
and faithless to new—leadership, they think each side
is in the right. And when he comes to see
all their apathetic fear and lethargy,
the empty night-watch posts along the ramparts,
he speaks to the worries that cause his mind to waver:

　　"Daring masks great fear. I'll take the field first.
March my soldiers down to level ground

while they are still mine. Free time changes minds.
Make them fight, they won't have time to think.   740
When they grip their sword and the bloodlust surges,
helmets masking shame—who can remember
what leaders contend? Who weighs the claims of causes?
Men favor the side they stand on. Like public shows,
the fatal arena's contenders don't clash together
to settle old grudges. They hate whoever appears."

So he thought as he arrayed his ranks
on the open plain. The fortune of war took him in
enticingly, to dupe him into future misery.
For he drove Varus off the field, an awful rout;   750
they cut up their unguarded rear all the way to camp.

But when Juba heard how Varus was overpowered,
the sad tales of the battle, the king just smiled:
this war's glory would fall to his contingents.
He rushes his troops in secret, enforcing silence
to ensure no reports get out. His only fear—
that he would be feared by his unwary foe.
Numidia's king sends out his right-hand man,
Saburra, to provoke a fight with a small brigade,
feigning that he'd been given full command of the war.   760
The king would hold back his forces, down in a hollow.

Like the ichneumon that outwits Egyptian asps
with a trick of his tail—its shadow drives them mad
and they'll strike the empty air until they're weary—
then he gets a safe tooth-hold on the serpent's throat
out of reach of deadly venom; spraying plague
without effect, his mouth drips wasted toxin.

Fortune rewards the ruse. Impulsive Curio,
without exploring his enemy's hidden reserves,
commits his cavalry to a nocturnal advance   770
to range far and wide a field they did not know.
At dawn's first light, he himself precedes

the standards out of camp, advised many times in vain
to beware of Libyan fraud and Punic tactics
always poisoned with guile. Doom was nearing,
fortune betrayed him to fate; the young man was pulled
down in the civil war he had helped to author.

    He leads his standards over arduous cliffs,
across crags with sharp embankments when, *there*,
from a hilltop rise the enemy is spotted.   780
In guile they feigned retreat, till he left the hill
and arrayed his lines in open formation on the plain.
Ignorant of the plot, believing they had fled,
he drove his men down, as if he were the winner,
and they plunged deep into the fields below.
When the ruse was revealed and Numidians raced
to fill the hills, imprison them on all sides,
the leader was dumbstruck along with his doomed throng.
No flight for the fearful, no battle for the strong.
No warhorse jumps at the trumpets' brass,   790
pounding rocks with his hooves, teeth grinding the bit,
tugging the reins, mane flying, ears pricked high,
stamping uneasy feet as he fights to break loose.
No, their weary necks droop, their sweating limbs steam,
panting tongues gape out of cracking mouths.
Hoarse and heavy breath groans in their chests,
and labored breathing drags their tired flanks on,
bloody spit caking round their hard-champed bits.
And now no lash, no goad, no constant spurring
of furious whips will speed the horses' gallop.   800
They stab their steeds to drive them—but no use
to break the horse to find its breakneck speed,
for no onslaught, no attack, was possible there.
Nearing the foe just made easier marks for their spears.

    But once the African rangers fired their horses in attack,
thundering down the plain, throwing up dirt—
as much as a Thracian tornado whirls in air—
a pillar of dust drew darkness down over the sky.

The battle's sad truth of doom enveloped the infantry.
The outcome was never in doubt. Mars had one face,   810
and death held the field throughout the time of fighting.
To rush in, fight hand to hand, was impossible.
Penned on all sides, the soldiers were overwhelmed
by sidelong swipes, straight-on, by spears from afar,
and died not only from blows and blood they lost
but were buried by the sheer hail of weapons and steel.

So a mighty army was squeezed to a small circle,
and if any man, afraid, tried to hide in the middle,
he barely got through unpunished by comrades' swords.
The ring compressed as front ranks took steps back,   820
tightening their own noose. There is no space
left to swing a sword. Crowding bodies grind;
as armored chests collide their armor breaks.
The victorious Moor could not enjoy the full spectacle
that Fortune granted. He missed the rivers of gore,
limbs falling, bodies ground into the earth—
crowded corpses, propping each other up.

Fortune, wake the spiteful ghosts of fallen Carthage
for these grim new sacrifices! May they appease
cruel Hannibal and the Punic shades!   830
Gods above, what a sin to make Libyan soil the site
of a Roman ruin, for Pompey, to serve the Senate's will.
Instead, let Africa conquer us for herself.

When Curio saw his lines poured out on the field,
when blood had settled the dust and he could behold
the massive slaughter clearly, he could not bear to save
his soul in its affliction, to hope for any escape,
but fell in with the fallen heaps of his men
and, forced into valor, hastened on his doom.

What good now is the Rostrum, the crowded Forum,   840
to you, who bore the plebeian standards as a tribune,
who drove nations to arms? Who betrayed the Senate's rights

and bade father- and son-in-law to clash in war?
You lie low before the chiefs meet at Pharsalia.
You won't get to watch the civil war.
For a city's misery your own blood is the price,
you pay for arms with your neck, all you mighty.
Rome would be truly happy, her citizens blessed,
if the gods took as much care for her liberty
as for its vindication.

                    Behold his noble corpse: *850*
unburied Curio feeds the birds of Libya.
But what does it profit me to be silent about
your worthy deeds, which fame preserves from decay
for all time? I eulogize the fine points of your life.
Rome never bore a citizen with such talent,
nor one who so obliged the state while he followed justice.
Then the times got lost and wrecked the city,
ambition, luxury, wealth, and dreadful plenty,
their undertow swept his wavering mind away.

   Curio radically altered the course of events   *860*
when Gallic spoils captured him, and Caesar's gold.
Others have gained the right to cut our throats with swords:
mighty Sulla, fierce Marius, cruel Cinna,
the entire chain of the dynasty of Caesar—
but who of them was granted the power he had?
They all bought their city, but he sold it.

BOOK FIVE

The Senate faction and Pompey convene a formal meeting in Epirus, confirming Pompey as leader of their party, among other business (1–66). Appius Claudius Pulcher visits the oracle at Delphi, long languishing in silence, to ask, in vain, about his future; the narrator foreshadows his imminent death and burial in Euboea (67–246). Returning from Spain, Caesar's tired and angry legions threaten mutiny (247–314), which Caesar suppresses with a haranguing speech and summary executions (315–96). Caesar sends his armies to Brundisium, with orders for ships to gather there for crossing to Greece (397–404), while he heads to Rome and becomes, with a travesty of normal constitutional procedure, dictator and consul (405–30). Caesar goes to Brundisium and crosses to Greece, despite poor weather and lagging winds (430–92). Caesar makes camp near Pompey's armies but must await the arrival of ships of men under the command of Mark Antony, who Caesar sternly enjoins in a letter to cross immediately (493–545). Caesar decides to go back alone to Italy to retrieve his men, and embarks in a tiny boat owned by Amyclas, with whom he faces a colossal storm and tempest, only to be washed back to where he started (546–748). His men abuse him for being so rash (749–78), and Antony finally arrives with the rest of the army (778–98). Pompey, seeing the moment of crisis upon him, sends his wife, Cornelia, away to Lesbos, although she strongly protests and does not wish to leave him (799–910).

BOOK FIVE

A SENATE MEETING IN EPIRUS

So both rival chiefs, having suffered wounds of war,
Fortune kept well matched, mixing successes and failures,
for the land of Macedon.

                        Already winter had frosted
Haemus with snow, the Pleiades set on cold Olympus,
and the day the calendar takes new names drew near—
New Year's, celebrating Janus, first of months.

But before their term of office expired, both consuls
exercised their right to summon to Epirus
senators away on diverse duties of war. Foreign,
squalid seats held the Roman elite. The Curia,
a guest under foreign roofs, heard secret matters of state.
Who would call it a "camp" where strict law wields
so many axes and rods? That dignified order
taught the people they were not the party *of* Magnus—
Magnus, rather, was a member of *their* party.

As soon as silence gripped that sad assembly
Lentulus, from high on his lofty seat, declared:
"If we live up to our Latin stock, if noble blood
floods our hearts with strength, let us not think of this land,
or how far we are from the roofs of our captured city.
Examine instead the faces here in this crowd,
and though you can order all, decree this first, fathers—

a fact clear to kings and nations—that we are the Senate.
For whether we meet below the Northern Bear's chilly wagon
or in the torrid zone, where the sky is clogged in hazy heat,
where night and day never grow unequal,
wherever Fortune takes us, high State and Empire
shall follow as companions.
                              "When Tarpeia's rock
was torched by Gauls, Camillus took up in Veii,
and that was Rome. Never has a change of location   30
annulled our order's rights.
                              "Caesar now possesses
our mournful halls, our empty homes, our muzzled laws.
The forums are closed in sad recess. The Senate House
sees only fathers we banished while the city was full.
Anyone not exiled from this great order is here.

"The war's first fury scattered us, while we
were unused to crime and sleepy from long peace.
But all our members have regrouped in one place.
See how the gods weigh Italy against the world's resources!
Illyrian waves bury our foes. On Libya's barren dunes   40
Curio, a great man in Caesar's 'senate,' has fallen.

"Raise our standards, captains! Drive the course of fate!
Declare to the gods your hope! And may fortune
muster your fighting spirit, as much as our cause
gave you when fleeing our foe!
                              "The rights of our office
end with the closing year. But you, fathers of Rome,
who shall never see a limit to your power,
consult among yourselves and make Magnus your leader."

The Senate welcomed that name with joyful clamor,
and placed on Magnus its own and the country's fate.   50

Then worthy kings and peoples are showered with honors.
They decorate Rhodes, the sea-power island of Phoebus,
and the rugged young troops of cold Taygetos. Athens

of antique fame is praised. For her Massilia,
Phocis is given her freedom. Then they commend
Sadalas and courageous Cotys; King Deiotarus
for faith in arms; Rhascypolis, lord of a frozen land.
Then the Senate commands Libya to obey
Juba's scepter.

        Then a bitter twist of fate—
Ptolemy, you shame of Fortune, crime of gods,   60
the worthiest king to rule a faithless people,
are allowed to ring your locks with Pella's diadem.
A boy received a brutal blade to wield against his people—
but would that he *had* used it against his people!
Given the kingdom of Lagus, with it came Magnus' throat,
stealing his sister's reign and the crime from a father-in-law.

APPIUS VISITS THE ORACLE AT DELPHI

  The meeting adjourns and the crowd begins to arm.
But while the nations and their leaders were preparing
for the blind spots of chance and uncertain outcomes,
only Appius feared the descent to the double-headed   70
dealings of Mars. He hassles the gods to divulge
the end of events. Though it was closed for many years,
at Delphi's shrine he unlocked Apollo's oracle.

  Sunset is just as far removed from Dawn
at Parnassus; its twin peak hinges up to the sky,
sacred to Phoebus and Bromius; both gods are feasted
as one by Theban Bacchae, every third year at Delphi.
When flood engulfed the earth this height alone stayed dry,
the only land left standing between the sea and stars.
Even your summits, Parnassus, were sundered by waters,   80
and one of your peaks lay buried in the waves.

To avenge his mother, expelled when heavy with child,
with his yet unmastered arrows Paean there unrolled
the coils of Python, when Themis still ruled the tripods.
When Paean saw in the earth the gaping chasm
breathing truths divine, its soil exhaling
whispering winds—Apollo hid in these sacred caves
and, occupying the shrine there, he became a seer.

Which higher power hides there? What ethereal force
deigns to dwell in the cell of those blind caverns?   90
Which god of heaven suffers in the earth,
conscious of the course of all, eternal secrets,
the world's future, and is prepared to offer
his knowledge to people? Bearing human contact,
he is great and powerful whether he just sings fate,
or whatever he chooses to sing then turns to fate . . .
Perhaps a large segment of Jupiter connects
to the earth, to govern and support the globe that balances
on a void of space. This wafts out of Cirrha's caves,
one with and derived from the Thunderer in the sky.   100

When this spirit has conceived in a virgin's breast,
striking her human soul it rings, and opens the mouth
of the priestess, like lava boiling out of Etna's peak
in Sicily, like Typhoeus, buried beneath Inarime's
eternal mass, smoking, quaking Campania's cliffs.

This spirit, open to all and denied to none,
alone can free one from the stain of human fury.
No curses are composed in silent whispers there,
for he sings what is fixed and forbids mortal to pray
for things that none can change. He is kind to the just   110
and often finds a new home for whole cities dispossessed,
as with Tyre. He has dispelled the threats of war,
as the sea of Salamis recalls. He has eased Earth's anger
by showing an end to famine. He has also cleared
pestilential skies.
                         No other gift of the gods

is missed more by our age. For the Delphic oracle
fell silent when kings began to fear the future
and forbade the gods to speak. But Cirrha's priestesses
do not complain that the voices stopped. They enjoy
the shrine's long holiday. For when the god enters her breast   120
her penalty—or reward—is premature death,
since the stinging lash and wave of frenzy
batters the human frame, and blows from the gods
shatter the fragile soul.

                     So for a long time
the tripods had not moved, the rocks had sat in silence,
when Appius queried them, prying into the ultimate fate
of Hesperia. He ordered the priest to unlock the awesome
temple, send in the fearful prophetess to the god.

    Phemonoë was carefree and wandering around
Castalia's springs, deep in its grove's recesses.   130
He grabbed and forced her in through the temple's doors.
Afraid to stand at the terrifying threshold,
the seer of Phoebus tries in vain to trick
and scare the general out of his ardor to know
the future:

               "What perverse hope for truth draws you here,
Roman? Parnassus' chasm is silent, dumb,
and its god suppressed. Either the spirit has left the gorge
or its path has turned, leading to some wasteland;
or when barbarians torched the Pythian temple,
ash and cinders poured down its vast caverns   140
blocking Phoebus' way. Or Cirrha is silent
by the will of gods, who thought it enough to entrust
secret songs of the future to your ancient Sibyl.
Or maybe Paean, who bars the guilty from his temples,
finds none in our age to whom he is willing to speak."

    The virgin's wiles were patent and her fearful denials
just proved her belief in the spirit. She twists a band
to bind up her hair in front; the locks let down her back
are wound with a white fillet and Phocian laurel.

Stalling, full of doubts, finally the priest shoved her   150
into the temple. The deep inner shrine made her shiver.
She resists, remaining in the oracle's outer foyer
and unmoved by the god she simulates ecstasy,
making up some speech.
                              No moaning garbles her voice,
her display of holy frenzy is not convincing.
Her false chanting would harm the general less
than it outraged Phoebus' tripod and his trust.

Her words weren't shaky, broken, her voice couldn't fill
the spacious cave. No bristling horror shook
the laurel out of her hair. The temple's doorsills   160
stood unmoved, no breezes swept through the grove.
These things betrayed her fear of trusting Apollo.

Appius knew the tripods had failed and raged:
"You'll pay dearly for that impious, false display,
to me *and* the gods, unless you get back down in that cave
and quit speaking for yourself when you are consulted
concerning a world that's being rocked by crisis!"

At last, terrified, the maiden fled toward the tripods.
She reached the cavernous depths and there remained,
and the power conceived in her virgin breast what the spirit   170
of the rock, unexhausted after so many centuries,
poured into the prophetess. At last he possessed
her Delphic breast—her body had never been fuller.

Paean burst in and drove Pythia out of her mind,
ordering all that was human to leave her heart.
Demented she raves about the cave, a Bacchant writhing,
a different person. Her garlands and bands of Phoebus
are flung from her wild hair on end. She whirls through all
the temple's corners, her neck two-headed, knocking over,
strewing tripods on her random path. She burns,   180
enduring the fire of your wrath, Apollo. Not only

do you lash her, goad her, sink flames deep in her vitals—
you also rein her in, not allowing her to reveal
all that she now knows.

Each age comes in a blur
chaotic, centuries of misery oppress her breast,
the great chain of events appears, every future
struggles to come to light, contending destinies
striving for a voice. The world's first day and last,
the compass of Ocean, the number of grains of sand—
like Cumae's Sibyl, in her Euboean chamber,   190
indignant that her frenzy must slave for many nations,
from such a heap of fates her proud hand picked out Rome's;
so Phemonoë, filled with Phoebus, labors to find
your name, Appius, who came to consult the god
hidden in the land of Castalia. She searches long and hard
and barely finds it, buried among so many great fates.
First, rabid madness pours from her frothing lips,
groaning, loud howling with heavy panting breath,
then sad wails of lamentation echo
through the vast caves. At last, the virgin is mastered   200
and her voice rings out:

"Roman, you will escape
the war's enormities. You've no share in the great dispute.
You'll rest in a deep hollow, alone off Euboea's coast."
But Apollo gagged her throat, suppressing the rest.

Keepers of Fates' tripods, secrets of the world,
and you, Paean, ruler of truth, from whom the gods
hide no future day—why do you fear to reveal
the final ruin of empire, leaders cut down,
the deaths of kings, and collapse of so many nations
into Hesperia's bloodbath? Have the divine powers   210
not yet decreed the crime? While the stars still doubt
how to damn Pompey's head, do they hold back every fate?
Do you keep silent so that Fortune can fulfill
the work of judgment's blade, the fury punished?
That tyranny meet again the vengeance of Brutus?

The doors fly open, dashed by the priestess' breast.
She bounds outside, driven from the temple.
Her madness lasts, and not having spoken all,
she has not expelled the god. He stays. Her eyes
roll wildly still, ranging across the entire sky.   220
Now she looks afraid, now scowls with menace.
Her face never stays the same. A fiery blush
dyes her cheeks, already black and blue.
Then a frightful pallor, worse than what fear causes,
overcomes her, unable to rest, heart-weary,
but like the raucous groans of the heaving sea
after northern gales, the seer sighs deep and speechless.

Then, returning from the holy light where she saw Fate
to the common glare of day, a shroud of darkness falls.
Paean had poured inside her Stygian Lethe   230
that stole away the gods' secrets. Truth fled her heart
and the future returned to Phoebus' tripods;
struggling to revive, she falls.
                              The nearness of death
doesn't frighten you, Appius, duped by ambiguous oracles.
You schemed to seize kingship over Euboean Chalcis,
caught up by empty hope in a lawless world.
Blind fool! What god besides Death can guarantee
that you'll feel no shock of war, that you'll be free
from a world in trouble?
                              Interred in a monumental grave
you shall own a secluded piece of Euboean shore,   240
where the sea's throat narrows with the rubble
of Carystos' marble quarries, across from Rhamnus,
where they worship the goddess who hates the proud,
where the sea constricts to surge through Euripus strait,
which draws the ships of Chalcis—with its breakers
and erratic current—to Aulis, port unkind to fleets.

CAESAR WARDS OFF MUTINY

    Meanwhile Caesar was returning from conquered Spain,
marching his eagles of conquest to the rest of the world,
when his whole career of fateful success and prosperity
was nearly overturned by gods.

                              Unbeaten in war,   250
the commander feared that among his own camp's tents
he would lose his criminal gains, when the hands
faithful through so many wars, now blood-sated at last,
almost deserted their leader—whether the furies of war
were driven out during the brief respite from
the grim blast of the trumpet, swords grew cold in sheaths,
or whether the soldiers now seek greater rewards
and damn their cause, reject their leader, and even
now are selling the swords they've stained with crime.
No crisis taught Caesar more clearly the lesson   260
that the height from which his eye beheld all things
was not stable but shaky, what shifty ground he stood on.
Maimed by the loss of so many hands, nearly left
alone with his sword, the man who dragged nations to war
now knows that soldiers, not a leader, draw the swords.

    They no longer fear to gripe, nor hide their anger
deep in the hearts. For the normal reason that binds
wavering minds to a cause—that each man is afraid
of those who also fear him, and each man supposes
that he alone feels troubled by tyranny's injustice—   270
this no longer holds.

                    A riot breaks out, banishing fears.
A mob gone wrong gets away unpunished.
They shower threats:

                "Caesar, let us quit
this criminal madness! You scour land and sea
for steel to cut our throats, to pour out our cheap souls
to any old foe. Gaul stole some of our comrades,

some fell in Spain's hard fighting. Some lie in Italy.
You conquer worldwide, while your armies perish!"

  "What good that we poured our blood out in the Rhine
and Rhône to conquer the North?"
                                        "For so many wars   280
you reward me with . . . civil war?"
                                    "When we seized
the roofs of our fatherland and drove out the Senate,
what men, what gods, did you permit us to loot?
Our hands, our swords, are guilty of all kinds of horror,
but we're still pious paupers."
                            "What end do you seek through arms?
What is enough, if Rome is insufficient?"
                                            "Look,
our heads turn gray. Look at our hands, sapped of strength,
our wasting arms. The pleasure of life is gone.
We have wasted away our years in warfare.
Dismiss these old men to die."
                                "Is it too much to ask?   290
Don't make us lay our dying bodies down
on hard heaps of sod, or make our fleeing spirits
strike a helmet, our eyes searching to find
a hand to close them in death. Allow us to fall
into our wives' tears, knowing that our pyre is heaped
for one body only. Let us die old, from sickness—
let a fate besides the sword take Caesar's men."

  "Do you think we're fools, luring us with hope
to train for horrors? Are we alone so clueless
that we don't know which crime pays best in civil war?   300
War has taught him nothing if he doesn't know
that *these* hands can do anything. No god or chains of law
prevent this daring. In the Rhine's currents Caesar
was the leader, here he's comrade. Crime levels
those it defiles."
                    "Add that when this ingrate judges

our merits, our valor is wasted. Whatever we do is 'fortune.'
Let him know that *we* are his fate. You may always
expect the gods to be compliant, Caesar—
but with disgruntled soldiers, you'll get peace."

So their words decreed, and running throughout the camp   310
they began to impeach their leader with hateful gazes.
So be it, gods on high! When faith and duty
desert, and our last hope is immorality,
let discord put an end to civil war.

What leader would not be scared by this revolt?
But Caesar is used to casting his fates to the edge
and revels in testing his fortune in utmost dangers.
He comes, not waiting until their rage dies down,
and rushes to try them in the midst of their fury.
He would not have denied them cities and temples   320
to spoil, and Jove's Tarpeian seat, and mothers and wives
and daughters of senators to suffer unspeakable things.
He wants them to beg him for every brutal act,
he wants them to love Mars' prizes. All he fears
is a sound mind in his untamed soldier.

                                      For shame,
Caesar! That you alone love wars your men condemn!
Will they get sick of bloodshed before you do?
Will the law of steel oppress them, while you rush on
through every right and wrong? Relax. Learn to get by
without armies. Let yourself put an end to crimes.   330
Madman, why do you pursue it? Why press unwilling men?
Civil war is deserting you . . .

                          He stood on a pile
of heaped-up sod, his gaze unshaken, inspiring fear,
fearless himself, his rage dictating this speech:
"I wasn't here to see your fists and faces raging,
soldiers! Here's my chest, bared and ready for wounds!
If it's end to war you want, leave swords *here* and flee.
This cowardly sedition has dared nothing,

except to expose your souls as unfit for war!
Just a bunch of boys with dreams of flight,   340
tired of successes and an undefeated leader.
Go! And leave the wars and me to my fates.
These weapons will find hands. As for you rejects,
Fortune will supply enough men to take your spears.
Magnus flees and Italian nations follow him
in a mighty fleet—don't you think Victory
will give me a crowd to take the prizes she offers
as wages for your labor in this all-but-routed war
and escort unwounded my chariot decked in laurels?
While you'll be bloodless old men just watching   350
our triumphs, part of the Roman rabble, despised.
You think Caesar's onward march would even
notice your desertion?
                            "As if all rivers threatened
to withdraw the waters they pour into the sea—
this wouldn't decrease the ocean's level surface
any more than they now raise it. You really think
your efforts for me have ever carried weight?
The gods don't care, they'd never stoop so low,
the Fates don't give a damn about your life or death.
Everything follows the whims of men of action.   360
Humankind lives for the few. You terrorized
Spain and the far north soldiering under my name;
had Pompey led, you would have fled. Labienus
was brave in Caesar's army. Now the vile traitor
tours lands and seas with the leader he prefers.
Your loyalty is no better to me, whether you battle
for or against me. Whoever abandons my standards
and doesn't surrender his arms to Pompey's faction,
never wanted to be mine.
                            "Without a doubt
the gods care for this camp, since it wasn't their will   370
that I wage so great a war without fresh troops.
How great a burden Fortune is lifting from your shoulders,
so weary from the load! She's given you a chance
to lay down arms, since you expect so much

and the entire globe would not suffice. Now,
I'll wage the wars for myself. Get out of camp!
Pass my standards to men, you spineless civilians.
You few responsible for this raving madness—
your punishment, not Caesar, detains you here.
Lie down on the ground and stretch your faithless   380
heads and necks out for the death blow. And you,
who now stand as the camp's last strength,
you raw recruits, observe these executions
and learn both how to kill and how to die."

   They trembled at his savage threatening voice,
a helpless mob afraid of a single man whom they,
so many strong young men, could have turned
back to private life—as if his orders
could wield against their will the very iron
of their swords. And Caesar himself was worried   390
that they might refuse their weapons for this crime.
But they submit to cruelty easier than he hoped:
not only a sword but throats came forward, too.
Nothing inures minds to crime like killing
and dying. So a grim pact was struck, restoring order;
the troops scattered, appeased by punishments.

   He orders that the tenth day's camp will be
Brundisium; he recalls every ship that's in the harbor
at distant Hydrus, old Tarentum, or on Leuca's
recessed shores; also the Salpine marshes and   400
Sipus beneath the hills, where Apulia's fertile
Garganus range—curving the Italian coastline
so it opposes both the north winds of Dalmatia
and Calabria's south winds—reaches the Adriatic.

CAESAR HEADS TO ROME AND
BECOMES DICTATOR

He himself heads, safely without troops, to Rome,
cowering and well versed already in serving him
even in his toga. Just to indulge the people's wishes,
of course, he assumed the highest honor of dictator,
and made the calendar joyful by becoming consul.
For all the words we've used for so long now   410
to lie about our masters, this age first invented,
when Caesar, so he'd lack no right of iron force,
willed to join his swords to Italy's civil axes,
to add the fasces rods to his standards' eagles,
snatching the empty name of legal imperium
he stamped worthy titles on those sorry times.
What better consul to name the year of Pharsalus?

The Campus Martius feigns its solemn proceedings:
they divide out the votes of the people (not admitted in),
the tribes are called out and they shake an empty urn.   420
To observe the sky is forbidden; it thunders but
the augur is deaf; they swear the bird auspices
are favorable (as an owl flies by on the left).
Then first perished that power once so revered,
now so deprived of rights; but just lest the time lack names,
our calendars mark the ages with consuls of the month.
So, too, the spirit who presides at Trojan Alba—
though hardly deserving its solemn rites, with Latium
now subdued—beheld the night of bonfires
that closes the Latin Games.

CAESAR BRAVES A WINTER
STORM AT SEA

                From there at full march   430
he crosses fields that idle Apulians no longer farm,
given over to useless weeds, and, quicker than lightning
or a mother tigress, reaches the Cretan rooftops
of curving Brundisium, finding the seas closed
by seasonal squalls, his fleets afraid of winter's stars.
To the chief it seemed a shame that times so ripe
for hastening war should waste away in slow delays,
stuck in port while others less favored by fortune
take safely to sea.

                So he inflates with courage
the minds of men untrained upon the deep: 440
"The blasts that seize both sky and strait in winter
hold steadier than those in spring, whose storms
you can't predict. They're shifty and can stop you
in your tracks. We won't have to follow
the curves of sea and shore, but can cut straight
across the waves using just the north wind.
Let it rage, bending our topmost mastheads,
sailing us through to the citadels of Greece
before Pompey's men from up and down Phaeacia's shores
dig in their oars and catch our sluggish sails.   450
Cut the ropes holding back our lucky bows.
We've wasted too long these clouds and savage waves."

    The first stars had emerged in heaven, beneath the waves
Phoebus had slid, the moon now cast her shadows,
when the ships cut off together. The cables stretch
the sails out full, as sailors bend the yardarms,
slant canvases to port and spread high the topsails
to gather breezes that otherwise would be lost.
At first a light wind propels the canvases,
which swell a little, then they fall slack against the mast   460

midship, and with land left behind, the very breeze
that drove the vessels is too weak to follow them.
The sea lies flat and calm, slow and lazy, stuck,
standing more still and sluggish than stagnant swamps.

So stands the idle Bosporus, freezing Scythian waters
when the Hister, choked with ice, no longer stirs
its channels; the whole vast sea is covered with frost.
The water holds fast whatever boats it catches,
the horseman cracks a surface impassable by sail,
and the nomad Bessian cuts his trail across the Maeotis,   470
resounding in hidden depths.
                                          A grim sea-silence,
swamps of standing water sluggish to gloomy depths.
As though nature had left it a frozen wasteland,
the sea stopped cold, the ocean forgot to observe
its age-old fluctuations and did not roll in surges,
no shiver nor ripple, no sun's reflection shimmers.
The ships were stuck, exposed to countless mishaps.
On one hand, hostile fleets might plow with oars
the motionless expanse; but then, a grievous famine
menaced those beleaguered by the calmed abyss.   480
New prayers were found for novel fears: they pled
for tempests, violent winds, if only the water
would shake itself out of its dismal doldrums
and be the sea. But clouds were nowhere and no
threat of waves. Lethargic sky and strait
removed all hope of shipwreck.
                                          But when night took flight,
weak, cloud-covered rays of daylight shone
and gradually struck the deep, driving the mariners
toward Ceraunia's peaks. At last the ships began
to pick up speed, and wakes pursued the fleet,   490
which glided now with favoring wind and wave
and fixed its anchors in Palaeste's sands.

The first land to behold the chiefs pitch camps
together was that enclosed between the banks

of swift Genusus and the gentler Hapsus.
A marsh with mild flow that hardly seems to drain
allows the Hapsus to carry ships; but the Genusus,
filled up both with snowmelt and with showers,
races headlong. Neither river grows fatigued
by a lengthy course, but with the shore nearby   500
each knows only a small extent of land.

                                    In this place
Fortune paired two names of such great fame,
and the sad world hoped in vain that chiefs divided
by a narrow field might condemn the nearing crime.
For they could see each other's face, hear each other's
voice there, and through so many years beloved
by you, Magnus, your father-in-law—after the birth
and death of grandchildren proved the tokens of love
were of unlucky blood—not once would see you nearer,
except upon the beaches of the Nile.   510

CAESAR WRITES TO ANTONY TO MAKE HASTE TO JOIN HIM

   Caesar's mind was thundering to join in battles,
but partisans left behind compelled him to endure
delays on crime. His officer Antony, always reckless
in combat, was during the civil war already
rehearsing for his Actium. Caesar summoned him
many times with threats and imprecations:

   "You're causing a lot of trouble for the world—
why are you detaining the gods above and Fates?
The rest has been accomplished at my pace;
Fortune now asks you to make the final effort   520
in a war that has raced through its successes.
It's not Libya with its broken coast of Syrtes,
shoals, and fickle surges that's dividing us!
Am I committing your army now to an untried deep

and hauling you into unknown hazards? Coward!
Caesar orders you to come, not go. Before you,
I broke right through the enemy's line to reach
a beach that they controlled. Do my camps scare you?
I'm bitter that fate's opportunities are slipping;
I'm wasting my prayers on the winds and sea lane.   530
Don't hold back the men now eager to cross
that precarious expanse. If I know them well,
the young men would risk shipwreck to meet up
with Caesar's army. I must add a harsh word here:
Our division of the world is not equal; Caesar
and the entire Senate hold Epirus, while you
are in Italy all alone."
                          Three and four times
he spurs him with such words, and when he sees
him loitering still—since he believes he is failing
the gods, not the higher powers him—he dares   540
freely to attempt the strait through the reckless darkness,
which others, when ordered, were scared of. For knowing
from life's trials that even rash deeds turn out well
if a god is tending, he hopes in a tiny vessel
to conquer swells that entire fleets would dread.

TO RETRIEVE ANTONY, CAESAR
VENTURES BACK TO SEA

Languid night had loosed war-weary men from cares,
a short rest for those pitiful ones whose hearts
a lowly fortune invigorates with sleep. Already
the camp was silent, the third hour woke the second watch,
when Caesar, pacing restless through dead silence,   550
got ready to do what slaves would hardly dare:
to leave all behind, make Fortune his sole companion.
Just outside the tents he jumped the bodies of
the guards given up to sleep—and grumbled quietly

that he could elude them. He scanned the curving shorelines
and found amid the surf a boat, tied by a line
to the hollow rocks. The skipper of the craft
and owner had his tranquil home not far from there.
No timber beam supported it, but wild rushes
and marsh reeds woven together; its open side was   560
sheltered by an upturned dinghy. Two or three times
Caesar rapped at the doorway, shaking the roof.
Up from his soft bed of algae Amyclas rose, saying,
"What shipwrecked sailor's come to my house now?
Who's forced by fortune to seek help at my shack?"
He spoke and took up a rope torch from a deep pile
of cooling ashes and nourished its slight sparks
into rolling flames. Untroubled by war, he knew
that in civil conflicts no one loots a shack.

What a safe means of life the poor man has   570
with his humble house divinities! What blessings
from the gods, not yet understood! What temples
or walled cities could be so lucky—not to panic
with alarm at the knock of Caesar's hand?

Then, when the door was unbolted, the general said:
"Expect things greater than your modest prayers, young man.
Unfurl your hopes! If you will follow my orders
and take me to Hesperia, you won't be bound
any longer to your boat and hands for everything
and forced to draw out a penniless old age.   580
Don't hesitate to yield your fate to a god who wants
to fill your scanty cupboards with sudden riches."
So he spoke; though cloaked in plebeian garb,
he was unskilled in common civilian speech.
Then Amyclas the pauper said:

                                        "Well, in fact,
many things keep me from trusting the sea tonight.
The setting sun didn't spin out any crimson clouds,
and its rays weren't of one mind. From the south
Phoebus called in Notus, but from the north, Boreas,

with its scattered light. Also, its sphere was hollow,   590
dim in the middle, dull as it sank, allowing
eyes to watch its sickly glow. And the moon
didn't raise her thin horn brightly, and her disk
wasn't hollowed out clearly in the middle.
She didn't stretch her slender crescents in an arc,
but turned red with a threat of winds, and then
she showed a sallow face, turning pale
and sad as she passed beneath a cloud. No,
I don't like the rustling woods, the crashing shore,
the dolphin who hesitates to try his luck at sea,   600
or when mergansers love dry land, or herons
trust their swimming wings and dare to soar on high,
or when a crow dips his head in the waves,
as though expecting rain, and paces the shores
with unsteady steps. But if the outcome
of weighty affairs demands it, I won't hesitate
to lend a hand. Either I'll reach the shores you bid,
or else the sea and its blasts will tell you no."

So saying, he unties his boat, gives sails to winds—
at their blast not only do stars shoot through   610
the upper air, plowing scattered furrows as they fall,
but even stars held fixed at the height of the poles
appear to quake. The dark sea's back bristles,
and far out across its swells that stretch for miles
a menacing wave is boiling. The turbulent sea
bears witness that ominous winds are breeding storms.

Then the skipper of the trembling boat said: "Look,
the savage sea is planning something big.
Whether he'll send out Zephyrs from the west
or Austers from the south is still unclear.   620
In fits the stern is pummeled by the deep
on every side. Notus' gusts grip clouds and sky,
but if we go by the roaring sea, a storm from Corus
is coming on. In such a maelstrom, no ship or
shipwrecked man will reach Hesperian shores.

The one safe thing is to give up hope of passage
and turn back from this journey. It's denied us.
Let's get to shore in this battered boat, before
even the nearest land is too far off."

    Confident every peril will retreat from him,   630
Caesar says, "Defy the ocean's threats and give
your sail to the raging wind. If heaven charges
you to avoid Italy, on *my* authority
press on. The only just cause for your fear
is that you don't know your passenger, whom the gods
never desert, and from whom Fortune deserves
but little when she arrives *after* my prayers.
So burst through the midst of these squalls, secure
with me as protector. The sky and sea can toil,
what does our boat care. Caesar's weight   640
will hold her down and guard us from the waves.
The winds' savage fury will not last too long.
This boat will even improve the rolling waters.
So don't turn the rudder, set sail to flee these
nearby shores. And trust that you will reach
Calabria's port even if no other land could give us
safety in this ship. This wrack and ruin brings
things that you don't understand: this turmoil
of sea and sky is Fortune looking for something
that can stand up to me."

                  He spoke no more—   650
when the ship was struck, its frazzled lines torn away
by a violent cyclone, snapping at the mast, it cracked
and the sails flapped above it. The hull's timbers
creaked aloud as its seams were overcome.
Then perils, stirred up worldwide, rushed together.
First from the Atlantic Ocean you raised your head,
Corus, rolling your breakers in, and now the sea
was raging as you rose up and crashed
its every surge against the rocks.

                    Freezing Boreas
rushed down and beat back the sea, which hung   660

in doubt to which wind it would succumb—but
the rabid madness of Scythian Aquilo won out,
churning up waves and making shoals of sands
concealed in the depths.
                          And Boreas didn't carry
the sea to the rocky coast but dashed its waters
against the swells from Corus, and even as the winds
withdrew, the stirred-up currents still crashed on.
Eurus' threats did not let up, and black with rainstorms
Notus did not hang back in Aeolus' rocky prison,
I'd suppose. All of them rushed from their own region,   670
defending their lands with violent hurricanes,
and as a result the sea stood steady in place.
For tempests snatch and haul off separate seas—
the Tyrrhenian crosses to the Aegean's waves,
the roving Adriatic echoes in the Ionian's basin.
Mountains pummeled by waters so often in vain
were buried that day! What lofty peaks the conquered earth
sank to utter ruin! Such powerful currents
don't surge from some shore, but out of another sphere
rolling they came, from the great outer Ocean   680
that binds and circles the world a wave drove on
these monstrous sea swells.
                          Just as the ruler of Olympus
called on his brother's trident to help his thunderbolt,
worn out against the ages of man, and so annexed
the earth into the second kingdom, that time when
the sea rolled over the nations, that time when Tethys
refused her shores' confines and strained to occupy heaven.
So this time, too, the mounting sea would have crested the stars
had not the ruler of gods suppressed the waves with clouds.
It wasn't the night sky. The air is hidden, cloaked   690
in murk from hell's house, weighed down with mists
it sinks, and showers pour in the overclouded flood.
Lightning bolts, even their dreaded light is snuffed,
and can't flash clear, but bursting darkly here and there
fizzle in the haze.
                          The vault of the lofty gods

feels tremors as the steep axis thunders,
laboring as the seams of the sky's pole falter.
Chaos frightens nature; its elements seem ruptured,
every boundary that fosters concord broken,
and Night is returning to confound the gods with ghosts.   700
Their one hope for safety? That such global ruin
had not killed them yet.

                  As high as when one gazes
down at calm seas from the clifftops of Leucas,
so high did those sailors shudder to see headlong below
the surf from the crest of the waves, and swelling again,
the breakers gape wide, the mast scarcely juts above surface.
In cloud the sails, the keel on bare ground,
since where sea ebbs it doesn't conceal the sands,
its billows consumed completely in surging heaps.
Terror defeats the aid of skill and the helmsman   710
doesn't know which swells to break, which to avoid.
The ocean's discord even helps those sad men
as wave crashes wave and can't capsize the ship.
Her side beaten, a wave knocks back and rights her;
with each wind gust the boat crests high and straight.
It's not the shallow shoals of Sason isle they fear
nor curving Chaonia's rocky shores, nor the coastline
of Ambracia with its hazardous harbors—
it's Ceraunia's craggy peaks the sailors quake at!

  At last Caesar believes that the perils measure up   720
to his own fates. "What great pains the gods are taking
to overthrow me," he declares, "hunting me down
with so mighty a sea as I sit in a tiny boat!
If the deep is granted the glory for my death
and I am denied battles, O spirits, I will stand firm
and accept whatever form of death you give.
Let the day the fates are speeding on cut short
colossal feats—my great achievements are enough.
I've tamed the northern nations, I've overcome
enemy arms through fear. Rome has regarded Magnus   730
second to me. At the people's bidding I've carried

rods of office denied to me through warfare.
No Roman power is absent from my titles.
Still, nobody will know but you, O Fortune,
the only one aware of my vows and prayers,
although I go down to the shades of Styx
heaped with honors, both dictator and consul,
I've died a mere private citizen. O gods above,
I don't need funeral rites. Hold back my corpse
mutilated amid the waves, let no pyre   740
or burial mound be given me, so long as I'm
dreaded forever and looked for in every land!"

He spoke and—marvel to tell—a tenth wave
lifted him in the feeble craft, not tossing it back
from atop the ocean's crest, but bearing it onward
the swell set them down on land where narrow shores
were free of jagged boulders. Touching land, at once
he got back so many kingdoms, cities, and his own fortune.

But returning now as dawn light neared, Caesar
did not deceive his camps and comrades as he had   750
when quietly escaping. Pouring around their chief,
a mob of his men weeping and groaning assailed him
with sad complaints he did not find unwelcome:

"Where did your reckless virtue take you, Caesar,
you hard man? To what fate did you desert our worthless souls
when you gave up your body to be dismembered
by spiteful gales?"
                    "When so many people depend
on that one soul for life and safety, when
so much of the world has made you its head,
to want to die is cruelty. Did none of your comrades   760
deserve the chance to *not* outlive you, *not* be witness
to your fate?"
                "While the sea was stealing off with you,
slothful slumber gripped our bodies. How it shames us!

You sought Hesperia yourself because it seemed
that sending another out on a sea so raging
would be harsh."

                    "Usually one hurls headlong
into dubious circumstances and sheer mortal dangers
when it's the last chance left. But for one at the peak
of world power to surrender so much to the sea—
why do you weary the gods so? Does it satisfy you   770
that Fortune's favor and effort toward this war's fate
were to dash you right back upon our beaches?
Are these the advantages from gods that please you,
to be not the world's ruler nor lord of its affairs
but a lucky shipwrecked sailor?"

                                        So they bantered
as night shattered and a bright sunny day overtook them,
the winds submitted and the weary sea laid down
its raging, swollen breakers.

ANTONY CROSSES FROM ITALY

                              Nor did his officers—
once they saw Hesperia's sea had exhausted its swells
and a brisk north wind was gathering strength in heaven   780
to break against the deep—fail to cast off ships.
Winds and skilled right hands kept them together
on even keel a good long time across the flat expanse,
like ground troops their ships advanced united.
But night was wild and ripped away from the sailors
the moderate gale and steady course of the sails,
driving the fleet out of order.

                              So driven by winter storms,
cranes take leave of the frozen Strymon, to drink
from your waters, Nile, and first taking to flight
they sketch out various patterns taught by chance.   790

But soon when a stronger south wind blasts their spread wings
they mix haphazardly, circle in heaped-up confusion—
the letter they drew disappears in a flurry of feathers.
When day returned, the air, incited by Phoebus rising,
pressed down on the ships more violently. In vain
they tried to beach at Lissus; passing it by, they reached
Nymphaeum. Here the south replaced the north wind
and made a harbor with waves free from Aquilo.

POMPEY SENDS CORNELIA TO LESBOS

On all sides Caesar's armies gathered in strength,
and Magnus, seeing the brink of Mars' harsh crisis   800
now beset his camps, decided to move to safety
his burden of marriage, and in distant Lesbos
to hide you, Cornelia, far from the noise of raging war.
Oh, how lawful Venus overpowers steady minds!
Even you, Magnus, Love made uncertain and anxious
to face battles. The only one you did not want
to stand fast under Fortune's lash, which threatened
the world and Roman Fates, was your own wife.
His mind made up already, words desert him.
Indulging in sweet delay pleases him more,   810
stalling what must come, stealing time from fate. . . .

At the end of night, with restful numbness banished,
Cornelia warms in embrace his chest heavy with cares
and seeks dear kisses from her husband, turned away.
Alarmed at his wet cheeks, a dark hurt strikes her;
she doesn't dare to catch her Magnus weeping.
"Not now," he groans, "sweeter to me than life,
which disgusts me now, but in a happy time, my wife—
a sad day has come, which we've put off too long,
and not long enough. Caesar is here, ready for battle.   820
We must succumb to war, and you will be safe from it

hiding in Lesbos. Don't tempt me with prayers. By now
I've even refused my own. You will not suffer
a long separation from me. Steep calamities
will come suddenly; it's a fast fall from the summits.
It's enough for you to hear about Magnus' dangers.
And your love has deceived me if civil wars
are something you can watch. For it brings me shame,
now that Mars stands ready, that I can sleep soundly
with my wife and rise up from your embrace   830
when the whole sad world quakes at trumpets of war.
If Pompey engaged in civil conflicts saddened
by no loss—I shrink with dread from that!
All the while you hide, safer than all peoples,
safer than any king, and lying there far off,
your husband's fortune will not weigh you down
with its whole load. And if the gods should rout
our ranks, the best part of Magnus will remain,
and I will have, if the fates and a bloody victor
beat me down, some place I'd want to flee to."   840

　　Scarcely had the sorrow struck her in her weakness
than her heart was stunned and her senses left her.
At last, her voice could utter troubled protests:
"I have nothing left, concerning our marriage fates
or the gods above, to complain about, Magnus. It's not
the grave that severs our loves, nor the final torch
that lights the dreadful pyre. It's just a case
of that all-too-common and low-class affair—
I have no husband, because he abandoned me.
At the enemy's approach let us break the vows   850
of our nuptial torch! Let's please your 'father-in-law'!
Is this how you acknowledge my faith to you, Magnus?
Do you think anything can be safer for me
that is not for *you*, too? Haven't we hung together
on the same turn of events for a long time now?
Are you telling me, cruel man, to hold my head high
to lightning bolts and utter destruction without you?
Does it seem to you a 'safe' and carefree lot

to lose my life while you are still praying to win?
If things go bad, I won't want to be a slave;   860
set on death, I'll follow you to the shades below;
but until the sad news strikes from far away
those distant lands, I'll survive you and live on.
It's also callous of you to habituate me
to this fate, teaching me to endure such heartache.
Forgive me saying this, but I am afraid
I could learn to endure. For if prayers work
and gods hear me, your wife will be the very last
to hear how things turn out. Even if you win,
I'll cling to the crags, afflicted, fearing what ship   870
will bring the news of so happy a fate. Nor will hearing
that the war goes well for you dispel my dread,
since cast off as I am in such a deserted place,
Caesar, even in fleeing, might take me captive.
My famous name will make those shores well known
as my place of exile; who will not be aware
that Mytilene is where Magnus' wife lies hiding?
This is my final plea: if your armies are conquered
and no safety is left to you except in flight,
when you take to the sea, steer your doomed ship   880
anywhere else you wish. On my shores
they will be hunting for you."
                                    Like fate she spoke,
then out of her mind she tore out of their bed,
unwilling to put off the torturing pain any longer.
She cannot bear to grasp the breast in sweet embrace
of her mournful Magnus, nor clasp his neck,
and she loses the last enjoyment of their long love.
They hurry their grieving and neither as they part
can bear to say "farewell." In all their lives
no day had been as sad as this. For later losses   890
they bore with sturdy minds, braced by sorrows.

    In her misfortune she falls and is caught up by her women
and carried to the watery sands, where she lies prostrate,
clutching the very shore. At last she's taken on board.

Less unhappily she had left her fatherland
and the ports of Hesperia when pressed by the armies
of savage Caesar.
                    Faithful companion of Magnus,
alone you go, bereft of the chief, fleeing from Pompey!
How sleepless the coming night will be for you!
For the first time in a widowed bed, cold, quiet,   900
unused to sleeping alone, your side bare,
no husband to hold you.
                        How often, oppressed by sleep,
hands embrace the bed but are deceived by emptiness!
Forgetful of exile, by night she seeks her husband!
For though flames burn her silently to the marrow,
she takes no pleasure in stretching out across the bed.
She saves his side for him.
                        She was afraid
she had lost Pompey. But the gods above were planning
far less happy things. The hour was fast approaching
that would bring Magnus back to her in misery.   910

BOOK SIX

With the armies and generals of both factions now together in northwest Greece, a first confrontation occurs around the coastal citadel of Dyrrachium (1–31), which Caesar besieges, surrounding it at a distance with impressive fortifications (32–69). Both armies suffer hunger, thirst, and illness (70–126). Pompey's armies attempt to break through the blockade, and are first successful (127–50), but then Scaeva, a decorated centurion in Caesar's legions, single-handedly fights back Pompey's forces and defends his position nearly to the death, a great but ironic example of valor (*virtus*) in civil war (151–287). The armies continue to skirmish (288–329), but Pompey misses an opportunity to press his advantage to victory, instead following Caesar, who retreats toward Thessaly (330–70). A long digression on the land of Thessaly, which begins and ends with the Gigantomachy, emphasizes all the ways in geography, mythology, and history that Thessaly is a cursed land, long fated and well prepared for this world cataclysm of Roman civil war (371–458). Fearing what is to come, Pompey's son Sextus consults a Thessalian witch, Erictho, the best at Thessaly's multitude of dreadful black arts (459–633), who engages in a gruesome necromancy to bring a dead soul back into its body (634–865), to tell Sextus about how famous Roman shades feel about the civil war and about his own family's coming doom (866–927).

BOOK SIX

After the chiefs, their minds on battle, had camped
on nearby slopes, both armies brought up face-to-face,
and the gods saw their contenders, Caesar spurned the capture
of any Greek walls and refused to owe Fate a victory
except for the defeat of his son-in-law in war.
All his prayers seek that world-lethal hour
that will hazard all on chance; a dice game of fate
is settled, which will sink one or the other head.

CONFRONTATION ROUND DYRRACHIUM

Three times he showed his squadrons, and the standards
threatening battle were arrayed on every hillside,   *10*
proof that he'd never abandon Latium's ruin.
When he sees that his son-in-law cannot be roused
to battle by any disturbance, but that he's trusting
the confines of his trenchworks, he takes up standards
and marches through fields, on paths hidden in thickets,
rushing to seize the citadel of Dyrrachium.
Magnus anticipates this move and makes his way
along the water. Pitching camp atop the hill
called Petra by the Taulantian residents,
he guards Ephyrean walls—defending a city   *20*
kept safe, in any case, by its citadel's site.
No work of the ancients guards it, nor massive structures

of human labor so easy—rising however high—
to fall in wars, or with the years that change all things.
Its fortress, which no weapon of iron can shake,
is its natural location. Enclosed by the deep
on every side and steep crags that spray seawater,
but for a small hill it would be an island.
Precipices terrible to ships uphold the walls,
and the Ionian's fury, when rabid south winds rouse it,   30
shakes its temples and houses, spews mist to the rooftops.

Here a contemptible hope gripped Caesar's mind
avid for war: the enemy was scattered widely
upon the hills; he would surround them unawares,
drawing in the distance mounded trenchworks.
He eyes the terrain to measure it, and not content
to build hasty walls with brittle sod alone,
he transports massive boulders and blocks of stone
stolen from mines, dismantling city walls
and homes of the Greeks. What they pile up   40
no savage battering ram could repel or break,
no violent war machine could ever shatter.
They tear mountains down and Caesar levels the work
across the peaks. He opens pits and situates forts
with towers high on the summits, retreating back
to encircle regions, forests, wooded wastes,
ranging wide to snare groves and beasts inside.
Field and forage are not lacking for Magnus;
he moves camp *inside* Caesar's encircling blockade.
Many rivers take their rise there, and there, too,   50
they weary and pour out their current; reviewing
how work is progressing at opposite ends of the field,
Caesar gets worn out and takes a break halfway.

Now let ancient fable raise the walls of Ilium,
ascribe them to the gods; let retreating Parthians
admire the brittle, clay-brick walls around Babylon.
See here, as much as the Tigris or quick Orontes circles,

enough land for a kingdom of Assyria's eastern peoples,
this hasty work amid the turmoil of war
seized and contained.
                         So much labor wasted.   60
That many hands could have yoked Sestos to Abydos,
displacing Phrixus' sea with great heaps of earth,
or severed Ephyra from Pelops' broad domains,
relieving ships of Malea's long winding circuit,
or anywhere in the world, however much nature opposed it,
changed it for the better.
                         War's stadium assembles.
Here is nourished blood to flow over every land,
here are contained the slaughters of Thessaly and Libya.
In a cramped arena, civil war's madness boils. . . .

BLOCKADE AND FAMINE

   At first the mounting war operations deceived   70
Pompey, just as one who is safe in the uplands
of Sicily does not notice Pelorus' rabid barking,
or when the tides of Tethys batter Rutupiae's coasts,
Britons in Caledonia aren't aware of turbulent waters.
When he first sees the vast rampart fencing the land,
he, too, leads troops outside the safety of Petra
and spreads them around the various high grounds, trying
to weaken Caesar's army, stretch the blockade thin
and exhaust his soldiers. For himself he lays claim,
with a fenced stockade, to a patch of ground no larger   80
than the distance from lofty Rome to little Aricia
with its grove sacred to Mycenae's Diana,
or that measure of land the Tiber passes
(if its stream never twisted) as it glides past our walls
and descends to the sea. No war trumpets sound
and, though unordered, spears fly back and forth;
arms just testing javelins commit many a crime.

A bigger worry stops the chiefs from engaging
their armies: Pompey now faced a land exhausted
of grazing supplies; the cavalry trampled it under   90
as hard hooves racing by pounded the budding plain.
With the fields mowed down, war chargers languish.
Although their mangers brim with import hay,
they grow deathly ill, longing to chew fresh grass;
wheeling round, their knees give out and they fall.
And as their corpses rotted, dissolving limb from limb,
stagnant air drew up the contagious, flowing plague
into a foggy haze, the sort of vapor Nesis sends up,
that Stygian mist from its steaming rocks, and as the caves
of Typhon exhale a lethal madness.
                                        Then the men   100
succumb; the water, which takes on any taint
more readily than air, stiffens their guts with filth.
Their skin hardens tight, their eyes swell up and burst,
a burning fire of sacred fever spreads to their faces;
men are so tired they refuse to lift their heads.
More and more, headlong fate takes everything.
The living aren't sick long before they die;
the ailment brings death with it. The crowd of fallen
worsened the plague, since unburied bodies lay there
mixed with the living; for those wretched citizens   110
their funeral was to be cast outside the tents.
Nevertheless these toils abated, because of
the sea at their backs and the gusting north-wind air
on the shores, and ships laden with foreign grain.

But the enemy, free on the spacious hillsides,
isn't troubled by sluggish sky and lifeless waters,
but suffers savage hunger, as though surrounded
in a cramping siege. While the grain is not yet swelling
ripe for harvest, he watches his miserable mob
dig into foods for beasts, pluck shrubs, strip leaves from trees,   120
and pull up suspicious plants with unknown roots
at the risk of death. Whatever flame would soften,
whatever teeth could grind, whatever rasping throats

could choke down into the belly—many things
yet unknown for human consumption the soldiers
grasped at, while they laid siege to a full-fed foe.

POMPEY ATTEMPTS ESCAPE, SCAEVA
PROVES HIS WORTH

As soon as it suits Pompey to break the blockade
and march out, deploying his men across the terrain,
he doesn't try it under the cloak of night's dark hours,
disdaining a stealthy passage while his father-in-law's   130
armies sleep. He wants to escape with widespread ruin,
assault the ramparts and beat down the towers,
resist every sword and make his way by bloodshed.

Yet a nearby section of rampart seems opportune,
where Minicius' fort lies idle and rough thornbushes
and dense trees give cover. No dust cloud gives away
the marching column that suddenly reached the walls.
All at once off the plain the Latin eagles gleamed,
all together the trumpets sang. His victory
owed nothing to the sword, for terror had struck   140
the enemy like thunder. Valor did all it could—
they were beaten down where duty bade them stand.
Now none were left to be wounded and the shower
of so many weapons was wasted. They send in torches
and pitch-black fires roll; the towers quake and nod,
threatening collapse; the piled rubble groans
as thick blows of timber dash against it.

And now Pompey's eagles had scaled the rampart's heights,
the world's rights were now in reach—a thousand squads
or Caesar's full force could not hold that position   150
with Fortune's favor, but one man robbed the victors
and fended off their capture. While he bore arms

and wasn't yet cast down, he denied Magnus victory.
Scaeva was the man's name; he was earning his due
living in camps before the wars with the wild tribes
of the Rhône. A lot of blood gained him promotion there,
and he ruled a large column with the centurion's staff.
Eager for any offense, he wasn't the sort to know
how great a crime is virtue in civil warfare.

Seeing his comrades already quitting the fight,   160
seeking safety in flight, he cries out: "Where are you
being driven by fear, so impious and unknown
in all of Caesar's armies? Turning backs on death?
Aren't you ashamed to be missing from the heap of men
and searched for among the corpses for the pyre?
Out of rage at least, boys, stand your ground
if duty is gone! Out of all we've been chosen
by the enemy, to make his break. Today
will not pass without some blood from Magnus!
I'd seek the shades a happier man if Caesar   170
were here to see. Fortune denies me that witness.
But I will fall and die with Pompey's praises!
Shatter their spears with the force of your chests!
Blunt their swords on your throats! Into the distance
the dust and noise of ruin are already traveling,
the clamor has struck Caesar's unworried ears.
We are prevailing, comrades! He will arrive
and win this fortress back while we are dying."

His voice arouses more fury than war trumpets
kindle with their first notes, and the youths admire   180
the man they follow, eagerly watching his moves,
ready to learn whether valor, when outnumbered
and in dire straits, can offer anything but death.
He stands on the crumbling rampart and, first thing,
rolls corpses from the cramped towers, overwhelming
the enemy, climbing up from below, with bodies.
All the destruction provides the man with weapons:
with logs, with rubble, with his very self

he harries the enemy. Now with a stake or sturdy pole
he shoves the chests that oppose him off the walls.   190
With his sword he hacks off hands that clutch
the tops of the rampart. He smashes a skull with a rock,
spilling brains from a structure too weak to defend them.
Flames kindle the hair and beard of another.
Fires hiss as eyeballs burn.

                              The growing heap
of corpses soon leveled the ground with the walls—
when it had, he leaped over their weapons and landed
in the midst of that great throng, quick as a leopard
will speed away through a volley of hunters' spears.
Hard-pressed among dense formations and hemmed in   200
by the whole war at once, he still overcomes a foe
glimpsed behind his back. His sword is losing its force,
its edge blunted and dull with thick-caked blood,
it breaks, but won't cut, limbs.

                              The whole heap
and every weapon presses him, no hand fails,
no lance is unlucky, as Fortune watches a new match
at equal odds contend: one Man fights a War.
His sturdy shield rings with constant blows,
his hollow helmet, in fragments, chafes and smashes
his temples; nothing now protects his naked vitals   210
except the very spears lodged in his bones.
Idiots, why are you wasting javelins now
and agile arrows? Those blows could never sink
down deep in his vitals. To overthrow *that* man
would take a ball of fire launched with twisted cords
or the wall-breaking weight of a massive boulder.
The iron ram and catapult would be needed
to budge *that* man out of the gate's threshold.
There he stands, a hard rock wall for Caesar,
holding off Pompey.

                              He does not protect his chest   220
with armor now—afraid someone might think
his left hand holding the shield was merely idle,
or that it's his fault he survived—he faces alone

so many wounds of war and bears on his chest
a thick forest of weapons, his stride now tiring
he chooses which enemy on whom he will fall. . . .

    Like a Libyan elephant, harassed by armed throngs,
who breaks every missile that bounces off his thick hide
and shakes his back to get rid of spears that stick,
his organs sit safely deep inside, the shafts that pierce   230
the beast do not draw blood, so many wounds
of arrows and javelins still cannot achieve one death.

    Look, in the distance—a Dictaean hand draws back
a Gortynian shaft against Scaeva, precise beyond hope
it goes for his head and pierces his left eyeball.
He tears the iron barb as well as the very bindings
of his nerves and plucks out the arrow along with
the eye hanging from it, undaunted he tramples on
the shaft and his own light.
                         A Pannonian bear
is no less wild after she's struck by a javelin   240
that a Libyan spins with a light sling—at the injury
she twists infuriated that the shaft she attacks
keeps retreating, she wheels herself around
at the fleeing spear.
                   Madness racked his face,
his features were distorted in a shower of gore.
A shout of joy from the victors struck the sky;
the sight of blood trickling from a wound
on Caesar himself would not have pleased them more.
Then he suppressed his fury deep in his mind,
hid his valor and put on a mild appearance: 250
"Citizens, spare me," he said. "Turn far aside your blades.
Wounds can now add nothing more to my death.
My chest needs shafts plucked out, not more hurled
against it. Carry and place me living in Magnus' camps.
Perform this for your chief. Let Scaeva be known
for deserting Caesar, not for honorable death."

Unlucky Aulus believed these feigning words
and did not see him holding his sword point upward—
about to lift the captive's body and his armor,
like lightning he got a sword blade through the throat.   260
His valor seethed and, refreshed by this one killing,
he said, "He'll pay the price, whoever had hopes
that Scaeva was beaten! And if Magnus wants peace
from *this* sword, let him lay down his standards
and beg mercy of Caesar. You think I'm like you?
Slow to face doom? Pompey and the Senate's cause
mean less to you than love of death to me!"

As he said this, plumes of dust announced
the arrival of Caesar's cohorts, saving Magnus
the disgraceful blunder of war that all his companies   270
had fled from you alone, Scaeva. With Mars withdrawn,
you crumble. Your blood was all poured out,
the fighting was giving you strength.

                                    A crowd of his men
catch him as he falls, hoist his worn-out frame
up on their shoulders rejoicing, they offer prayers
to the spirit that seems housed in that pitted chest,
a living image and likeness of Great Virtue.
Competing to remove the shafts that pierce his limbs
they decorate the gods and bare-chested Mars
with your armor, Scaeva. And you'd have been happy   280
in this claim to fame if hardy Iberians
had turned tail from you, or Cantabrians
who wield light arms, or, carrying heavier arms,
the Teutons. But you cannot adorn the temple
of the Thunderer with your spoils of war,
nor cry aloud in joyful triumph, wretched man—
you gave up so much valor to gain a master!

POMPEY MISSES AN
OPPORTUNITY TO PREVAIL

Though beaten back at that corner of his camps,
Magnus did not dally within his enclosure
lying quiet, delaying Mars, just as the sea   290
is not worn out when east winds heave its waves
that crash and break against a crag or steep hillside
that water washes over till a landslide looms.
So he aims at fortresses alongside the placid deep
and hurries a double attack, on land and sea,
strewing his army widely, spreading out the tents
haphazard on the plain, pleased that freedom
gives him license to move and shift his ground.
Like the Po when it swells full at its mouth and overruns
its banks buttressed up with levies, devastating   300
every field—if anywhere the earth gives way,
its mass unable to stand the raging of waters,
it falls to pieces, the whole river invades
and buries lowlands never flooded before.
Some masters lose their ground, while other farmers
receive from the Po an expansion of their fields.

Caesar had hardly noticed the battles; a watchtower
sent up a signal fire relaying the news.
He finds the walls battered, the dust already settled;
the traces he sees are cold, like ancient ruins.   310
The spot's very peacefulness burns him; he falls in a rage
that Pompey had beaten Caesar then taken a nap.
He's hot even for defeat, so long as it interrupts
their pleasures. Menacing, he rushes on Torquatus,
who sees Caesar's armies and, quicker than a sailor
furls all sails when his mast trembles in Circe's gales,
calls back his troops within a narrower wall
so he can position them tight, in a smaller ring.

Caesar had crossed the stockade's first defenses
when over every hillside Magnus sent his forces   320
spreading out his battle lines against a boxed-in foe.
Inhabitants of Henna's vales do not shudder
at the giant Enceladus, when the south wind blows,
and when caverns over the whole of Etna quake
and pour out burning flames onto the plains,
as much as Caesar's soldiers were overwhelmed
by dust rolling before the troops; they trembled
in a cloud of blind terror, and as they flee
they meet their enemy, rushing afraid into the hands
of fate.

       All the blood shed in the civil wars   330
could have achieved peace right then and there,
but the chief himself restrained their raging swords.
You might have been happy, Rome, free of kings
and enjoying your rights, if Sulla had been there
and gained that victory for you. Oh, how it grieves
and always will grieve us that the worst of your crimes,
fighting against a dutiful son-in-law,
was to your profit, Caesar.

          What heartbreaking fates!
Libya and Spain would not have to weep for the slaughters
at Utica and Munda; the Nile, unspeakably polluted   340
with blood, would not have carried a corpse more noble
than Pharos' king, nor would Juba have lain
stripped naked on Marmaric sands, nor would Scipio
have poured out his blood to placate Punic shades,
nor would life be bereft of holy Cato.
It could have been your last day of evils, Rome.
Pharsalia could have escaped its central place in Fate.

BOTH ARMIES MAKE FOR THESSALY

Deserting a position he held against god's will,
Caesar leads his mangled troops to Emathian lands.
The arms of his father-in-law, wherever they fled,   350
Magnus would follow; his comrades tried to urge him
to turn aside and seek instead his fathers' land,
Ausonia, now free of enemies. But he said,
"I'll never take Caesar's example of how to return
to our fatherland—Rome will never see me
returning without disbanding my soldiery.
I could have held Hesperia when the unrest began,
if I had been willing to commit armed troops
in the temples of our fathers and to fight
in the middle of the Forum. But as long as I can   360
banish wars, I will march beyond the world's extremes,
both of Scythian cold and the torrid zones.
Shall I, now victor, rob you of peace and quiet, Rome,
when I fled so that battles would not oppress you?
Before you suffer in this war, I would prefer
that Caesar think you his own."
                                        So he declared
and settled on a march toward Phoebus' rising;
pursuing the land's byways, where Candavia
opens its vast ravines of forest, he reached Emathia,
which the Fates were getting ready for the war.   370

THE LAND OF THESSALY—GEOGRAPHY, HISTORY, MYTHOLOGY

Thessaly, on that side where on the shortest days
of winter Titan rises, is bound by crags of Ossa;
when deepening summer draws Phoebus to the heights

of heaven, Pelion's shadows resist his newborn rays;
but the sky's midday flames and the solstitial head
of fierce Leo are repelled by wooded Othrys;
Pindus catches the crosswinds of Zephyr and Iapyx,
cutting short the light as evening hastens on;
and he who dwells at the foot of Mount Olympus
has no fear of Boreas, nor awareness of the Bear,   380
who shines the whole night through.

                                          Between these mountains
the fields hemmed in the middle valley once
were hidden under endless swamps, the plains
held in the rivers and Tempe's channels gave
no outlet to the sea, so all that it could do
was rise and fill up one vast marsh.

                                          Later, Hercules
by hand severed weighty Ossa from Olympus
and Nereus felt the downfall, an onslaught of rushing waters,
then Emathian Pharsalus, watery Achilles' kingdom,
emerged—better had it stayed beneath the waves!—   390
along with Phylace, whose ship first beached at Rhoetion
in Troy, and Pteleos, and Dorion, which mourns
the Pierian Muses' wrath, and Trachis, where Hercules'
quiver was paid to Meliboea's hero
for lighting his funeral pyre, and Larisa
powerful in the past; an Argos once was famous
there, they plow it over now, and stories point out
the *old* Thebes of Echion, and where once Agave
carried in exile the head and neck of Pentheus
and gave them to last flames, lamenting that this had   400
been all she'd salvaged of her son.

                                          So the swamp
was broken up and parted into several streams.
From here the Aeas, clean but shallow, flows
west into the Ionian Sea; no stronger, the father
of kidnapped Isis glides, and nearly your son-in-law,
Oeneus, slimes the Echinad islands with thick waters,
and stained with Nessus' blood the Euhenos cuts
through Meleager's Calydon. With its rapids

the Spercheos strikes the Malian gulf, and the Amphrysos
with clear waters irrigates the pastures where   410
Phoebus served as herdsman.
                                    Here the Asopos
takes its course, the Phoenix, Melas, and Anauros—
which exhales no humid mists nor dewy vapors
nor any light breezes—and all those streams
that don't know the sea but donate their waters
to the Peneus: in goes the Apidanos, its flood seized,
and the Enipeus, never quick until it merges;
only the Titaresos, though joining up in name,
defends its waters, gliding above the Peneus' current
treating it like dry fields. Tradition has it that   420
this stream drips out of the Stygian swamps and
remembering its source it spurns contamination
from worthless rivers and preserves for itself
the fear of the gods.
                                    When the rivers first subsided
and the fields lay bare, the Bebryces broke rich furrows
with their shares, and soon the plow dug deep,
pressed by Leleges' hands; Aeolidae and Dolopian
farmers cut the soil, with Magnesians and Minyans,
the first known for horses, the second for their oars.
There a pregnant cloud gave birth in Pelethronian   430
caves to Ixion's spawn, the half-beast Centaurs:
you, Monychus, who broke Pholoë's jagged rocks,
and you, fierce Rhoecus, hurling ash trees plucked
below Oeta's peak, which Boreas could hardly knock down,
and you, Pholus, hosted great Alcides, and you,
wicked ferryman, had to suffer the arrows
that slew Lerna's Hydra, and you, old man Chiron,
are a star that shines in the chilly season,
hunting the larger Scorpion with Haemonian bow.

    In this land the seeds of savage Mars flashed forth.   440
When the rocks were struck by the ocean's trident
the first Thessalian stallion, omen of deadly wars,
leaped out, first champed the steel bit and bridle,

foaming at the strange reins of its Lapith tamer.
First from Pagasae's shore a ship cut the strait,
casting land-bound man onto unknown waves.
A ruler in the land of Thessaly, Ionos,
was first to pound masses of hot metal into shape;
he poured silver over flames, and stamped gold pieces
with a die, and smelted bronze in massive forges.   450
With this, which drove peoples into wicked arms,
one could now count up one's riches.

                              The monstrous serpent
Python came from here and slithered down
into Cirrha's grottoes (and so the laurels come
from Thessaly for the Pythian Games).

                                From here
impious Aloeus spurred his sons against the gods,
when Pelion nearly rose up to the lofty stars
and Ossa attacked and stole the planets' paths.

SEXTUS POMPEY AND ERICTHO,
A THESSALIAN WITCH

   When in this fate-damned land the chiefs had pitched
their camps, a mind foreboding the coming war   460
troubles everyone—it's plain that the grave hour
of utmost crisis is approaching, nearer now
the fates are stirring . . .

                        Cowardly minds tremble
and ponder the worst; a few rehearse their strength
for doubtful circumstances and suffer both
hope *and* fear . . .

                   Amid this idle mob
was Sextus, unworthy son of his "Great" father,
who soon, as exile, would loiter in Scylla's waves,
a Sicilian pirate dishonoring sea-won triumphs.
Spurred by fear to foreknow the course of Fate,   470

impatient with waiting, sick from everything coming,
he doesn't consult Delos' tripods, or Pythia's caves,
nor is willing to find out what Dodona—who nursed us
with first fruits—would sound from Jupiter's bronzes,
or who could discern fates in entrails, or read birds,
or watch the flashing sky and scrutinize the stars
with Assyrian worry, or any other kind of secret
that *is* permissible. *He* investigated things
the gods above detest, savage Magis' arcane
lore and altars sad with funeral rites,   480
trusting in shades and Dis, and pitifully he
was certain the gods above know far too little.

   The place itself abets his empty, raving madness,
and nearby camp are the walls of Haemonian women,
whom no free rein to conjure imaginary monsters
could surpass, whose art is anything beyond belief.
Thessaly's ground, too, grows noxious herbs
upon its crags and the rocks are affected by
the deadly spells magicians chant; many things
grow there that can force the wills of gods,   490
and the stranger from Colchis picked in Haemonia
herbs she hadn't brought with her. That cursed tribe
with their impious spells charm the sky-dwellers' ears,
which are deaf to so many peoples and nations.
Only *their* voice carries to the corners of heaven,
bringing words to bind an unwilling deity
whose attention is never diverted from the concerns
of wheeling heaven and its pole. But when that unspeakable
mumble has reached the stars, then even if Persian
Babylon and mysterious Memphis opened   500
every inner sanctum of their ancient mages,
Thessaly's witch would still attract the gods
away from others' altars.
                         With a Thessalian charm,
love, aroused against fate, has flooded hard hearts,
and stern old men have burned with illicit flames.
It's not just their potions that have noxious power—

as when they steal the juice a foal's forehead exudes
which makes its mother love it—even with no poison
extract to infect it, a mind can perish when
cursed by a chanted spell. Men unfettered   510
from conjugal harmony, not bound by potent allures
of beauty, have succumbed to the magical twirling
of a twisted thread.
                      Nature's cycles have ceased—
night has run long and day has slowed, the sky
has disobeyed its law, the rushing world has stalled
on hearing a spell, while Jupiter urges the poles
to spin on their quick axles, wondering why
they are not moving. Now they soak everything
with showers, cloaking the heat of Phoebus in clouds,
and the sky thunders though Jove is unaware of it.   520
With the same charmed voices they have shaken out
deep wet fogs and disheveled locks of storm clouds.
In calm winds the sea has heaved, or been silent
as the south wind blusters, commanded not to feel
the blasts, and sails that bear a ship have swelled
against the wind.
                   From a sheer crag a waterfall
has hung suspended, and a river has rushed
where it did not run before. The Nile has failed
to rise in summer, the Maeander has straightened
its waters' course, and the Arar has hurried along   530
the loitering Rhône.
                     Mountains have leveled their peaks
and laid low their summits. Olympus has gazed up
at clouds, and though winter bristles and no sun shines,
Scythia's snows have melted.
                             When Tethys' tides
rise with the moon, a Haemonian witch's song
can drive it back and defend the shore. The earth
has also quaked at the axis of its unmoved mass,
and the pressure that strains toward the world's center
has wobbled—struck by a voice, the whole great weight
has drawn back to reveal a view of Olympus revolving.   540

Every lethal animal born for harm both dreads
and teaches the deadly arts of Haemonia's witches:
bloodthirsty tigers and the infamous wrath of lions
fawn on them with licking tongues; for them
the adder spreads his chilly coils, unwinding
in frosty fields, and, though dismembered, vipers
collect and reconnect their joints, and serpents
fall when blasted by their venomous human breath.

Why do the gods above toil to follow, and fear
to spurn, magic chants and herbs? What pact of trade   550
holds gods duty-bound? Is it a necessity
or a pleasure to obey? Do they deserve it
for some secret piety? Or do they prevail
through tacit threats? Do they have this right
over every god, or do these tyrant songs
dictate to one certain god who can compel
the world however he himself is compelled?
                                        They were first
to draw down planets, too, from their headlong orbits,
and bright Phoebe dims when she's beset by their dire
venom of words, she burns with black, earthly fires,   560
as when the earth bars her from her brother's image
when her shadows fall obstructing celestial flames,
and she suffers great labors when pressed down by song
until, being nearer, she rains dew on plants below.

These wicked rites and crimes of a dire race
would be damned as still too pious by savage Erictho,
who had applied her polluted art to novel rites.
To submit her funereal head to a city's roof
or to household gods is an unthinkable deed.
She haunts deserted graves and lurks in sepulchers   570
from which ghosts have been driven, a welcome friend
to the gods of Erebus. To hear the gatherings
of the silent dead and know the Stygian halls
and buried secrets of Dis, neither the gods above
nor being alive prevents her. Her ill-omened face

is thin and filthy from neglect, her features frighten
with Stygian pallor, never knowing the light of day;
her head droops heavy with matted, knotted hair.
Whenever black storm clouds conceal the stars,
Thessaly's witch emerges from her empty tombs   580
and hunts down the nightly bolts of lightning.
Her tread has burned up seeds of fertile grain
and her breath alone has turned fresh air deadly.
She doesn't pray to gods above, or call on powers
for aid with suppliant song, or know the ways
to offer entrails and receive auspicious omens.
She loves to light altars with funereal flames
and burn incense she's snatched from blazing pyres.
At the merest hint of her praying voice, the gods grant her
any outrage, afraid to hear her second song.   590
She has buried souls alive, still in control
of their bodies, against their will death comes
with fate still owing them years. In a backward march
she has brought the dead back from the grave
and lifeless corpses have fled death. The smoking cinders
and burning bones of youths she'll take straight from the pyre,
along with the torch, ripped from their parents' grip,
and the fragments of the funeral couch with smoke
still wafting black, and the robes turning to ashes
and the coals that reek of his limbs.

                             But when dead bodies   600
are preserved in stone, which absorbs their inner moisture,
and they stiffen as the decaying marrow is drawn off,
then she hungrily ravages every single joint,
sinks her fingers in the eyes and relishes it
as she digs the frozen orbs out, and she gnaws
the pallid, wasting nails from desiccated hands.
With her own mouth she cuts the fatal knotted noose,
plucks down hanging bodies and scours crosses
ripping at guts the rains have pounded and innards
exposed to the sun and cooked. She takes the nails   610
piercing the hands and the black decaying poison
and coagulated slime oozing through the joints.

If a tendon resists her bite, she throws her weight into it.
Whatever corpses lie out on the naked ground
she seizes before the beasts and birds; not wanting
to pick the bones with iron or her own hands,
she waits and snatches the pieces from the thirsty jaws
of wolves.

             Her hands don't flinch from slaughter either,
if she needs fresh blood, first gushing from opened throat,
if her graveyard feasts demand still-throbbing entrails.   620
So, too, from a belly's wound, not as nature would do it,
a fetus is removed and placed on blazing altars.
And every time she needs forceful savage shades,
she makes the ghost herself. She finds a use for
every death of man.

                 She plucks from a youthful body
the blossom on its cheek, and her left hand shears off
the lock from a dying teen. And at a relative's funeral
the dire Thessalian often bends down over the body
and feigning kisses she mutilates the head,
opens the clenched mouth with her teeth and, biting   630
the tongue that cleaves in a dry throat, pours
her murmurings into the chilly lips, sending commands
for secret crimes down to the shades of Styx.

SEXTUS VISITS ERICTHO

   Once Pompey's son had heard the country's rumors
about *her*, when night was high in heaven—
that time the Titan draws midday beneath our earth—
he makes his way . . .

              His faithful servants, used to crime,
wandered about the grave mounds and plundered tombs
and spied her afar, seated on a sheer rock cliff
where Haemus slopes down reaching Pharsalia's hills.   640
She was trying out words unknown to magicians
and their gods, crafting a spell for strange new purposes.

For fearing lest fickle Mars go elsewhere in the world
and the land of Emathia lose out on so much slaughter,
the sorceress had forbidden Philippi to let
the wars pass through, polluting the land with charms
and strewing her dire poisons, so that she would have
so many deaths for her own and she would enjoy
the profit from the world's blood. She hopes
to mutilate the slaughtered carcasses of kings   650
and to steal the ashes of the Hesperian nation
and the bones of nobles, and to own *so many* souls.
Her passion now and final toil is what she'll snatch
from Magnus' downcast body, what pieces of Caesar
she'll manage to pounce on.

                              Pompey's worthless offspring
addressed her first: "Splendor of Haemonia's ladies,
you can reveal people's fates, and deflect things coming
from their course. I pray you, let me learn for certain
the end that this war's fortune is preparing.
I'm not some lowly member of the Roman mob,   660
but a most illustrious child of Magnus—either
the world's master, or heir to a mighty funeral.
My mind quakes, stricken by doubts; nonetheless,
I'm ready for definite horrors. Take away from chance
the power to rush down blind and all of a sudden.
Either torment divine spirits with questions or
spare them and disclose the truth from ghosts.
Unlock the abodes of Elysium and call forth
Death herself, and force her to confess to me
which ones of us she's hunting. It's no small task.   670
It's worth *your* trouble, too, to ask what way
this weighty die of fate is leaning and will fall."

    The evil Thessalian, thrilled to hear her name
was famous and well known, responded, "If you'd asked
of lesser fates, young man, it would have been easy
to rouse unwilling gods and attain your wish.
My art can cause delay when the rays of stars
have marked one death, or even if all constellations

would grant one an old age, we can cut his years
in half with magic herbs. But once a series of causes   680
has descended from the world's first origin
and all fates struggle if you want to change anything,
when the human race is subject to a single blow,
then Thessaly's ilk admits it—Fortune is stronger.
But if you're intent on knowing events beforehand,
there are many easy paths that open onto truth.
The earth and skies and Chaos, the seas and plains
and crags of Rhodope speak to us. But it's simple—
since there's plenty of fresh dead—to lift one body
from Emathia's fields, so that the mouth of a corpse   690
just slain and still warm will speak with full voice,
and not some deathly ghost with sunburned limbs
rasping out things dubious to our ears."

                                              She spoke,
and with her craft redoubled the shadows of night;
her dismal head shrouded in squalid mist, she wanders
among slain bodies cast off and denied their burial.
Straightaway fled wolves, hungry birds of prey
pulled out their talons and fled, while the Thessalian
selects her prophet; probing entrails chilly with death,
she finds the fibers of strong, unwounded lungs   700
and seeks the voice in a body discharged from life.
Many fates of slain men already hanging there—
which *one* would she want to call back up to life?
If she had tried to raise up all the ranks
and return them to war, the laws of Erebus
would have obeyed, and that powerful monster
would have hauled out of Stygian Avernus
a people ready to fight. At last she picks a body
with its throat cut, takes and drags it by a hook
stuck in its fatal noose, a wretched corpse   710
over rocks and crags, then lays it high up under
a mountain's cave, which gloomy Erictho damned
with her sacrifices.

                             The ground sheers off and sinks down
nearly to the blind caverns of Dis; it's hemmed in by

a dreary wood with stooping branches, and a yew,
which no sun penetrates nor crown beholds the sky,
throws shadows over it. Darkness droops inside
the caves and, due to long night, gray mold hangs;
no light shines, except that cast by spells.
The air in the jaws of Taenarus doesn't sit so stagnant—   720
a dismal boundary between the hidden world
and our own, where the rulers of Tartarus wouldn't fear
to let ghosts enter. For though the Thessalian witch
can ply the Fates with force, it's doubtful whether she
visits with shades of Styx by drawing them up
or by descending to them.

                         Clad in motley dress
like a Fury's mottled robe, she bares her face
and binds her tangled hair up with a crown of vipers.
When she sees the young man's friends are quaking
and he himself is trembling, his fixed eyes staring   730
with the life drained from his face, she says, "Put off
the fears your fretful minds have conjured. Now
new life in its true form will be restored, so that
even the horrified can hear him speaking.
If indeed I show you swamps of Styx and the shore
that roars with fire, if by my aid you're able
to see the Eumenides and Cerberus, shaking
his necks that bristle with snakes, and the conquered backs
of Giants, why should you be scared, you cowards,
to meet with ghosts who are themselves afraid?"   740

   First she fills the chest with boiling blood
through new wounds that she opens, then washes out
the bowels of putrefaction and liberally applies
poison from the moon. To this she adds whatever
nature has brought forth in inauspicious birth.
She doesn't leave out froth of dogs afraid of water,
nor guts of lynx nor joint of dread hyena
and marrow of a stag that has fed on serpents;
nor *echenais*, which hinders ships although east winds
strain at their ropes, and eyeballs of dragons, and stones   750

that sound when warmed under a pregnant eagle;
nor Arabia's flying serpent and the Red Sea's viper
that guards the precious oyster, nor the skin
that Libya's horned snake sheds while still alive,
nor ash the phoenix left on its eastern altar.
And once she'd mixed together these common banes
with well-known names, she added leaves soaked through
with evil spells, and plants her wicked mouth
had spat on as they grew, and every other poison
she herself gave to the world. Last, her voice—   760
stronger than any plant to bewitch the gods of Lethe—
pours forth cacophonous murmurs in great discord
with the human tongue. It contained the bark of dogs
and howl of wolves, the fearsome eagle owl's
and nocturnal tawny owl's laments, the shrieks
and cries of beasts, the serpent's hiss, and it expressed
the crash of waves that beat upon the rocks,
the rustle of forests and thunder from fractured clouds—
one voice held all these things.
                                        The rest she then spelled out
in a Haemonian chant, piercing Tartarus with her tongue: 770
"Eumenides, Stygian crime and punishments of the guilty,
Chaos, greedy to pour disorder on countless worlds,
Ruler of the earth, tortured through long ages
by Death, delayed for gods, Styx and Elysium,
which no Thessalian witch deserves, Persephone,
loathing heaven and her mother, and the third
last part of our Hecate, through whom commerce
between the ghosts and me occurs with quiet tongue,
doorman of the open halls who throws our guts
to the savage dog, and sisters who will spin out   780
threads anew, and you, O ancient ferryman
of the burning river, weary by now from bringing
shades back up to me. Pay heed to my prayers!

     "If I call on you with a mouth that's sinful
and polluted enough, if I never sing these songs

while still famishing for human entrails,
if I've often bathed a hacked-up breast
still full of soul divine and brains still warm,
if any infant whose insides and head I've laid
upon your platters would have lived if I had not—   790
obey me as I pray!

        "We don't want one
hiding out in Tartarus' chasm, long accustomed
to the darkness, but a soul who has just been
exiled from the light and is just now descending,
who still clings in the jaws of murky Orcus
and will, so long as it pays heed to my drugs,
go to the ghosts but once. For the general's son
let the shade of this one who is now our soldier
sing all the Pompeian affairs—if civil wars
deserve your gratitude."

        With these declarations   800
she lifted her head and frothing mouth and saw
stand forth before her the shade of the cast-off corpse,
afraid of its lifeless limbs, those hateful confines
of its old prison. It dreads to enter that opened chest
and guts and innards ruptured by lethal wounds.
Poor man, unfairly stripped of death's last gift—
to not be able to die!

        Erictho is astounded
that fates are so free to linger, and, angry at the dead,
she whips the motionless body with a living serpent,
and down the gaping fissures in the earth her spells   810
had opened up she barks at the ghosts of the dead,
disturbing their kingdom's silence:

        "Tisiphone!
Indifferent to my voice? Megaera! Aren't you driving
with your savage lashings through the emptiness
of Erebus that hapless soul? Soon I'll conjure you
by your real names and then abandon you
Stygian dogs in the light above. I'll stand guard,
hunt you down through graveyards and burial grounds,

expel you from tombs, drive you from every urn.
And I will reveal you, Hecate, to the gods   820
in your pale, wasting form when you are used
to going before them in a different guise,
but I will forbid you from changing the face you wear
in Erebus. And I will declare what banquets
hold you, lady of Henna, under earth's great weight,
by what marriage bond you love night's gloomy king,
what pollution you suffered that your mother, Ceres,
would not call for your return. And against you,
worst of the world's rulers, I'll send the Titan Sun,
bursting your caverns open and striking with sudden daylight.   830
Will you obey? Or must I address by name
that one at whose call the earth never fails to shudder
and quake, who openly looks on the Gorgon's face,
who tortures the trembling Erinys with her own scourge
and dwells in a Tartarus whose depths your eye can't plumb?
To him, *you* are the gods above; he swears, and breaks,
his oaths by waters of Styx."

                                        Just then the cold blood-clots
warmed and nourished the dark wounds, running into veins
and to the ends of every limb; his insides pulse,
shaking under his frozen chest, as new life creeps   840
back into unused marrow, mingling with death.
Every muscle palpitates, every nerve goes tense—
then the body rises from the ground, not slowly,
limb by limb, but thrown straight up from the earth
all at once. He did not yet look alive, but like
someone who was now dying. Still pale and stiff,
he stands dumbstruck at being thrust back in the world.
But no sound comes from his closed mouth; his voice
and tongue are only allowed to answer.

                                        "Speak,"

said the Thessalian, "at my command and great   850
will be your reward. For if you tell the truth,
we promise to make you immune for all the ages
from Haemonian arts; I will burn your body

on such a pyre of such logs, with Stygian chants,
that your shade will never be summoned by spells
of any magicians. Living twice is worth this much!
No words or herbs will dare disturb your slumber
of long forgetfulness once you've died at my hand!
Ambiguous sayings are suited to tripods and seers
of the gods. But anyone who bravely comes and seeks   860
true oracles of callous death from the shades
should leave with certainty. Don't hold back, I pray—
give names to events, give places, and give voice
so that the Fates may speak with me."

                                        She added a spell
that gave the shade the power to know whatever
she asked of it.

                        Dripping with tears, the wretched corpse
said: "Well, I did not see the sad threads of the Parcae
since I was called back from the edge of the silent bank.
But what I happened to learn from all the shades
is that brutal discord troubles the Roman spirits   870
and impious arms have disrupted the quiet of hell.
Some leaders have left their homes in Elysium, others
come up from sad Tartarus; they have made it clear
what the Fates are preparing.

                                "The blessed shades
wore sorrowful faces. I saw the Decii, son and father
who offered their souls in battle, Camillus weeping,
the Curii and Sulla, complaining about you, Fortune.
Scipio mourned that his ill-fated offspring would fall
in the land of Libya. Carthage's greater enemy,
Cato, cried for the fate of his great-grandson   880
who would not be a slave. Only you, Brutus,
first to be consul after the kings were expelled,
I saw rejoicing among the dutiful shades.

    "Suddenly, Catiline the menace, breaking his chains,
ran riot, thrilled, with the fierce Marii and Cethegi,
their arms bared. I saw delighted demagogues,

the Drusi, immoderate legislators, the Gracchi,
who dared outrageous deeds. Eternal chains of steel
bound their hands applauding in the prison of Dis—
a criminal mob demanding the plains of the pious.   890
The landlord of that idle kingdom is opening
his gray estates and sharpening his jagged rocks
and solid adamant for fetters, putting in order
his punishment for the victor.

                 "Take this solace with you,
young man: the spirits await your father and his house
in their peaceful hollow and are reserving a place
for Pompey's line in a calm, clear part of that realm.
Don't let the glory of this brief life disturb you.
The hour comes that will level all the leaders.
Rush into death and go down below with pride,   900
magnanimous, even if from lowly tombs,
and trample on the shades of the gods of Rome.
Which tomb the Nile's waves will wash and which
the Tiber's is the only question—for the leaders,
this fight is only about a funeral.

                 "Don't ask
about your fate. The Parcae will grant you knowledge
where I am silent. A clearer seer will sing you all,
your father, Pompey, himself, in Sicily's fields,
but he, too, will be unsure where to call you,
where to drive you from, which tracts or skies   910
of the world he should order you to shun.
Unhappy men, beware of Europe, Libya, Asia—
Fortune is doling out tombs upon your triumphs.
O pitiful house, you will look on nothing
in all the world safer than Emathia."

   So once he finished the words of fate, he stands
with muted face and sad, then asks again for death.
She must resort to magic spells and drugs before
the corpse will fall, since Fate's law had been used once
and could not take the soul back. Then she heaps up   920
a great wood pyre; the dead man approaches the fire.

Erictho left the youth lying on the kindled pile
and let him die at last.
                              She accompanied Sextus
back to his father's camp as dawn's light drew
its colors in the sky; but till they bore their steps
safe into their tents, she ordered night to keep
day back; it complied with deep, dark shadows.

BOOK SEVEN

The day of the Battle of Pharsalus has come, and the sun rises slower than usual (1–7). Pompey dreams of his happy past, seated in his theater in Rome, applauded by adoring crowds, but the poet foreshadows his coming death (8–52). His pleasant dreams are broken by his soldiers clamoring for battle (53–72), and Marcus Tullius Cicero delivers a speech rousing Pompey to action (73–99). Pompey responds with a vacillating speech that consents to battle but effectively gives up control of events, like a pilot who abandons the rudder in a storm (99–150). Panic and fear in the camps as they ready their arms for a battle like that waged between the Olympian gods and Giants (151–79). Portents and omens of the battle are reported around the world, enabling the world to watch the fall of Rome in the signs provided by the gods (180–244). The poet predicts posterity will read the wars in his poem, feel again all the hope and fear, and still root for Magnus (245–52). The Battle of Pharsalus: Pompey's lines, under Lentulus and Domitius, are formed, his allies' positions listed (253–77); Caesar addresses his troops (278–396), and Pompey his (397–453). The poet pauses for historical commentary: Pharsalus will depopulate the Roman world, which steadily rose in might and glory until Pharsalus, when all her good fortunes reversed, Liberty fled beyond the Tigris and Rhine, and now sad Rome has divine Caesars as masters (454–539). With Caesar's centurion Crastinus leading the way, battle begins with raucous trumpet blasts and the first flurry of weapons (540–605). Pompey's cavalry is routed, and then his panicked lines are demolished (606–30). Then Pompey's center, with senators and leading Romans, fights and dies, hacked down by Caesar's ferocity (631–76). Brutus, who survives for greater things, and Domitius, who dies here defying Caesar, are singled out for attention (676–711), before generic universal carnage (712–46). Pompey, seeing defeat, prays for others to be saved, and tries to convince his lines to surrender before he himself flees the battle (747–827) and is received in Larisa (828–47). Caesar finishes fighting and sends his men to plunder the enemy camp, full of the riches of Pompey's many allies (848–82). They pass the night in evil, tortured dreams (882–915), and the next day Caesar feasts before the battlefield to take in the gory spectacle (915–29); Caesar refuses burial to the dead, which leads the poet to ruminations on the universality of death, the coming conflagration that will end the whole world, and the grisly feast of birds and beasts on the dead (930–88). The book closes with a eulogy and curse of the fatal land of Thessaly, where another battle, Philippi, is still to come (989–1019).

BOOK SEVEN

Slower from the Ocean than eternal law calls for,
sorrowfully the Titan Sun—and never harder
against the upper heavens—drove his horses on
their backward course upon the whirling pole;
he wanted to suffer eclipse, the toils of stolen light,
and so drew clouds in, not to feed his flames,
but so over Thessaly he would not shine clearly.

POMPEY DREAMS OF HAPPIER DAYS

That night, for Magnus the end of a happy life,
deceived his troubled slumbers with an empty image:
he sees himself seated in the Theater of Pompey,   10
perceives the countless shapes of Roman plebs
extolling his name to the stars with ecstatic voices,
roaring sections contending with their applause.
Such was the people's appearance, such the clamor
of their praise, back in youth, his first days of triumph
after he'd mastered the tribes that the Hiberus
rushes around, along with every army Sertorius,
that fugitive, hurled at him. The West was pacified,
and in a plain white toga—as worthy of veneration
as the chariot with its ornaments—he sat   20
applauded by the Senate while still a Roman knight.
Perhaps his mind, anxious for the future

and the end of good times, was taking refuge
in happier days; or else prophetic rest was bringing—
through its usual ambiguities—omens
of great mourning contrary to his visions;
or else since you'd been banished beyond your fathers'
homelands, Fortune granted you to see Rome thus.

   Don't interrupt his slumbers, watchmen of the camp,
lash no ears with your horn. Tomorrow's sleep   30
will bring sorrowing dreadful images of the day,
everywhere the lines of death, everywhere war.
Where might the people find a night as blessed
with restful sleep? Your Rome would be happy indeed
if only she saw you thus! Would that the gods above
had granted one day as a gift to the country and you,
Magnus, when each, certain of its fate, might snatch
the last sweet fruit of their great love!
                             As though
you are to die in Ausonia's city you go, and she,
knowing her vows for your safety have been fulfilled   40
forever, does not think this crime is the fault of Fate,
that she'll lose even the tomb of her beloved Magnus.
You would have been wept for by elder and youth
in mixed lament, and even by children unprompted.
Their hair unbound, a crowd of women would have
beat their breasts as they did at Brutus' funeral.
Even now, they may fear the unjust victor's darts,
Caesar himself may announce your funeral, still
they weep, as they offer incense and laurel wreaths
to the Thunderer. Pitiful! How they groaned   50
and swallowed their grief, when they could not mourn
all together for you in the crowded theater.

CICERO CALLS FOR POMPEY
TO JOIN BATTLE

Light had defeated the stars when a mob from the camps
came roaring chaotic complaints, and since the Fates
were drawing the whole world in, they plead for standards
and signals of battle. Most of that miserable crowd
would not see day's end. Surrounding their chief's tents
they protest, passions inflamed by the great upheaval,
hastening ever nearer the sudden hours of death.
A dreadful madness rises. Each man craves to plunge   60
headlong with the others down to a common fate.
Pompey is slow and timid, they say, and far too patient
with his father-in-law; he is indulging in monarchy
over the world; he wants to keep so many nations
all at once beneath his authority; he fears
to settle a peace. The kings and eastern peoples, too,
complain that the wars drag on and hold them back
far from the lands of their fathers.
                              Does this please you,
gods above, when you've determined to topple all things,
to add crime to our errors? We rush into disasters,   70
pleading for perilous arms. In the Pompeian camps
they pray for Pharsalia!
                              All these voices are conveyed
by the greatest author of Roman eloquence,
Tullius, under whose command, and in a toga,
Catiline the savage had cowered at the axes
that keep peace. He's angry at the wars and longs
to mount the Rostra in the Forum. Fluent speech
adds vigor to a feeble cause:
                              "For all her many
favors, Magnus, Fortune's only prayer is that
you will take and use her. All the nobles of your camps,   80
these prostrate kings of yours—the world's on its knees—
we beg you, let your father-in-law be overthrown!

Will Caesar cause the human race to war so long?
Nations you defeated as you were racing through
deserve to resent that Pompey is slow to conquer.
Where has your passion gone? Or your trust in fate?
Do you fear you're unpleasing to the gods above,
and hesitate to entrust to them the Senate's cause?
The troops themselves will pluck up your standards
and venture forth. It's shameful to be constrained   90
into a victory. If you've been commanded to lead,
if the war is waged in our interest, then, it's right
to let them lead the attack on any field they wish.
Why are you holding back the world's swords
from Caesar's blood? Their fists are shaking spears,
and hardly a man can wait for the slothful standards.
Hurry, or your trumpets will leave you behind!
The Senate longs to know, is it following you
as soldiers, or your entourage?"

POMPEY CONSENTS TO ENGAGE IN BATTLE

                       The leader groaned,
sensing the gods' tricks, that the fates were contrary   100
to his purpose. "If all agree with this," he said,
"and if the time needs Magnus as a soldier,
not as leader, I won't transgress the Fates by stalling.
Let Fortune envelop the nations in one downfall,
let this day's light be the last for a large portion
of humankind. But I call you to witness, Rome!
Magnus welcomes this day when all will perish.

  "This work of war might have ceased without slaughter
from you. I could have subdued and handed over
as captive the leader who violated the peace.   110
Blind men! Why this madness for crimes? Civil wars
waged and won without bloodshed—is that what they fear?

We've seized the lands, barred him from the whole sea,
driven his starving troops to ransack unripe grain,
and forced our foe to vow that now he would prefer
to be laid low and share in the wanton death
that awaits his men upon my swords. This war's almost over,
accomplished by what makes raw recruits not fear a fight—
if sheer virtue goads them, and in a flush of rage
they're calling for the standards. Many are flung   120
into the utmost perils by the very terror
of coming doom. But the most courageous man,
one ready to suffer a dreaded impending challenge,
can also stand delay . . .
                              "It is Fortune's pleasure
to betray us when things are going as we hope,
and to submit the world's crisis to the sword.
They want their chief to *fight* more than to win.
You gave me the Roman state to rule over, Fortune.
Take it back now greater, guard it amid Mars' blindness.
For Pompey the war will be no crime or glory.   130
Among the gods above you've beat me, Caesar,
with your hostile prayers. The fight is on!
What great wickedness, how many miseries
will dawn today upon the world's peoples!
So many kingdoms will be laid low! With blood
of Romans how the Enipeus will seethe and boil!
I'd wish the first lance of this deadly war
would pierce *this* head, if it could fall without
upsetting the balance, or destroying our party.
For victory will not bring more joy to Magnus.   140
Today, once this massacre's been committed,
Pompey will be a name that's either hated
or pitied by all peoples. This final cast of lots
for everything will bring all evils on the vanquished.
All the guilt will fall upon the victor."

    So speaking, he commits the nations to arms
and rage lets loose the reins upon their raving,
as when a sailor, beaten by violent northwest blasts,

gives up his skill and hands the rudder to winds,
like worthless cargo of his ship he's dragged along . . .   150

    Anxious panic, the camps roar with confusion,
wild souls are pounding out of chests,
their pulse erratic, many faces pale
with coming death, looking as though they've met
their fate already. The day had come that would
establish the fate of human affairs for ages,
and in that clash they were struggling over
what Rome was to be—this was clear to all.
No one is aware of his own danger,
stricken by a greater fear . . .
                          Who, beholding the shores   160
buried under ocean, the sea flooding mountain peaks,
the sky falling to earth, the sun dislodged from orbit,
the end of so many things, could feel fear for himself?
No one is free to feel such selfish worry.
Their fear is for the city and for Magnus.

    They do not trust their swords unless the edge
has showered sparks when sharpened on the stone.
Every lance is straightened on a rock; they stretch
their bows with better strings, and then take care
to fill their quivers up with new, picked arrows.   170
The horsemen strengthen spurs and tighten up
the reins tied to the bit—
                      If it is allowed
to match up human labors with the gods above,
it was just like when Phlegra raised the rabid Giants
and Mars' blade was pounded hot on Sicily's anvils;
Neptune's trident again glowed red in the flames
and Paean, with Python slain, reforged his arrows;
Pallas spread the Gorgon's locks upon her aegis
and the Cyclops restored Jove's bolts to blast Pallene.

PORTENTS ON THE EVE OF PHARSALUS

Fortune even now did not avoid revealing   180
coming events through various signs. For as
they pushed through Thessaly's fields, the entire sky
opposed their going: torches of comets and columns
of colossal fire drove against them, typhoons
of torrential rain mixed with sheets of lightning;
in the men's eyes thunderbolts shattered the clouds
blinding them with the assault of splendor; it shook
the crests from their helmets, it melted their swords
till the hilts poured away, and took their javelins
turning them to liquid; the wicked iron smoked   190
with reeking brimstone from the ether of heaven.
The standards, which all the way to Thessaly had
belonged to Rome and her people, suddenly swarmed
with countless bees, and could hardly be plucked
out of the ground; they wept tears and their extra weight
overwhelmed the head of the standard-bearer.
A bull brought forth for the gods shattered the altar
and fled, charging headlong across Emathia's fields,
and no other victim was found for disastrous rites.

But what gods of wickedness, what Furies did you summon   200
in solemn rites, Caesar? What powers of Stygian realms,
infernal abomination and madness sunk in darkness,
did *you* placate when about to wage savage, impious war?

Then—whether they had faith in the gods' omens
or believed from excessive fear—many claimed to see
Pindus clash with Olympus, and Haemus collapse
into sudden sheer ravines, Pharsalia raise
nocturnal voices of war, and blood pour forth
from Ossa into nearby Lake Boebeis . . .

By turns they marvel at faces shrouded in darkness,   210
the day, pale and fading, night roosting on their helmets,
and dead fathers and shades of blood relations
flutter before their eyes. Out of their minds, they had
one solace: conscious that their vows are wicked,
the crowd, expecting to slit the throats of fathers
and pierce the hearts of brothers, derives some pleasure
from monstrous signs and the mind's revolt,
thinking that sudden insanity presaged their crimes.
Is it a wonder that people whose last light awaited them
shook in frantic terror, if man has been given a mind   220
that forebodes troubles? Every Roman—whether he
had settled as a foreign guest near Tyrian Gades,
or drank the waters of Armenia's Araxes,
in any climate, under any constellation—
began to grieve and, ignorant of the reason,
rebukes his soul for its sadness, unaware
what he was losing on Emathia's fields.

An augur, some recall (if we can trust them),
was seated in Euganean hills, where from the ground
the misty Aponus springs and the Timavus—   230
Antenor's stream—spreads out its waves, he said:
"The crucial day has come, the whole affair decided—
Pompey's and Caesar's impious arms are clashing!"
Perhaps he observed Jove's ominous bolts of thunder,
or he discerned how the whole ethereal pole
resisted the strife of heaven. Or maybe the sad sky god
made note of the fight in the sun's pale darkness.
What is sure: in Thessaly nature rolled out a day
unlike any other, and if the mind of man
had read through skillful augury all the heavens'   240
strange new signs, the whole world could have watched
the spectacle at Pharsalia.
                                How mighty were those men!
Fortune broadcast signs of them throughout the world,
the entire sky stood idle to watch their fates!

And among later nations, our populous progeny,
perhaps their fame alone will carry them into your ages,
or maybe my diligent labor can also bring some profit
to these great names: whenever these wars are read,
hope and fear and dying prayers will waver,
all will stand rapt, enthralled, as though their fates   250
are even now approaching and not yet finished . . .
they'll read and, Magnus, they still will cheer for you.

POMPEY'S ARMY MOVES INTO
BATTLE FORMATION

  The troops descend, ablaze against the rays of Phoebus,
flooding all the hills with light they take up position,
hardly at random, on the plains; those doomed ranks
stand firm in their lines. Lentulus, you take charge
of the left flank; two legions in your care, the Fourth
and First, which at that time was best in battle.
The army's vanguard on the right is handed over
to you, Domitius, sturdy fighter against   260
a hostile god. But the middle line of battle
is packed with the strength of the bravest throngs
that had come from Cilicia, brought by Scipio
(who was a soldier here but would in Libya
hold chief command).

               Along the channels and pools
of billowing Enipeus rides the mountain cohort
of Cappadocia and the horsemen of Pontus
free with the rein. But most of the dry ground
is held by tetrarchs, kings, and mighty tyrants,
all the regal purple that is slave to Latin steel.   270
Numidians from Libya, Cydonians from Crete
were gathered there, from there Ityraean arrows flew,
from there you marched against your usual foe,

ferocious Gauls, and there Iberian warriors
shook their hide-bound shields.
                              Drain the world of blood,
Magnus! Rob the victor of nations over whom
to triumph! Just annihilate them all at once!

CAESAR MARSHALS AND ADDRESSES
HIS TROOPS

   That day by chance Caesar had left his position,
was pulling up the standards for a raid on grain crops,
when suddenly he spies the enemy marching down   280
into the open plains. He sees the time he's asked for
in a thousand prayers has now been offered to him,
the chance to hazard all on one last throw of dice.
Sick of delay and burning with lust for empire,
he had begun to condemn the sin of civil wars
as one too slow in coming and much too small.
But now he sees the arrival of the last pitched battles
that would decide between the leaders; he senses
the ruins of fate now teetering on the brink of collapse,
and even that frenzy for steel so quick and ready   290
subsides a little, that mind, so bold to promise
successful outcomes to events, stands wavering . . .
his own fates don't allow him to fear, but neither
do those of Magnus allow him to hope . . .
                              Suppressing dread,
his confidence soars, the better to hearten his throngs:
"Breaker of the world, in all my affairs the fortune,
soldier, the riches of battle so often longed for
lie at hand. There's no more need for prayers.
Summon fate now with your sword! In your hands
you hold the greatness of Caesar! Today is the day   300
I remember was promised me at the Rubicon's waves,
and looking forward to *this* we took up arms,

postponing our return for triumphs denied to us
until today, which will prove, with Fate as witness,
who took up arms more justly. This engagement
will render the loser guilty. If for me you've assaulted
your fatherland with fire and iron, fight now
all the more savagely and with your swords
free yourselves from guilt. For if the other side
becomes the judge of war, no hand will be clean.   310
This struggle is not for me, but so that the lot of you
might be free, hold power over all nations,
that's my prayer. For me, I long to return
to private life, wear a toga of the people
and be a modest citizen. Just so long as you
are free to do all things, I will not object
to having no position. You can be king!
The hatred can be mine.

           "Without much blood
you can win the world you wish for. The youth of Greece
will come, rounded up from their gymnasia, sluggish   320
from wrestling practice and barely able to carry arms,
also barbarian hordes, a dissonant babel of tongues,
who will not endure the sound of the war trumpets,
much less their own screams once the army is moving.
Few will lift their hands in *civil* war. Most of the fight
will purge the world of these peoples, trample down
the enemies of Rome. March right through these
spineless nations, these notorious kingdoms,
your first sword-stroke will lay the world low.
Make it plain that these nations whom Pompey drove   330
into the city so often before his chariot, now
will not supply one triumph. Do Armenians care
whose leadership the Roman power is under?
Is any barbarian willing to pay with his blood,
however little, to put Magnus in charge of
Hesperia's affairs? They hate every Roman
and resent their masters, especially those they know.

"But Fortune has placed me in the hands of my own men,
whom Gaul so many times made me witness in war.
What soldier's sword will I not acknowledge as mine?   340
Every quivering lance that crosses the sky
I'll note without fail whose arm hurled it. And if
I see those signs that never fail your leader—
grim, savage faces and menacing eyes—you've won!
I seem to see rivers of gore and kings trodden down
along with the Senate's scattered corpse and peoples
swimming through immense slaughter—

                                          "but I'm stalling
my fate, I'm holding you back with words when you
are furious for weapons. Forgive me for hindering warfare.
I tremble with hope. I've never seen the gods above   350
so near me and so ready to give such mighty gifts.
How small a stretch of field divides us from our prayers!
I am the one who, once this war is finished,
will be free to dispose of the wealth of kings and nations.
By what motion of the sky or shifting of the planets
are you granting so much to Thessaly, O gods?

"Today we'll earn the wages or the penalty of this war.
Imagine the chains, the crucifixions of Caesar's men,
my head stuck on the Rostrum, my body cast aside,
another Saepta massacre, clashes locked in the Campus—   360
It's a Sullan leader we're waging civil war against!
You are my concern. My own lot will be safe,
secured by my own hand: whoever looks back
upon the unconquered foe will also see me
eviscerate myself. O gods, whose care has turned
away from heaven to earth and the trials of Rome,
may he conquer who does not think he must
draw his cruel blade against the conquered,
whoever does not believe it the worst transgression
that fellow citizens took up standards against them.   370
When Pompey had pinned your lines in a tight spot,
unable to move despite your valor, how much blood

did it take to sate his sword? But I implore you, men,
don't cut down any enemy in the back!
Whoever flees, count him your fellow citizen.
But as long as weapons flash, don't let any shadow
of piety move you, not even if you see your father
in the enemy's front ranks. With your sword
dismay those reverend faces! And if your brutal blade
does run through a heart that shares your blood,   380
or even if the wound does not breach some bond,
even for unknown foes, every throat you cut,
treat it as a crime.
                              "Now, level the rampart,
fill in the trenches with rubble, and be ready
to march out in full force and tight formation.
Don't spare the camp. You can pitch your tents
in *that* rampart, from where their troops are coming
out to meet their doom!"
                              Hardly had Caesar finished
saying all this when each man falls to his duty, in haste
seizing arms and grain. They take the omens of war   390
and trample the camp in their rushing, stand in no order,
follow no plan of their leader, leave it all to the Fates.
If all of them had been fathers-in-law of Magnus,
all of them seeking to dominate their own city,
and you set them down there in that fatal warfare,
they still would not have stormed so headlong into battle.

POMPEY AND LUCAN PLEAD
FOR ROMAN FIGHTING COURAGE

When Pompey sees the enemy throngs march straight out,
allowing no more delay to war, and that the gods
approved the day, he stands dumbstruck, his heart goes cold—
for such a great leader to fear arms was an omen . . .   400

He stifles the dread and rides down the front of the line
to address them from high on horseback:
                                                   "The day your virtue
has pressed for, the end to civil discord that you've sought,
is here! Unleash your full strength! One last great labor
is left for our steel, a single hour to haul in nations.
If you yearn for home and the household gods you care for,
your offspring and marriage bed, forsaken bonds of love—
seek them with your sword! God has placed it all
in the middle of the field! Our greater cause urges us
to hope for favor from powers above. *They* will guide   410
your shafts through Caesar's vitals, it's *their* will
to ratify Roman laws, sanctified with his blood.
If they were ready to hand my father-in-law
the kingdom and the world, they could have hurled me
in old age down to my fates. No, it is not
because of divine anger against the people and city
that Pompey is saved as leader. All that can conquer
we have gathered and planned for. Illustrious men
are freely submitting to dangers, and our old soldiers
strike a hallowed image. If the Fates brought back   420
to our own times the clans of Curius and Camillus,
or Decius, who devoted his life unto death,
they would take our side. Nations from the East
and countless cities have assembled. Never before
have so many forceful hands been roused to battle.
The whole world at once is ours to wield!
Whatever is bound by the limit of heaven's signs,
from south to north, all men are here with us
and armed to march! Will we not drive the enemy
crowding into the middle and onto our flanking horns   430
that will come flooding around them? Victory needs
just a few hands. Most of our mighty throngs
will wage war only with shouts! Before our arms
Caesar is no match!
                              "Picture mothers straining
from the city's lofty walls, their hair streams down,
urging you into battle; picture the Senate elders,

prevented by age from bearing arms, but bowing
their hallowed gray heads to your feet, and Rome herself
running to take refuge with you in fear of a master.
Picture the people now and the people to come   440
offering their united prayers: the one crowd wants
to die, the other to be born, in freedom.

"And after these great bonds of duty, if there is room
for Pompey, I would—if I could preserve the dignity
of my command—kneel down before your feet,
entreat you as a suppliant with my wife and sons.
Magnus, unless you win, is an exile, a laughingstock
to my father-in-law, on you a disgrace—I plead
to avoid the ultimate fate, the shame as my years unwind
of learning, as an old man, to be a slave."   450

The voice of their commander speaking such sad words
inflames their spirits, and Roman virtue stiffens,
resolved to die if what it feared proved true.

So both lines rush forward, each side driven
by equal rage: on one side fear of tyranny,
hope for it rouses the other . . .

                                 Those right hands
will do things that no age can ever make up for,
that the human race can never restore, no matter
if it is free from war for all time. That work of Mars
will bring down future nations and plunder the day   460
of birth of peoples yet to come into the world.
At that time, every Latin name will be a myth:
Gabii, Veii, Cora, mere ruins buried in dust
which one can hardly trace; the Alban Lares
and Penates of Laurentum, empty countryside
where no one dwells except unwilling senators
complaining that they're forced by Numa's law
to spend one night. It's not "devouring time"
that's gnawed these monuments of history
and left them rotting in decay. We see the crime   470

of civil war in our droves of empty cities.
How the human multitude has been reduced!
The peoples born around the world cannot refill
the walls or fields with men. One city fits us.
Chain-gang planters farm Hesperia's crops,
the roofs of ancient homes stand rotting, ready to fall
on nobody; Rome is packed, but not with citizens,
stuffed with the scum of the world we've given her up
to disaster, so that now in such a bloated body
a *civil* war could not be waged!
                        Pharsalia   480
is the cause of so much evil. The gloomy names
of Cannae and Allia, disasters long since damned
on Roman calendars, ought to yield their place.
Rome has marked the times of lighter troubles,
but wills to forget this day.
                    O sorrowful Fates!
Airborne plagues that infect the breath, wasting diseases,
maddening famine and cities abandoned to flames,
crowded walls demolished flat by earthquakes—
these might equal the men whom Fortune hauled in
from everywhere to pitiful death; displaying the gifts   490
of a long age and snatching them away, she stood up
peoples and their leaders together on the field
to show you, Rome, through them, as you toppled,
how mighty was your fall.
                  Who has possessed
the world more widely, or through fate's successes
raced so quickly? Each war gave you nations,
every year the Titan Sun watched your advance
toward both the poles. Just a small stretch of earth
remained in the east, until the night was yours,
all day was yours, the heavens would run for you,   500
and all the wandering stars beheld would be Roman.
But your fates went backward equal to all your years
that lethal day in Emathia. In its blood-soaked light
it made India feel no horror at Latin rods,
and now no consul stops the Dahae's wandering

and leads them inside walls, then girds himself up
to mark out Sarmatian colonies with the plow;
and Parthia owes you, as always, harsh penalties,
and fleeing civil horrors, never to return,
Liberty has withdrawn beyond the Rhine and Tigris,   510
and though we've sought her often with our throats,
she wanders, a blessing to Germans and Scythians,
no longer looking back on Ausonia.
                                        How I wish
our people never knew her! Ever since Romulus
founded your walls when a vulture flew by on the left
and filled them with men from that grove of infamy,
down to your collapse in Thessaly, Rome,
you should have remained in slavery. I blame you
for Brutus, Fortune. Why did we have an era of laws
with years named for the consul? Happy are Arabs   520
and Medes and Eastern lands, whom fate has kept
perpetually under tyrannies. Out of all peoples
who bear the rule of kings our lot is lowest:
we are ashamed to be slaves!
                                    In fact, there are no powers
over us; blind chance ravages the centuries;
we say "Jove reigns," we're lying. Would he behold
Thessaly's bloodbaths from high heaven and still
hold back his lightning bolts? So he himself indeed
would blast Pholoë and Oeta with fire, along with
the innocent groves of Rhodope and pines of Mimas—   530
and *Cassius* is the assassin? He brought down the stars
on Thyestes and doomed Argos to sudden night.
Will he grant daylight to Thessaly, which also wielded
swords of brothers and fathers? No god has ever cared
for mortal affairs. Yet for the calamity we have
vindication, as much as gods consent to give:
the civil wars will make gods equal to those above.
Ghosts will be adorned with lightning bolts, sun rays,
and stars, and in gods' temples Rome will swear by shades.

THE BATTLE OF PHARSALUS

As their rapid advance devoured the space delaying   540
the climax of Fate, when only a patch of earth divides them,
the men see where their spears will fall or what hand there
is holding their own fates, and now they recognize
what atrocities they soon would be committing:
in the enemy's vanguard they saw their fathers,
their brothers' weapons ready for combat, and did not care
to shift their positions. Still, every heart went numb
and tightened, the blood ran cold and froze inside them
as family duty was overthrown, and all the cohorts
long held back their spears, ready and waiting   550
on arms stretched taut . . .
                           Crastinus! May the gods
damn you not to death (the punishment waiting for all)
but to feel pain after death, because your hand heaved
the lance that started the battle and first stained Thessaly
with Roman blood. Sheer madness! As long as Caesar
restrained his weapons, did any hand prove more eager?

   Then the air shook with a harsh blast from the trumpets,
the horns let loose the battle cry, the brass made bold
to give their signals, and the crashing noise
strains to heaven and shatters against the vault   560
of highest Olympus, where storm clouds never reach
nor peels of thunder endure. The clamor resounded,
echoing down the valleys of Haemus, which sent it on,
ricocheting through Pelion's caverns, Pindus howls,
Pangaea's crags ring out, the cliffs of Oeta groan,
till the whole earth had shared their story of madness,
and the sound filled them with dread.
                                   Countless missiles fly
buoyed by diverse prayers: some wish for wounds,
some hope their weapons stick in the ground, so that their hands
stay clean. But chance takes them all and random fortune   570

makes guilty whomever she wishes. But what a small part
of the blood was shed by javelins and flying steel.
For civil hatreds, only the sword suffices
to draw right hands down deep into Roman vitals.

Pompey's forces crowded in dense bands,
weaving their shields together, boss on boss,
so tight that hands and spears could hardly move,
so packed they even feared to swing their swords.
Caesar's insane troops speed headlong against
these dense columns, clearing a path through arms   580
and enemies; breastplates of heavy chain mail
conceal the heart safe beneath their covering—
even here they penetrate the vitals, aiming
every stroke to reach the goal below all armor.
One army suffers civil war, while the other
is waging it. Over there, the blade stands cold;
with Caesar, every sword is hot with guilt.
In no time Fortune toppled a colossal state
and swept its massive ruins down a torrent of Fate.

Pompey's cavalry split into detachments   590
and spread out around the battlefield's edges,
then light infantry took the outside squadrons
and assaulted the fierce strength of the enemy there,
each nation warring with its own style of weapon,
all seeking Roman bloodshed. Arrows, torches,
and rocks all fly, and balls of hot lead liquefy,
soaring through the fluid air. Then Ityraeans,
Medes, and Arabs with flowing robes, keen mobs
of archers, aim their arrows nowhere but up
into the air that looms above the plains—   600
and from there death descends. But foreign steel
is not polluted with any heinous crime.
All the guilt stood heaped around our legions.

Iron shrouds the sky and over the fields
hovers a night of interwoven weapons . . .

Caesar, afraid his front might collapse before
this onslaught, holds back cohorts at an angle
behind the standards and, on that side of battle
where the enemy wavered, sends a sudden surge
while the main lines hold position—
                           Forgetting the fight,   610
shameless cowards fled headlong and made it clear
that barbarian hordes do not win civil wars.
When one charging stallion took a blade through the chest,
threw its rider on his head, then trampled his body,
the whole cavalry fled the field, a rolling cloud
that reined around and stormed on its own ranks.
An all-out bloody rout, no one puts up a fight,
just throats on steel, and the front ranks were too few
to slay all the men whom they could have killed.

O Pharsalia, would that this bloodshed had glutted   620
your fields! That no gore stained your springs except
what flowed from barbarian chests! And that their bones
would be enough to clothe your every field!
Or if you'd rather take your fill of Roman blood,
spare these others, I pray. Let Galatians live,
and Syrians, Cappadocians, Gauls, Iberians
from world's end, Armenians and Cilicians—
for after the civil wars, they'll be the Roman people!
But once it had arisen, panic spread to all,
and doom was on the march for Caesar's cause . . .   630

It reached the main vigor of Magnus, his center battalions.
Combat had ranged at random across the whole field.
Now it stood right here, Caesar's fortune hit the mark.
These weren't bands of boys, forces rounded up
from royal auxiliaries and begged to take up arms.
Their brothers stood this ground, their fathers stood here.
Here is raving insanity, here are all your crimes, Caesar.
Flee this part of the war, my mind, leave it in darkness,
and let no age learn of such evils from me as poet,
or just how much becomes licit in civil wars.   640

Let our tears fall dead, fall dead our lamentations.
Whatever you did in this clash, Rome, I'll keep silent. . . .

   Here Caesar goads the crowds to rave and rage,
and so that no part miss out on crime, he ranges
around the lines, adding fire to blazing spirits.
He inspects their swords—which are dripping blood,
which ones still shine, only the point is gory,
what hand shakes as it grips its sword, who is lazy
and who strains to thrust his weapons, who performs
when ordered and who enjoys the fight, whose face   650
betrays emotion when killing a fellow citizen.
He tours the corpses strewn widely on the fields.
His own hand stanches open wounds of many
whose blood is draining out. Wherever he wanders—
like Bellona cracking her bloody whip, or Mars
impelling Bistones onward, savagely lashing
his chariot stallions thrown into mayhem by
the aegis of Pallas—a vast night of felonies falls,
slaughter springs up, and some gigantic voice
howling, clattering shrieks of armor on chests   660
collapsing, sword blades shattering sword blades.
He hands back fallen swords and furnishes weapons,
orders them to bewilder with iron the faces
of adversaries, he pushes the front lines forward,
drives on the rear, spurs those hanging back
with a blow from the butt of his spear.

                        He bars his men
from advancing on the plebs, and points out senators.
He knows where the blood of empire runs, where the state's
vital organs lie, just how to wear Rome down,
and where the world's last Liberty must be struck   670
to bring her to a standstill.

                   The orders are confounded,
knights of second rank with nobles, honored bodies
are hard-pressed by the steel. They cut down Lepidi,
they cut down Metelli, Corvini, and those named Torquatus,
so often leaders of state and (next to you, Magnus)

the very best of men.
                    There! Hiding his face
in a foot soldier's helmet, unnoticed by the foe . . .
what is that sword you're clutching, Brutus?
                                    Glory of empire,
highest hope for the Senate, and last man bearing
the name of a family so mighty down the ages,   680
don't rush so recklessly through the enemy's ranks
or undertake that deed before fatal Philippi—
Thessaly is preparing a death for you. Here now
you'll gain nothing by aiming at Caesar's throat.
He hasn't attained the citadel, or climbed beyond
the lawful human summit and trodden on all things,
so meriting from Fate such a noble death.
Let him live and—so that he may plummet,
the victim of Brutus—let him also reign!

All the fatherland's glory is perishing here.   690
The patrician order lies dead on the field, unmixed
with plebeians, one giant heap of corpses. Yet,
amid the carnage of famous men, one death stood out:
fierce Domitius, whom the fates had carried
through every disaster. The fortune of Magnus never
surrendered without him. Beaten by Caesar so often,
he dies with Liberty still alive. Rejoicing
in his thousand wounds he sinks down, happy
not to be pardoned a second time.
                                Caesar saw him,
his body writhing, caked with blood, and abused him: 700
"At last you abandon Magnus' army, Domitius,
my 'successor.' The wars go on now without you."

So he spoke; but the spirit pounding the other's chest
sufficed for speech, and he set free these dying words:
"You haven't grasped the fatal wages for your crimes,
Caesar. Your fate's uncertain, lesser than your son-in-law,
I see that, and with Magnus as leader I go down,
free and secure, to the shades of Styx. May savage Mars

subdue you, paying harsh penalties to Pompey and to me—
that is my dying hope."

                              He spoke no more.   710
Life fled and his eyes were buried by deep darkness.

   It's shameful to shed tears for the uncounted dead
at the world's funeral, or to pursue the fates
of individuals and ask whose lethal wound passed
right through his vitals. Who trampled his own bowels
poured out in the mud? Who faced the enemy
and pushed out the sword lodged deep in his throat
as he gave up the ghost? Who fell down with a thud?
Who stood there while his limbs fell off? Who took
weapons straight through the chest? Or whom did a spear   720
pin down on the plain? Whose severed veins
shot blood through the air and splattered his enemy's armor?
Who slew his brother, then cut off his head and threw it
far away so he could plunder his relative's corpse?
Who slashed his father's face, and with excessive rage,
to prove to those who watched that it was *not* his father
that he murdered?

                      No death deserves its own lament,
nor do we have the time to mourn for any one man.
Pharsalia was a different kind of battle
than other disasters. In those, Rome was undone   730
by the deaths of men; here, by the deaths of peoples.
Then, a soldier would die; now, entire nations.
Here flowed the blood of Achaea, Pontus, Assyria,
but the Roman torrent kept all that gore from settling
or clotting on the fields. The nations in that conflict
were wounded worse than their own age could bear.
What was lost was worth even more than health
and life itself. To the end of time we are crushed.
By those swords all ages are conquered in war
and carried off into slavery. But what did their children   740
or their grandchildren do to deserve to be born
under a despot? Were *we* the cowards in battle?
Did we hide our throats? For the fear of others

the penalty sits on our necks. If you were planning
to give a master to those born after the battle,
Fortune, you should have also given them a war.

MAGNUS FLEES PHARSALIA

Now Magnus understood the gods and fates of Rome
had left him, out of luck, but still he was not forced
by the sheer disaster to condemn his fortune.
He stood high on a battlement, beyond the fighting,   750
from where he could behold the slaughter strewn
across the acres of Thessaly, which had been hidden
by the screen of warfare. He saw so many weapons,
all seeking to end his life, so many bodies drained,
and saw his own death there in all that blood.
But as the wretched often will, when they are sunk
they drag down all else with them—he has no desire
to make the nations share in his own ruin.
That a multitude of Latins might survive him,
he continued to believe that the gods in heaven   760
even now deserved his prayers, and he pondered
consolations for his downfall:
                              "Gods above, spare them!
Do not destroy all nations! Let the world stand,
let Rome survive! Magnus can be the one to suffer.
If more pain would please you, I have a wife and sons.
I've pledged them all as security to the Fates.
Is it not enough if the civil war wipe out
both me and mine? Are we too small a loss
when the world is spared? Why do you devastate
and labor to destroy all things? By now,   770
Fortune, I have nothing left."
                              So he declares,
and around the army and standards—troops afflicted
on every side—he goes and calls back those

rushing to early doom, tells them he's not worth it.
Their chief did not lack the nerve to face the swords,
to suffer a lethal blow in the heart or throat,
but he feared when the body of Magnus was laid low
his soldiers would not retreat, and over its leader
the world would fall. Or else he wanted to steal
his death away from Caesar's gaze—in vain,   780
unlucky man! Your father-in-law will want to see,
and demand to be presented with, your head,
wherever it happens to be.

                 Dear wife, you, too,
are reason for flight, your face, and his will to die—
denied by fate—with you at his side.

                      So he spurred
his horse, which carried Magnus away from the war,
without fear of the weapons at his back,
leading his mighty spirit to its fatal doom.
You did not weep or moan, your sorrow kept
its awesome dignity, as was proper for you,   790
Magnus, when you answer for Roman losses.
You gaze upon Emathia with equanimity.
Successes in war never saw you arrogant
nor will adversities see you broken now.
As faithless as she was to you when happy,
through three triumphs, now in misery
Fortune is beneath you. Now you depart untroubled,
your burden of fate laid down. Now you are free
to reflect on happy times. Your hopes recede,
never to be fulfilled. Now you are allowed   800
to know what you have been.

                   Flee dire battles
and call the gods to witness that who persists in arms
no longer dies for you, Magnus. Like the losses
in woeful Africa, like ruinous Munda, and the defeat
by the bay of Pharos, so the greater part
of Thessaly's conflict after your departure
is no longer for Pompey's world-famous name
nor zeal for war, but it will be the matched duel

that we always have: Liberty versus Caesar.
And once you had fled, the Senate made it clear   810
that they were fighting and dying for themselves.
Is there not some satisfaction to be beaten
and retreat from war, and not to have observed
its horrors? Look back and see the heaps that froth
with gore, the rivers troubled by a rush of blood,
and pity your father-in-law. What must he feel
when he enters Rome exultant from *these* fields?
Whatever you suffer abroad in lonely exile,
whatever the tyrant of Pharos subjects you to,
trust the gods and fates who long gave you favor: 820
it was worse to win. Forbid the people to weep
and sound laments, put off tears and wailing.
The world will honor Pompey's trials as much
as his successes. Not bowed in supplication,
calmly survey the kings, survey the cities
you've occupied and realms bequeathed to you,
with Egypt and Libya, and choose a land to die in.

    The first to witness your downfall was Larisa,
which saw your noble head unconquered by fate.
In full force all its citizens poured out of the walls   830
as though to meet you in joy. They promise favors
shedding tears, they open their temples and homes,
and want to be your allies even in defeat.
Clearly your name still carries much abundance,
and inferior now only to your former self
you could again arouse all nations into arms,
again pursue your fate.
                        But he says: "What use
can the defeated be to cities and peoples?
Display your loyalty to the victor."
                                    (Caesar,
while you still tromp through deep mounds of death   840
and the entrails of your fatherland, your son-in-law
is already giving you peoples!)
                                    His charger carries

Pompey away as the people follow with groans
and tears and complaints against the cruel gods.
Here was true assurance of the favor you had gained,
Magnus, and your reward to enjoy: the prosperous
never know if they are really loved.

CAESAR'S TROOPS PLUNDER
THE BATTLEFIELD

When Caesar saw the fields swimming with enough
Hesperian blood, he reckoned it time to spare
the steel and strength of his men, and so grants life   850
to worthless souls and troops who would die for nothing.
But lest their fugitives return to camp and a night
of rest dispel their fear, he decides to press on
right to the enemy's stockade, while his fortune is hot
and terror is mopping up everything. He had no fear
that his men, combat-weary and worn down by Mars,
would take this order badly. Not much urging
was needed to draw the soldiers to the spoils.

"Victory is lavished on us, men! One thing left:
for our blood, the wages, which I will show you.   860
For I won't call a gift what each will give himself.
Behold! Their camps stand open, stuffed with cash.
The gold stolen from the nations of the West
rests here, and tents bulge with Eastern treasures.
The fortune of so many kings and that of Magnus
is heaped here, waiting for masters. Hurry, soldiers!
Overtake the men you're chasing. Whatever riches
Pharsalia made yours are being hauled away
by those you conquered."

                              What mound or trench could hold back
men seeking the prize of wickedness and war?   870
They race to learn how great it pays to be criminals.

And indeed they found a great many heaped-up masses
of gold and silver plundered from round the world
for the expenses of war. But minds that want it all
were not filled full. Even if they had seized the gold
the Spaniards mine, all that the Tagus River spits out,
and what the rich Arimaspian picks from the sands,
they would think their crime had come to little.
When the victor had promised himself the strongholds
of the Tarpeian heights, when he had vowed his all   880
in hopes of plundering Rome, he now feels cheated
to loot a camp.
                    Plebeian soldiers take their rest
impiously on patricians' cots, couches spread
for kings have foul men lying on them, criminals
relax their limbs on the beds of fathers and brothers.
Insane nightmares harass them, fitful raging sleep
churns the battle of Thessaly in their wretched breasts.
In each a brutal crime is watching wakeful, weapons
utterly disturb their minds and hands shake
sword hilts that are not there. I would believe   890
the battlefields groaned and the wicked land
breathed into and inflamed their souls, as ghosts
fully infest the air, the night above is steeped
with Stygian dread. From deserving men
victory exacts stern penalties, and in sleep
hisses and flames assail them, shades of slain
fellow citizens appear, and each is haunted
by a specter of what frightens him the most.
One sees old men's faces, another the shapes
of boys, another's dreams are troubled by   900
corpses of his brothers, or his father
haunts another's heart.
                    But *all* of the phantoms
are inside Caesar—just as Orestes, in Pelops' line,
before he had been purged at the Scythian altar,
beheld the Furies' faces, or like the mutiny
of mind, utter bewilderment, that Pentheus felt
while he was raving, or that Agave felt

after her madness faded—so is he overwhelmed
that night by every sword Pharsalia saw,
or all that would be drawn on that day of vengeance   910
in the Senate. Infernal monsters torture him.
And how much punishment is his guilty conscience
sparing the wretch, when he sees in his dreams
the river Styx and Tartarus with its crowds of dead
while Pompey is still alive!

        Yet having suffered all this,
once daylight has revealed the losses at Pharsalus,
no feature of the landscape can draw his eyes away
from those fields of death. He stares at rivers
overflowing with bloodshed, bodies piled
in mounds as high as hills, the multitudes   920
beginning to decay, reckons up the number
of Magnus' peoples, and has a feast prepared
on that spot, from which he can identify
the faces and the features of the dead.
He likes that he can't see Emathia's ground
and that his eyes take stock of fields hidden
beneath a massacre. In the blood he makes out
his fortune and his gods above. And lest he lose
this spectacle of crimes that gratifies his madness,
he begrudges the poor souls fire for cremation   930
and rails against heaven, blaming it for Emathia.
That Hannibal buried a consul and a Libyan torch
lit the pyres at Cannae does not convince him
to observe the rite that all men grant to enemies;
yet he remembers that they are his fellow citizens,
and his wrath is not yet sated with the slaughter.

   "We do not ask for individual pyres
and separate burial mounds. Give the nations
fire once and let the bodies burn in flames
that never stop. Or if you'd like to punish   940
your son-in-law, heap up Pindus' groves,
haul in Oeta's oak forests and pile them up,
let Pompey at sea watch Thessaly on fire."

AFTERMATH AND MEANING, A FEAST
FOR BIRDS AND BEASTS

Your wrath does nothing. Whether the corpses rot
or a pyre undoes them makes no difference.
Nature welcomes everything back to her
peaceful bosom, and bodies owe their end
to themselves. All these peoples, Caesar,
if fire does not burn them now, it will
burn them with the earth, burn them with   950
the sea's abyss; a common pyre awaits
the world, it will mix their bones with stars.
Wherever Fortune calls your soul, *these* souls
are there too. You won't ascend any higher
into the breezes, or lie in a better place
beneath the night of Styx. Death is free
from Fortune. Earth takes all that she gives birth to,
and heaven covers whoever has no urn.

You who punish the nations by denying them
burial, why are you fleeing this atrocity?   960
Why leave these fragrant fields? Try these waters,
Caesar, enjoy this air, if you are able.
But no, the rotting nations take the soils of Pharsalus
from you. They hold the fields once the victor leaves.

To the funeral feast of Haemonia's war
came not only Bistonian wolves, but lions, too,
left Pholoë when they smelled the rotting blood
of slaughter. Bears deserted their dens, and filthy dogs
their roofs of home, and whatever else has a keen nose
for noxious air and comes to the scent of corpses.   970
Now the birds, which had long followed the camps
of civil war, assemble. You, who are accustomed
to leave the Thracian winters for the Nile, flew
later to the mild south. Never had so many

vultures veiled the sky or more feathered wings
overwhelmed the air. Every forest sent its birds
and every tree dripped bloody dew from wings
bespattered. Often from high in the air above
onto the victor's face and impious standards
putrid gore poured down, and even body parts   980
dropped from the weary talons of the birds.

    Even so, not all those people were reduced
to bones and picked apart by beasts. They don't bother
with the inmost entrails or greedily suck out
all the marrow, they merely taste the flesh.
Most of the Latin mob lay there neglected, loathed,
which sun and rainstorms and a long stretch of days
decomposed and mulched into Emathia's soils.

    Thessaly, unhappy land, what crime of yours
so outraged gods above that you alone were weighted   990
down with so much death and fated wickedness?
How much time must pass before this war's losses
are out of mind and you can be forgiven?
What crops will not rise blighted and with stalks
discolored? What plowshare will not violate
the shades of Roman dead? Before long, new ranks
will come and you will offer them your fields—
with *this* blood not yet dry—for a second crime.
We could wreck the tombs of all our ancestors,
those still standing and those that ancient roots   1000
have cracked the joints and poured out their urns,
still, more ashes are plowed into Haemonia's furrows,
and more bones are struck by its farmer's hoe.
No sailor at the shore of Emathia would have
tethered his rope, nor plowman dug your earth,
the Roman people's tomb, settlers would have fled
your fields of ghostly shades, no flocks would prune
your hedges, no shepherd would have ever dared
to let his herd graze on the grass that rises
from our bones, but like some marginal land   1010

where, from brutal heat or cold, no humans dwell,
you would have lain neglected, barren and unknown—
if you had been the last and only, not the first,
to bear the unspeakable wickedness of war.
Gods above, let noxious lands be reviled.
Why did you oppress, and thus absolve,
the whole wide world? Slaughters in the West,
Pachynum's tearful waters, Mutina and Leucas—
with all these Philippi has been washed clean.

BOOK EIGHT

Pompey steals away in disgrace from Pharsalus and Greece (1–38), then sails to Cornelia in Mytilene on Lesbos, whose people greet and send him off in sorrow (38–190). Pompey wavers, unsure where to go or what to do, and talks with the ship's captain about the stars (191–237). Pompey meets up with his son and King Deiotarus of Galatia, whom he sends east, to seek alliance with and aid from Rome's enemy Parthia (238–91), before sailing on to Cilicia (292–307). The defeated senators gather here, Pompey speaking first and urging them to enlist the Parthians against Caesar (308–91). Lucius Lentulus Crus, the recent consul, speaks vehemently against Pompey's rash and treacherous plan, which is rejected, and urges instead that they seek aid in Egypt (392–555). Pompey sails for Egypt (555–67), and in Ptolemy's court his counselor Pothinus argues that they must side with the victor and Pompey must die (568–687). Ptolemy's henchman Achillas and a Roman mercenary, Septimius, who formerly served under Pompey, kill Magnus when he joins them in their boat (688–749). Pompey turns over his life in his mind and dies in silent dignity (750–81), while Cornelia watches in horror and mourns from their boat before they flee (781–814). The murderers hack off Pompey's head and stick it on a spear to take to Ptolemy as proof, while the great commander's body is left to be battered in the tide (814–74). Cordus, a quaestor under Pompey, hastily and in secret burns and buries Pompey on the beach (875–977). The poet offers his own honorific eulogies to Pompey, buried in this lowly tomb, unworthy of him, but fitting in its humble lack of pomp and luxury (977–1076).

BOOK EIGHT

   Now over Hercules' gorges and wooded Tempe,
pursuing costly byways through Haemonia's wastes
and forests, his horse exhausted from travel and now
ignoring the spurs, Magnus beats a wavering trail
of flight and wanders baffled paths. He startles
every time the winds crack through the forest,
and when one of his comrades rides up from behind
he jumps out of his wits, trembling for his life.
Though fallen from the summit, he knows the price
placed on his blood is not yet cheap, and brooding   10
on fate, he deems the bounty on his own throat
is still as much as he himself would pay
for Caesar's severed neck.
                          Seeking desolate places,
he can't find any safe spots to hide his fate
because of his famous face. Many who were heading
to the camps at Pharsalus, and had not heard the news
of his defeat, were awestruck to encounter the chief
and, dumbfounded by the wheeling turn of events,
hardly believed it when he himself was telling
of the disaster. It weighs heavy on Magnus   20
whenever anyone witnesses his troubles.
He'd prefer to be unknown in every nation,
to pass safe through the cities as a nobody;
but for long favor Fortune makes him pay
with misery: his fame becomes a weight
of hardships that she crushes him under, prodding him
with his former fate.

          Now he feels his honors
came far too hastily, he damns his youthful laurels
and his deeds with Sulla. Now even his fleets
sailing off Cilicia and his standards in Pontus   30
grieve him, in his dejection, to recall.
So are mighty souls destroyed by a long life—
when it outlives their authority and power.
Unless one's last day comes when good times end,
outstripping sorrows with a rapid death,
former fortune is a disgrace. Who would dare
surrender himself to the fair successes of fate
unless he's ready for death?

POMPEY HEADS FOR LESBOS

                He touched the shores
where the Peneus River, now red with blood
from Emathia, meets the sea. From there a boat,   40
unequal to winds and waves and barely safe
even in river shallows, took him nervously
out upon the deep. His own ships are still rowing
off Corcyra and the bays of Leucas, but the master
of Cilicia and the lands of Liburnians slunk
as a timid passenger onto a tiny bark.
He bids them turn the sails toward the shores
of Lesbos, distant keeper of his secret love . . .

   the land where you were lying hidden, Cornelia,
with more distress than if you stood in the middle   50
of Emathia's plains. Tortured by foreboding,
sick with worry, trembling dread shatters your dreams,
and every night is obsessed with Thessaly.
And once the darkness has withdrawn, you run
to the rocks of a sheer cliff at the shoreline's edges

and gazing far out to sea you always are the first
to see the sails of a coming ship tossing on the waves.
You do not dare inquire about your husband's fate . . .
There, a ship! Sails tending toward your ports—
you don't know what it brings, but your worst fears
right now are sinister rumors or sad news
about the war. Your husband has come, defeated.
Why waste the time you have for grief? You fear,
when you could be weeping.

            The boat drew near—
she leaped up racing, and saw the crime and cruelty
of the gods: the general stood disgraced and pale,
every feature showed his anguish, his gray hair,
his clothes so ragged, filthy with black dust.
Night reared up before her in her sorrow
and stole away the bright sky into darkness
as grief surrounds her soul. Her strength gives out
and body falls, her heart goes cold and long she lies
deceived by hope for death.

            At last the line is tied
to shore and Pompey walks the empty beach.
When her faithful servants see him coming near,
silent, inward groans are the only rebukes of fate
they allow themselves, as they try in vain
to raise their half-dead mistress from the ground.
Magnus takes her to his breast and wraps her
in embraces to revive her chilly limbs with warmth.
Once the flush of blood had returned to her skin
she started to feel Pompey's hands and could endure
to look on her sad husband's face.

            Magnus forbids her
to yield to fate and scolds her intemperate sadness:
"Woman, granddaughter of great and honored men,
why does your strong noble heart break at the first
blow of Fortune? There is for you a road to fame
that will last for ages. Your sex cannot gain honor
in the forum of laws, or by force of arms. A husband

in misfortune is your only resource. Take heart,   90
let your devotion stand up to the fates, and love
the very fact that I am beaten. For you I am
a greater glory now that the rods of office,
the Senate's loyal mob, the vast host of kings,
all have abandoned me. You can be the last
lone follower of Magnus. Inconsolable grief
is unsightly when your husband's still alive.
Mourning your man is devotion's final debt.
You've lost nothing in my war. After the battles
Magnus is alive, though his fortune has died.   100
That's what you're bewailing, and what you loved."

  Rebuked by her husband's words, she forced herself
to get up off the ground, frail as she was,
and in her pain these grievances burst out:
"I should have been the bride of hateful Caesar!
An unlucky wife who makes no husband happy,
I've harmed the world twice. A Fury is my bridesmaid
along with the shades of the Crassi, since I'm vowed
to their spirits unto death and brought their bad luck
from Assyria into the camps of our own citizens.   110
I drove nations over a cliff, and all the gods
away from the greater cause. Most cherished husband,
I'm unworthy of your bed. Did Fortune have
so much claim on a head so great? I was unfaithful
to marry you if I was bound to bring you sorrow.
Punish me now, I will gladly pay it,
to calm the seas for you, restore the faith of kings,
make the whole world more obedient—just scatter
your partner over the sea! For luck in battle
I prefer to trade my life. Now, Magnus!   120
Atone for your defeat at last! And you come too,
wherever you lie—you've already taken vengeance
against our bed with the civil wars. Impose
your punishments, cruel Julia! Slay your rival
and be appeased. Just spare your beloved Magnus!"

She spoke, then melted back into her husband's
caring embrace, causing all eyes to well up into tears.
She softened the hard heart of Magnus, and his eyes,
dry since Thessaly, now poured freely in Lesbos.

By now a crowd from Mytilene filled the shore,   130
addressing Magnus: "If it will be our greatest glory
ever after that we safely harbored your dear pledge
of marriage, we pray that you yourself may deign
to make our walls, devoted to you by a sacred pact,
and our allied homes your own, for this one night.
Magnus, make it a site that all ages may come visit,
where Roman travelers may come and pay respects.
No other walls are better for you to enter in defeat.
The rest can hope for goodwill from the victor;
ours by now are criminal. Also, we're an island   140
out in the sea—isn't Caesar lacking ships?
Most of the chiefs and nobles will be informed
and gather here. You must restore your fate
on our famous shore. Take the gold and gifts
from our gods' temples. Take these young men,
use them on land or ship as needed. Take them.
You should have them in defeat, or Caesar will
just steal them. But rid our land that has served well
of this one charge, that the faith you counted on
in success, you then found fault with once you lost."   150

Made happy in his adversities by such devotion
of these men, and pleased for the world's sake
that loyalty does exist, he told them: "No soil
in all the world has been more obliging to me,
as I've made known by placing in your hands
no small pledge, and by this hostage Lesbos
has held my fond affections. Here I've found
the safety of home and sacred household gods—
just like Rome to me. In flight I turned my ship
to no other shores before these, though I knew   160
that Lesbos already deserved Caesar's anger

for harboring my wife, nor was I afraid
to present you even greater means and chance
to gain his mercy. But I have made you guilty
enough by now. My fates drive me onward
across the entire world.

                "Ah, Lesbos, your name
forever will be extremely blessed, whether you
convince other peoples and kings to take Magnus in,
or you alone prove loyal to me. For it's settled:
I go to learn what lands hold justice or iniquity.   170
Accept my final prayers, whatever god may still
attend me: grant me peoples similar to Lesbos,
who won't forbid a man beaten down by Mars
to enter their ports, though Caesar may harass them—
or stop me from leaving."

                He spoke, and set down
his partner in the boat. You would have thought they all
were leaving the land and soil of their fathers,
the way they wailed up and down the shore and stretched
defiant arms toward heaven. Pompey's fortunes
had moved their pity, yes, but watching *her* depart—   180
whom throughout the war they had regarded
as their own citizen—the populace truly groaned.
Even if she had left to join her husband's camps
in victory, the matrons would hardly have been able
to let her go without tears, she had so won their love
with modesty, her honest ways, the sober restraint
of her chaste demeanor. With her humble retinue
she was a guest whom none found too oppressive.
Even while her fate stood high, she lived with them
as though her husband had already been defeated.   190

POMPEY SAILS SOUTH

The Titan Sun had fallen, with half his fires
now in the sea, his orb not wholly visible
to those from whom he hid nor those, if any,
on whom he rose . . .

                         The restless cares in Pompey's breast
turned now to the cities allied in treaty with Rome
and the fickle minds of kings, now to the world's trackless
expanses of too much sun lying beyond the South . . .
Often in sad toils of worry, loathing the future,
he banished his heart's strenuous storm of doubts
questioning the ship's pilot about all the stars.   200
From which does he mark the lands? To cut a path
in the sea what measure is in the sky? Which star
keeps Syria in view? Or which of the Wagon's fires
steers well toward Libya?

                         The expert observer
of silent Olympus addressed his queries: "Whichever
rise and fall on heaven's zodiac wheel, which never
stands still, those deceive poor sailors and we
don't follow them. But one doesn't go under sea,
the unsetting axle, brightest in the twin Bears,
that one governs ships. When it's rising for me   210
ever toward the zenith and the Little Bear climbs
up the top of the yard braces, we're heading for
Bosporus and Pontus, with Scythia's curving shores.
But when the Bear Guard slides down the topmast
and the Dog's Tail sweeps into the sea, the ship
is aiming for port in Syria. Then Canopus appears,
a star that keeps its roving to the southern sky,
afraid of the north wind. Keep that one on your left
and press on past Pharos, mid-sea the ship hits Syrtis.
What are your orders then? Whither do we give sail?   220
What sheet should stretch the canvases?"

                                        His mind in doubt,

Magnus answered: "Over the entire ocean
keep one thing in view, that your ship is always
farther away from Emathia's coast. Abandon the sky
and sea of Hesperia. Leave the rest to the winds.
I rescued my dear companion whom I had placed in trust.
Then I knew for certain what shores I wanted most.
But now, let Fortune choose our port."

                    At his word
the pilot turned the sails hanging straight and true
upon the yardarms, swinging the ship hard to port,   230
and to cut the waves that billow rough between
Psyria's crags and Chios, he slackens the bowlines
and tightens those at the stern—

                    the prow changed course,
the keel wheeled round, the sea sensed the motion
and made a new sound.

                    No horseman so adroitly
circles his left axle round on the right-hand wheel,
forcing his chariot near the turn post without a foul.

ALLIES REGROUP, DEIOTARUS
SENT EAST TO SEEK AID

Revealing lands, the Titan Sun veiled the stars.
Scattered by Emathia's tempest, all who escaped
catch up with Magnus. First off the coast of Lesbos   240
his son overtakes him, and soon a host of loyal chiefs.
For even cast down by fate, his troops put to flight,
Fortune had not deprived Magnus of attendant kings.
Masters of the world who wield Eastern scepters
were an exile's entourage.

                    He sends Deiotarus—
who tracked the general on his far-flung trail—
off to remote regions of the world, saying,
"Since that part of the world which was Roman

was lost in Emathia's ruins, what is left,
most faithful king, is to test the faith of the East,   250
the peoples who drink the Tigris and Euphrates,
they are still safe from Caesar. Don't let it irk you,
when chasing fate for Magnus, to work your way
into the strange and distant halls of Medes,
reach Scythian retreats, under a different sky,
and to report my words to proud Arsacides:
'If our original treaty holds, which I swore
by the Thunderer of Latium, and your Magi
bound in confirmation, then fill Armenia's quivers,
stretch their bows, and add the Getae's muscle—   260
if, when I was laying siege at the Caspian Gates
and hunting the Alans, tough from endless warfare,
I suffered you Parthians to range the open plains
of the Achaemenids and never drove you
frightened inside Babylon for safety.
Beyond the fields of Cyrus, out to the limits
of Chaldean realms, where the rapid Ganges
and Hydaspes of Nysa reach the sea, I went,
and was nearer to the rising fire of Phoebus
than Persia is—though conquering everywhere   270
I held back, and in my triumphs only you were missing.
Alone of all the kings over lands in the East
the Parthian approaches me on equal terms.
Nor was it only one act of kindness from Magnus
that keeps the Arsacidae standing. For after the trauma
of Assyrian defeat, who restrained the Latins,
justly angry as they were? So bound to me
by so many benefits, now let Parthia extend
her borders, break her bonds and cross the banks
at Alexander's Zeugma, barred to her for ages.'   280
Tell the Parthians that if Pompey is conqueror,
Rome will *want* to be conquered."

                            Hard requests,
but compliance didn't pain the king, and putting off
his signs of royalty, he wraps himself in garb
taken from a slave, then disembarks. It's safe

in doubtful times for tyrants to masquerade
as poor men (proof of how much more securely
than the world's masters the real pauper
spends his days).
                            On shore he parts with the king
and sails on, past Icaria's bluffs and leaving   290
Ephesus behind and Colophon's placid waters,
skirting the frothing rocks of slender Samos.
A fluent breeze blows from the coast of Cos,
and he passes Cnidos and leaves famous Rhodes
behind in its brilliant sunlight, making good
the time spent in the choppy bays off Telmessos
once out in the open sea.
                            The land of Pamphylia
looms up on the ship and—not yet having dared
to trust any walls enough to go inside—you first,
little Phaselis, Magnus enters. For your scarce residents   300
and houses drained of people removes all cause of fear;
their ship had a bigger crowd than you did.
                            From there
he sets off again and sees the Taurus range and, plunging
down from Taurus, Dipsus Falls.

THE DEFEATED SENATE FACTION
DELIBERATES IN CILICIA

                            Would Magnus
have believed it, when he brought peace to these waves,
that he was looking out for his own interest?
Along the coast of Cilicia his little boat
flees in safety. A large part of the Senate
follows, gathering round their fugitive leader.
In small Syhedra, near the harbor where Selinus   310
sends and receives ships, to a gathering of chiefs
at last the somber mouth of Magnus opens
with these words:

                    "Comrades of war and in flight,
likeness of the fatherland, although on a barren shore
in the land of Cilicia, with no armies encircling me,
I deliberate our new state of affairs and search
for some beginning—bear your souls with pride:
I did not fall completely on Emathia's fields,
nor is my fate so downtrodden that I am unable
to raise my head and shake off the tragedies   320
that I am saddled with. If after exile in Libya
Marius was able to regain his high command
and get his name yet again onto the calendar,
will Fortune hold me down when a lesser hand
has ousted me? I have a thousand ships, riding
the waves in Greece, and a thousand captains.
Pharsalia scattered our resources, but it did not
diminish them. But even so, the fame of my deeds
around the world all alone could sustain me,
and my name, which the world loves.

                              "Weigh the kingdoms,   330
in strength and in trust, of Libya, Parthia, Pharos—
which one, I ask you, is best suited to lend aid
to Roman affairs? Now, I will lay out for you
my secret concerns, what carries weight in my mind.
The age of the Nile's dynast raises suspicion,
since steep loyalty demands more hardy years.
And then, the shrewdly wavering, two-faced Moor
raises fears. For he is mindful of his birth,
that shameless son of Carthage, and poses a threat
to Hesperia, his vain heart so full of Hannibal,   340
whose blood stains the kingdom indirectly
and pollutes his Numidian ancestors. Already
when Varus entreated him, it puffed him up to see
Romans taking second place. For this reason,
my comrades, come, let us hasten to the East.
Across the Euphrates' torrent a mighty world
awaits, the Caspian Gates draw back to reveal
limitless haunts and refuges, and in Assyria
nights and days are turned by a different sky,

they have a sea, distinct from ours, with waves   350
of a different color, and their own ocean, too.
Their only pleasure is empire. Their steeds are loftier
on the plain, their bows are stronger. Neither
young nor old is slow to stretch their lethal strings,
and from every arrow death is swift and sure.
With the bow they were first to break the lances
of Macedon, and they took Bactra, seat of the Medes,
and Babylon, home of Assyrians, proud of its walls.
Nor do our javelins scare the Parthians much.
They boldly come to war, having tried and proven   360
their Scythian quivers the day that Crassus died.
It's not just the iron they trust when scattering darts;
their missiles hiss by, fully soaked in venom.
Small wounds, but harmful, the slightest graze means death.

    "I wish my confidence in the fierce Arsacidae
were not so great. Fates that inspire the Medes
too closely rival our Fates. Their nation has many gods.
I will uproot the peoples from this other land
and pour them out, rouse the Orient from their homes
and set them loose. Or if the loyalty of the East   370
and treaties with barbarians delude us,
let Fortune carry my shipwreck beyond the world's
common routes of trade. I will not beg
from kingdoms that I made. Death will bring me
quite enough relief, if in that other world
I lie at rest, without my father-in-law
treating my body with cruelty or devotion.

    "But when I go back over the whole fate of my life,
I always remember how venerated I was
in that part of the world, how great I was   380
beyond Maeotis, how high I stood along the Tanaïs,
gazing all the way to where the sun is born.
Into what lands did my name go forth with greater
success in action, or from which return with greater
triumphs? Favor my endeavors, Rome.

For what greater happiness could the gods above
have ever offered you, than to wage your civil wars
with Parthian troops, and destroy so great a nation
by drawing them into our troubles? When Caesar's armies
clash with the Medes, Fortune will be forced   390
to avenge either me or the Crassi."

                            Once he'd spoken,
their grumbling told him that the men condemned
his counsel—that this whole assembly was doomed.
Lentulus outstripped them all in virtue's zeal
and noble heights of protest with his speech
worthy of one who'd just been consul:

                                    "So!
Did Thessaly's ruins shatter your mind? One day
has doomed the world, has it? Does Emathia
determine such a huge dispute? This brutal wound
lies beyond all help? Has Fortune stranded you   400
at the feet of the Parthians? Magnus! Why
are you deserting the world, detesting every
region of earth and sky, pursuing foreign stars
and heavens estranged from ours—are you planning
to worship Chaldean fires and to partake in
barbaric rites as a lackey of the Parthians?
Was 'love of liberty' just a pretext for this war?
Why did you deceive the wretched world
if you're so ready to be a slave?

                                 "You!
The one he shuddered to hear was ruling Rome,   410
the one he saw lead captive kings away
from Hyrcania's woods and even Indus' shore—
now he will see you thrown down by the Fates,
humbled and broken, his mind will go insane
with lofty designs against the Latin world,
having measured himself and Rome against
the sight of Pompey begging. Nothing you say
will be worthy of your spirit or your fate.
In his ignorance of Latin, he'll demand that you
implore him with your tears.

"Great Magnus!   420
Are we to suffer this shameful blow, that Parthia
avenge Hesperia's disasters before Rome does?
Granted, she chose *you* to take command
in this civil war. But why are you broadcasting
to Scythia's nations news of our wounded state,
debacles we should keep quiet? Why are you telling
the Parthians how to invade! Rome is losing
this solace for her troubles, that she invites
no kings in, but instead becomes enslaved
to one of her own citizens. Would it please you   430
to march across the world leading savage tribes
against the walls of Rome—behind the very standards
captured by the Euphrates with the Crassi?
He was the only king *not* in Emathia,
when fate was still hiding her favor. Will he now
want to challenge the victor's massive resources
when he hears of him, or join his fate to yours?
Magnus! Their race doesn't have such confidence.

"All peoples who are born in Arctic frosts
are unbreakable in war and in love with death.   440
But as one approaches the warm regions of Dawn,
a mild climate makes those nations soft.
There you even see men wear loose-fit robes
and flowing dresses. The Parthian, across the fields
of Media, among the Sarmatian plains and level
acres of flatland along the Tigris—there
no enemy can top him, because of his freedom
for retreat. But where the earth has swelled,
he will not climb rough mountain peaks, or fight
through murky shadows where his bow is weak   450
and imprecise. He won't swim straight across
a river's violent current, or hold out in battle
limbs all drenched in blood, hot in the dust
under a summer sun. With no battering rams
or any machines of war, they have no strength
to fill in trenches, and when a Parthian chases you

any wall whatever can withstand his arrows.
Trifling fighters whose war is retreat by bands
who wander at will—soldiers better at ceding
than gaining ground. Trickery smears their shafts,   460
no virtue that dares to suffer fighting hand to hand
like men, just stretching strings from far away
and letting wounds fall where they will on the winds.
A blade has *vigor*, and any race of *men*
wages war with swords! For Medes are disarmed
in the very first skirmish, then they must turn back
with empty quivers. There's no strength in their hands,
all their courage relies on poison.

                           "Magnus,
do you trust men for whom it is not enough
to send them to the fray armed with a steel blade?   470
Is seeking shameful support worth that much,
just to die cut off from the world, far
from your own land, barbaric soil settling
over you, a tiny, worthless tomb covering you—
yet enviable to Crassus, still not buried?

   "But your lot is easy, since the penalty of death
is final and holds no fear for men. But Cornelia,
it's not death she fears under that awful king.
Or don't we know about that barbarous lust,
blind in the manner of beasts, that corrupts the laws   480
and vows of marriage with countless consorts
and opens the solemn secrets of the bedroom
for a thousand young wives to share? Deranged with wine
and feasting, royalty tries out forms of sex
that aren't spelled out in law codes. All night long
entwined with so many women, one man still
is not worn out. Sisters lie in the beds of kings
and mothers, violating hallowed bonds.
The tragic tale of Thebes and Oedipus,
forced unwillingly into sin, is censured   490
by all nations. But how many times is
a son of Arsaces born from just such incest

to be lord of the Parthians! Who finds it holy
to impregnate the one who gave him birth,
what deed can I suppose he holds unholy?
The illustrious daughter of Metellus will stand
at his barbaric bed, one of a thousand wives.
Still, the king's libido will devote free time
to none of them more often than her, Magnus,
aroused by brutality and her glorious husbands.   500
For it will thrill his monstrous fantasies more
to know that she was also the wife of Crassus—
as though Assyria's fates had long deserved her,
he'll take her like a captive of the former defeat.

   "Keep the pitiful wound of that Eastern mishap
firmly fixed in mind, and you will be ashamed
not only to beg support from that deadly king,
but also that you were waging *civil* war *first*!
For which crime of your father-in-law and you
will people consider greater than that the vengeance   510
due the Crassi was lost while you were clashing
in arms? All of our generals should have marched
on Bactra, leaving none of our armies in reserve,
even exposing the empire's northern frontier
to Dacians and the Rhine's great hordes, until
treacherous Susa had crumbled over the tombs
of its rulers and Babylon was laid in ruins.
Fortune, we pray for an end to peace with Assyria!
And if Thessaly has brought civil war to an end,
let the victor march against the Parthians,   520
the only race in the world that I could enjoy
watching in Caesar's triumphs!
                              "But against you,
once you cross the cold Araxes, the old man's
sorrowful shade, transfixed with Scythian arrows,
will he not hurl these words? 'You whom we expected
to avenge our unburied shades and ashes after death,
have you come to settle a peace?' Then many more

reminders of the slaughter will assail you:
walls that our generals, mutilated and headless,
were dragged around, where the Euphrates sank   530
such mighty names, and the Tigris washed away
our men's corpses underground then spat them
out again. If you can pass through *these* things,
Magnus, then you can also find your father-in-law
sitting in the midst of Thessaly and make peace.

"Why not reconsider the Roman sphere?
If you fear the realm that spreads to the south
and faithless Juba, we can head to Pharos
and Lagus' fields. On one side, Libya's Syrtes
keep Egypt safe, and there the rapid river   540
with seven streams clears a path to the sea.
It is a land content with the goods it has;
in need of neither merchandise nor rain
from Jove, its great trust is in the Nile alone.
Young Ptolemy holds his scepter thanks to you,
Magnus, since it was entrusted to your care.
Who fears the shadow of a name? His age
is innocent. It's in the halls of an old king
where one can't hope for justice or loyalty
or respect for the gods. Well-worn scepters   550
stop short at nothing. Kingdoms find the mildest
treatment under a new king."
                                      Saying no more,
his view convinced their minds. O last hope for the state,
you give tongues too much liberty! The resolution
of Magnus was overruled.

MAGNUS SAILS TO EGYPT

                                      They left Cilician soil
and let loose their ships at full sprint toward Cyprus,

whose altars are favored above all by the goddess
who is mindful of Paphos' swells (if we believe
that divine powers are born, or hold it true that gods
had a beginning). When Pompey departed these shores,   560
passing Cyprus' rocky peaks which stretch southward,
he turned into the vast sea's heaving crosscurrent,
and did not hold on course to that grateful tower
with its light by night, but reached the lowest
shores of Egypt with difficulty, fighting the sail,
where the seventh stream, the largest part of
the divided Nile, dumps into Pelusium's shallows.

PTOLEMY'S COURT PLOTS THE
MURDER OF POMPEY

   The season was when Libra weighs out equal hours
balanced no more than a day, and the declining light
pays back the winter night damages for spring losses.   570
Learning that the king was camped on Casius Hill
he turns that way. Phoebus was not yet sinking
nor sails drooping . . .

                       A rider on the lookout had
already sped off and filled the court with panic
about their guest's arrival. There was barely time
to convene a council. Still, all the monsters
of Pella's palace gathered, among them Acoreus,
mild now with age and sobered by broken years—
born in Memphis, city proud of pointless rites,
it oversees the Nile's cresting into the fields;   580
while he tended the gods, more than one Apis bull
lived out the span of years from its mother, Phoebe.
Of the council his voice was first, a high-flown speech
on loyalty and just deserts, on the sanctity
of promises of his father, now deceased.
But better at knowing the ways of tyrants, how

to coax them into evils, Pothinus dared
to condemn Pompey to **death:**

                        "Justice and decency,
Ptolemy, lead many into injury. One pays
a penalty for loyalty, so lauded, when   590
it holds up those whom Fortune has pulled down.
Take sides with the Fates and gods and promote
the fortunate. Flee the wretched. As distant as stars
from earth and fire from sea lies advantage
from the straight and true. A scepter loses all force
once it starts weighing justice, and citadels
that care for honesty topple. The liberty
for crimes is what props up hated regimes—
that and an extravagant number of swords.
You can't get away with all your brutal deeds   600
unless you keep on doing them. If being devout
is what one wants, let him leave the court.
Virtue and absolute power do not mix.
Those who feel ashamed at cruelty live
in constant fear.

                 "Magnus can't get away with
treating your age with condescending scorn.
He thinks that you cannot defend our shores
from even a beaten army. We need not let
a stranger rob us of the scepter. You have nearer
bonds of trust. If ruling them is grievous,   610
return the Nile and Pharos to your ousted sister.
But surely let's guard Egypt from Latin armies.
It didn't belong to Magnus during their wars,
and it will not be the victor's. He's been driven
out of the rest of the world already, and now,
when his cause has lost all confidence, he is seeking
some nation to join him in his fall. He's on the run,
from ghosts of fellow citizens. It's not just the army
of his father-in-law he's fleeing. He's fleeing
the face of the Senate, a large part of which stuffs   620
the birds of Thessaly, and he dreads the nations,
which he left there to mingle their blood in one,

and he fears kings, whose everything he sank—
the culprit for Thessaly, whom no land lets in,
he now hassles our realm, which he hasn't destroyed,
yet.
      "Magnus has given us a more just cause
for grievance against him, Ptolemy. Ask him, 'Why
are you staining secluded, ever-peaceful Pharos
with the guilt of wars, making our fields suspect
to the victor? Why as you fall did you choose   630
to charge our land alone with Pharsalia's fate
and your punishment? We already have a crime
that must be purged by the sword. For your Senate
placed us on the throne by your own urging,
and so we cheered your armies in our prayers.
This blade, which fate commands I draw, is ready
not for you, but for the defeated. Magnus,
I'll strike your guts. I'd prefer your father-in-law's.
We are rushing where everything else is carried.
Do you doubt that I *must* do you violence   640
while I'm free to do so? What confidence
in our realm drives you here, unfortunate man?
Don't you see our people, unarmed, struggling
to dig their fields softened by the receding Nile?'
It's fitting to appraise our kingdom and admit
its resources. Ptolemy, are you able to prop up
Magnus' collapse, beneath which Rome is lying?
Do you dare kick up the mound of Thessaly's ashes
and declare war on our kingdom? Before the fight
in Emathia, we joined neither side in arms.   650
Do Pompey's camps now suit us, when the world
abandons them? Will you challenge the victor now,
with all his riches, with Fate so clearly known?
It's decent not to abandon one in adversities—
but leave it to those who followed in good times.
No loyalty ever chooses wretched friends."

    They all approve the crime. The boy king thrills
at the unusual honor of being permitted by servants

to give the order for such great deeds. Achillas
is chosen for the crime. Where that treacherous land   660
strikes out into beaches at Casius, and the shallows
of Egypt bear witness to the neighboring Syrtes,
he stocks a modest vessel with swords and partners
in monstrous crime . . .

                    Gods above! Do the Nile
and barbarous Memphis, Pelusium or Canopus
with their soft mobs, possess such daring spirits?
Has the fate of civil wars so oppressed the world?
Are Roman affairs so sunk? Is there any place
for Egypt in these tragedies? Is the blade of Pharos
going to be set loose?

                  O civil wars!   670
Keep at least *this* faith—let hands of relatives
step forward, and be rid of these foreign monsters!

    If Magnus deserved, with his illustrious name,
for Caesar to bear the guilt, doesn't the downfall
of such a mighty name give you any terror,
Ptolemy? And do you dare, you unclean half-man,
to lay your unholy hands on a thundering heaven?
Not because he was a master of the world
or three times rode a chariot up the Capitol,
or a lord of kings and protector of the Senate   680
and the victor's son-in-law—to Pharos' tyrant,
it might have been enough that he was Roman.
Why are you reading our entrails with your sword?
Don't you know, you vile boy, do you not know
your place according to Fortune? Already you have
no right to hold the Nile's scepter, for civil discord
has overthrown the one who gave you the kingdom.

THE DEATH OF GNAEUS
POMPEY MAGNUS

By now he had furled his sails out of the wind
and was rowing in toward those unspeakable shores,
when a short bireme pulled up before him, carrying   690
that wicked band, who feign that Magnus is free
to enter the realm of Pharos, inviting him down
from his own ship's high stern into their small craft,
claiming the shore is perilous, with the swells
from two seas' tides crashing against the shallows,
preventing foreign fleets from putting in to land.
If the laws of the Fates, and an eternal Order
bent on drawing his sad death ever nearer, were
not hauling Magnus to shore to suffer his doom,
none of his companions would now neglect   700
the omens of wickedness. For if his allegiance
were sincere, if the palace were open in true
devotion to Magnus, by whose authority he held
the scepter, the tyrant of Pharos would have come
with his entire fleet.
                          But he yields to Fate
and, when asked to leave his ships, he obeys,
preferring death to cowardice—
                                    Cornelia rushed
to board the enemy's boat, all the more unwilling
to let her husband leave without her because
she feared disaster. "Wife, do not be reckless.   710
Stay here, and you, my son, please stay and watch
what happens to me from far away offshore.
My neck will be the proof by which you'll know
the tyrant's faith."
                      But deaf to his refusal,
Cornelia, frantic, stretched forth both her hands:
"Cruel man! Where are you going without me?
Am I to be left again, already sent away

from evils in Thessaly? Never a happy omen
marks our wretched partings! Why did you
change course when you fled across the deep?   720
You could have left me hiding out in Lesbos
if you were going to keep me barred from every land.
Or am I only a pleasing companion out at sea?"

    Her words she poured in vain, but still she hangs
off the edge of the stern, anxious and thunderstruck
with fear, she can't turn her gaze away or bear
to look at Magnus. The fleet stood anxious about
the outcome for their general, fearing no crime
or conflict in arms, but that Pompey would submit
with humble prayers to a scepter his own hand gave.   730

    As he is preparing to cross, a Roman soldier
salutes him from the Pharian ship, Septimius,
who—disgrace on the gods—was bearing arms
in the king's bodyguard, dishonoring himself
by setting aside his javelin. He was inhuman,
violent, untamed, no beast was more bloodthirsty.
Who would not have thought that you were sparing
the nations, Fortune, when his hand missed the war,
and you kept such noxious weapons far from Thessaly?
You deal swords widely, so all corners of the world   740
can accomplish civil-war felonies for you!
The story's an outrage even to the victors,
and it will always bring shame upon the gods,
that a Roman blade was so compliant to a king,
and Pella's boy lopped off your head, Magnus,
with a sword that once served you. What infamy
will carry Septimius down the ages? What name
will they, who call what Brutus did "unspeakable,"
use when they speak of this foul deed?
                        The end
of his last hour had come. Swept away   750
in the Pharian boat, he had already lost
power over himself. The king's monsters

get ready to bare the steel. He sees the swords
closing in and covers his face, refusing in rage
to bare his head to Fortune. He shuts his eyes
and holds his breath, lest any cries of pain
escape and spoil his endless glory.
                                        But once
Achillas dug in his side the sharp deathblow,
he accorded the stroke no groans nor took regard
of the wicked deed. Holding his body still,   760
he proves himself in dying, and in his heart
these thoughts roll:
                        "The ages are listening now
and they will never keep Roman struggles silent.
The future the world over is watching this boat,
seeing the faith of Pharos. Now reflect on fame.
Fate has given me a long and prosperous life.
People do not know—unless you prove it
by your death—if you could endure misfortunes.
Don't give in to shame, and so deprive of joy
the author of your death. Whatever strikes,   770
believe it to be the hand of your father-in-law.
Let them mangle and scatter me, still I am
happy, gods above! No god has the power
to take that away. In life prosperity rises
and falls, but no man turns miserable in death.
Cornelia is watching my murder, and my Pompey—
so conceal your pain and groaning all the more
with patience. My son and wife will love me slain
if I die with dignity."
                        So did Magnus keep
a close watch on his mind, and as he died   780
kept in command of his soul.
                                But Cornelia,
with less patience watching the brutal crime
than she will have enduring it, fills the air
with words evoking pity:
                            "Oh, my husband!
My cursed self has killed you! Lesbos, off your path,

caused you deadly delay, and Caesar reached
the Nile's shores before you. For who else
would order this crime? But whoever you are—
set loose by the gods against so great a head
and looking out for Caesar's anger or your own—   790
you do not know, for all your savagery, where
Magnus' true heart lay! You rush to level blows
where he would pray to be beaten. Let him watch
my own head fall, if you want him to pay
a penalty worse than death. I am hardly free
from blame for these wars. Alone of all the matrons
I was his partner at sea and in camp. No fear
of doom, when he was beaten, would deter me.
Though even kings were scared, I took him back.
Husband, do I deserve this? Left safe in a ship?   800
Faithless man! You spare me, while for yourself
you seek out the end? I don't deserve to live.
I'll die, and not in a spectacle for the king.
Sailors, let me leap headlong overboard!
Or twist the cables in a noose around my neck!
Or some worthy friend of Magnus use his sword!
Do it for Pompey, blame it on Caesar's armies.
Don't hold me back! I want to die, you savages!
You're still alive, O husband! Cornelia has already
lost her rights. Magnus! They're stopping me   810
from gaining death, saving me for the victor!"

    These were her words as she fell into the arms
of those around her, trembling as their ship
sped away in flight.
                    But when the steel struck
his back and cracked against his chest, Magnus
maintained a splendid dignity and holy figure,
his face cursing the gods, his mortal end
changing nothing in the man's appearance
or behavior—so they acknowledge who saw
his severed head. For savage Septimius finds   820
within his wicked act a deed yet more wicked.

Cutting back the toga to reveal the holy face
of Magnus—half-alive, his mouth still breathing—
he falls upon his head and, as it languishes,
he sticks it in a crossbeam of the boat.
He hacks at nerves, muscles, and tendons, taking
a long time to break the knotted bones (rolling
heads off a sword had yet to become an art).
But after his head was cut off and his trunk
had fallen away, Achillas the Egyptian seized it   830
as his own, showing it off in his right hand.
You worthless Roman soldier, of a second class,
your dreadful sword chops off the sacred head
of Pompey, but you yourself don't carry it?
What a disgraceful fate! So that a shameless boy
could identify Magnus, his matted hair that kings
revered and the locks that graced his noble brow
are gripped in a fist, and on a Pharian spear
the head is stuck—with its face still living, its soul
gasping, rattling in the mouth, its eyes empty   840
and stiffening—which when it called for war
there was never peace, which set the laws,
the Campus, and the Rostra into motion,
the face that had pleased you, Fortune of Rome.
It wasn't enough for that awful tyrant to see it,
he wants some proof of the crime, so they drain
the head of decay by their forbidden art,
take out the brain and desiccate the skin,
wash out rotting fluid from deep inside,
and firmly set the face with drugs infused.   850

    Last in the line of Lagus, worthless offspring
about to die and give up the scepter to
your incestuous sister, while you preserve
the Macedonian in a hallowed cavern,
and ashes of kings rest in artificial hills,
while the shades of Ptolemies, that shameful series,
are shut up in pyramids and mausoleums
too good for them, tides are battering Pompey,

his headless trunk is tossed back and forth
in swampy waters. Was it too much hassle   860
to keep his corpse intact for his father-in-law?

    Fortune kept the faith and carried Magnus
successfully through to the end of his fate,
pursuing him in death from the heights of power
to make him pay on one lone brutal day
for all the disasters from which she kept him safe
for all those years. Pompey was one who never
saw blessings mixed with sorrows, his happiness
no god disturbed, nor any spared his misery.
Fortune held back, then struck him down at once.   870
Beaten by sands, torn on the rocks, his wounds
drinking the waves, a laughingstock of the ocean,
when nothing of his form is left, one last sign—
the missing head—will tell you it was Magnus.

CORDUS BURIES POMPEY

    But before the victor reached the sands of Pharos,
Fortune granted Pompey a hasty burial, lest
he have a better tomb, or none at all.
Out of fearful hiding Cordus runs down
to the sea; as quaestor he had come with Magnus
under evil omens from the Idalian shore   880
of Cinyras' Cyprus. Under shadows he risks
approach, devotion overcoming his fear,
to search out the body amid the waves, lead it
landward, and haul Magnus up on the beach.
Mournful Cynthia gives too little light
through thick cloud cover, but the torso's color
stands out against the gray sea. He holds his leader
against the clutching grip of riptide hauling
him back out, but when he's beaten by the weight

he watches for a wave and lets the ocean   890
help drive the body in. Once he's seated
on dry sand he falls down over Magnus;
shedding tears on all his wounds he calls out
to gods above, in the darkness of the stars:
"Your dear Pompey, Fortune, does not ask for
a costly burial, a mountain of incense wafting
rich smoke of Eastern odors from his body
to the stars, for pious Romans to carry
on their shoulders their dear parent, while
a funeral march presents his ancient triumphs,   900
a sad song resounds throughout the forums,
the whole army, disarmed in mourning, forms
a circle round the fire. No, give Magnus
a cheap box for a commoner's funeral
to place his mangled body on parched flames,
give the wretched man some logs to burn
and a squalid undertaker to ignite them.
Gods above, may it be enough for you
that Cornelia is not lying here, her hair
flowing over her husband in embraces,   910
insisting that the torch be cast below them—
unhappy wife, still not far from shore
but missing the final service of burial."

     The young man's words. Off in the distance he sees
a small fire, cremating a poor man's body
with no guardian. From there he snatches flames
and, stealing some half-burned logs out from under
the limbs, says, "Whoever you are, so neglected
by your own, unloved, but still a happier shade
than Pompey, please forgive this stranger's hand   920
which violates your grave after it's arranged.
If any awareness survives death, you yourself
would give up your pyre and accept these losses
from your mound, you would feel the shame
of being burned while Pompey's spirits scatter."

He spoke, and filling his tunic's folds with hot embers
dashes back to the mangled body on the beach
before the surf can wash it out again. He digs down
into the sand, then gathers some ragged wreckage
of a keel that lies some way away and, trembling,   930
places it in the shallow trench. No framework
of strong timbers supports that noble corpse at rest.
With no space to slip the flames up underneath,
he simply sets fire to Magnus, and it takes him.
Seated beside the flames, he says, "O mightiest
commander, single majesty of Hesperia's name,
if this burial distresses you more than being
cast off at sea, or having no grave at all,
turn your spirit and powerful soul away
from the rites I offer. Fate's insult   940
makes this right by force. . . .
                            "Lest a sea monster,
beast or birds, or the wrath of savage Caesar
venture anything, take what you can get,
a meager flame, lit by a Roman hand.
If Fortune lets you return to Hesperia,
your sacred ashes won't rest in this place.
Cornelia will receive them from me, Magnus,
and pour them into an urn. But for now,
let me mark the beach with a little stone
to make your gravesite known, so that perhaps   950
if anyone would like to appease your murder
and render you full honors due to the dead,
he'll find your body's ashes and know which strip
of sand, Magnus, to bring your head back to."

He said this, and stirs up the feeble flames
with kindling, till it snaps and tears at Magnus,
dripping slowly down into the supple fire,
nourishing the grave with melting flesh. . . .
But now the light that heralds in the dawn
had overrun the stars—he breaks off the rites   960

in sudden shock and seeks a place to hide
along the shore.
                              What punishment are you afraid of,
in your folly, for this crime that fame
has rumored down the years? His impious father-in-law
will praise the burial of Magnus' bones.
Now go, sure of pardon, acknowledge the gravesite
and demand the head.
                              Duty constrains him
to finish off the service. He grabs the bones,
half-burned and not yet fully free of muscle,
still full of smoldering marrow, puts them out   970
with seawater, heaps them in a pile and hides them
in a patch of ground. Then so that no light breeze
uncover and blow the ashes away, he packs
the sand down with a rock and, lest some sailor
tie his line off there and disturb the grave,
with a charred stick he writes the sacred name:
HERE RESTS MAGNUS.

EULOGIES FOR POMPEY

                              Does it please you, Fortune,
to call *this* the tomb of Pompey? His father-in-law
preferred him to be buried there than be withheld
from earth. Thoughtless hand! Why do you hinder   980
Magnus in a grave and jail his roving spirit?
He rests where the farthest border of earth hangs
over the Ocean's wheeling flood, the Roman name
and empire are the bounds of Magnus' grave—
tear down those stones that are nothing but a crime
committed by gods. If the whole of Oeta
is Hercules', and all the peaks of Nysa
are kept free for Bromius, why in Egypt
does Magnus have just a tombstone?

                                    He could possess
all the fields of Lagus, if his name were not   990
attached to a plot of ground. People would always
wonder, Magnus, where your ashes were
and, in dread, would never walk the Nile's sands.
But if you honor a stone with a name so sacred,
add his mighty deeds, preeminent monuments
of his dealings, add the armed rebellion
of wild Lepidus, Alpine wars, and armies
of Sertorius, defeated after the consul
had been recalled, the victory chariot he drove
while just a knight, commerce made secure   1000
for the nations, Cilicians scared from the sea.
Add the barbarians subdued, the nomad tribes
and all the kingdoms that lie in the east and north.
Tell how he always, after wars, returned
to his civilian toga, after driving three
triumphal chariots he was satisfied
and gave up many others for his country.

    What tomb can hold all this? A sorry gravestone stands
empty of honorifics, no long list of annual
magistracies. People were used to reading   1010
above the vaulting ceilings of the gods
and on arches built from enemy spoils
the name of POMPEY, now not far above
the lowliest sand, so low down on the tomb
that passersby can't stand up straight and read it;
if not pointed out, Roman travelers miss it.

    Land of Egypt, guilty of civil-war doom,
it was hardly undeserved when in her verses
the Sibyl of Cumae warned Hesperia's soldier
not to touch Pelusium's mouth of the Nile   1020
and the banks that flood in summer. Savage land!
What can I pray befall you for such a crime?
Let the Nile run backward and keep its waters
in that zone where it rises, let the fields

be barren and in need of winter showers,
let it all vanish down soft Ethiopian sands.
Into Roman temples we have accepted
your Isis and demigod dogs, sistra summoning
lamentations, and the one all your wailing
declares to be mortal, Osiris. Rome, you also   1030
have now given temples to the brutal tyrant,
but Pompey's ashes you haven't asked for yet.
The shade of a general still lies ignored in exile.
If the first years were afraid of the victor's threats,
now rescue at least the bones of your Magnus,
if they haven't been washed away in the waves
and still reside in that hated land.

                         Who fears tombs?
Who will dread to disturb a shade so worthy
of sacred rites? O how I wish Rome commanded
me to commit the deed and wanted to make use   1040
of my toga's folds. O too great a blessing!
If it fell to me to uproot his spirit
and bring it back to Ausonia, if I get
to violate *that* gravesite of our leader.
Perhaps when Rome is longing for the gods
to bring some end to barren furrows, or deathly
south winds, or fiery waves of heat, or rooftops
shaken by earthquakes, then at the advice and bidding
of gods, you will come back to your city, Magnus,
and the highest priest will carry your remains.   1050

   For whoever, touring the Nile, goes to Syene,
which parching Cancer burns, and Thebes, a desert
even when the Pleiades bring their showers,
or any merchant of Eastern wares who heads
for the deep Red Sea basin and Arabia's ports—
which of them will not be turned aside
by your venerable gravestone and your ash
kicked up, perhaps, into the top of the sand,
bidding him to appease your spirit, Magnus,
in preference even to Jove of Casius?

                                 Your fame   1060
won't suffer any harm from that grave. Your shade
would be cheapened if enshrined in temples of gold.
Now it is FORTUNE lying in this mound,
equal to the highest divinity; a rock
battered by Libyan sea is more "AUGUST"
than altars for the victor.

                         Often men refuse
the Tarpeian gods their incense, while revering
a Tuscan lawn that fences a lightning strike.
Someday it will profit that no lofty mass
of marble was hoisted to last into the future.   1070
The small heap of dust will scatter in no time,
the grave will fall, all evidence of your death
will pass away. A happier age will come,
when no one will trust those who point out that stone.
And maybe our descendants will call Egyptians liars—
like Cretans with Zeus—about the tomb of Magnus.

BOOK NINE

Pompey's spirit ascends to the heavenly spheres, sees and laughs
at his headless corpse, then descends and lodges in Cato and Bru-
tus as an avenging spirit (1–19). The routed forces with Cato now
in command sail to Libya (20–52), where Cornelia's ships catch
up with them; the scene flashes back to Cornelia's reaction upon
seeing Pompey's death and her reporting to Sextus of Pompey's
last wishes that they fight on (52–138); then Sextus tells his
brother Gnaeus, who is with Cato, about their father's death
(139–76). At the news he vows in rage to go to Egypt and ravage
the whole land in retaliation, but Cato restrains him (176–99);
weeping and funeral rites are held in absentia for Pompey and the
dead of Pharsalus, and Cato eulogizes Pompey (200–63). The
Cilician king Tarcondimotus intends to desert and Cato tries to
restrain them, but another speech arguing for desertion requires a
more forceful, and this time effective, harangue from Cato about
the cause of liberty (263–364). Cato puts the men to work, to
harden them, then they sail for Libya across the treacherous
Syrtes shoals, with storms and some shipwrecks along the way
(365–430). They make landfall near Lake Triton, and the poet re-
lates myths about its name (430–57). Cato lectures his men on
virtue and sets out to march by land around the Syrtes (458–513),
which occasions a long digression on the land of Libya (514–57).
The troops are overcome by a sandstorm and suffer thirst (558–
638), before coming to the oracle of Ammon, which Labienus
urges Cato to consult, but he declines, there being nothing he
wants to know (638–737). The march goes on, and the men begin
to be attacked and killed by snakes (737–77), which occasions a
long digression on the story of Perseus and Medusa, the mythical
cause of Libya's serpent infestation (777–884). A catalogue of
Libyan serpents and fabulous monsters precedes a series of vivid,

grisly deaths, which take their toll, and the men begin to go mad
(885–1091). But Cato's example of patient virtue gives them
strength (1091–1105), and then the native Psylli, who know how
to repel snakes and heal snakebites, come to their aid (1106–64).
The men make it to Leptis, where they spend the winter (1165–
77). Caesar, following Pompey, visits the ruins of Troy and vows
to rebuild it for Rome's Trojan ancestors (1177–1242). Sailing to
Alexandria, Caesar is met at sea by Pothinus, who welcomes him
with assurances of Ptolemy's allegiance before revealing to him
the head of Pompey (1243–80). Caesar, though secretly pleased
that he is dead, rebukes them sharply for their crime and openly
mourns for Pompey, telling them he must be buried with all hon-
ors (1281–1375).

BOOK NINE

ASCENT OF POMPEY'S SPIRIT

But his spirit did not lie in Pharian embers
nor scanty ash confine such a mighty shade.
It leaped from the pyre, leaving the half-burned limbs
and useless remains, and sought the Thunderer's dome.
Where with its stars the axis joins the black sky—
what spreads out between the earth and lunar orbit—
demigod spirits dwell; innocent in life,
their fiery virtue has made them able to endure
the lowest heaven and has gathered them together
as Soul in the eternal spheres.

                               Not there go those   *10*
laid to rest in gold or entombed with incense.

Once he had taken his fill of true light there
and admired the wandering planets and the pole's fixed stars,
he saw how deep a night covers our day's light
and laughed at the mockery of his headless corpse.
Then over Emathia's plains and bloody Caesar's standards
and the fleets strewn on the sea he flew, an avenger of crimes
he settled down in the righteous breast of Brutus
and took up a place in the mind of unconquered Cato.

CATO REGROUPS IN AFRICA

He, while events still hung in air and doubt remained   20
whom civil wars would make the world's master,
had hated Magnus, too, although he had gone
as comrade-in-arms, caught up by his country's omens
and the Senate's command. But after the slaughter in Thessaly
now with his whole heart he was a Pompeian.
He took his fatherland which lacked a guardian
into his care, warmed the people's trembling limbs;
to cowardly hands he gave back cast-down swords.
Without desiring kingship he waged civil war,
not fearing slavery. Nothing he did in arms   30
was for his own cause. After the death of Magnus
his whole role and mission was for Liberty.

They were scattered up and down the coasts,
and so that Caesar could not speed to victory
rounding them up, he heads for hideouts in Corcyra,
stealing away in a thousand ships the wreckage
of Emathia's downfall. Who would believe
that so many boats full of troops were on the run?
Or that the sea was cramped with routed ships?
Toward Doric Malea first, rounding Taenaros,   40
an open door for shades of the dead, from there
he heads for Cythera and, with Boreas bearing down
Crete eludes their ships, they sail on past
Dicte's shores with waves that yield before them.
Then, when it dared to bar their fleet from harbor,
they assaulted Phycus and laid it waste in plunder
with a savagery it deserved. From here they glide
on calm breezes over the deep to your shore,
Palinurus, for not only on Ausonia's sea
do you have monuments, and quiet harbors   50
of Libya proclaim that the Phrygian pilot
once found them pleasing.

ARRIVAL OF CORNELIA'S SHIPS

　　　　　　　　　　　　　　Far away, out in the depths,
ships with straining sails held their minds in doubt—
was it allies of their troubles that they carried,
or was it enemies? The sheer speed of the victor
makes everything frightful, and he is believed to be
on every boat. But *these* ships brought sorrows
and lamentations, troubles that would move
even stern Cato to tears.

　　　　　　　　　　　　　　For after Cornelia
had pleaded with the sailors and stopped her stepson's　　　　　60
flight in vain—in case his body were cast off
on the shores of Pharos and washed back out to sea—
and flames made known the pyre of unjust burial,
she said, "So I was unworthy, Fortune, to light
my husband's pyre? To lie down over my man
and cover his cold limbs? Or tear and burn my hair?
To gather the limbs of Magnus scattered on the sea?
To flood his every wound with tears and fill
my garment's folds with bones and warm ashes,
take whatever I could from the burned-out pile　　　　　　70
to distribute among the temples of the gods?
Without funeral honors, a grave is burning.
Maybe some Egyptian hand has offered
this service, which is grievous to his shades.
How good that the Crassi's ashes lie unburied!
Pompey has met with a fire that shows a greater
hatred of the gods. Will my troubled lot
always be the same? Will I never be allowed
to give my husband's proper funeral rites?
Will I never weep at an urn that is not empty?　　　　　　80
But what's the use of tombs, or why, my grief,
do you need any ornaments? Don't you carry
Pompey in your heart, you faithless woman?
Isn't his image fixed deep down in your bones?

Let her long for ashes who is also looking
to go on living. . . .
                            "Yet now, far off from here,
shines the spiteful light of a fire. Rising
from the Pharian shore it offers me still
some small part of you, Magnus. . . .
                                     "The flame has subsided,
and vanishing smoke bears Pompey into the sunrise,   90
as hateful winds are straining at my sails.
I don't want to leave the shores of Pelusium—
if one can believe it. To me, no land that gave
Pompey triumphs of conquest is dearer now,
not even his chariot treading the lofty Capitol.
'Magnus the Blessed' has fallen from my heart.
I want the man the Nile holds! It grieves me
not to stay in that guilty land. Its crime
has graced its sands.
                        "Sextus, pursue the perils of war
and rouse your father's standards over the globe!   100
For Pompey left behind these orders for you,
entrusting them to my care: 'When that fatal hour
dooms me to death, take up this civil war, my sons,
and as long as my line survives at all on earth,
don't let the Caesars have any leisure to reign.
Use the glory of my name to stir up kingdoms,
as well as cities whose liberty gives them strength.
These are the causes I leave you, and the allies
and armed forces to fight them. Whichever Pompey
sets out on the waves, he will find fleets.   110
My heir will take these wars to every nation.
Just hold your spirits proud and never conquered,
in memory of your father's rightful power.
Only one man is it proper for you to obey,
if he takes sides for Liberty—and that is Cato.'
    "I've kept my promise, Magnus, and done what you asked.
Your wiles prevailed, you tricked me into living
lest I prove unfaithful, carrying off to death
the words you trusted me with. And now, at last,

I will follow you, husband, through empty Chaos   120
and through Tartarus, if they exist. I don't know
how long before my fated end. But until then,
I'll punish my soul for living on, for watching you die,
Magnus, and not being able to flee into death.
It will be bruised and beaten and perish in sorrows,
it will flow away into tears. I won't resort
to swords or nooses, or plunge headlong through the air.
It's a disgrace if I can't die, after you have,
from grief alone."

                This said, she draped her head
in a funeral veil; determined to suffer the darkness,   130
she hid in the depths of the ship, holding fast
to her bitter grief, taking pleasure in tears,
and, in place of a husband, loving her sorrow.
Neither the sea's surge nor the east wind whining
through the rigging moves her, not even rising shouts
as dangers loom; her prayers are opposite
to those of the nervous sailors. She lies calm,
fixed on death and cheering on the storms.

GNAEUS POMPEY LEARNS OF HIS
FATHER'S DEATH

    The frothing surf of Cyprus first receives their ship.
From there the east wind—which still held the sea   140
but now more temperately—drove them on
to the Libyan front and the camps of Cato.

    Sad, his mind foreboding amid its many fears,
Magnus the younger beheld his father's comrades
and his brother from shore, then rushed headlong
waist-deep into the waves.

                "Tell me, brother,
where is Father? Does the world's highest head

still stand? Or have we fallen? Has Magnus carried
the Roman state off with him to the shades?"

His words, to which his brother said in turn: 150
"How fortunate that chance had cast you up
on other shores and you only hear of the horror.
Brother, my eyes are guilty with the sight of Father.
It wasn't Caesar's arms that slew him. His fall
came at the hands of one unworthy of it.
It was that filthy king who lords over Nile's fields—
relying on the gods who watch over guests and hosts
and on his great benefaction to their dynasty,
he fell victim to the kingdom he had given.
I watched them slashing at our father's chest—   160
with his great soul inside it—and couldn't believe
the tyrant of Pharos could accomplish such a thing.
I thought his father-in-law already must have
reached the Nile's banks. But it wasn't his blood
or the wounds of our aged father that tortured me
as much as seeing the general's face paraded
through the city, stuck high on a pike.
We heard report that they were saving it
for the cruel victor's eyes, and that the tyrant
had asked for proof of the crime. As for his body,   170
I don't know if Pharian dogs and greedy birds
tore it apart, or whether it was consumed
in a stealthy fire that we saw. Whatever
outrage of fate stole his limbs, those crimes
I can forgive the gods. But the part they saved—
that makes me indignant."

                                When Magnus heard this,
he did not pour his grief into groans and tears,
but raged in righteous duty and cried out:

"Rush the ships out off the dry sand, sailors!
The fleet can break through adverse winds with oars.   180
Come with me, captains, for the greatest wages
ever offered in civil war—inter his spirits,

which lie unburied, appease Magnus with the blood
of that unmanly tyrant! Why shouldn't I sink
those Pellaean citadels in the swamps
of Mareotis, haul the body of Alexander
out of its shrine and throw it in there too?
Why not dig Amasis out of his pyramid mound,
the other kings too, send them swimming down
the Nile's torrent? Let all their tombs be punished   190
for the fact that you lie naked, Magnus. I will roll
from her tomb that goddess of the nations, Isis,
to the mob I'll scatter the linen-wrapped Osiris,
and to Magnus' ashes I'll slaughter sacred Apis.
With their gods I'll build a pyre for his head!
I'll punish the land itself, leave the fields
empty of farmers, the Nile will rise for no one,
I'll drive out the people and the gods so you,
Father, will be the only one left in Egypt!"

He had spoken and now in his rage was rushing   200
the fleet down to the waves. But Cato stopped him,
curbing the praiseworthy anger of the youth.
Meanwhile, as news of Magnus' death went up
and down the coastline, cries of grief shook the sky,
mourning unlike anything any age had known,
as nations wept for the death of a mighty man.
But even more, when Cornelia appeared,
worn-out with weeping, her hair streaming down
over her face as she disembarked the ship,
again they keened aloud and beat their breasts.   210
Now that she had reached these friendly shores,
she gathered up the garments and glorious medals
of her poor Magnus, his arms and gold-stamped spoils
that he used to wear, his fine embroidered togas,
the clothes three times beheld by highest Jove,
and offered them up to a funeral fire. To her,
in her misery, these were the ashes of Magnus.
All with a sense of duty followed her example,
and all along the shore pyres rose, offering

fire to the spirits of those who died in Thessaly.   220
It looked like when Apulians ready the fields
for winter grass to grow again, after their pastures
have been grazed down they nourish the earth with fire,
and all at once Garganus and Vultur's plowlands
and the cattle fields of warm Matinus blaze.

CATO EULOGIZES POMPEY

   But still more pleasing to the shades of Magnus,
than all the crowd who dares to reproach the gods
and blame them for Pompey, are the words of Cato,
few though coming from a heart filled with truth.
"A citizen has passed," he said, "who though no match   230
with our great ancestors in knowing the limits of law,
still, he was a benefit to this age, which showed
no reverence for justice. He asserted power
and liberty survived. He kept to private life
when the people were ready to be his slaves.
He was a guide to the Senate, but it still ruled.
He demanded nothing by right of force, but wanted
to be given only what could also be denied him.
His wealth was excessive, but he gave more than he kept.
When he drew his sword he knew how to put it down.   240
He preferred arms to the toga, but loved peace
even when he was armed. It pleased him to take command,
it pleased him to lay down power. His house was pure
and not extravagant, never corrupted by the fortune
of its master. His name is famous and revered
among nations, and has been a great profit to our city.
Real belief in liberty, with the return of Sulla and Marius,
passed away long ago. With Pompey now removed,
even its figment is dead. Shameless kingship at last,
no pretense of sanction, no Senate as a screen!   250
Lucky man! His last day crossed paths with defeat,

and an Egyptian crime offered him the swords
he should have asked for—or maybe you could have learned
to live on during the reign of your father-in-law?
The best lot for men is to know when to die,
but next best is to be forced. As for myself,
if by fate I succumb to another's control,
Fortune, make Juba play the part. I won't beg
to be spared for the enemy. He can save me
after he cuts off my head."

                                    By these words   260
he gave greater honor to the noble shade of the dead
than if the Rostra in Rome had sounded praises
for the commander.

ALLIES AND SOLDIERS THREATEN
TO DESERT

                        Meanwhile the crowd is howling
in discord, tired of war and life in camp
after the death of Magnus. When Tarcondimotus
raised the standards for abandoning Cato
and now was stealing off with his fleet, pursuing him
in his flight down to the shore's very edge,
Cato called him out with words like these:
"Cilician! You have never been brought to peace!   270
Are you going back to plunder on the waves?
Fortune has taken Magnus—so back to sea now
for the pirates, is it?"
                        He looked around
at all the men swarming and in commotion,
and one of them whose plan to flee was clear
accosted the man in charge with words like these:
"Forgive us, Cato, love for Pompey, not civil war,
drew us to take up arms, and we took sides
out of goodwill to him. He has fallen,

whom the world preferred to peace, and so   280
our cause has also perished. Let us go,
to see again the gods of our fathers, our homes
that we deserted, and our own sweet children.
For what end will there be of fighting, if not
Pharsalia or Pompey? We've wasted our lives away.
Let us die in safety, let us in our old age
look forward to the flames that we deserve.
Civil war can hardly bury its leaders!
It's not a barbaric kingdom that awaits us
now that we're beaten, Fortune is not so cruel   290
that a Scythian or Armenian yoke now looms.
I go to become a citizen, under the laws
of one who wears a toga. Whoever was second
while Magnus was alive, he'll be first for me.
The highest honor will go to the holy shades.
Whom loss forces on me, I'll take as master.
But no one else will be my leader, Magnus.
I followed only you in war, and after you—
I will follow Fate. For I've no right to hope
for any luck to hold; the fortune of Caesar   300
possesses everything. His victory has scattered
the swords of Emathia. Assurances are cut off
to us in our plight, and he alone in the world
can choose to offer safety to the conquered.
With Pompey dead, civil war is a crime,
even if it was loyalty while he lived.
If you always follow the laws of your people
and your nation, Cato, let's seek out the standards
behind the Roman consul."
                                    So he declared
and jumped aboard with a mutinous band of youths.   310

CATO REBUKES THE DESERTERS

   It was all over for the Roman Republic
as on that shore the entire mob was raving
in need of slavery, when these words burst forth
from the holy heart of the leader:
                                    "So,
the same prayer kept you young men waging war,
you, too, were fighting on behalf of your masters!
You were Pompeian, not Roman forces. But now,
you aren't toiling toward a kingdom. Now
you live and die for yourselves, not for your leaders.
Now you aren't seeking the world for anybody,   320
now you are free to conquer for yourselves.
You're fleeing war and longing for the yoke
now that your neck is free! You don't know how
to bear life without a king! But now the cause
is worth the hazard for men. Pompey might have
spilled your blood—*now*, for your fatherland,
you pull back your throats and deny your swords,
when liberty is so near? Fortune has left just one
out of three former masters. What a shame!
The royal court of the Nile has done more for law,   330
so has the bow of some Parthian soldier. Go!
Worthless cowards, spurn the gift of Ptolemy
and the force of arms. Who would ever think
your hands are guilty of bloodshed? He'll believe
you easily turned tail, he will believe that you
were first to flee from Emathian Philippi.
Go in safety! You deserve for Caesar
to grant you life, having never been beaten down
in battle or under siege. Wicked slaves!
After your former master has met his fate   340
you're running to his heir. Why not aim at
earning greater things than mere life or pardon?
Abduct the wretched wife of Magnus—a daughter

of Metellus—take Pompey's sons to sea with you,
outdo Ptolemy's gift! My head too—
whoever shows my face to that vile tyrant
will gain no small reward! That band of men
will know by the price on my neck that following
my standards was well worth it. Come on, then!
Reap the bounty on a grander murder.   350
But mere desertion, that's a coward's crime."

His words called all the ships back from mid-sea,
as when the swarms at once are leaving the combs
of wax from which they've hatched, forgetting the hive,
their wings don't interweave or densely mingle
but each flies lazily off on her own, no longer
tasting bitter thyme. But when the sound
of Phrygian bronze rattles its rebuke, they halt
their flight, thunderstruck, and go back to work,
zealously hunting among the scattered flowers   360
for honey that they love; the shepherd thrills
in Hybla's meadow, relieved that his hut's riches
have been preserved. So the voice of Cato
impressed upon the men endurance for just war.

CATO'S FLEET TAKES ON THE SYRTES

He decided to spur them on with constant work
and labors of war, to exercise their minds,
which had not learned to hold their peace. First,
he drives the soldiers to exhaustion on the beach.
Next, they toil against Cyrene's fortified walls.
When they lock him out he takes his vengeance   370
not in anger. Their only punishment for defeat
is to be beaten by Cato. Then he determined
to head for Libyan Juba's realms that shared
a border with the Moors. But Nature blocked the way—

the Syrtes were in between. Intrepid Virtue
dared to hope that she would yield before it.

It may have been that Nature, when she first
was giving shape to the world, left the Syrtes
wavering between land and sea, for it did not
sink down fully so that the waters of the deep   380
could rush in, nor does the land fend off the water;
instead, the region is ruled by uncertain laws
that make it hard to cross, the sea's expanse
is broken up by shoals, the land gives way
to sudden depths, and waves crash up against
many beaches before they die down spent.
So has Nature sadly abandoned this part
of herself and gets nothing useful from it.
Or maybe the Syrtis once had deeper water
and it swam far beneath, but the swift Titan   390
fed its lights on ocean, drawing off the waters
that here lie near to the parching torrid zone.
For now, the sea fights Phoebus in his attempts
to dry it out, but soon, as sun rays over time
wreak their damage, the Syrtis will be earth.
For the water above it is already shallow,
and far and wide the sea is disappearing.

As soon as the weight of the fleet was under way,
driven by oars across the sea, a south wind,
black and heavy with storms, began to howl.   400
Running riot against its own realms, its cyclone
defended the sea that the fleet was attempting,
and it drove the waves far away from the Syrtes
and shattered the sea against invading shores.
When the wind caught canvases straight on a mast
it tore them from the sailors' grip—in vain
the rigging tried to keep the sails from Notus,
their folds swelled out, passing the length of the ship
and flapping beyond the bow. If any with foresight
had tied up all his sails to the upper yards,   410

he, too, was beaten, swept away with tackle stripped.
Some ships had a better lot: thrown to open sea
they reached deeper waters. Others cut their masts
to lighten the ship and weaken the force of the blast
bearing down on them, but the surge more freely
rolled them against the winds and overcame them,
hauling them off and pressing them up against
the resistance of the south wind. These lie stranded
on the shoals, the land jutting out of the deep
batters the ships, subjecting them to an unsure fate: 420
part of the boat is aground, the rest hangs in the waves.
Then the more they are dashed, the more the sea shrinks
and land rises up in their path. Although the south wind
churned the surf, it could not conquer the sand berms
that now rose high off the sea's back, miles away
from any fields, a rampart of dry dirt
that water could not breach. Wretched sailors
stand there out of luck, their keel stuck in land
with no shores in sight.

                So the sea caught some
along the way. But most of the boats followed   430
their rudder's guidance and escaped in safety,
and by assigning duties to those sailors
experienced with this place, they reach unharmed
the stagnant lake of Triton.

                    The story goes
that it is dear to the god whose wind-filled conch
the ocean hears, when it blasts its marble surface
and echoes up and down the shores, and dear
to Pallas, too, who, sprung from her father's head,
first touched land in Libya (since it is closest
to heaven, as proven by its heat), and saw her face   440
in the lake's still waters. She planted her feet
there on the edge and called herself Tritonis
from the waters she loved.

                   Nearby, the silent river
Lethon glides past, which (the story goes)
draws up oblivion from its infernal channels,

and once there was a dragon that never slept,
which guarded the garden of the Hesperides,
which now is poorer with its branches robbed.
(It's spiteful to impair the glory of bygone years
and demand the truth from poets!)

There was a golden wood,   450
where branches were heavy with riches and yellow fruit,
and a maiden chorus protected the shining grove,
and a serpent whose eyes never dimmed in sleep
coiled the trunks, which stooped with gold-red metal.
Alcides stole the prize from the trees and left
the grove without its work, stripped its branches bare,
and took the gleaming apples back to the king of Argos.

CATO MARCHES OVERLAND THROUGH
THE LIBYAN DESERT

So the place diverted them and the Syrtes
ran the fleet aground. They hardly made it past
the Garamantian waters, but with young Pompey   460
taking command they stayed along the coast,
the better part of Libya. But Cato's manly virtue
cannot bear to wait around and dares to drive
the troops—confident in their strength of arms—
against unknown nations, skirt the Syrtes by land.
Winter prompted this too, since the sea was closed,
and those afraid of excessive heat could hope for
rain showers. The way would not be harsh from sun
or bitter cold, and the season should be mild,
both from Libya's climate and the winter.   470

And so before they set out into those barren sands
he spoke to them:

"You who have chosen to follow my standards
as the one safe thing, with unconquered necks

and unto death—train your minds on our great task,
the utmost toils of virtue. We are heading
for barren plains, the world's burned-out wastes,
where Sun is too hot, water rare in the springs,
and dry fields crawl with deadly serpents.
The path to law and order is hard, and so is
the love of our fatherland, now falling to ruin.   480
Come along, right through Libya, attempting
to cross impassable tracts—if you are the sort
who never prays to make it through, the sort
for whom the going is enough. For I don't plan
to mislead anyone or try to seduce the crowd
by hiding the peril. Let those be my comrades
who are drawn by danger itself, those who think—
and prove it to *me*—that it is lovely and truly Roman
to suffer even the most deplorable things.
But any soldier who needs a formal vow of safety   490
and who is smitten with life's sweetness, he can
go to his master by some better road.
I'll be first to walk the sands, my footsteps
will first mark the dust and heaven's heat
will beat down on me. I'll run into the snake
when it's full of venom, and you can determine
what dangers you face by watching my own fate.
Whoever sees me drinking, he, too, can thirst,
or seeking trees for shade, he can feel heat,
or riding on horseback before the foot soldiers,   500
then he may feel weary—if there is any way
to tell whether I'm commander or common soldier.
To virtue, serpents, thirst, the heat of the sand
are sweet. Endurance delights in adversities.
The more integrity costs, the happier it is.
And Libya is the only thing that can put forth
such a swarm of suffering that it will seem right
for men to have fled from battle."
                                    So he kindles
their timid souls with virtue and love of toils,
and strikes out on a desert road, for a journey   510

from which he would not return. His holy name
was to be locked in a humble tomb in Libya,
which had seized the fate of fearless Cato.

THE LAND OF LIBYA (THAT IS, AFRICA)

Libya is the world's third part, if you're willing
to follow all the beliefs of popular opinion.
But if you go by the heavens and the winds,
it is part of Europe. For the Nile's mouths
are the same distance as Scythian Tanaïs
from Gades, where Europe begins and parts
from Libya and their curving shores make room   520
for the ocean. But more of the world goes into
Asia alone—since while the first two together
send forth the western Zephyrs, it alone
touches the left side of Boreas in the north
and the right side of Notus in the south
and possesses Eurus, stretching to the sunrise.
The fertile ground in Libya lies in the west,
but even it has no streams to soften it.
Sometimes north winds blow Arctic showers in,
refreshing its fields while our own skies are clear.   530
The land is not despoiled for the sake of riches,
not smelted for copper or gold, there is no crime
to be had from its clods, it's just pure earth
all the way down. Its people's only wealth
is Mauritanian timber, for which they had no use
but lived content in the shade of the citron's branches.
(Our axes have now reached these foreign groves
as we have hunted to the ends of the world
for foods and tables for our sumptuous banquets.)
But that whole coastline that bounds the fickle Syrtes   540
and lies stretched out under too much daylight,
too near a parching sky, burns up all crops

and withers the vine of Bacchus in its sandy soil
too soft for roots to hold. It lacks the moderation
of climate needed for life, and for that land
Jove has no concern. It's a sluggish world,
with an idle nature and unchanging sands,
that does not feel the passage of the year.
Yet this dormant soil grows sparse grasses,
which the hardy race of Nasamonians gather.   550
They live naked in seaside fields, thriving
on the world's losses, which the barbarous Syrtis
tosses up—they comb the sandy beaches
salvaging wreckage, and so although no ships
reach harbor there, they still know of riches.
So the Nasamonians from shipwrecks
engage in commerce with the entire world.

BRUTAL SANDSTORMS BLAST THE TROOPS

   This is the land that hardy virtue urges
Cato to traverse. There the troops were safe
from winds and had no hurricanes to fear—   560
but on land they suffered watery terrors.
For the Syrtis catches the south wind more violently
against the dry shore than out at sea, and does
more damage to the land, since Libya does not break
its rising force against opposing mountains
or drive it back and scatter it on any cliffs
breaking up its cyclone into flowing breezes.
Nor does it crash against forests and wear itself out
winding round ancient tree trunks.
                                    The whole ground is flat,
so the wind is free to range, whipping all that sand up   570
with Aeolian madness, as it drives with all its violence
twisters of whirling dust but no clouds bringing rain.
Great masses of earth are lifted up and hang,

caught in a whirlwind that never weakens.
The poor Nasamonians watch their kingdom drifting
on the wind, their homes scattered in pieces,
the Garamantians' huts fly away, their roofs
ripped from over their heads. What fire has seized
does not rise any higher, but just as smoke can soar
and blot out the daylight, so does that dust   580
possess the sky.
               At that time too, the wind
with more than its usual violence assaults
the Roman line, no soldier can gain a footing
on anything, he stumbles as even the sand
he's stepping on is snatched away—
                      It could shake
the world and knock every land down to its base,
if Libya could lock the south wind up in caverns
hollowed out of rocky crags, with airtight seams
and mass that did not budge. But since its sands
are loose and easily unsettled, the lower ground   590
stays put by not putting up a fight and letting
the topsoil vanish—
             Helmets and shields and javelins
are torn from the men by a violent blast of air
that, gaining momentum, whirls them aloft
through the emptiness of mighty heaven.
Perhaps in some far-distant land they were
a prodigy, the people there afraid of armor
fallen from heaven, thinking that what was ripped
from the arms of men was sent down by the gods.
Just like those, in fact, that fell while Numa   600
sacrificed, which now are brandished by a band
of picked patrician youths. The south or north wind
stripped our sacred shields from those who owned them.

So with the south wind torturing the world,
the Roman troops hunker down, afraid to be taken.
They cinch up their cloaks, stick their hands in the ground,
and have to struggle just to lie down flat,

hardly able to keep still in the south wind,
which heaped up over them huge mounds of sand
and covered the men with dirt. A soldier can barely   610
lift his limbs, stuck in a big pile of dust.
A great sand dune spread out in front of them
stopping them in their tracks, holding them back
as the earth kept rising. The wind dashed walls
utterly to pieces, hurling down their stones,
flinging them far away, a marvel of misfortune
to those who saw no houses but saw their ruins.

The path is now long lost, all landmarks gone.
They find their way by the stars, but the horizon
of Libya does not display all the stars, for many   620
are hidden by the sloping edge of the earth.
Then as heat disperses the air that the wind
had whirled, and as day burned on, their limbs
drip with sweat, their dry mouths parch with thirst.
Off in the distance a stingy little stream
of water is spotted! A soldier struggled to catch it
from the dust, got some in the round of his helmet,
and stretched it out to his leader. Everyone's throat
was rough with dust, and holding those few mere drops
of flowing liquid, their leader became the object   630
of spiteful envy.
                    "Soldier!" he said, "are you so base
as to think that in this crowd I'm the only one
devoid of virtue? Did I seem so soft, no match
against the first flush of heat? How much more
do you deserve this punishment—to drink
while your own people are thirsty!"
                                   His anger flared
and he knocked the helmet away, making the water
available to all.

THE ORACLE OF AMMON

They came to a sanctuary,

the only one among the nations of Libya,
which uncultured Garamantians maintain.   640
Jupiter there gives oracles, so they say,
but Ammon does not brandish thunderbolts
or look like ours, but instead has twisted horns.
The Libyan nations have not built wealthy temples
in that place, no altars for gift offerings
gleam with oriental gems. Although the people
of Ethiopia, Arabia's blessed nations, and
the Indians have no god but Jupiter Ammon,
still the god is poor, and lives in shrines which
down the ages have not been spoiled by riches,   650
and following ancient custom the spirit protects
his sanctuary from Roman gold. The grove of trees—
the only green in all of Libya—gives clear proof
that gods are in that place. For all the dry dust
between blazing Berenicis and cooler Leptis
doesn't know what tree boughs are. Ammon
has taken all the woods for himself. The trees
arise in that place because of a spring whose water
binds the crumbly earth, tames and joins the sands.

But even here nothing stands against Phoebus   660
when day stands high, balanced at the zenith.
A tree can barely protect its trunk, its shadow
is so short, the sun's rays constrain it to the center.
It has been discovered that this is the place
where the sun's circuit, when it pauses high in summer,
cuts across the middle of the zodiac wheel.
But among the people (whoever you are) cut off
from us by the fire of Libya, shadows fall
to the south, while ours turn toward the north.
For you the Dog's Tail rises slowly, you think   670

the dry Wagon sinks in the deep, and you have
no star at the summit always free from the sea.
Either axle is far away, and the swift flight
of the constellations rushes everything
through mid-heaven instead of at a slant.
Taurus and Scorpio rise at the same angle,
Aries does not donate its time to Libra,
nor does Virgo force Pisces to set slowly.
Chiron matches Gemini, Cancer burns
as long as Capricorn rains, and Leo climbs   680
no higher than the Water Bearer's Urn.

Before the doors stood crowds, sent from the east
to seek the advice of Horned Jove and learn
what changes Fate would bring. But these gave way
to the Latin general, and Cato's comrades
clamor for him to investigate these spirits
spoken of throughout Libya, and pass judgment
concerning its fame, which went back for ages.

The one who pushed him most to probe the future
in the voice of the gods was Labienus, saying,   690
"Luck and Fortune have placed in our path the words
of a great spirit and the counsel of a god.
We can use a guide like that through the Syrtes,
and learn, too, the outcome of these wars.
For to whom should I think the powers above
will grant their secrets and speak what is true
more than to sacred Cato? Surely you have always
steered your life by higher laws and followed god.
And now, look, you are given the liberty
to speak with Jove! Inquire about the fates   700
of Caesar—I should not even speak that name—
and search out our country's future norms of living:
will the people be free, with their rights and laws,
or has civil war come to nothing? Replenish
your sacred heart with his voice. You are a lover

of stern virtue, ask at least what virtue is,
and request a model of upright integrity."

    And he, full of the god that he carried quietly
in his mind, poured forth words from his heart
worthy of a god's inner sanctum:

                                    "What, Labienus,   710
do you want me to ask? Whether I'd prefer
to die free in battle or to look upon tyranny?
Whether it matters one bit if one's life is long?
Can violence ever harm the good? Does Fortune waste
her threats when Virtue stands up to her? Is it enough
to be intent on things that will merit praise,
or does integrity ever increase with success?
We know these things, and Ammon will not plant them
any deeper in us. All of us are joined
to the powers above, and even if this temple   720
falls silent, we can do nothing without god's will.
Spirit does not need words; our maker spoke
once at our birth all we are permitted to know.
Did it choose barren sands, so it could sing
just to the few? Did it sink truth in this dust?
Is there a seat of god besides the earth and sea
and air and sky and virtue? Why do we seek
powers above and beyond these? Jupiter is
everywhere you look, wherever you move.
Let those who doubt and always waver unsure   730
of future events resort to diviners in their need.
It's not oracles but the certainty of death
that makes me certain. The coward and the brave
both must fall. *That* is Jove's word, and it is enough."

    Declaring this, he departs the temple's altars;
its credence preserved, he made no examination
but left Ammon to the people.

THE DESERT MARCH CONTINUES

                    In his hand
he carries his own javelins and marches on foot
before the face of his soldiers, who gasp and wheeze,
showing them how to bear up under labors.   740
He gives no orders nor is carted lying down
across men's shoulders or seated in a wagon.
He himself sleeps least, and is the last to drink
when water is finally found. As the thirsty troops
are forced to fight at the stream, he stands and waits
while the camp followers drink.
                                If true goodness
secures great fame, and if you strip success
from virtue, look upon her naked, all the things
that we praise in our ancestors were Fortune.
Who has ever deserved a great name for conquest,   750
for shedding people's blood? A march through the Syrtes
out to the edge of Libya, this is the triumph
I'd choose to lead, not to climb the Capitol Hill
thrice in Pompey's seat, or break Jugurtha's neck.
Rome, behold the true father of his fatherland,
one most worthy of your altars. To swear by him
would be no shame—and if you ever stand up
and free your necks, now or in time to come,
you will make him a god.

THE SERPENTS OF LIBYA

                        Now the fire deepened,
as they trod the region farthest to the south   760
that the gods have made for mortals. Water
grew more scarce. They found a single spring

out among the dunes, with plenty of water,
but a mob of serpents lived in it, so large
the place could hardly hold them all. Thirsty asps
crowded its banks, while out in the waves *dipsades*
drank their fill. When the general saw the men
were going to die if they abandoned the spring,
he said:
     "The fear of death that holds you back
is empty. Do not worry, soldiers, you can drink   770
these waters safely. The venom of snakes is harmful
when it mixes with blood. Their bite holds the poison
and the threat of doom is in their fangs. But cupfuls
of it will not kill."
       He spoke and drained a drink
of the doubtful poison. In all of Libya's desert
this was the only spring where he demanded
to be first at the water.

THE STORY OF MEDUSA

       Why the air of Libya
abounds in so many plagues and is fruitful of death,
or what secretive Nature has mixed in its harmful soil,
our study and toil to know has been to no avail,   780
besides the story that has spread throughout the world
beguiling it for centuries, in place of the true cause.
At Libya's farthest edges, where burning earth
meets the Ocean heated by the sinking sun,
sprawl the wastelands of Medusa, daughter of Phorcys.
No forest canopy covers them, no sap softens them.
A harsh land, rough with the rocks of those who beheld
the gaze of its mistress, in whose body Nature,
being cruel, first gave birth to nasty pests.
From her throat snakes poured their piercing hisses   790
with trembling tongues, and flowing down her back

like a woman's hair, they lashed Medusa's neck,
which gave her pleasure. The serpents rose up straight
above her brow, and viper venom streamed down
when she combed her locks.
                              Poor Medusa,
these are what she had that everyone was free
to gaze at with impunity. For who ever feared
that monster's face and gaping jaws? Who ever looked
Medusa straight in the eye did she allow to die?
She snatched fates while they wavered, preventing fear.   800
Limbs perished with breath still in them, shades
did not escape but froze deep down in the bones.
The Eumenides' hair would only stir up fury,
Cerberos calmed his hissing when Orpheus sang,
Amphitryon's son saw the Hydra he was beating.
This monster was feared by her own father, Phorcys,
the waters' second power, and her mother, Ceto,
and her sister Gorgons. She could threaten heaven
and sea with uncommon sluggishness and cover
the world with earth. Suddenly birds grew heavy   810
and fell from the sky, beasts clung fast to rocks,
whole tribes of Ethiopians living nearby
were hardened into marble. No animal could endure
the sight of her, and even her own serpents
recoiled to avoid the face of the Gorgon.
She turned Atlas, the Titan who holds up
the Western Pillars, into rocky crags,
and long ago when heaven feared the Giants
rearing up on serpent tails in Phlegra, she
turned them into mountains, and so the Gorgon   820
on the breastplate of Pallas brought an end
to that monstrous war of gods.
                              Here came Perseus,
after his birth from Danae and the shower of gold,
carried on the Parrhasian wings he got from
Arcadia's god (inventor of the kithara
and wrestling oil), swift and sudden he flew,
carrying the Cyllenian saber—a saber

already bloody from another monster,
for it had killed the guardian of the cow
that Jove had loved—and maiden Pallas helped   830
her flying brother, getting from the bargain
the monster's head. She instructed Perseus
to turn round toward the sunrise once he reached
the border of Libya, and to fly backward across
the Gorgon's realms. For his left hand she gave him
a gleaming shield of burnished bronze, in which
she ordered him to watch out for Medusa,
who turns things to stone.

                  The deep sleep that would drag
her down into the eternal rest of death had not
completely overwhelmed her. Much of her hair   840
is awake and watching, snakes stretch out from her locks
and defend her head, while some lie sleeping
down over her face, shadowing her eyes.
Pallas herself guides Perseus' trembling hand,
and as he turns away she aims the shaky saber
that Hermes gave him, breaking the broad neck
that bore all those snakes.

                  What did the Gorgon's face
look like then, with her head cut off and the wound
from that hooked blade? I would imagine her mouth
exhaled a mass of poison, and how much death   850
poured out of her eyes! Not even Pallas could look,
and they would have frozen the averted gaze
of Perseus, if Tritonia had not shaken
that thick hair and covered the face with snakes.
So he grabbed the Gorgon and fled on wings to the sky.

   He was about to change course and cut a shorter path
through the air by plowing straight through the middle
of Europe's cities, but Pallas told him not to harm
those lands and to spare their peoples, For who would not
gaze up in the sky at such a marvelous flight?   860
He bends his wings into the west wind, heading
over Libya, which sows and tends no crops

and lies empty, exposed to stars and Phoebus:
the beaten path of the sun furrows into it,
burning out its soil. Nor does night fall deeper
over the heavens in any land, obstructing
the course of the moon if she forgets the slant
of her wandering and runs straight across
the zodiac signs, instead of fleeing north or south
to avoid the shadow. Although that land is barren   870
and its fields grow nothing good, it draws in
the poison of Medusa's dripping gore,
the dreadful dewdrops of that savage blood
which heat gave strength, cooking it down into
the stinking sand.

             Here the gore first stirred a head
out of the dust and raised up the neck of the asp,
swollen with the sleep it gives. More blood fell there
with a thick drop of poison, and so no serpent
contains more of it. Needing heat, she doesn't pass
into chilly regions and by her own will ranges   880
the sands as far as the Nile. Nevertheless
(when will our greed for profit give us shame?)
Libyan forms of death are sought out here
and we have made a commodity of the asp.

  But the bizarre *haemorrhois* unrolls its scaly coils
and stops its victims' blood from clotting at all.
And the *chersydros* was born, it dwells among
the Syrtes' pools and shoals, and the *chelydros*,
which draws a smoking trail, and the *cenchris*,
which always glides along in a straight line.   890
The many markings on its belly are finer grained
than the flecks of color in Theban serpentine.
The *ammodytes* looks exactly like burned sand,
and the *cerastes* roves with curving spine.
The *scytale* is unique in shedding its skin
even when there's frost; the *dipsas* is hot and dry;
the *amphisbaena* is burdened with two heads,
each trying to turn it. The *natrix* pollutes its waters,

the *iaculus* has wings; the *parias* is content
to furrow a path with its tail, and the *prester*   900
opens wide his ravenous fuming mouth;
the *seps* corrupts the body, even dissolving bones.
And raining hisses that terrify all other pests,
harming without venom, the basilisk
clears out all the rabble far and wide
and reigns over desolate sands.
                              You dragons, too,
who creep along in every land and are regarded
as harmless spirits, gleaming bright as gold,
scorching Africa makes you deadly. High in the air
you mount on wings and hunt entire herds,   910
winding your tails around enormous bulls
you lash them into submission. Not even elephants
are big enough to be safe. You deal death
to everything without resort to venom.

DEATHS BY SNAKEBITE

   Among these hazards Cato and his hardy soldiers
make their arid trek. He watches as many of them
meet sad fates, strangely dying from small wounds.
A standard-bearer named Aulus, a youth of Etruscan blood,
stepped on a *dipsas*, which reared back its head and bit him.
He hardly felt the teeth or any pain—the face   920
of death itself is free of malice, and the bite
does not seem threatening. But suddenly the venom
silently steals in and gnawing fire chews
his marrow and a wasting fever burns
his insides up. Disease consumes the fluid
that surrounds his innards and his tongue begins
to bake on his parched palate. There was no sweat
for his exhausted limbs and the flow of tears
deserted his eyes. Neither the glory of empire

nor the power of Cato in all his severity   930
could stop the fevered man from recklessly tossing
the standards down and madly searching for water
in every field, driven by the poisonous thirst
deep in his heart. He could be thrown in the Don,
or the Rhône or Po, and still would be on fire,
or even drink the Nile flooding over the fields.
Libya adds to his death, the aid of that hot land
diminishing the fame of the lethal *dipsas*.
He grubs for moisture deep in the filthy sand.
Now he goes back to the Syrtes and fills his mouth   940
with its waves, the flowing seawater gives some relief
but does not satisfy. He does not know the nature
of his suffering or that he is dying from venom;
he thinks it is just thirst, and so he goes so far
as to slash open his swollen veins and glut
his mouth with blood.
                      Cato issued orders
for the standards to move out quickly, unwilling
to let any learn that thirst can come to this.
But a sadder death than his was right before their eyes—
a tiny *seps* struck poor Sabellus on the leg.   950
Its curved fangs stuck there till he tore it off by hand
and with his javelin pinned it to the sand.
Just a little serpent, but no other holds
so much bloody death. For the broken skin
around the bite drew back, exposing to view
the pale white of the bones, and as the abscess widened
the wound stripped off his flesh. His limbs are awash
in putrefaction, his calves have melted away,
the back of his knee is laid bare, and all the muscles
of his thighs dissolve, while from his groin   960
a black pus oozes. The membrane holding the belly
burst and his guts spilled out, but not as much
poured on the ground as should have from one body,
since the brutal venom boiled down his limbs
and death constricted it all into potent poison.
The unholy nature of that plague reveals

all there is to man—the ligaments that bind,
the texture of the rib cage, the hollow chest
and everything concealed by the vital organs
is laid bare in death. His shoulders and stout arms   970
melt away, his neck and head flow down,
quicker than snow thaws in the warm south wind
or wax gives way to sun. It's not saying much
that his flesh was dripping, burned by the venom
in his blood. Flame can do this too—
but what pyre ever consumed the bones?
These also disappear, along with the marrow
that goes to rot, leaving no traces of his sudden fate.
Of all the pests on Libya's river Cinyps,
the palm for harmfulness goes to you: the rest   980
may take the soul, only you take the corpse.

    But there! A face of death slinks near, the opposite
of turning to liquid. Nasidius, a Marsian farmer,
was struck by a scorching *prester*. His face turns red
and burns like fire, swelling stretches his skin so tight
that everything is misshapen and he loses form—
and now as the venom's corrupting force spreads over
all his limbs, puffing his whole body out beyond
its human measure, he himself is hidden,
so deeply sunk within his bloated body   990
his breastplate can't contain his swollen chest.
A boiling pot does not pour forth so great
a cloud of soggy steam, nor do sails billow
in a northwest gale with such bulging folds!
Now the shapeless blob of his torso's busted mass
can't hold his tumid joints. The beaks of birds
won't touch him, beasts can't safely feast on him.
They don't dare burn and bury him but—still
not done with its growing—they flee his corpse.

    But Libya's pests have greater spectacles ready: 1000
a harsh *haemorrhois* sank its teeth in Tullus,
a great-hearted youth and admirer of Cato.

And as it will exude over all the planks alike
when Corycian saffron is pressed out, so, too,
his every limb at once lets loose an orange ooze
instead of blood; his tears are blood, each pore
and hole where liquids pass drips copious gore;
his mouth and nostrils overflow, his sweat is red,
his every limb flows as from full open veins.
His whole body is one wound.

But you, poor Laevus,   1010
the blood from the wound of a Nile serpent struck,
held fast, and attacked your heart; no pain made you
confess the bite, but in a sudden fainting darkness
you met your death and descended in a slumber
to your companions' shades.

Death is not *that* quick
to infect the cups in which the conjurers of Saïs
steep their dreadful stalk of speedy toxins that
they pick to falsely look like Sabaean spice sticks.

But look! Far off, a nasty snake on a dead tree trunk
whirled and hurled itself—a *iaculus*, Africa calls it—   1020
right through the head of Paulus; piercing his temples
it then sped off. Venom played no role there:
with the wound he seized his fate. It struck them, too,
how slow the stones fly that a sling wheels off,
how weak is the hiss of air from a Scythian arrow.

What good did it do poor Murrus that he speared
a basilisk clean through? The venom raced through the shaft
and penetrated his hand—in a flash his sword came out
and he hacked it off at once, his whole arm up to the shoulder
fell away, and he stood there safe, just watching   1030
his hand die, a pitiful likeness of his own death.

Who would have thought that a scorpion held doom
or the force of sudden death? But the savage threat
from its knotted, upraised lash bears off the glory,
with heaven as witness, for bringing down Orion.

Who would fear to trample your dens, *salpuga*?
But to you, too, the Stygian sisters have given
power over their threads.
                                    So neither bright day
nor black night gave any quiet rest to the wretches,
who held suspect the very ground they lay on.   1040
For they had no leaves to pile up as beds,
nor straw to thatch into couches, but exposed to fate,
their bodies toss and turn on the earth, attracting
with their heat the pests, cold in the nightly chill—
for a while their venom is harmless, inert, until
they warm up their jaws among the limbs of men.

   Ignorant of both the measure and the method
of their journeys, with heaven as guide, they often
complain, crying out: "O gods, give us back the arms
we abandoned in our miseries! Take us back to Thessaly!"   1050

   "Why are we suffering such slow, lingering fates,
when we vowed to die by the sword? These *dipsades*
are fighting on Caesar's side. These horned *cerastae*
are finishing off the civil wars!"
                                    "I'm happy to go
to the red-hot zone, right to the sky's very axle
branded by the sun's steeds, it's a pleasure
to ascribe my death to celestial causes, to say
I died for heaven!"
                         "Africa, it's not you,
or you, Nature, that I'm protesting. You took
this part of the world that bears so many monsters   1060
away from human tribes and gave it to the serpents.
You condemned its soil to grow no grain and so,
by refusing the farmer, it was your will that men
never encounter these poisons. It's we who've entered
this place of snakes. Exact your punishments, god,
whoever you are who detests our trafficking here
where you've parted the world into a scorching desert
and the shifting Syrtes, and placed between them death.

Our civil war is penetrating your secret hiding places,
our soldiers conspire to learn your realm of mystery   107○
and strike at the bolted gates of the world! Maybe
greater things abound for those who enter there,
where fires gather and unite with hissing waves
and heaven's nature is hidden. . . ."

                    "—But no land lies
beyond this, none we know of from report,
but the sad domains of Juba. Perhaps we should have
explored these serpent lands. There is one comfort
under this sky: at least there is something alive."

   "I don't ask for our country's fields, not Europe
nor Asia, which look on other suns. But Africa—   108○
by what quarter of sky or tract of land
did I leave you? Just lately in Cyrene
it was brisk with winter. On this short march
are we fulfilling—perhaps reversing—the law,
the ordinance of the year? We're heading toward
the opposite poles, released, evicted from the world,
bearing our backs to the blasts of the south wind.
Maybe Rome herself is already beneath my feet!
We ask this consolation for our fate—
let our enemies come, let Caesar pursue us   109○
here where we have fled."

                 So does stern endurance
of suffering disburden them of their protests.
They are forced to tolerate such massive labors
by their leader's peak of virtue, who stands guard
stretched out on the bare sand and every hour
calls Fortune out for challenge. He is the one
who is there, at hand for every fatal event.
Wherever called he flies and offers a vast service,
greater than saving life: strength unto death.
They felt ashamed to cry in pain when he   110○
stood witness as they died. What rightful power
could any pestilence exercise against him?
He conquers accidents in the heart of others

and, by the way he watched as witness, teaches
that great pain and anguish can be nothing.

RELIEF FROM THE DESERT AT LAST:
THE PSYLLI

At last, worn out by such peril, Fortune gave
late and grudging aid to the wretched men.
The only tribe that dwells on earth immune
to the nasty bite of serpents are the Psylli
of Marmarica. Their tongue has force that equals   *1110*
potent herbs, their blood itself is safe and able
to resist all poisons even if a charm should fail.
The nature of the place prescribed that they
should mingle free and clear among the snakes.
It proved to their advantage to make their seat
in the midst of venoms, and they have settled
terms of peace with death.
                                      So greatly do they trust
their blood that whenever a baby drops to the earth
too small, they fear a taint of Venus from outsiders
and test these doubtful children with a deadly asp.   *1120*
Just as the bird of Jove, when warm from the egg
its featherless offspring come, turns them toward
the rising sun. Those able to endure its rays
and withstand the straight sunlight of day are saved
for heaven's use; those that yield to Phoebus
are cast away to die. So, too, a Psyllus has sure proofs
of tribal birth: if any infant did not shudder
at the touch of snakes, or has played with serpents
given to it. Nor does this nation rest content
with its own safety but keeps watch for its guests,   *1130*
and a Psyllus helps the people that he hosts
against these noxious monsters.
                                      One now followed

the Roman standards—once the general has ordered
the tents be raised, first this man would purge the sands
encompassed by their rampart, with charms and words
that set the snakes to flight. A fumigating fire
surrounds the limits of camp.
                                        Here dwarf elder crackles,
exotic galbanum sweats gum resin, the tamarisk
not blessed with foliage and oriental gingerroot
and potent panacea and Thessalian centaurea,   1140
sulfurous peucedanum and Erycinian thapsos
all resound in the flames, larch and southernwood
burn with smoke that serpents find oppressive,
and horns from a kind of deer born far away.

    So by night the men are safe. But if anyone
is plagued by day and dragging out his fate,
then there are marvels from this magical tribe,
as the Psyllus firmly fights the hastening venom.
For first he marks the limb, tracing it with saliva
that contains the toxin, keeps back its infection   1150
in the wound; then off his frothing tongue
many spells roll in an unbroken mumble—
the wound's pace doesn't let him take deep breaths
and the fates allow him but the least bit silence.
Very often the pest, once fixed in the black marrow,
by these charms has been expelled. But if a poison
is slower to respond, if when allured and ordered
to come out it fights back, then he gets right down
over the injury growing pale, and licks it,
drawing out the venom with his mouth,   1160
and stanches it tight with his teeth.
                                        Now in possession
of the death he's extracted from the chilly flesh,
he spits it out. And what kind of snakebite he's beaten
the Psyllus easily knows just from the taste of the venom.

    And so at last the Roman youths, relieved
by this assistance, freely range the wild wastes.

Twice had Phoebe quenched her flames, and twice
reclaimed her light, in watching as she rose and set
Cato roaming the dunes. Now more and more
the dust beneath him starts to harden, Libya   1170
is packed back down to earth, and now far off
scattered boughs of woods rise up, uncultured huts
of gathered thatch appear. What glad delights
it gives those wretches just to see wild lions
stand against them!
                        Just nearby was Leptis,
a quiet station where they finished out the winter
free from fires and storms.

CAESAR, HUNTING POMPEY, VISITS TROY

                                    Caesar, once he was sated
on Emathian carnage and had withdrawn,
threw off the weight of his other concerns
and focused on his son-in-law, whose tracks   1180
he traces in vain, scattered over the land;
then rumor leads the chief down to the surf,
he coasts the Thracian narrows, scans the deep
that was swum for love and the towers of Hero
on that tearful shore, where Nephele's daughter Helle
lost her name to the sea.
                        No thinner flow of water
anywhere severs Asia from Europe—although
the channel may be tight that parts Byzantium
from Chalcedon's oyster beds and brings the Euxine
rushing into Propontis through a tiny mouth.   1190

   In awe of its fame, he seeks Sigeum's beaches
and the waters of the Simoïs, the glorious tomb
of the Greek at Rhoetion, and other shades
that owe so much to poet-seers. Round he goes,

touring the memorable name of burned-out Troy,
hunting for any great vestige of Phoebus' walls.
Barren groves and rotting trunks of trees
now bury the halls of Assaracus. Tired roots
now hold the temples of gods. All Pergamum
is hidden in thorns. Even its ruins have perished.   1200
He looks at Hesione's crags, and a grove
where Anchises made his secret marriage bed;
a cave where a judge once sat, and where a boy
was snatched to heaven; a peak where a Naiad wept,
named Oenone. Not one rock goes nameless.
Not knowing it he crossed a creek bed, winding
in dry dust—it was the Xanthus; without a thought
he walked into some tall grass—a Phrygian local
warned him not to trample Hector's ghost.
Some stones were lying scattered without a trace   1210
of sacred purpose. His tour guide said, "Do you
have no regard for the altars of Zeus Herkeios?"

O sacred mighty work of poet-seers,
you rescue everything from fate and grant
eternal life to mortal peoples. Caesar,
don't be touched by envy of sacred glory.
For if Latin Muses have a right to make a promise,
as long as Smyrna's singer endures in honor,
the future will read you and me: our Pharsalia
will live, not condemned to shadows in any age.   1220

When reverence for antiquity had filled his eyes,
the general heaped up sod, raised hasty altars,
and poured his prayers over fires burning incense,
nor were they in vain:
                    "Gods of the ashes—
whoever you are who inhabit these Phrygian ruins—
and of my Aeneas, who settled your household gods
at Lavinium, and Alba now preserves; whose altars
still shine bright by Phrygian fire—Pallas,
never beheld by any man, concealed deep

within your shrine, a lasting pledge of safety—   1230
the most illustrious grandson in Iulus' line
offers pious incense on your altars, duly
calling upon you in your former home.
Grant me happy outcomes for what remains
and I will restore your peoples. In grateful return
the Ausonidae will pay back walls to Phrygians
and a Roman Pergamum will rise."
                                    So he declared
and made for his fleet, giving full sail to winds
favoring out of the northwest. He was eager
to press the breeze, make up for Iliadic breaks,   1240
and so passes by the power of Asia, leaving
behind Rhodes also, amid the foaming sea.

CAESAR IN EGYPT FACES POMPEY'S HEAD

  The seventh night, with west winds never slackening
on their cables, Egypt's coastline comes into view,
lit by the flames of Pharos. But dawn of day
hid its nocturnal torch before he reached safe waters.
There the shores are full of turmoil—voices
of disorder, from vague murmurs that he hears—
so fearing to trust himself to a dubious kingdom
he keeps his ships from land.
                                    But the king's attendant   1250
bearing his ghastly gifts sails out on mid-sea,
carrying Magnus' head veiled in Pharian linen,
first commending his crimes in his despicable voice:
"Tamer of countries, mightiest of the Romans,
and—since you do not know—quite safe from
your son-in-law, now slain. The king of Pella
spares you labors in war and on the sea;
the only thing you missed of Emathia's armies
he sets before you. Civil war in your absence

has come to an end. Magnus came here seeking   1260
to make good his utter downfall in Thessaly,
and lies low by our sword. By this great pledge
we have bought you, Caesar. Our treaty with you
is sealed with this blood. Accept the kingdom of Pharos
pursued without bloodshed. Accept the lawful right
over the Nile's flood. Accept . . . whatever
you would have given for the throat of Magnus.

     "Trust that we're a worthy client of your camp,
to whom the Fates were willing to grant such license
over your son-in-law. Don't deem this service cheap   1270
just because the murder was easy for us to achieve.
He was a very old friend, he restored the scepter
to a banished father. What more can I say?
You'll find names for such a deed. Or else
consult its fame in the world. If it's a crime,
you will confess you owe still more to us,
since *this* crime you didn't do."
                              So he declared—
then he exposed his secret and held up the head.

     Now the likeness, weak in death, had changed
the bearing of his face that he was known for.   1280
At first sight Caesar did not condemn the gift
or avert his eyes. He lingered on its features
until he could believe it . . . and once he saw
that he could trust the crime and thought it safe
to be a good father-in-law, he let tears flow
(they did not fall unforced) and squeezed out groans
from his happy breast—the only way he could
suppress the manifest pleasures of his mind
was by his tears; demolishing the merit
of the tyrant's monstrous service, he prefers   1290
to mourn for its removal rather than to be
indebted for the head of his son-in-law.

   The man who could trample the Senate's limbs
with stone-cold face, and with dry eyes had viewed
Emathian fields, only for you, Magnus,
he doesn't dare refuse to moan.
                                          This lot of fate
is hardest of them all! Caesar, did you hunt down
this man for illegal warfare, to whom you owed
his due of mourning? Do your shared bonds of kinship
touch you now? Does your daughter now urge your grief,   1300
your grandson, too? Do you think it will help your camp
among the peoples who love the name of Pompey?
Perhaps you're plagued by envy for the tyrant,
you're sad that others captured Magnus, taking
such license against his life, and you lament
you lost war's vindication, that your son-in-law
was snatched from his proud victor's rightful power. . . .
Whatever impulse it was that forced you to weep,
it fell far short of true devotion.
                                          This, no doubt,
was what you had in mind ranging lands and seas—   1310
make sure your son-in-law was nowhere humbled
and died abased? It's good his death was stolen
from your adjudication! What huge crimes
did somber Fortune waive from Roman shame
when she did not endure you, traitor, to pity
Magnus while still alive!
                                          He doesn't dare
to not deceive them with these words, and gains
their trust by feigning grief upon his brow:
"Get these deathly gifts of your king, you lackey,
out of my sight. Your crime has earned you worse   1320
from Caesar than from Pompey. We have lost
civil war's sole prize, granting life to the beaten.
If the tyrant of Pharos did not despise his sister,
I could have paid back what the king has earned
and sent to your brother *your* head, Cleopatra,
in return for a service like this.
                                          "Why did he raise up

these arms in secret, intruding his own weapons
into my efforts? So, was it on Thessaly's fields
that we gave sanction to Pella's blade? Did your realm
ask to act with such free license? I couldn't bear   1330
for Magnus to rule the Roman world with me.
Am I to bear you, Ptolemy? All for nothing
we've embroiled the nations in our civil wars,
if any power is left in the world but Caesar,
if any land has two masters.

                         "I would have turned
my Latin prows clear of your shore, but a concern
for rumor prevented it, lest I seem to fear,
rather than condemn, the bloodlust of Pharos.
Do not for a minute think you've fooled the victor.
The same hospitality was ready for me as well—   1340
the fortune of Thessaly makes it that *my* neck
is not being handled that way. Greater indeed
than any could have feared was the hazard risked
when we took to arms. I was afraid of exile,
my son-in-law's threats, and Rome. But for flight,
the punishment was Ptolemy!

                         "But we'll be lenient
because of his age and we forgive his crime.
Let the tyrant know that for his butchery
he can get nothing more than pardon.

                         "You will bury
the head of such a great leader in a grave,   1350
but not so that your land simply hides its crimes.
Offer incense to a proper burial due him,
appease his head and gather up his ashes
scattered on the beach, give a single urn
for his spirits that have been dispersed.
Let him know that his father-in-law has come;
may his shade hear my pious words of sorrow.
So long as he preferred everything to me,
since he chose to owe his life to Pharos,
his own client, our people have lost a joyful day: 1360
our coming to an accord within this world

has died. No gods have been in favor of my prayers
that I might lay aside my successful arms
and embrace you, ask for your old affections
and your life, Magnus, and be satisfied,
as worthy reward for my labors, to be your equal.
Then, with peace secured, I could have convinced you
to pardon the gods for defeat, and you could convince
Rome to pardon me."

                       Such were his words,
but he found no friend to share in his weeping,   *1370*
nor did the crowd believe that he was mourning.
They hid their groans and concealed their hearts
behind a happy face, brazenly looking upon
that bloody wickedness—what fine liberty!—
while Caesar spoke his sorrowful lament.

BOOK TEN

Caesar warily enters Alexandria, tours the city, and visits the burial crypt of Alexander the Great (1–24), whose life and career of mad world conquests is recalled (25–64). Cleopatra gets into the palace and supplicates Caesar for support against Pothinus and Achillas, finally bribing him with a night of illicit passion (65–132). Cleopatra throws a lavish, luxurious feast for Caesar (132–213), during which Caesar asks Acoreus the Memphite priest to tell him all about Egypt, especially the source of the Nile and its annual flood (214–40). Acoreus discourses about the Nile's secrets, the source of its flooding, where it arises, and the extent of its course (241–412). Pothinus sends word to Achillas urging him to attack Caesar in force, or else their own fates are sealed (413–97). Achillas brings on his army, composed mostly of Roman mercenaries, but missing an opportunity to kill Caesar in the night, they besiege the palace where Caesar is now cooped up and outmanned (498–615). They attack the palace also by ship but Caesar sets fire to their sails, which spreads to the city (616–37), giving Caesar a chance to break out on ship and take the lighthouse island of Pharos (638–47). With control of access to the port, he executes Pothinus by beheading, and Arsinoë, Cleopatra's sister, escapes and takes over the royal armies, putting Achillas to death (648–69). Battle continues, and Caesar is trapped on Pharos and about to be taken, when he looks around for Scaeva, the great fighter who fended off Pompey's army in Epidamnus—and so the poem ends (670–91).

BOOK TEN

BOOK TEN

CAESAR IN THE CITY OF ALEXANDER

As soon as he touched land, hunting Pompey's head,
once Caesar had trod those dreadful sands,
the general's fortune and the fate of criminal Egypt
were at war: would Lagus' kingdom submit
to Roman arms, or would a sword of Memphis
take the head of the victor out of the world
along with that of the vanquished? Your shade, Magnus,
came to his aid, your spirit rescued your father-in-law
from bloodshed, lest the Roman people might
come to love the Nile just less than it loves you.   10

He then came safely into that African city
which had sealed its pledge to follow his standards
with such savage crime. But rumbling in the crowd,
complaints that Roman authorities and rods
were being set up over them, informed him
that discord held their hearts, their minds were split,
and Magnus had not perished for his sake.
Calmly then, and ever masking the fear on his face,
he tours the seats of the gods, the temples of ancient
divinity attesting to Macedon's bygone strength.   20
He is not taken in by anything's charm,
not by gold or the reverent care of gods,
nor by the city's walls—eagerly he descends
into the cave hollowed out for a tomb.

There, Philip of Pella's crazy offspring,
the lucky bandit, lies, carried off by Fate
avenging the world. The limbs of a man, which ought
to have been scattered over the entire world,
were laid in a consecrated crypt. Fortune spared
his spirit, and his empire's fate has lasted   30
right to the end. For if Liberty ever restored
the world to itself, he would have been preserved
as a laughingstock to teach the world
this useless lesson, that so many lands can be
subject to just one man.
                          He left his own confines
and haunts of Macedon deserted, spurning Athens,
which his father had conquered, through Asia's peoples
driven by fates bearing down on him, he stormed
with human slaughter and finished off all nations
with a sword. He muddied unknown streams, mixing   40
Persian blood in Euphrates, Indian blood in Ganges.
A fatal evil on the earth, a bolt of lightning
that struck all peoples alike, an adverse star
unto the nations.
                    He was readying a fleet
to launch out on the ocean's outer sea.
No flame or wave, not barren Libya nor
Ammon in the Syrtes could resist him.
He could have gone to the west by following
the world's curve, he could have rounded both poles
and drunk from the source of the Nile.
                                    His final day   50
overtook him and this was the only end
that Nature could impose on the crazy king.

With the same hateful envy by which he captured the world
he took his supreme power with him and left no heir
to his whole fate, and offered up the cities
to be torn to shreds. But in his own Babylon
he fell and Parthians revered him.
                                What a shame

that eastern peoples feared the long pikes of Macedon
just more than they now fear our legions' spears!
We may rule the north and where the west wind dwells,   60
we may tread the lands beyond the blazing south wind's back,
still we give way in the east to the Arsacidae's master.
Parthia, so unlucky to the Crassi,
was once a settled province of tiny Pella.

THE ADVENT OF CLEOPATRA

  Coming up from the Nile's Pelusian mouth,
the boy king had by now allayed the angers
of his unwarlike people; as a hostage of peace
Caesar was safe inside the Pellaean palace—
when Cleopatra, in a little bireme,
bribed the guard to relax the chains of Pharos   70
and got herself inside the Emathian halls
without Caesar knowing.
                          Egypt's disgrace,
to Latium a lethal Fury, her unchastity damaged
Rome as much as the Spartan's harmful face and figure
battered Argos and knocked down the homes of Ilium,
so much did Cleopatra swell Hesperia's frenzies.
She terrified the Capitol with her sistrum
(can it be?), and with her unwarlike Canopus
sought Roman standards to stage Pharian triumphs
with Caesar as captive. And in the gulf off Leucas   80
there was a dangerous chance that she, a woman—
not even one of our own—would rule the world!

  Such daring spirit she got from that first night
when our own generals lay wrapped up in bed
with Ptolemy's incestuous daughter. Who
will not forgive your raving love for her, Antony,
when fire even consumed the hard heart of Caesar?

In the midst of all the madness and fury,
with Pompeian shades inhabiting the halls
and drenched in blood from Thessaly's massacre,   90
he committed adultery, let Venus join his cares,
confused the arms of war with unlawful couches,
and fathered offspring that were not his wife's.
What shame! Forgetting Magnus, he gave you, Julia,
a brother from a filthy mother, permitting
the partisans he had routed to regroup
in Libya's distant kingdoms while he chose
to give away Pharos, not conquer it for himself. . . .

    Trusting her beauty, Cleopatra came to him,
sad but not in tears, decked out in false grief   100
(which suited her well), her hair disheveled
as though it were torn, and began her speech like this:
"If there is anything, O most mighty Caesar,
in noble birth, I—a most illustrious child
in the line of Lagus and the founder of Pharos—
am exiled, outcast forever from my father's scepter,
unless your right hand raise me up, restore me
to my former fate.
                    "I, a queen,
embrace your feet. You have come to us
as a fair star of support unto our nation.   110
I will not be the first woman to possess
the cities of the Nile. Pharos has learned
to have a queen—sex makes no difference here.
Read my father's final dying words—
he gave me an equal share of royal power
and marriage with my brother. The boy loves me,
his sister, if only he were free. But his affections—
and his swords—are under the sway of Pothinus.
I do not ask for any of my father's power.
Just free our house from the deep shame of its error,   120
remove the deadly arms from his attendant
and order the king to rule! How that servant

struts around, his mind so puffed with pride!
The severed head of Magnus—he's already menacing you
with that (but may the Fates keep this far off).
Dishonor enough, to you and the world, Caesar,
that Pompey was murdered, and Pothinus took the credit!"

She would have tried to tempt the stubborn ears
of Caesar in vain, but looks support her prayers
and, summing up, her figure closes her filthy speech.   130
She reaps a night too wicked to speak of, spent
corrupting her judge with bribes.

AN ALEXANDRIAN FEAST FOR CAESAR

                                    Once her peace
was born with the chief, bought with monstrous gifts,
they consummated their pleasures in such grand affairs
with a feast, and Cleopatra rolled out
in great commotion her own display (not yet
exported into Roman life and times)
of lavish luxuries.
                        The place itself
was like a temple, any age more decadent
could hardly build one like it. Coffered ceilings   140
vaulted their riches, the beams hid thick with gold.
No thin veneer of choicest marbles gleamed
encasing the house's walls: freestanding agate
was put to good effect, and royal porphyry,
and spread throughout the hall to walk upon
is onyx; vast doorposts are wrought of ebony
from Meroë (not cheap wood overlaid with it),
not just for looks but holding up the house.
Ivory decks the entryways, and hand-dyed shells
of Indian tortoise rest upon the doors,   150

their mottled knobs all adorned with emerald.
Jeweled couches flash and furnishings
of yellow jasper. All the coverlets glitter—
most of them long cooked and not just once
in vats of Tyrian dye, absorbing its full force,
some embroidered with radiant plumes of gold,
others on fire with crimson, the threads laced
in the Pharian style together on the loom.

Then there were the servants, a mob in number,
an entire population of attendants helping,   160
some distinct in color and blood, some by age,
some with Libyan hair, still others so blond
that Caesar says in all the fields along the Rhine
he never saw such ruddy locks. Some with dark skin
had heads tortured into shape and wore their hair
pulled far back off the brow. Unlucky boys
were those whom steel had rendered delicate
and soft, their manhood cut off. Standing opposite
were stronger youths whose chins, despite their age,
had yet to darken with the slightest fuzz.   170

Reclining there were kings and a greater power,
Caesar. And with her harmful beauty painted on
excessively, not satisfied to hold her scepter
or with her brother as husband, loaded down
with the Red Sea's spoils, around her neck
and in her tresses Cleopatra wears her riches,
and labors under refinement. Her white breasts
are clearly shining through the Sidonian fabric
(a Nilotic needle loosened the compact threads
of Chinese weave and then relaxed the texture   180
by stretching out the cloth).
                              On snow-white tusks
they set down wheels, hewn from an Atlantic forest,
the likes of which did not meet Caesar's eyes
even when Juba was conquered.
                              What blind desire

for favor, what senseless frenzy of ostentation,
to reveal their own riches to a man engaged
in civil wars, to set on fire the mind
of a guest who comes in arms!
                                    Even supposing
it wasn't that man full ready for wicked war
and hunting for resources in the world's rubble,   190
put ancient leaders in, names from poverty's age,
Fabricius or grave Curius, have him lie down,
bring in that consul, dusty from Etruscan plowing—
he will pray to lead such a triumph for his country!

  They pour out dishes on gold, things that earth and air
and sea and the Nile had given, things that luxury,
raving to show its vanity, hunted the world over
though no hunger demands it. Many birds and beasts
they served were gods of Egypt. Over their hands
crystal pours Nile waters, and gemstone goblets   200
take ample shares of wine, not from the grapes
grown on Lake Mareotis, but famed Falernian,
which Meroë takes untamed and with a few years
of age compels to ferment. They put on crowns
woven with flowering nard along with roses
that never fail, and drench their hair with cinnamon
whose strength had not yet faded in foreign air
nor lost its native land's aroma, and cardamom
picked fresh and carried in from nearby farms.

  Caesar is learning to waste the rich resources   210
pillaged from the world, and feels ashamed
for waging a war with his poor son-in-law,
and prays for causes for war with Pharos' peoples.

CAESAR INQUIRES INTO
THE NILE'S SOURCE

Once their pleasure grew weary, setting a limit
on feasting and Bacchus, Caesar begins to draw out
the night with lengthy conversations, calling on
Acoreus, robed in linen, reclining on his high seat,
in gentle words as these:
                        "My dear old man,
devotee of sacred things—and your age proves
the gods do not neglect you—would you set forth   220
the origins of the Pharian race, the lay of its lands,
its people's customs, the rites and forms of its gods?
Explain the inscriptions on the ancient temples.
Pass down those gods who are willing to be known.
If your ancestors taught their sacred matters
to Plato of Athens, was ever a guest here worthier
to hear them, or more able to grasp the world?
It's true that the rumors of my son-in-law
drew me to the city at Pharos, but your fame
drew me, too. Even in the middle of battles   230
I've always had free time for the powers above,
their regions up in the sky among the stars.
Nor will my year be beaten by the calendar
Eudoxus made, but while such strength of virtue
lives inside my breast, and such a love of truth,
there's nothing I'd rather discover than the causes
of the river's flood, hidden for so many ages,
and its unknown source. Give me a certain hope
of seeing the springs that lie at the head of the Nile,
and I will quit this civil war."
                              So he ended,   240
and holy Acoreus began his reply this way:
"Divine law gives me the right to publish, Caesar,
our great ancestors' secrets, up until this time
unknown to outsiders, those people uninitiated.

Let others think it piety to keep such wonders silent.
I deem, instead, the powers in heaven are pleased
by the effort to go through every sacred matter
and make people know their laws.

        "To those stars
that moderate alone the swift flight of Olympus
and run opposite round the pole, the world's first law   250
gave diverse powers. The sun apportions time,
exchanges day for night, and with its potent rays
keeps the stars on course, blocks them from ranging
outside their station. The moon, with changing cycles,
keeps earth and ocean churning. Cold and ice
and the snowy zone pay heed to Saturn. Mars
holds sway with winds and unpredictable lightning.
Under Jove the sky is mild and never stormy.
But fertile Venus has the seeds of everything
in her possession. Cyllene's son is arbiter   260
of the boundless swell.

        "When that one holds
the part of heaven where the stars of Leo
mix with those of Cancer, when Sirius wields
violent flames and the circle that alternates
with the changing year has settled around
Capricorn and Cancer, to which the Nile's mouths
are subject and kept hidden—once the lord of waters
strikes them with his fire hurled from above,
then the Nile comes out, its source set free,
and the ocean is urged on by the waxing moon   270
to offer aid, and it does not curb its growth until
night recoups the hours it lost to summer days.

 "The ancient belief is false, that the Nile crests
into the fields because of Ethiopian snows.
There's no north wind or Great Bear in those mountains.
As proof, the very color of its sunburned people
and the humid heat of its south winds. Add to this,
that any river which falls headlong from ice melt
begins to swell in spring, when snow first thaws.

But the Nile does not rouse its waves before   280
the Dog Star shines, nor bind its stream in banks
before the Scales judge night and day as equals.
So it does not know the laws of other waters:
it does not swell in winter, since the sun is far
away and so its flow is then free of its duties.
Its order is to temper the cruel, excessive sky,
and so it emerges midsummer in the torrid zone
lest fire ravage the earth. The Nile aids the world,
swelling up to counter Leo's burning jaws
and answering the call for help from his Syene   290
when Cancer is scorching it. Nor does he set free
the fields from his waves until the sun veers
over into autumn and the shadows stretch
out at Meroë. Who can explain the causes?
This is how Mother Nature told the Nile to range;
the world needs it this way.
                                "Ancients were also wrong
to ascribe these waters to the westerly winds,
which blow for a fixed season throughout the day
and long hold power over the air—either by driving
clouds out of the west, crossing the south wind   300
and forcing rainstorms to bear down on the river;
or by beating the shores with an unrelenting tide
and forcing the Nile, which breaks up its waters
so often, to come to a standstill. So its course,
stalled by the obstacle of the sea against it,
roils up over the plains.
                                "Some think the earth
has air vents, a hollow network of vast chasms.
In these depths flows water silently back and forth,
and from the cold Arctic it returns to the equator
when Phoebus assaults Meroë and parched earth there   310
attracts the waters. Both the Ganges and the Po
are drawn through this world unheard; then the Nile
spews forth all the rivers from just one source
and bears them not in one stream back round to sea.

"One story says an abounding Ocean binds
all lands—the Nile breaks out of it by violence,
and on its long trail its salty waters freshen.
Nor do we doubt that Phoebus and the skies
feed on the ocean; this is what the sun grabs up
when it has touched the arms of Cancer, taking   320
more water than the air is able to distribute.
Nights bring it back and pour it in the Nile.

  "But if I have any right to settle this great dispute:
certain waters, Caesar, may break forth many ages
after the world was made, from fissures that crack
open during earthquakes, and no god is involved;
but some, I believe, are part of the very structure
and began with the whole; the creator and maker
of things keeps *these* bound under a definite law.

  "This desire of yours to know the Nile, Roman,   330
was felt by the rulers of Egypt, Persia, Macedon;
no age has not wanted to bestow this knowledge
on the future. But so far its hidden nature is winning.
Greatest of kings, Alexander, looked with envy
on the Nile, which Memphis worships, and sent
picked men to the ends of the Ethiopians' land.
But that flushed-hot zone with its sky ablaze
blocked them; the Nile they saw was heated.
Sesostris went west, toward the world's edges;
his Egyptian chariot drove down necks of kings.   340
Yet he reached your streams, the Rhône and Po,
before he drank the Nile at its source.
Mad Cambyses raved into the east and came
to the long-lived people, ran out of food,
killed his own men for dinner, then came back—
but you, Nile, were still unknown. Nobody
has even dared to make up lying tales
about your source.

                    "Wherever you are seen
you cause more questions, and the glory falls

to no one nation that can call itself happy   350
with the Nile as its own.
                         "I will expose
your rivers, Nile, to the extent that the god
who keeps your waters in hiding has granted
me to know you. At the equator you rise,
daring to raise your banks against blazing Cancer,
and your waters run straight north, toward Boreas
and the middle of Boötes, bending your course
both west and east, now to Arabia's advantage,
now to Libya's sands. The first who see you
(though they, too, have their questions) are the Seres;   360
then into the plains of Ethiopia you bring
your flood from outside, and they do not know
to which of all its lands the world owes you.
Nature has not betrayed your secret head to any,
nor allowed her peoples to see you as a baby,
causing your curves to vanish and preferring
the nations to marvel about your origins
rather than to know them.
                         "By right you rise
in the heart of the tropics, right at midsummer,
surge at a strange sort of wintertime, occasion   370
your own kind of rainy seasons, and are given
freedom to wander through both hemispheres.
One seeks your water's beginnings in the one,
and finds its end in the other.
                         "Your depths divide
and widely surround Meroë, fertile for black farmers,
blessed with its boughs of ebony, which, despite
the tree's large number of leaves, still offer
no relief of shade against the summer heat,
so upright is the line that strikes the Lion there.
Then you track the regions of Phoebus, without   380
suffering loss of waters, traversing many miles
of sterile sands, now gathering all your forces
into a single stream, now wandering scattered
with fragile banks that give you easy passage.

A sluggish bed again calls back your waves
from many channels where Arabia's peoples
are separated from Egypt's crops at Philae,
the gates of the kingdom. Soon you will be cutting
through the deserts where commerce joins our sea
with the Red Sea, gently gliding along.   390
Who would think that you, flowing so softly,
Nile, were going to incite your torrent
to all-out rage and violence?

                                "But when sheer falls
and steep cataracts catch your tumbling streams
and you resent that your waters, never before resisted,
must fight the opposition of any bedrock,
then your froth assaults the stars, your waves
make everything roar with a mountain-rumbling groan
as your stream goes white with foam, its floods unconquered.

     "Next is Abatos, as our old tradition calls it   400
out of reverence; this powerful land is struck
and notices the first upheavals; and the rocks
that they like to call the river's 'veins' because
they give the first clear signs of the new swell's pulse.
Below this, Nature has posted mountains around
the wayward waves, which bar you from Libya, Nile.
Between these, deep in a valley, the water runs
in silence now, returning to its customary ways.
The first to spread out fields for you is Memphis,
where no banks limit your flood of open croplands."   410

     So, as though they had nothing to fear and peace
had been secured, they spun out midnight's passage.

POTHINUS AND ACHILLAS PLOT
AGAINST CAESAR

But Pothinus, his raving mind was already stained
with one sacred murder; now it had no freedom
from criminal impulse. With Magnus eliminated,
he now thinks there's no wickedness off-limits.
Spirits now dwell in his heart; the goddesses
of vengeance give him fury for new horrors.
He deems that his vile hands are also worthy
of that blood which Fortune is getting ready   420
to drench the conquered city fathers in—
punishment for civil war and the Senate's
vindication was almost given to a slave!
Far away, O Fates, drive off this crime,
that *his* neck is cut and Brutus is not there!
A Roman tyrant's punishment would become
a mere Egyptian crime, and the example
that it sets would die.
                        He boldly plots events
the Fates had rendered void: he does not plan
a murder in covert fraud. Instead, he assaults   430
in open warfare a general who had never lost.
His misdeeds gave him the nerve to issue orders
that Caesar's neck be severed—send your father-
in-law to join you, Magnus.
                        He tells his loyal servants
to convey his words straight through to Achillas,
his partner in Pompey's murder. The feeble boy,
unable to fight, had appointed him the head
over all his armies and thus given him a sword—
retaining no right for himself—to wield at once
against all others and himself.
                        He tells him: 440
"Now lie there on soft couches, getting fat
and drowsy. Cleopatra has overrun the house.

Pharos is not just betrayed, it's given away.
Are you alone too lazy to jump into bed
with our mistress? The sister marries her brother
despite the impiety, since she has already married
the Latin chief. She's running back and forth
between her husbands, holding on to Egypt
and buying off Rome. Cleopatra had her drugs
to wear the old man down. You'll trust that boy   450
to your own doom: a single night, just one embrace
of her incestuous breast, if he drinks that passion—
calling it devotion to cloak its loathsomeness—
your head and mine will be hers, his gift, perhaps
for nothing more than a kiss. We have no ally left.
The king is her husband. Caesar is her lover.
And let me tell you, we're the ones responsible
in the eyes of that harsh judge. And Cleopatra,
which of us does she not count as guilty—
of those she has not slept with?

                                    "By our joint deed,   460
by the wickedness we wasted and by the pact
we struck on the blood of Magnus, take a stand!
Provoke some sudden disturbance to stir up war,
then make your attack. Let's snuff out with a death
her nightly marriage torches, butcher our cruel mistress
right in her bed, along with any man she's with.
Don't let our daring exploits be deterred
by the Hesperian leader's fortune, which has raised
and set him on top of the world. A share of glory
is ours as well. Magnus has exalted us.   470
Look to the shore. *There* is the hope for our crime.
Those waves, stained by a consul—what do they
permit us to do? Look at that little heap of dust,
it doesn't even cover all of Pompey's limbs.
And he was the equal of the man you fear.
So what if our blood is not noble? Or if we can't
summon all the riches of nations and kingdoms?
In crime, our fate is huge. And into our hands
Fortune is seducing those men. Behold, another

victim has come, one still more illustrious.   480
Let us mollify the tribes of Hesperia
with a second slaughter. Caesar's throat,
drained of blood, can do me this benefit:
the Roman people will love the perpetrators
of Pompey's murder. Why should such big names
and all the forces of their leader make us shudder?
Apart from them, he is just one soldier.
Tonight will bring the civil wars to an end
and offer funeral gifts to the crowds of dead
by sending down to the shades the single head   490
that still owes a debt to the world.
                               "Go, you warriors,
have at Caesar's throat! Let your Lagus boys
serve their king in this; let Romans serve themselves.
Spare all delay. You'll find him stuffed from feasting,
drunk on wine and ready for Venus. Make bold,
and the gods above will reward you with everything
that any Cato or Brutus has ever prayed for."

   Not slow to yield to criminal persuasion,
Achillas gave the signs for breaking camp,
but not so loud as usual, not giving away   500
his army with the peal of any trumpet.
In haste he snatches up all his instruments
of savage war. A very large part of his throng
came from the common mass of Latin poor,
but such oblivion had seized the minds
inside this soldiery debased and bought
and they had so adapted to foreign customs
that they will march behind a slave as leader
and at an attendant's bidding, when even to obey
a Pharian tyrant was beneath their dignity.   510
There is no loyalty, no sense of duty, in men
who just follow army camps, their muscle for hire.
Their next payday tells them what is right.
They earn a bit of copper and agree to march
for Caesar's throat, but not for their own good.

By all that's right! Where does the miserable fate
of our empire *not* find civil wars? The troops
who snuck out of Thessaly down to the Nile's shore
now madly rage, as is their country's custom.
What more could the house of Lagus have dared to do,   520
if it had taken you in, Magnus? Every right hand
is evidently paying its debt to gods above,
and not one Roman is allowed to be at leisure.
So has it pleased the gods to cut up the body
of Latium; people are not dividing their favor
between a father- and son-in-law: the civil wars
are being incited by an attendant, and playing
the role of a Roman is Achillas. And unless
the Fates ward off their hands from Caesar's blood,
their party will win!

                 Both were there, ripe and ready,   530
and the palace, distracted with feasting, was open
to every insidious plot; they could have drenched
the royal hall in Caesar's gore and thrown his head
slumping onto the table. But they were afraid
to cause a disturbance and panic of war at night,
in case sheer random carnage hand you also,
Ptolemy, over to fate and haul you down.
So great was their trust in steel, they did not rush
the crime, disparaged the easy opportunity
for this, their utmost work. The slaves assumed   540
the loss could be recovered, and let the hour slip
for Caesar to be slaughtered. He is spared
his punishment, will make it to open daylight.
The chief was granted a night, a gift of Pothinus;
Caesar's life was prolonged into the sunrise . . .

THE ALEXANDRIAN WAR BEGINS

The morning star looked out from Casius rock
and sent day into Egypt, even in first sunlight
heating up, when far from the walls a line of troops
is spied, its columns neither loose nor drifting,
but coming on as against a fair and lawful enemy,   550
straight and true the vanguard rushes forward
ready to clash and suffer in combat hand-to-hand.
But Caesar doesn't trust the city's walls
and takes cover behind the palace's bolted gates,
enduring cowardly hiding-places. Nor was he free
under this constraint to move throughout
the king's compound, and had gathered his forces
into one tight corner of the house. Anger
knocks his spirits; so do fears: he's afraid
of their incursion, and angry that he fears.   560

Like a noble beast, cramped in a tiny cage,
roars and rages, biting at the bars until
he breaks his raving teeth,
                          nor would your flames
be any less furious, Mulciber, if your summit
at Etna were blocked off—
                          just lately he had dared,
in Thessaly, beneath the crags of Haemus,
to face without fear all of Hesperia's nobles,
the Senate's battle line with Pompey as commander,
and though his cause prevented his being hopeful,
he promised that hostile fate would fall his way;   570
but now this servile crime has terrified him;
indoors, with household gods, he is overcome
by hurled spears. No Alan or Scythian could have
injured him, no Moor who mocks the foreigner
his arrow has pierced, this man for whom the span
of the entire Roman world is not enough,

who thinks that a kingdom from Tyrian Gades
to India would be small, now like a child
who has never faced battle, or like a woman
inside captured walls, he seeks a house for safety.   580
He puts his hope for life in a locked doorway,
and wanders corridors at random and in doubt,
yet not without the king, whom he takes everywhere,
ready to exact the penalty and atonements
to appease his death, and if no weapons or fire
are at hand, to hurl against your servants
your head, Ptolemy.
                        Like the barbarous woman
of Colchis is thought to have done, when she was afraid
of an avenger from the kingdom for her flight,
with sword held ready at her brother's neck   590
she waited for her father.
                            Yet these dire straits
compel the leader to test his hope for peace,
and a royal servant is sent to rebuke the brutal slaves
in the voice of their absent tyrant, demanding
by whose authority they were inciting war.
But the law and sacred pacts that hold among
the nations of the world did not prevail:
the king's ambassador and emissary for peace
determines just how much must be included
in the tally of your crimes, Egypt, already   600
guilty of so many monstrous deeds. The land
of Thessaly, or Juba's vast domains, or Pontus
and the impious standards of Pharnaces,
or the realm around which cold Hiberus flows,
or barbarian Syrtis—none has dared so many
wicked deeds as it has amused you to do!

   War is pressing on every side; already spears
are falling on the house, shaking its Penates.
No ram is set to rock the doorways with one blow
and batter down the house, nor are any other   610
machines of war or flames entrusted with the work.

Instead, the bands of youths, blind without a plan,
spread out to surround the house's vast precincts;
they never mount an assault with their full force.
The Fates forbid and Fortune guards him like a wall.

They also try by ship to take the palace,
where that luxurious house extends right out
into the midst of waves on a bold retaining wall.
But on every side Caesar is its defender,
hindering some attacks by sword, others by fire,   620
and though besieged he carries on the work—
so steady is his mind—like one laying siege.
He orders torches smeared with sticky pitch
be launched against the sails of each ship.
Nor was the fire slow to burn through ropes
of flax and make the decks all drip with wax,
then all at once the crossbeams for the rowers
and the upper yardarms blazed. And now the fleet
is half burned up and sinks down in the sea;
now the foe must swim, their weapons float.   630

Fire did not take just the ships, but rooftops
near the sea caught fire from the lasting heat
and south winds added their warmth to the disaster—
their gales blast the flame and send it whirling,
racing across the rooftops, the way a comet's torch
will range and trace a furrow across the heavens
though lacking matter and burning only air.

This catastrophe somewhat called off the mobs
from the gated palace, in order to aid the city.
Not wasting the time of this emergency in sleep,   640
in the blind night Caesar leaped on board some ships—
always one to put the rapid pace of wars
to lucky use—and in the stolen moment
he captured Pharos, gateway to open sea.
Once this island had stood out in mid-sea,
in the time of the seer Proteus, but now

it meets up with the Pellan walls. It served
a double use in battle for the general:
he deprived his enemy of outlet and all access
to the sea; and so when Caesar saw the harbor   650
free for reinforcements to enter on the deep,
he put off no longer the punishment and doom
that were due Pothinus. But in his wrath
he does not go as he deserved, by cross, by flame,
or tooth of beasts. Ah, the misdeed! His neck hung,
a poor sword chop—he dies the death of Magnus.

   Then, by ready wiles of her servant Ganymedes,
Arsinoë was secreted through to Caesar's enemies;
and since the king was absent from the camps
and she was a daughter of Lagus, she took over,   660
and finished off Achillas, that dreadful minion
of the tyrant, with a righteous blade of steel.

   So now a second victim is offered to your shades,
Magnus, but Fortune does not think that this suffices.
Banish the notion that this brings to conclusion
your just retribution. The tyrant himself
would not be vengeance enough, nor would all
the royal court of Lagus. Until the fathers' swords
reach Caesar's guts, Magnus will not be avenged.

   But once the author of the frenzy suffered,   670
still the madness did not cease. For back in arms
they go, under the auspices of Ganymedes,
and wage many battles, and Mars is kind to them.
In this pitched contest for Caesar, a single day
could have gone down in glory for the ages.

   On the tiny causeway, with his army cramped,
as he readies to move the fight to open ships,
suddenly all the terror of war surrounds
the Latin chief—on one side crowds of ships
fringe the shores; at rear, infantry taunt him.   680

No path of safety, neither flight nor valor,
scarcely even hope for death with honor.
No routed line or any great heap of carnage
was needed then for Caesar to be conquered,
nor any blood at all.
                Caught by his chance position
he hesitates, unsure if he should fear or pray
for death. . . . He looked back in the crowded throng
for Scaeva, who already had earned titles
of eternal glory on your fields, Epidamnus,
when all alone, with the battlements breached,   690
he blocked the walls being trampled on by Magnus.

Appendix

THE *CIVIL WAR* OF EUMOLPUS

Petronius, *Satyricon* 118–24

Introduction

The *Satyricon*, attributed in some manuscripts to T. Petronius Arbiter, is a fragmentary work of fiction that is often considered among the very first novels in European literature. While much of the work is lost, and the surviving passages are often textually corrupt and lacunose, large sections of what appear to be books 14–16 are extant and give the reader a broad outline of the work's scope. Though conclusive proof is lacking, the author is usually identified with the Petronius described by Tacitus (*Annales* 16. 17–20), a courtier known for his decadent lifestyle and given by the emperor Nero the title of *arbiter elegentiae*, or "judge of taste," a position that seems to have involved the selection of the most debauched luxury items for Nero's increasing self-indulgence. The novel's details seem appropriate for a Neronian dating, and the work's most famous passage, the *Cena Trimalchionis* ("Dinner with Trimalchio"), seems to be the work of one familiar with imperial extravagance. Another clue to the date of the work is the passage translated below, a hexameter poem on the same theme as Lucan's *Civil War*. Eumolpus' *Civil War* echoes, in miniature, the plot of the first three books of Lucan's poem, which according to the *Life of Lucan* had been published separately by the author while he was alive. This strongly suggests that Petronius knew Lucan personally; both authors were close to Nero, and both would be forced to suicide after conspiring against him.

The title *Satyricon* seems to play on the lascivious activities of

317

the protagonists Encolpius, Ascyltus, and Giton, who are continually involved in sexual escapades worthy of the satyrs, the perpetually randy half-goat figures from Greek mythology. But the title also echoes the Latin *satur*, an adjective meaning "stuffed" or "full," and also referring to a mixed medley of hors d'oeuvres; the word would later be applied to the Latin genre of satire, which was similarly a mixture of biting observations on everyday life in various stylistic registers, often in a combination of both poetry and prose (like the contemporaneous *Apocolocyntosis* attributed to Seneca). Thus the *Satyricon* of Petronius is stuffed with satiric portraits of the decadent Roman demimonde, with slaves, freedmen, and the nouveaux riches coming under the author's comic microscope. The novel, narrated by Encolpius, ridicules people but also parodies a wide variety of literature, with generic pastiches of epic, tragedy, folktale, and mime recurring throughout the work. The generic farrago includes many representations of poets at work, with various characters extemporizing poems on often banal topics.

The passage translated in this appendix is of particular interest to the study of Lucan, as Petronius presents a direct poetic response to Lucan's poem on the civil war between Pompey and Caesar. This poem is usually labeled a parody, but attempts to divine Petronius' motivation for including nearly three hundred lines of Latin have proved quite difficult. Some have read the piece as direct criticism of Lucan's style, in particular his decision to exclude the Olympian gods from the poem's action. Reverting back to traditional mythological epic practice common from Homer onward (and also standard in historical epic), Eumolpus' poem includes a council of the gods Dis and Fortuna, followed by a theomachy similar to the one in *Iliad* 20–21, where the gods come to earth and line up on the battlefield. Lucan's exclusion of the gods from his epic seems to have been quite a break from tradition, and some have seen Petronius' response as a critique of Lucan's narrative strategy. But the fact that the *Civil War* in Petronius is uttered by Eumolpus muddies the waters. For Eumolpus (whose Greek name, probably ironically, means something like "good singer") is consistently portrayed in the novel as the worst sort of poetaster, always declaiming his bombastic poems at inappropriate times and to almost universally unappreciative audiences; at *Sat.* 90 he is even pelted with stones for his poetry. In addition to his unwanted versifying, he is also portrayed as a sexually omnivorous lecher. Thus Petronius, filtering his response to Lucan's poem through a character of low repute, seems to invite the reader to contrast and compare the two poems, while at the same time disassociating himself from any critical position. (Hence, also, its value placed alongside Lucan, its parodic intertext.)

The poem itself is rarely praised. The narrator Encolpius, after Eumolpus ends, simply notes that the poet had been prattling on for some time, and quickly the narrative changes direction. Modern critics have found it mediocre, usually criticizing the bombastic tone, the lack of real action, and the occasionally repetitive language. Stylistically, Eumolpus does echo Lucan's predilection for epigrammatic statements, moralizing, and gore, but there are also many resonances with Virgil and Ovid: Eumolpus' Discord has a clear ancestor in Virgil's Allecto in the *Aeneid* and Ovid's personifications of Envy and Hunger in the *Metamorphoses*. Eumolpus' prefatory remarks, naming Homer and Virgil as models, profess his allegiance to traditional epic. He also seems to allude to ancient stylistic debates about epic, frequently using the image of rushing and flooding water to describe proper epic poetry. By the first century AD, the description of poetic styles as ranging from raging muddy torrents (endless, bombastic, boring) to thin, clear rivulets (concise, refined, witty) was standard, and even somewhat trite. Eumolpus, in his attempt to parse his literary affiliations, ends up sounding like a hack. While Lucan's stylistic innovations earned him some censure, as ancient reports suggest, Eumolpus' *Civil War* is evidence of the epic style Lucan's poem assiduously avoids. Petronius' poem, then, offers the reader an opportunity to see a clearer picture of Lucan's achievement.

PETRONIUS, *SATYRICON* 118–24

[118] "Poetry, young men, has deceived many," said Eumolpus. "For once someone has constructed his verse in meter and woven in a more refined meaning with clever phrases, he thinks he has gone straight to Mount Helicon. In the same way, those who are

worn out by their work in the law courts often take refuge in the tranquillity of poetry as if they had reached some lucky harbor, believing that a poem is more easily heaped together than a declamation coated in glittering witticisms. But the nobler spirit does not love such foolishness, and the mind cannot conceive or give birth to offspring unless soaked in a mighty flood of literature. One must take refuge from all cheapness of language, as I call it, and expressions must be adopted that are far removed from plebeian usage, as in Horace's words *I hate the vulgar mob and shut them out.* Furthermore, care must be taken that statements be expressed without protruding from the stylistic register; they should be as rich as the colors woven into a piece of cloth. Homer is an example of this, and the lyric poets, and, among Roman authors, Virgil and the prudent care of Horace. Others, though, either have never seen the path by which poetry is reached or, if they have seen it, they are afraid to tread there. For example, whoever takes on the massive theme of civil war will collapse under the weight unless he is fully versed in literature. For it is not the historical events that are to be related in verse, as historians do this far better; instead, the inspired and unfettered soul should catapult through labyrinthine allusions and divine interventions and mythological twists and turns, so that it appears more like the prophecy of a raving mind than a reliable and accurate statement before witnesses. If you like, here, I've taken a stab at the theme myself, although it hasn't yet received the finishing touches:

[119]

By now the conquering Roman owned the world,
where sea and lands extend, from east to west—
but this was not enough. Plowed by laden vessels,
still the ocean waters are explored;
any cove still hidden far away, or land
that offered yellow gold, became a foe,
and wealth was sought as Fate planned gloomy wars.

Familiar pleasures now no longer pleased,
nor decadence worn out by common use.
Corinthian bronze was praised by troops at sea,   10
the glint of gems sought in the earth now vied
with purple, Numidian marbles, Chinese silks,
and the Arab peoples plundered their own fields.
But more disasters loom as broken peace lies hurt.
The wild beast is sought in woods for gold,
from distant African Hammon they extract
the beast whose tusk is precious for the kill;
the fleet is burdened with a strange new beast,
the hungry tiger, brought to stalk the gilded halls
and drink up human blood to loud applause.   20
Alas! what shame to utter and reveal
the Fates, which now are doomed! Manhood stripped
from boys who've barely reached maturity,
their organs chopped by knife, in Persian style,
and ruined, all for lust; the lapse of time
is tricked, the bloom of flighty youth delayed,
and Nature seeks but cannot find its course.
So now these hustlers find themselves in vogue,
effeminate bodies taking swaying steps,
with hair let down, dressed in exotic gowns—   30
whatever lures a man.

        Look! dug from African soil,
citron-wood tables reflect with polished sheen
the troops of servants and the purple dye,
their dazzling speckled marks worth more than gold.
A mob now swallowed up by wine surrounds
this useless and ignoble plank of wood,
and roving soldiers hunger for the world
and all its plunder, weapons drawn for war.
Gluttony is resourceful. From deep in Sicily's seas
exotic fish are shipped to banquets still alive;   40
oysters shucked from the shores of Lucrine Lake
add value to the meal, as cost alone
revives the appetite. Already the waters of Phasis
are emptied of their birds, and on its quiet shores

lonely breezes blow through now-deserted leaves.
No smaller is the madness now in Rome. Bribed citizens
raise their shouts and change their votes for cash.
The People and the Senate, all for sale,
and influence and favors now come cheap.
The elders, too, their fearless courage lost,   50
exchange authority for showered gifts
and let their very dignity kneel to gold.
Conquered Cato is rejected by the mob;
but he who won now has it even worse,
ashamed to have plundered Cato's leadership.
This sent the nation's laws to shame and ruin,
for not just one man met defeat; instead,
through one, all Rome's power and honor fell.
And so, already lost, Rome found herself
a prize that cost itself, with none to save her.   60
Furthermore, plebeians, too, were drowned
in a double whirlpool, consumed and devoured
by debt and filthy loans with interest. No house is safe,
no man lacks a mortgage, and like a pestilence
will silently infect the vitals, madness makes its way
through their limbs as pains and worries howl.
To the wretched, war is welcome: property lost in vice
can be retrieved with blows. The poor have nothing to lose.
What arts or sense or reason could wake Rome
as she lay mired in filth, heavy with sleep,   70
other than rage and war and lust urged on by steel?

                                  [120]

    Fortune had sent forth the triumvirate;
deadly Enyo, goddess of war, buried all three
beneath a heap of arms. Now Crassus lies
in Parthia, great Pompey on the Libyan shore,
while Julius soaked ungrateful Rome with blood.

As if Earth could not bear all these tombs,
she portioned out their ashes. Such is power's reward.
There is a place carved deep in a sunken gorge,
between great Dicarchis and Parthenope,   80
infused with Stygian waters, where vaporous wind
rolls out its fury in polluted blasts.
The soil here sees none of autumn's color,
no fertile fields here nourish grassy turf,
no soft green shrubs resound in springtime song
with the noisy chatter of squabbling birds—
just an abyss, black pumice, darkened rock,
and gloomy cypress trees exulting over tombs.
In this locale Lord Dis raised up his head,
aglow like a funeral pyre and white like ash,   90
and with these words provoked winged Fortune:

"O Fortune, whose power rules both gods and men,
you tolerate no power that seems secure,
you love the unforeseen, and soon desert
what you possess—can you not see at all
that you are foiled by heaving Rome's collapse,
that trying to raise a structure doomed to fail
cannot be? Young Romans now resent their strength,
and can't maintain the riches they've accrued.
All you see is extravagance far and wide,   100
plunder and wealth raging till it's bankrupt.
They build their homes of gold to reach the stars,
displace the waves with stone, carve inland seas,
rebel against the world by putting it up for sale.
Look! Now they even eye my realm. New trenches yawn
for foolish building schemes; gutted mountains
groan with grottoes; while they find a way
to use their useless stones, infernal ghosts
profess their hopes of reaching heaven. Come then,
Fortune, turn your peaceful face toward war,   110
provoke the Romans, send my realm their dead!
For too long now no blood has wet my lips,
my Tisiphone has not bathed her parching limbs

since the blade of Sulla drank its fill
and the wild earth brought into the light
a bounteous harvest fertilized by blood."

[121]

These were the words he spoke, and as he strove
to join right hands and seal the pact, he cracked
the earth and opened wide a cleft.
The capricious heart of Fortune then poured forth: 120

"O Father, master of Cocytus' secret realm,
if it is right for me to speak the truth
candidly, your wishes will prevail.
For this heart of mine feels no less wrath;
the swift flame of revenge now boils my blood.
I hate the power I conferred on Roman might;
the gifts I gave now rouse my ire. The god
who built their empire now will tear it down.
Indeed, my heart is cheered to torch their pyres
and glut myself on blood. Already, yes! I see   130
corpses strewn again at Philippi,
Thessalian pyres, the Iberian race entombed—
already crashing arms ring in my keen ears—
Libya, too, I see, and you, O river Nile,
your groaning barricades, and those who flee
Apollo's army in the Actian gulf.
Make haste, throw open the doors to your confines,
your thirsty realm, and summon down new souls!
The ferryman's gondola will scarce suffice
to sail the souls of men to the other side;   140
he will need a fleet. And you, O pale Tisiphone,
be satisfied with such colossal ruins
and gnaw on all the freshly opened wounds:
the mangled world is marched down to the Styx."

[122]

Scarcely had she stopped when a rumbling cloud,
shattered by forked lightning, split in flames.
The father of the shades sank back below,
closing up the chasm of the earth
in pale dread of his great brother's might.
At once, ill omens sent down by the gods   *150*
presaged impending doom and loss of life.
For now, the Titan Sun, turning bloodred,
hid himself in darkness out of shame.
You'd think that he already had in view
lines of citizens at war. Elsewhere Cynthia
extinguished her full moon, and so refused
to illuminate such wickedness. Now broken crags
rumbled down from falling mountaintops;
dying rivers refused to wander in their banks.
The sky is enraged with the sound of crashing arms,   *160*
a blaring trumpet up amid the stars
stirs up the god of war. Mount Etna is engulfed
with freakish flames, and sends its blasts on high.
And look! Among the graves and bones not laid to rest
ghosts appear with threats and dire shrieks.
A shooting star portends the fires to come,
and Jupiter dumps a fresh rainstorm of blood.
What these omens meant the gods soon showed.
For Caesar now rejected all delays
and, driven by his passion for revenge,   *170*
abandoned Gaul to start a civil war.

In the Alps that touch the sky there is a place
where once a Greek god broke crags to form a pass,
with holy altars built for Hercules.
Packed snow and wintry storms still block the way
and raise the whitened peak up to the stars.
You'd think the sky itself dropped down from there;
it knew no taming rays of the warming sun,

no spring breeze—just frozen ice stiff with cold and frost;
its overhanging ridge could shoulder the globe.   180
When Caesar trampled over these heights with cheering troops
and spied this spot, down from the mountain's peak
he gazed out far and wide on Hesperian plains,
stretched his hands up to the stars, and spoke aloud:

"Jupiter Almighty, and you, O Saturn's land,
once happily laden with my triumphant gains,
I swear I summon Mars against my will,
to battle lines I bring unwilling hands. No—
I'm forced to strike back, insulted by my city;
all the while I stain the Rhine with blood,   190
driving Gauls away from our Capitol
as they seek to cross the Alps again.
By winning am I destined for exile?
With sixty wins and so much German blood
I've become a threat. But who are they
who only watch the fights and fear my fame?
Day laborers, hired cheap—my Rome's not their kin.
But I think (and it's no idle threat)
no coward will tie these hands and escape my wrath.
March on in rage, men, my victorious troops,   200
march on, and plead your case by sword.
We have all been summoned on one charge;
a single verdict hangs above us all.
Thanks must now be rendered to you all.
I have not won alone; and so, since penalties
threaten our prize, our victories earning disgrace,
let fall the die with Fortune as our judge!
Begin the war, and try your strength of hand.
I've pled my case by now; it is complete.
Armed amid such men, I cannot lose."   210

His voice echoed. Down from the sky
a Delphic bird (good omen) beat the air,
and on the left from some old holy grove
strange voices cried out, followed by a flame.

The face of Phoebus, brighter than before,
glowed and flashed, an orb all ringed in gold.

[123]

Emboldened by omens, Caesar stirred his martial flags,
moved first to seize upon his bold new task.
At first the snow and frost refused to fight,
the ground was neutral in its sluggish chill.
But after squadrons broke through tightened clouds
and quaking horses cracked the icy bonds,
the snows relented. New rivulets soon flowing
down high mountains—these, too, as if so bid—
stood still, in awe, their torrents now in check,
a danger once, now knots ready to be cut.
Then what before had barely been secure
now fooled their steps and tripped their marching feet.
Troops of men, together with their gear,
fell sprawling, massed in cursing tangled heaps.
Now, too, harsh gales cracked the clouds,
which dumped their burden; winds broke in swirls
and bulging hailstones cracked the sky to pieces.
The clouds themselves fell crashing on the troops,
a frozen sea of ice rolling down in waves.
The earth and sky and stars were conquered by snow;
conquered, too, the rivers in their banks.
Caesar, though—not yet: with his great spear
and steady steps he broke the harsh terrain,
like the very son of Amphitryon
marching down the steep peak of Caucasus;
or like Jupiter's stern gaze, when once
down from the heights of Mount Olympus
he smote and hurled the dying Giants' darts.

While Caesar's anger flattened the swelling peaks,

220

230

240

meanwhile frightened Rumor took to flight
and winged her way to the lofty Palatine
to strike thunder and fear with omens dire for Rome:
fleets are swarming the sea already, armies
spattered with German blood now melt the Alps;   250
weapons, bloodshed, slaughter, fire, war—
all buzz before the eyes. Now in the chaos
frightened breasts are beaten, torn between two paths:
flight by land seems best to some, to others
the sea seems best, safer than the homeland,
and some decide to stay and test the Fates
by making trial of their force of arms;
each person's fright decides his mode of flight.
Amid the tumult, wretched sight to see,
the citizens are swift to leave their homes,   260
led by broken spirits to desert the town.
Rome herself is happy for the flight,
as crushed citizens, heeding Rumor's call,
leave behind their dwellings in the gloom.
One leads children with a shaking hand,
another cradles household gods close to his chest,
wailing as he bids his doors farewell,
with deadly curses for the coming foe.
Some press their spouses to their mourning hearts,
youths unused to toil lead aging sires;   270
each person's dread decides what he will bring.
A fool drags all he has, takes possessions off to war.
As when the mighty Auster bristles on the deep
and roils and beats the waves, no tackle helps,
no rudder saves the crew; one lashes the planks of pine,
another seeks safe harbor and placid shores,
another sails in flight, trusting all to Fortune.

But why do I complain of minor woes?
Together with both consuls, Pompey fled,
great Magnus—once the very bane of Pontus,   280
who once found the wild river Hydaspes,
who once broke up the pirates like a rock,

who once, with triple triumphs, challenged Jove,
who wore down the waters of the Pontic Sea
and forced the Bosporus to kneel and pray—
for shame! he fled, deserting his power and sway,
as fickle Fortune watched him turn in flight.

[124]

   This mighty plague infected gods as well,
as fear in heaven assented to the flight.
Now look! Throughout the world the gentle mob   290
of gods gives up, deserts the fury on earth;
they turn away from the throng of men condemned.
The goddess Peace first bruises her snow-white arms,
hiding her head in a helmet in defeat,
and leaves the world in flight for the dire realm of Dis.
With her, broken Trust, and Justice, hair unbound,
and Harmony, mourning and tearing at her robes.
But on the other side all hell erupts,
Erebus yawns open, the gangs of Dis emerge:
the savage Erinys, menacing Bellona,   300
Megaera, armed with flaming torches,
Doom, Deceit, the ghastly sight of Death.
Among them Rage, like a horse that snaps its reins,
tosses his bloody brow, and in his gory helm
conceals a face pocked with a thousand wounds.
His left hand holds the heavy shield of Mars,
dented by innumerable darts,
and in his right—a threat to all the earth—
he bears the searing fires of a torch.
Knocked off balance, stars shift their weight,   310
and all the sky's domain rushes to take sides.
First Dione drives her Caesar to his task,
with Pallas and Mars, shaking his huge spear.
Magnus is joined by Phoebus and Diana,

Cyllenian Mercury, and the one so like himself,
Tirynthian Hercules, known for his great deeds.
Trumpets blare and Discord, with torn hair,
lifts her Stygian head to the world above.
On her face dried blood, eyes bruised with tears,
her brazen teeth all scaly and caked with rust,   320
her tongue dripping with gore, face besieged by snakes,
above her throbbing breast and tattered cloak
with quivering hand she shakes a bloody torch.
She left Cocytus' gloom and Tartarus,
climbing the lofty peaks of the Apennines,
where she could scan the earth and every shore,
and all the troops that swarmed over the globe,
and from her furious chest poured out these words:

    "Seize your weapons, nations, with hearts aflame,
seize torches and cast them down on every town.   330
Whoever tries to hide will be subdued;
no woman, or child, or old man weak with age
should yield in the fray. Let the earth shake,
fallen buildings rise up in revolt.
You, Marcellus, you: uphold the law!
You, Curio, you: shake up the plebs!
And you, O Lentulus: do not restrain
bold Mars. And you, too, godlike Caesar,
why delay in arms? Why don't you break the gates?
Why don't you crumble the walls of every town   340
and seize the treasuries? And Magnus, can't you
figure out how to guard Rome's hilltop strongholds?
Seek the safety of Epidamnus' walls,
and stain the Thessalian bays with human blood."
What Discord ordered came to pass on earth.

    When Eumolpus had gushed all this out in a monstrous torrent
of words, at long last we entered Croton . . .

Greek and Latin Names for the Winds

In the translation the winds are normally rendered in English, for example, "north wind" for Boreas or Aquilo in the original, except that occasionally the original name is kept when it seems especially pertinent to the context. In either case, the following list will enable translating back and forth between the Latin name and English cardinal direction. In ancient as in modern usage, a wind blows *from* the named direction: that is, a Zephyr, or west wind, blows eastward, out of the west.

Wind	Direction
Aquilo (L)	N/NE/NNE
Boreas (G)	N
Auster (L)	S
Notus (G)	S
Zephyr (G)	W
Eurus (G)	E/SE
Corus (L)	NW
Circius (G)	NW
Iapyx (G)	WNW, favoring passage to Greece from Iapygia in southeast Italy
Etesiae (G)	Seasonal northwesterlies in the eastern Mediterranean

Notes

In addition to explaining historical and mythological references, the notes also indicate some of the more prominent allusions to earlier texts in the Greek and Roman literary tradition. Such "intertextuality" is a basic feature of Latin poetic style, and ancient, as well as medieval and early modern, readers could draw on their familiarity with these texts in order to appreciate the densely textured crosscurrents of allusion in the *Bellum Civile*. The notes aim to open up these dimensions of the poem for modern readers.

For many issues regarding the war, especially chronology and dating of events, we have often relied on the authority of M. Gelzer's *Caesar: Politician and Statesman* (Harvard, 1968), for its clarity and excellent annotation, and because he consistently gives both pre-Julian dates and their reformed Julian equivalents, which is important for assessing and making sense of the many places where Lucan uses the seasons and constellations to date events. Line references to Lucan are to those of the translation; references within the same book do not include the book number. Authors and works are cited following standard conventions, with occasional variations to facilitate retrieval by readers less familiar with classical texts and scholarship. The occasional reference to scholarly works, unless cited fully in the note, is listed by author and date and will be found in the Suggestions for Further Reading.

BOOK ONE

1–8. *Of civil wars and worse . . .* : Lucan's conventional epic proem is, as in both the *Iliad* and *Aeneid*, seven lines long. Line 1 mixes verbal echoes of Virgil, *Geo.* 1.492, and Ovid, *Met.* 12.58 (and *Met.* 5.313–20). The wars are literally "more than civil," meaning (1) Pompey and Caesar are related by marriage, so their war is a family feud, between son-in-law (*gener*) and father-in-law (*socer*); (2) the civil wars will embroil nearly all Rome's foreign allies and subject peoples, making it a world war as well (see the summary, influenced by Lucan, in Florus, *Epit.* 4.2.1–6, "the rage of Caesar and Pompey swept up the city, Italy, tribes, nations, and finally the whole extent of the empire like a flood or fire, so that it is right to call it not just a civil war nor a social war nor external war but something common to all these *and more*"); (3) for Lucan it is also a cosmic war, akin to and recapitulating the primeval wars between the Olympian gods and the Titanic Giants (see 37–39).

1. *Emathian fields*: A Homeric name for the region north of Mount Olympus and Pieria in northeastern Greece (*Il.* 14.226), in historic times the heart of Macedon, home of Philip and Alexander the Great. Roman poets (Catullus 64.324, Virgil, *Geo.* 1.492, Ovid, *Met.* 15.824) conflated Emathia with Thessaly to the south, where the Battle of Pharsalus took place, as well as with Philippi, east of Macedonian Pella, where Brutus and Cassius were defeated by Antony and Octavian in 42 BC (see map). Following Virgil, Lucan conflates Pharsalus with Philippi as though the battles occurred in the same place, and subsumes this fanciful and geographically inaccurate poetic doubling under the name of Emathia. The mantic matron at 719–41 will make this doubling explicit. Administrative geography contributed to this poetic convention, since the Roman province of Macedonia included Thessaly. The mythical and historical resonances of geography are important throughout the poem.

2. *crime made law*: On one level, a reference to the criminal nature of civil war; also likely refers to (from the Republican perspective) the unconstitutional and revolutionary character of the Principate regime (see 5.410–29). Civil-war poets had spoken of right and wrong being confounded, but not quite of wrong becoming right (cf. Virgil, *Geo.* 1.504–5, Catullus 64.405).

4. *broken pact of rule*: The "First Triumvirate," an alliance of convenience formed in 60 BC by Caesar, Pompey, and Crassus, which fell apart when Julia, Caesar's daughter who was married to Pompey, died in 54 (see 122–31), and Crassus died in battle at Carrhae in 53 BC (see 13, 106–18).

7–8. *standards . . . partisan eagles . . . spears*: Characteristically Roman military equipment ("spear" is the Roman *pilum* or javelin), emphasizing not just the clash of arms but of Roman arms against themselves. A scholiast to Lucan quotes a line of Ennius' *Annales* that Lucan reworks here. More literally, the eagles of the military standards are "equals, well matched" (*pares*), a term regularly used of a matched pair in a fight, especially gladiators (the same term is used at 142, "the rivals were no equals"). But "partisan" succinctly captures the factionalism of the struggle, preserving the *par-* element, which Lucan uses extensively, and "party, partisan" (*partes*) is similar.

9–35. *What fury . . . :* As in Virgil, *Aen.* 1.8, Lucan seeks the causes of the civil wars he will narrate. Fury or madness (*furor*) is, especially in poetry, divine madness; a close synonym is *ira*, "frenzy, rage," both Latin terms used to evoke the *mênis*, "rage," of Achilles in the *Iliad*. Compare *Aen.* 5.670 and Horace, *Epod.* 7.13, with many echoes of tone, theme, and language.

9.   *iron:* Also translated as "steel," iron is used throughout the poem as metonymy for the sword. It also evoked the Iron Age, fourth and last in the myth of the ages first found in Hesiod, *WD* 106–201; cf. Ovid, *Met.* 1.127–150. In 40 BC, after Philippi, Virgil prophesied an end to the Iron Age and restoration of the Golden Age (*Ecl.* 4.9); Lucan paints the dying Republic with the anarchy, bloodlust, and wickedness that characterized the Iron Age.

11–13. *Crassus' ghost:* When Crassus died in the Battle of Carrhae in 53 BC, the Parthians ("Babylon") took the legionary standards, a grievous insult to Roman pride. Avenging the death of Crassus and the memory of Carrhae continued to be a Roman patriotic slogan well into the Principate.

14.   *no hope for triumph:* A triumphal victory procession had to be voted by the Senate, and could be awarded to a commander only for victory over foreign enemies. Cf. Horace, *Carm.* 1.2.21–22.

15–25. *how much of earth:* Lucan evokes the idea of Roman world domination, Virgil's "empire without end" (*Aen.* 1.279), but civil war has weakened the state's full potential for power (cf. Horace, *Carm.* 3.6.1–20, for the same theme). The Chinese (*Seres*) were known only through long-distance trade (the main import was silks) and by vague rumors. The Araxes is a river in Armenia.

26–35. *now that walls are teetering . . . :* The image of an Italian landscape ravaged by warfare mainly refers to the time of the civil wars and draws on lines in Augustan poets (e.g., Horace, *Carm.* 1.2.23–26, Virgil, *Geo.* 1.505-8); but even in Lucan's own day the landscape of Italy, with its hundreds of years of history, would have already displayed, as it does today, the ruins of ravaged and abandoned towns and other traces of large-scale shifts in settlement.

30. *Hesperia*: "The evening land" in Greek, a traditional poetic term for Italy as a whole, which occurs throughout the poem.

32. *Pyrrhus, nor can Hannibal*: Two of Rome's most formidable foreign enemies at the height of the Republic; Hannibal of Carthage, who invaded Italy from the north in the Second Punic War, and King Pyrrhus of Epirus in northwestern Greece, who invaded southern Italy and Sicily in the early third century BC, costing the Romans dearly in war.

36–72. *if the Fates could find*: "The Praise of Nero" (*laus Neronis*). Lucan invokes Nero as the Muse for his poem and dedicates his work to the emperor. It had become standard in the Julio-Claudian period to dedicate poems to the *princeps*. Nevertheless the passage displays some ironies: e.g., the notion that Nero's reign was a worthy exchange for all the horrors of the civil wars from Pharsalus to Actium seems hyperbolic. But the tone of the passage, satiric or sincere, has been much debated. The apotheosis of Nero is foretold here, also standard for epic dedications; Virgil's *Geo.* 1.24–42, which similarly offers the *princeps* his choice of cult locations in the heavens, is a conspicuous source (also Ovid, *Met.* 15.868–70). Cf. also Phoebus' advice to Phaethon (Ovid, *Met.* 2.126–49). Another irony is Lucan's reversal of the Augustan poets' "refusals" (*recusatio*) to write epic (e.g., Propertius 2.1): Lucan will not refuse the commission of a truly Roman epic, civil wars and all.

38. *Thunderer*: Augustus built the temple to Jupiter the Thunderer (Tonans) on the Capitoline, and thereafter the emperors were closely connected with Jupiter, especially as the wielder of the thunderbolt. Caesar will soon be characterized via a simile to thunder and lightning (see 166–72).

39. *Giants*: Both the civil wars between Caesar and Pompey and between Octavian and his rivals were allegorized with the myth of the Gigantomachy, with the Caesars always playing the role of the gods and their rivals the hubristic Giants attempting to overthrow the Olympian regime. This is a prominent motif throughout the poem, though Caesar's Olympian identity will be complicated.

42. *Hannibal's shade*: The ghost of the defeated Carthaginian general would drink in satisfaction the blood of his Roman enemies murdering themselves. It also alludes to the "Punic curse," the idea that the Romans were doomed to eternal enmity with Carthage (incurred in the *Aeneid* by the curses of Dido, 4.622–29).

43–46. *Munda . . . fiery Etna*: List of the major civil-war battles, looking past the poem's narrative down to the ultimate victory of Octavian in 31 BC. At Munda in southern Spain Caesar defeated the sons of

Pompey in 45 BC. The siege of Perusia by Octavian in 41 BC caused bitter famine. Mark Antony besieged Mutina (modern Modena) in 44–43 BC, killing the two consuls Hirtius and Pansa in battle. Leucas is the naval battle of Actium in 31 BC, when Octavian's navy defeated Mark Antony and Cleopatra. The "slave wars" with Sextus Pompey, based in Sicily, were ended with the Battle of Naulochus in 36 BC. This is one of the few places where Lucan refers explicitly to events that occur *after* his narrative time frame. Earlier historical events and persons (e.g., Sulla, Hannibal, Alexander) he refers to freely; those after the assassination of Caesar in 44 BC almost never.

67. *belligerent Janus*: The gates of the temple of Janus, closed when Rome was not at war—Augustus closed them three times—recalls Virgil, *Aen.* 1.292–96.

70–71. *Delphi . . . Nysa*: Apollo, god of Delphi, inspires prophecy and poetry, as does Bacchus (one of whose homes was the mythical Mount Nysa); Nero fashioned himself as a terrestrial Apollo. Lucan summons the emperor to be the sole muse for his poem.

73–87. *I've in mind*: An allusion to the first line of Ovid's *Met.*, Lucan's other great epic model besides Virgil. Ovid begins with creation out of primal Chaos; Lucan dissolves it back into Chaos, describing the universal conflagration (Gr. *ekpyrosis*) theorized in Stoic cosmology, in terms that also recall the disastrous ride of Phaethon in the chariot of his father, the Sun (Ovid, *Met.* 1–328). Lucan's uncle Seneca was much obsessed with what he supposed was an imminent universal destruction, whether by flood, fire, or a combination of natural causes (cf. *Nat. Quaest.* 3.27–30).

90. *did Fortune lend her envy*: The first mention of Fortune, long worshipped as a goddess in Rome. Fortuna became a key idea in Stoic philosophy, and along with Fate or the Fates (Fata) she is the principal divine power in the poem. Fortuna was also the usual Latin translation for the Greek term *tuchê*, "luck, chance," important in the traditional arsenal of explanatory ideas in historiography going back to Herodotus. Fortune's "envy" (*invidia*, also "hatred" or "spite") is aroused against the greatness of the very mortals (whether individuals or cities) whom she raises by her favor: the same principle of "power is impatient of equals" (100) holds between gods and mortals.

92–93. *three masters . . . fatal bonds of tyranny*: the first Triumvirate.

102–105. *a brother's blood*: To boost the population of their new settlement, Romulus and Remus offered "asylum" to outlaws from surrounding areas. When Remus leaped over the city's walls, joking about their small size, Romulus killed him. "This was how

Romulus obtained sole power" (Livy, *AUC* 1.6.3). The story was often used as a cautionary tale about fratricidal (and by extension, civil) strife. Horace says the civil wars are the Fates' punishment of later generations for Remus' murder (*Epod.* 7.20). Ovid has a colorful version at *Fasti* 4.807–56.

118. *Arsacides*: The hereditary name for kings of Parthia, descendants of Arsaces, the first king of the Parthian dynasty.

124. *Julia*: Daughter of Julius Caesar, married to Pompey 59–54 BC, an alliance that cemented the bonds of the Triumvirate. Her death was seen as a major contributing cause of the leaders' falling into conflict, and Pompey made their estrangement explicit by refusing to marry Caesar's grand-niece Octavia and marrying instead Cornelia, the younger Crassus' widow and daughter of Caesar's enemy Quintus Metellus Scipio.

129–30. *Sabine women*: When Romulus' band of asylum seekers needed brides, they invited the nearby Sabine tribe to a festival, then seized and married their daughters. When the Sabine men came to take them back by force, the women stepped between their fathers and new husbands and stopped their fighting (see Livy, *AUC* 1.11–13).

133–35. *former triumphs . . . conquered Gauls*: Pompey's glory rested on his three great triumphs for conquests in Numidia (81 BC), Spain (71 BC), and Asia (62 BC), and on his defeat of the Cilician pirates (67 BC). But by 50 BC Pompey had long been resting on his laurels in the city. Caesar spent nearly ten years successfully campaigning in Gaul (58–50 BC); his triumph for the subjugation of Gaul was delayed until his magnificent quadruple triumphal celebration in 46 BC (which many are said to have resented, since several of his victories had been over fellow Romans).

141. *Cato*: the first mention of Marcus Porcius Cato the Younger, a prominent senator and staunch enemy of Caesar, the third major character of the poem (see note to 2.258).

146. *his theater*: Pompey had built the first permanent stone theater in Rome, dedicated in 55 BC, the year of his second consulship, with magnificent shows (see Plutarch, *Pomp.* 52–53). Until then Romans had resisted a permanent theater, and Pompey got around this resistance by incorporating into it a temple to Venus Victrix. Ironically, the theater complex would be where Caesar was murdered in 44 BC. See also 7.8–52.

148. *his great name's shadow*: A play on Pompey's honorific name Magnus "the Great," examples of which went back to Pompey's own time; the grandeur of his title is belied by his long inaction. By contrast, Caesar, at 158, has "no mere name" or "not (yet) so great

a name": his current achievements already appear more substantive than Pompey's and his star is still rising.

149–72. *Like a mighty oak . . .*: Two well-crafted epic similes compare the heroes with an old and revered oak tree and with lightning, devoting the same number of lines to each. Like Homeric similes, the heroes are characterized through natural phenomena. The image of lightning striking an oak tree occurs in *Iliad* 14.414ff. The custom of devoting spoils of war to sacred oaks is described in *Aen.* 11.5–11 (cf. also *Aen.* 4.441–46).

170. *raging against its precincts*: A difficult wordplay in the Latin that both suggests the belief that Jupiter often struck his own temples with lightning and refers to the Etruscan division of the sky into zones (*templa*) for purposes of divination. The images seem to foreshadow the truncation of Pompey in Egypt and to the damage Caesar will inflict on the state.

174–86. *public seeds of war*: In Neronian authors the sordid details of Roman moral and civic decline had become standard commonplaces, but Lucan's treatment also parallels contemporary civil-war texts, especially (of those that survive) Sallust, *Cat.* 5–14. The civil-war narratives of Livy and Asinius Pollio do not survive, but Livy's *Preface* gives a brief taste: "Of late years wealth has made us greedy, and self-indulgence has brought us, through every form of sensual excess, to be, if I may so put it, in love with death both individual and collective" (trans. of de Selincourt, Penguin, 1960). These general, long-term explanations for discord in Rome can be contrasted with Caesar's own account of immediate and specific causes of strife in *BC* 1.4.

184–85. *Camillus . . . Curius*: Examples of sturdy Roman manhood from the good old days of the Early Republic, both from plebeian families: Marcus Furius Camillus, illustrious Roman of the early fourth century BC, star of book 5 of Livy, triumphed four times, was dictator five times, and undertook the reconstruction of Rome after the Gallic invasion; Manius Curius Dentatus (consul 290 BC) was known for his stern probity and frugality, exemplified in the story about his refusal of bribes from an embassy of Samnites.

197. *Campus Martius*: During the Republic the annual polling for public offices was conducted within an outdoor enclosure on the Field of Mars, outside the gates west of the city, traditionally the place where soldiers trained for war, but already much built up in the 50s BC (including with Pompey's new theater).

200. *Now the cold Alps*: Caesar's infamous illegal entry into Italy under arms, sparking the civil war, calls to mind Hannibal's crossing of

the Alps to invade Italy during the Second Punic War (218 BC). A likely historical source for the drama of this event was the civil-war history of Asinius Pollio, who, as Plutarch relates, was also an eye-witness to it: "when he came to the river . . . he became full of thought . . . his mind wavered as he considered what a tremendous venture he was engaged upon. He began to go more slowly and ordered a halt. For a long time he weighed matters up silently in his own mind, irresolute between the two alternatives. . . . He thought of the sufferings his crossing of the river would bring upon mankind and he imagined the fame of the story of it which they would leave to posterity. Finally, in a sort of passion, as though he were casting calculation aside and abandoning himself to whatever lay in store for him, making use too of the expression frequently used by those on the point of committing themselves to desperate and unpredictable chances, 'Let the die be cast,' and with these words hurried to cross the river" (Plut., *Caes.* 32, trans. of R. Warner, Penguin, 1958).

202. *narrow Rubicon*: This small river in northeast Italy (see map) was the boundary of the province of Cisalpine Gaul (see 233–34); by law a general was not allowed to leave his province and bring his army into Italy. Caesar, conveniently but understandably, neglects to mention this crossing (*BC* 1.7–8).

205. *head crowned with towers*: The iconography of goddesses often included a turreted crown representing a city wall. Alternative versions of the story have a divine power urge on the army to cross the river (Suetonius, *Jul.* 32). Plutarch (*Caes.* 32) relates the tradition that the night before crossing, Caesar dreamed he had committed incest with his mother.

213–16. *Tarpeia's Rock . . . Vestal fires*: The Tarpeian Rock was the southern crest of the Capitoline Hill, where there was a huge temple to Jupiter Optimus Maximus and one to Jupiter Tonans ("Thunderer"), which had been dedicated by Augustus. The Phrygian Penates were the household gods that Aeneas was believed to have rescued from Troy as it fell (cf. *Aen.* 3.148). The Julian family traced their ancestry to Aeneas' son Iulus/Ascanius, as celebrated in the *Aeneid*. Jupiter Latiaris was worshipped in Alba Longa, 35 kilometers south of Rome, an ancient Latin city supposedly founded by Ascanius. Quirinus is the deified Romulus, caught up in a cloud by the gods; he had temples dedicated to his cult in Rome. The eternal Vestal fires were tended in the temple of Vesta by the priestly college of Vestal Virgins; the temple also housed the Phrygian Penates. Caesar's prayer to this host of divinities is an attempt to associate himself with all of Rome's most ancient gods;

Caesar had been Pontifex Maximus, the highest priestly office, since 63 BC, and would have been knowledgeable in the religious formulae for addressing the state gods.

223–30. *Libya a lion*: For similar lion similes cf. *Il.* 20.164–73 (of Achilles) and *Aen.* 12.4–8 (of Turnus).

236. *Cynthia's horn*: Phoebe, the moon; i.e., it had rained for three nights.

245–46. *Fortune . . . Let war decide*: Most accounts of Caesar's words upon crossing the Rubicon have him saying in Greek "the die is cast." Lucan instead invokes his favored terms "Fortune" and "Fate."

248–49. *Balearic . . . Parthian*: The Balearic islanders were famed for their skill with slings; Parthian archers were similarly famed.

250. *Ariminum*: Town just south of the Rubicon (modern Rimini, see map). Caesar makes no mention of how the townspeople reacted to his arrival (*BC* 1.8).

258. *people's rest*: Cf. Virgil, *Aen.* 7.458–62.

273–75. *Senones . . . Teutons*: The Gallic Senones, who established themselves in northern Italy in the fourth century, marched on and sacked Rome in 387–86 BC. The Cimbri and Teutons were Germanic tribes that invaded Italy in 101 BC and were defeated by Gaius Marius. "Libya's Mars" is Hannibal.

286. *The Curia*: "Assembly place," name for the Roman Senate house and, by extension, the Senate itself.

288. *reminders of the Gracchi*: Tiberius and Gaius Gracchus were tribunes of the people assassinated by senatorial opposition in 133 and 121 BC, respectively. They represented the "populist" (*populares*) party and its agenda; ancient and modern historians have usually taken their assassination as a starting point for the following century of Roman civil strife, culminating in the Principate. When Caesar relates the treatment of the tribunes he says not even "the most revolutionary tribunes of earlier times" had been treated so outrageously (*BC* 1.5) and names the Gracchi a bit later (*BC* 1.7).

290. *Curio . . .*: Tribunes of the people Marcus Antonius (Mark Antony) and Quintus Cassius, supporters of Caesar, were expelled from the city by the Senate and fled to Caesar in Ariminum, joined by Gaius Scribonius Curio, tribune the previous year, who had aided Caesar with vetoes and obstruction after Caesar paid him off. Cf. Caesar, *BC* 1.1–7.

293. *turning many cares*: A formulaic phrase in Virgil (*Aen.* 1.305, 5.701–2).

297. *Rostrum*: The platform for public speaking outside the Senate house in the Forum.

310–11. *Capitol . . . sacred laurels*: Triumphal processions ended at the Capitoline Hill, where spoils were deposited in the temple of Jupiter Optimus Maximus.

319–21. *Olympic stallion*: A very common epic simile; cf. Virgil, *Geo.* 1.511–14; *Aen.* 11.492; Homer, *Il.* 6.506–14; Ennius, *Ann.* 85. "Olympic" refers to the quadrennial Olympian Games held in Olympia, Greece.

332. *whole forests fall*: Lucan will consistently associate Caesar with deforestation, which is a sign of hubristic militarism ultimately going back to the myth of the Argonauts and their building of the first ship (cf. 6.445–46). Cf. 3.411ff., where Caesar cuts down a sacred grove near Massilia.

335. *savage tribes of Gauls*: All sources mention the panic and false rumors that spread when Caesar entered Italy (cf. Caesar, *BC* 1.14, Appian, *B Civ.* 2.35). In his flustered letter to Atticus on this occasion, Cicero derides the panic and flight, mentioning Hannibal and the Gauls (*Ep. ad Att.* 7.11.1, 10). The notion that a Gallic invasion will follow Caesar partly motivates Lucan's catalogue of Gallic tribes; cf. also the panicked city at 514–17.

338–40. *peacetime leader . . . Marcellus . . . Catos*: The peacetime leader is Pompey. Cato is Marcus Porcius Cato, strident enemy of Caesar. Three members of the Claudius Marcellus family were consuls in 51, 50, and 49 BC, all opponents of Caesar. G. Claudius Marcellus (consul 50) was married to Caesar's great-niece Octavia. M. Cl. Marcellus (consul 51) was famously pardoned by Caesar after the wars, the circumstances of which are related in an impassioned public speech by Cicero (*pro Marcello*).

343. *before the age*: Pompey was just twenty-five at his first triumph, over Numidia (81 BC), and his age was only one of its improprieties: since to triumph a commander had to have held the office of praetor or consul, one could scarcely hope to triumph before the age of forty. Worse was that Pompey was technically a private citizen, having never been elected to a magistracy, and was thus not even a member of the Senate. His second triumph in 71 BC, still as a private citizen, had the same taint of illegality. Caesar does not mention that the Numidian campaign followed directly on *civil conflicts* against Marian forces in Sicily.

346. *world hunger*: In 57 BC Pompey was given a five-year command with authority to stabilize the grain supply, a position with extensive real and symbolic power.

346–50. *Milo's trial*: When Titus Annius Milo was tried in 53 BC for the murder of Clodius Pulcher, Pompey stationed an armed guard outside the courthouse, contrary to law, but ostensibly only to prevent public disturbance; this intimidating tactic prevented Cicero from delivering his defense of Milo (cf. Cicero, *pro Milone*, Plutarch, *Cicero* 35).

353. *Sulla's student*: Lucius Cornelius Sulla Felix, the most prominent Roman leader of the previous generation, had led a civil war against Gaius Marius in 88–86 BC, and was dictator in 82–81 BC, during which time he conducted bloody proscriptions and confiscations of land. Pompey had married Sulla's stepdaughter Aemilia and his early successes were under his wing. The political conflicts of the Triumvirate period were inherited from the times of Marius and Sulla, as bitter old veterans will recall in 2.70–247.

354–55. *wild tigers . . . Hyrcanian woods*: Near the Caucasus and Caspian Sea; Dido compares Aeneas to a Hyrcanian tiger at *Aen.* 4.367.

363. *Cilician pirates . . . Pontic wars*: By the *lex Gabinia* of 67 BC Pompey was tasked with suppressing the rampant piracy in the Mediterranean, based largely out of Cilicia, which he accomplished with spectacular rapidity. Mithridates VI of Pontus was defeated by Pompey and committed suicide in 65 BC, after waging wars against the Romans since the early 80s BC. Particularly, he had been "tired" out by several seasons of warfare against Lucius Licinius Lucullus, whom Pompey's supporters (including Cicero and Caesar) maneuvered to have replaced by Pompey in 66 BC.

365. *final province*: Each year the commands of Rome's provinces were doled out among the most prominent leaders, highly prized honors for their promise of great profits through campaigns, taxes, and extortion. Caesar suggests that he has been reduced to the mere status of a province.

387. *Laelius*: Otherwise unknown, perhaps Lucan's invention, but the name would have called to mind the great general of the Second Punic War era, Gaius Laelius (consul 190 BC), and his son Gaius Laelius Sapiens ("the Wise," consul 140 BC), the titular character in Cicero's dialogue on friendship (*de Amicitia*). But why Lucan would draw this association is obscure. Laelius Sapiens was known for his eloquence and for not pursuing a political program that would increase civil dissension; perhaps Lucan's Laelius is an ironic reversal of such a "wise" temperament.

397–401. *Scythian nations . . . Rhine's north currents*: A standard topic of debate in the rhetorical schools was whether Alexander, halted by his troops in India, should continue his march to the ends of the earth. Laelius' speech is full of rhetorical colors familiar from the declamation schools (cf. Seneca the Elder, *Suasoria* 1). During the Gallic campaigns Caesar and his troops had crossed the "waves of

Ocean" to Britain and had also bridged the Rhine. Scythia, north of the Black Sea, and the Syrtes, dangerous shoals off the coast of Libya, represent climatic extremes at opposite ends of the world.

413. *Tuscan Tiber*: The Tiber flows through Rome but rises in Etruria to the north.

421–24. *clamor . . . Ossa . . . the sky*: This simile mixes two others from the *Iliad* (2.334, 3.1–14), directly preceding and following Homer's catalogue of ships; here it introduces the catalogue of Gallic tribes left free by the retreat of Caesar's legions. The clamor striking the heavens and the mention of Mount Ossa both call to mind the Giants who piled Mount Pelion on Mount Ossa in their assault on Olympus. Cf. also *Aen.* 12.409.

429–98. *The tents pitched . . .*: Catalogues of troops are standard epic fare (*Iliad* 2.484–877, *Aen.* 7.641–817), and Pompey's forces will be treated in Book Three. This passage is distinct in that its real focus is not the anonymous recalled cohorts but the ethnography and topography of the frontier's barbarian enemies now left unchecked (for which Caesar's *Gallic War* was a main source); some of these tribes are noted on the map.

429. *Lake Leman*: Lake Geneva.

430. *Vosegus*: A mountain range in northeast Gaul (modern Vosges, in Alsace and Lorraine), between the Rhine and Moselle. Caesar mentions the mountains in conjunction with the Lingones (*B. Gall.* 4.10).

431. *Lingones*: A tribe living in central Gaul, southwest of the Vosegus Mountains; modern Langres was their chief town.

432. *Isara*: Modern Isère River, flows into the Rhône.

435. *Ruteni*: A people of Gallia Aquitania just west of the border of the Roman province of Gallia Narbonensis.

436. *Atax*: Modern Aude River in southwest Gaul.

438. *Var*: River in southeast Gaul, in Lucan's time the boundary of Italy.

440–42. *Hercules' sacred harbor*: Monoecus (modern Monaco). Though Lucan's use of wind names has raised critical doubts, his Circius is likely referring to the mistral.

443–54. *that uncertain coastline*: Lucan now shifts north, to the tidal maritime coasts along the North Sea, probably Belgium. Atlantic tides, absent in the Mediterranean, were a source of wonder to the ancients and provoked much theorizing as to their natural causes (Caesar mentions his men's ignorance of high ocean tides at *B.Gall.* 4.29; Pliny discusses the tides at *Nat. Hist.* 2.99-102; Cicero, *Nat. Deo.* 3.24, registers skepticism at invoking divine agency for the tides). This is the first of Lucan's many passages on natural history. Hexameter had always been the meter of didactic treatises too (e.g., Hesiod, *WD*; Empedocles; Lucretius; Virgil, *Geo.*), but by the Hellenistic period heroic epic had begun to take on natural science as part of its repertoire.

447. *second heavenly body*: The moon.

448. *Tethys*: Wife of Ocean, metonymy for the ocean.

449–50. *Titan . . . raises the ocean*: The sun; in Stoic cosmology, the fiery sun and stars were nourished by vapors that rose up from the earth's waters (see note on 10.318–22).

455. *Nemetes*: A German tribe along the Rhine, in the Hercynian forest.

455–56. *Atyrus . . . Tarbelli*: Modern Adour River in southwest France, near the Pyrenees; it flowed through the territory of the Tarbelli, who lived along the Atlantic coast.

457–58. *Santoni . . . Bituriges*: Peoples living near the coast in western Gaul.

458–61. *Suessones . . . Leuci and Remi . . . Sequani . . . Belgian drivers*: All tribes in Gallia Belgica. The Remi gave their name to modern Reims; the river Seine is named for the Sequani. The Belgae were one of the larger tribes in northern Gaul.

462. *Arverni*: A tribe in south-central Gaul (modern Auvergne); Vercingetorix was of the Arverni.

464. *Nervii*: A people in Gallia Belgica; Lucan refers to the death in battle of Caesar's legate Lucius Aurunculeius Cotta in 54 BC (Caesar, *B.Gall.* 5.24–37). According to Caesar, it was the Eburones who killed him and destroyed the legion, but the warlike Nervii were then persuaded to rise up and attack the legion under Quintus Cicero stationed in their territory (5.38–45).

465. *Vangiones . . . Sarmatians' dress*: A German tribe on the banks of the Rhine, north of the Vosegus Mountains (near modern Worms). The Sarmatians lived along the Danube near the Black Sea and were known for their loose-flowing pants.

466. *Batavi*: A German tribe living in the modern Netherlands.

468. *Mosa*: Modern Meuse, river in northeast France, Belgium, and the Netherlands. The manuscript reading—Cinga, a river in Spain—is corrupt and requires emendation; unfortunately, all previous suggestions are poorly attested in classical sources or otherwise fail to convince. Mosa has therefore been adopted as the most likely reading on geographical and philological grounds (Caesar mentions the Mosa often and prominently in his *Gallic Wars*, and the Batavi, mentioned just before, lived along it; cf. Caesar, *B. Gall.* 4.10). Another possibility is the Sulga (modern Sorgue), a tributary of the

Rhône (not mentioned by Caesar). Liger (modern Loire) would also be convincing, if only it fit the meter (cf. Tibullus 1.7.9–12).

469. *Arar*: Modern Saône, joins the Rhône at Lyon.

470–71. *that tribe . . . Cebennes*: A mountain range in southern Gaul (modern Cévennes); Lucan does not name what tribe he has in mind, if any, but he may mean the Helvii, who Caesar says live by the Cebennes Mountains (*B. Gall.* 7.8). After this line some manuscripts include five additional lines, which were added in the Middle Ages by a patriotic interpolator eager to praise his homeland. All editors now exclude them.

472. *Treviri*: A tribe living along the Mosella (modern Moselle) River in Gallia Belgica. They gave their name to Triere.

473–74. *Liguri . . . long-haired folk*: The Liguri lived on both sides of the Italian Alps; once among the *comati*, or "long-haired" peoples, they had given up their practice of wearing their hair long upon becoming Romanized (*togati*).

476–77. *Teutates . . . Esus . . . Taranis . . . Diana*: Three Celtic gods whom Roman authors mention in connection with practices of human sacrifice (cf. Caesar, *B. Gall.* 6.16–17); this provokes Lucan's comparison with the Scythian Diana, goddess of the Tauri of Crimea known for human sacrifice (cf. Euripides, *Iph. in Taur.*).

478–95. *Bards . . . Druids*: the Bards were oral poets among the Celts who, just as Lucan describes them, sang praise songs of traditional Celtic heroes. The Druids were the educated social caste among the Celts who maintained the traditional religious knowledge and practices. Caesar discusses them briefly in his *Gallic Wars* (6.13–16). They abstained from warfare and did not pay tribute; Caesar emphasizes their extensive memorization of oral lore, and mentions, as does Lucan, their belief in the transmigration of souls. This treatment of the Bards suggests a sense of authorial identification as a heroic poet, and epic commonly includes poets in the poem (e.g., Thamyris in the *Iliad*, Demodocus and Phemius in the *Odyssey*). Cf. 9.1213–20 for another comment on poetry and its purpose. The theme of transmigration also recalls Pythagoras' didactic speech in Ovid, *Met.* 15 (cf. also the speech of Anchises, *Aen.* 6.724ff.), and perhaps points forward to Nigidius Figulus (684ff.), infamous for his Pythagorean mysticism.

486–87. *Erebus . . . Dis*: Erebus is the underworld, Dis is the Roman god of the underworld (Greek Pluto/Hades).

490. *the Bear*: The constellation Ursa Major, our Big Dipper, in the northern sky, thus looking down on the peoples of the north.

496. *Cayci*: Or the Chauci, a German tribe living in the far northwest of Germania. Caesar does not mention them, probably because they were outside his sphere of exploration and conquest; but by Lucan's time they were familiar names in Rome since their involvement in a rebellion against G. Domitius Corbulo in AD 47, after which Claudius Caesar drew back the frontier garrisons to the Rhine (see Tacitus, *Ann.* 11.16–20). They would later take part in the massive German rebellion under Julius Civilis in AD 69 (see Tacitus, *Hist.* 4.12–37). Their mention last in the list therefore heightens the terror that contemporary readers would feel at the thought of being "exposed to every tribe." *Belgae* is a textual emendation; the manuscripts read "fend off in war [*bellis*]."

502. *Empty rumors*: Recalls Ovid's personification of *Fama*, "fame, rumor," whose vast echoing halls are abuzz with panicky noise at the arrival of the Achaeans in Troy (*Met.* 12.39–63).

506. *Mevania's bull pastures*: A town in Umbria (modern Bevagna) famed for its bulls (cf. Propertius, *El.* 4.1.123–30, a reference to his family's loss of land in the civil wars).

508. *Nar*: Modern Nere, a tributary of the Tiber between Umbria and Etruria.

523. *decree of war*: The "Senate's final decree" (*senatus consultum ultimum*) that the *res publica* be defended from harm, used several times since the days of the Gracchi, was in effect a declaration of a state of emergency, and as a result constitutional law and order was put at considerable jeopardy.

533–39. *As when the stormy south wind*: The "ship of state" metaphor has an ancient pedigree, occurring as early as the Greek lyric poet Alcaeus; cf. Horace, *Odes* 1.14. The storm and shipwreck in *Aen.* 1.81ff. also lies in the background: the Trojans are similarly driven by the south wind (and others) to the treacherous Syrtes. When Neptune pacifies the storm he is compared to a great statesman calming civil unrest (1.148–56). Lucan inverts the metaphor: the outbreak of civil turmoil and panic is likened to the violent shattering of a storm-wrecked ship.

542. *gods of the family hearth*: The Lares, the tutelary gods of a Roman house.

564. *prodigies*: Both Virgil, *Geo.* 1.464–88, and Ovid, *Met.* 15.779–98, give civil-war prodigies. Omens and portents were a regular feature of Roman historiography, and Lucan probably drew on accounts in Livy and/or in Asinius Pollio (cf. Appian, *B.Civ.* 2.36, who mentions raining blood, statues sweating, lightning strikes, a mule giving birth, and "many other prodigies which por-

tended the destruction and permanent transformation of the con-
stitution").

567–68. *the comet*: A dire omen signifying a change of rulers; recalls
the comet seen upon the death of Julius Caesar in 44 BC, the
so-called *sidus Iulium* that was represented in the temple of the
deified Julius and on Octavian's coinage. In AD 60 a comet ap-
peared, causing Nero anxiety and leading to the removal of Rubel-
lius Plautus, a potential rival (Tacitus, *Ann.* 14.22.1). For an
extended description of comets and their meaning, see Manilius,
Astr. 1.809 ff. The Greek word "comet" means long hair; thus
Lucan is etymologizing the name.

572–74. *Latin Alba*: the Alban Mount, near the site of ancient Alba
Longa, southeast of Rome. The portent realizes the comparison of
Caesar to a lightning bolt striking temples of Jupiter; cf. notes on
170 and 213–16.

583. *Thyestes' Mycenae*: When Atreus killed the children of his brother
Thyestes and served them to him unawares at a feast, the Sun was
disgusted by the crime and refused to rise. Lucan probably has in
mind his uncle Seneca's tragedy *Thyestes* (cf. ll. 789–883). The
house of Atreus was a classic paradigm from Greek myth for the
horrors of internecine strife playing out over several generations.

584. *Mulciber*: Another name for Vulcan. The volcanically active
Mount Etna on Sicily was believed to be the foundry of Vulcan,
god of fire and metallurgy.

587–88. *Charybdis . . . Scylla*: Mythical monsters, the one a violent
whirlpool, the other a woman with barking dogs from the waist
down, were believed to haunt the narrow Strait of Messina be-
tween Italy and Sicily (cf. 4.485).

590. *Latin Games*: The *feriae Latinae*, annual festival of Rome and her
Latin allies for Jupiter Latiaris, celebrated on Mount Alba in April
since early Republican times or even earlier. Though its original
purpose and character had long since declined, it was still crucial
to Roman state religion, since the annual magistrates could not
begin their duties before its rituals had been duly and successfully
conducted (cf. 3.92, 5.427–30, 7.463–67). In fact, it seems that the
festival was either not held this year, or was held improperly with-
out the consul presiding.

592. *Theban pyres*: The civil war between the sons of Oedipus, Eteocles
and Polyneices, was another standard mythic paradigm for interne-
cine strife, prominent in Athenian tragedy; when the warring broth-
ers died, even the flames of their joined pyre split apart and refused
to mingle (cf. Seneca, *Oed.* 321–23, Statius, *Theb.* 12.429–32).

Thebes (city of Ares) as a double of Rome (city of Mars) is promi-
nent in Ovid, *Met.* 3.1ff., and Statius, *Thebaid*.

595. *Calpe . . . Atlas*: Gibraltar and the Atlas Mountains in northwest
Africa, indicating the far western Mediterranean in general.

596. *native gods . . . Lares*: The Di Indigetes were various native Italian
gods; the Lares were household gods; specifically, Lucan may
mean the Lares of the city (*Lares praestites*), which had a temple
on the Via Sacra near the arch of Titus and/or a shrine on the Pala-
tine Hill, or again may have been housed within the large complex
of the Vestal Virgins' house. At *Geo.* 1.498ff., Virgil prays to the
Di Indigetes, Romulus, and Vesta to help Octavian bring aid to the
troubled times (the civil wars).

598. *birds of bad omen*: Probably owls.

604. *Cumaean Sibyl*: The oracular Sibyl of Cumae, on the Bay of Na-
ples, would be immortalized, and drawn into close connection
with Augustus, by Virgil in *Aen.* 6. Poems of omen and prophecy
ascribed to the Sibyl were common during the strife of the Late
Republic and into the Imperial period.

605–07. *Bellona . . . Galli*: A Roman goddess of war (L. *bellum*) whose
fanatic worshippers gashed their arms during their rites. The Galli,
orgiastic priests of Cybele (also Cybebe or Magna Mater, "the
Great Mother"), were infamous for their self-castration (cf. Catul-
lus 63). Generally despised as a foreign cult, Galli were not allowed
to be Roman citizens.

613–18. *Fury . . . Hercules*: Greek Erinyes, chthonic goddesses who orig-
inally avenged bloodguilt, especially in the family, though in Latin
poetry they became general agents of divine wrath and madness.
Their definitive literary treatment was in Aeschylus' *Oresteia*. Tisi-
phone, Megaera, and Allecto were their usual names (Allecto ap-
pears in *Aen.* 7.324; Tisiphone in *Met.* 4.474). Agave was the
mother of Pentheus, who, like Lycurgus in the following line, de-
nied the divinity of Bacchus, who then drove her mad. Both are led
to kill their own children. Hercules, driven by Hera (Juno) on his
labors, descended to the underworld and on returning was inflicted
with madness, causing him to kill his wife, Megara, and their chil-
dren (Seneca told the story in his tragedy *Hercules Furens*). All the
examples raise again the theme of internecine destruction and vio-
lence, closely tied to divine agents of wrath (cf. 2.1–17).

621–25. *Sulla . . . Marius*: Sulla had been buried in the Campus Martius
(an extremely rare honor for a Roman citizen). Marius' body had
been disinterred on Sulla's orders and dumped in the Anio River.
The rising of their ghosts obviously portends a renewal of the civil

discord they had led. Moreover, the distance between the living and the dead, the earth and the underworld, is being effaced. This foreshadows the reminiscences of the civil war between Sulla and Marius in Book Two, as well as the gruesome scene of necromancy with Sextus Pompey and the Thessalian witch in Book Six.

627–28. *Arruns . . . Luca*: Roman state religion called on traditional Etruscan *haruspices*, diviners expert in the inspection and interpretation of omens, whether lightning strikes, birds, strange births, or the entrails of sacrificial animals, as here. The Senate would officially summon haruspices to come assess the omens and prescribe ritual remedies. Arruns is an authentic Etruscan name, but the figure is otherwise unknown. Luca is modern Lucca near Pisa, on the northern edge of Etruria.

635–37. *circle the city . . . boundary space*: The *lustrum* was a regular purification rite conducted every five years after the census was taken and during times of trouble; the priests, followed by a parade (*pompa*) of citizens, would make a circuit around the ritual boundary of the city (*pomerium*).

638. *Gabine priests*: A quick survey of Rome's various official priesthoods; the Gabine priests were recognized by their uniquely girded togas.

639. *Vestal choir*: They wore a ribbon in the hair, signifying their chastity. Trojan Minerva was the Palladium of Troy supposedly brought to Italy by Aeneas and housed in the temple of Vesta.

641. *secret songs*: A fifteen-man college (*quindecemviri*) was responsible for consulting the Sibylline Books, a supposedly ancient collection of oracles kept a state secret.

642. *Cybele*: A priestly college to the cult of Cybele once a year bathed the image in the Almo, a small tributary of the Tiber near Rome.

643. *augurs*: They observed bird omens.

644. *Seven Men . . . Titian Guildsmen*: The *septemviri* were in charge of sacred feasts for Jupiter; the Titian college was founded by the Sabine king Titus Tatius during the reign of Romulus; the guild may have preserved early Sabine ritual.

645. *Salii*: The "Leapers," known for their festive songs and dances, guarded the ancient Shields of Mars (*ancilia*); when one shield fell from heaven, King Numa ordered eleven copies to be made to protect the identity of the authentic shield (cf. 9.603 and note).

646. *Flamen*: There were fifteen flamens, high priests selected from noble families, who wore a distinctive pointed cap, divided into three orders sacred to Jupiter, Mars, and Quirinus.

654. *struggled long against it*: The physical appearance and behavior of sacrificial animals was strictly observed and regulated. Any infelicity,

such as the animal struggling at the altar, was ill-omened. The victim had to appear willing for the sacrifice to be propitious. Similarly, the many irregular physical signs in the entrails in the following lines all indicate the gods' displeasure and the victim's unsuitability.

664–69. *the liver . . . hostile side . . .* : This passage uses several technical terms from the art of inspecting entrails; for divination the liver was divided into two parts, the "hostile" and "familiar." Here the "hostile" side has menacing veins, signs of impending conflict.

672–73. *One part hangs sick . . . pound too quickly*: The two lobes, one sick and sluggish, the other overly aggressive, seem to describe the leaders of the two factions, Pompey and Caesar respectively.

681. *Tages*: A mythical figure, who came out of the earth and taught Etruscans the arts of divination (cf. Ovid, *Met.* 15.552–58). His name was said to mean in Etruscan "a voice emitted from the earth." The story of how he was plowed up from the earth is told, with great suspicion, by Cicero, *de Div.* 2.23.

684. *Figulus*: Publius Nigidius Figulus, whom Aulus Gellius called the most learned man after Varro, was a friend of Cicero and partisan of Pompey; he died in exile in 45 BC. Deeply interested in natural philosophy, including astrology and Pythagorean ideas (Lucan's wording makes clear allusion to Ovid's Pythagoras in *Met.* 15), he wrote treatises on grammar, the gods, dreams, augury, and meteorology. Here he provides the second panel in a triptych of doom closing Book One: augury (Arruns), astrology (Figulus), and mantic possession (the Roman matron), three standard modes of foretelling the future. Suetonius (*Aug.* 94) tells a story that, he says, "everyone believes," about the birth of Augustus Caesar: his birth coincided with the Senate debates about Catiline's conspiracy, and when his father, Octavius, arrived late and told the hour of his son's birth, Figulus declared, "The ruler of the world is now born." Lucan's use of Figulus may rely on this story's currency, while quite reversing its pro-Augustan thrust.

685. *Egyptian Memphis*: The Egyptians were famous for their knowledge of the heavenly movements (cf. 10.248ff.).

687. *world wanders*: Whether the world was governed by cosmic fate or was chaotic and random was an entrenched debate in ancient philosophy, and is a recurring theme in Lucan (cf. 2.1–17). The Stoics believed in a world of fate and divine providence; but Lucan's toying with such theological doubts adds dramatic and existential tension to the poem.

691. *earth crack open*: The cataclysms Figulus foresees recall the Stoic cosmic conflagration referred to in the poem's opening (see note to 73–87).

697–711. *Saturn . . . Aquarius . . . Orion*: Astrology involved interpret-
ing the locations and movements of the planets (including the sun
and moon) within the constellations. As Housman showed, this
passage has no accurate relation to astral positions at this time (late
November 50 BC), and thus is to be read purely on astrological and
literary symbolic grounds. Saturn and Mars both exerted a negative
influence; Jupiter and Venus were positive; Mercury was by nature
variable; the sun and moon were of neutral influence. Aquarius (the
Water-Bearer) is portending another flood, like that of Deucalion
and Pyrrha at the beginning of the world (cf. Ovid, *Met.* 1.26off.). If
the sun were in Leo (equated here with the Nemean Lion killed by
Hercules) the world would be destroyed by fire. Mars is moving into
Scorpio and thus "ignites his tail." The overbright shining of Orion,
the sword-bearing hunter, is offered here as a hostile sign. The epi-
thet of Mars used, Gradivus, meaning perhaps the Pursuer or the
Hunter, may likewise be significant in this context.

720–23. *as from the peaks of Pindus*: The Pindus range extends from
western Thessaly in Greece north into Macedon and western
Thrace. The ecstatic worship of Dionysus, born in Thebes, was
closely associated with Thrace. Here the god of prophecy Phoebus
Apollo (Paean is another of his cult names) inspires the unnamed
Roman matron, who becomes a raving Bacchant like Agave and
an unwilling prophetess like Cassandra, offering grim glimpses
into a bloody future.

725–26. *Pangaea . . . Haemus . . . Philippi*: Mount Pangaea is in south-
ern Thrace near Philippi, where the critical civil-war battle in 44 BC
was fought. Haemus is another range on its northern boundary.
Besides the Bacchic associations of Thrace, there seems to be a
clever wordplay here: *Pangaea* is (or sounds like) the Greek "the
whole world," *Haemus* sounds like Greek for "blood"—thus she
sees in Philippi "the whole world" bathed in blood. This passage
reworks Virgil's *Georgics* 1.490ff., a crucial civil-war text.

727. *What fury*: The matron repeats the poet's question from line 8,
giving Book One a ring composition.

730–31. *Lagus' Nile . . . headless trunk*: Lagus was one of Alexander's
successors, father of Ptolemy I, the founder of Egypt's Ptolemaic
dynasty. She foresees Pompey's murder and decapitation in Alex-
andria, narrated in Book Eight.

732–33. *Syrtes . . . Libya . . . Enyo*: She now sees the theater of war
moving to North Africa, as it did after the Battle of Pharsalus.
Enyo is a Homeric goddess of war, whom the Romans associated
with their Bellona.

734-35. *Emathian . . . Alps . . . Pyrenees*: Emathian identifies the troops following the Battle of Pharsalus (see note on 1); the Alps and Pyrenees both evoke the entire western theater of the civil wars, including the sieges of Massilia and Spanish Ilerda, and the later Battle of Munda.

737. *middle of the Senate*: The assassination of Julius Caesar; the Senate here refers to the meeting of the Senate and not the Senate house. The senators met, and killed Caesar, in the portico of Pompey's theater on the fateful Ides of March.

740. *already seen Philippi*: Conflates the two battles, 350 kilometers apart, of Pharsalus and Philippi. Virgil did this in *Geo.* 1.489-92, and Ovid followed in *Met.* 15.823-24.

BOOK TWO

1-17. *Now gods' wraths . . .*: Whether the world was ruled by fate or chance was a common philosophical topic. Stoics believed the world was controlled by an all-encompassing Fate and that portents and omens were warnings from the gods to humans about fated events. The Stoic "creator of things" was akin to Mother Nature, but was also thought of as the soul (*animus*) or mind (*mens*) of Nature, in which case it was masculine. That the creator "obeys the law himself" reinforces the "natural law" ethical component of Stoic belief; the poem tends to present the civil war as a perversion of the order of things and thus contrary to Stoic ethical norms. The alternative view, on which Lucan spends only two lines and which he seems to reject, is the Epicurean and Atomist notion that the universe is made up of and created by blind, will-less atoms moving and interacting at random. In Latin poetry Lucretius' *De Rerum Natura* looms large behind these lines, as well as providing a model for such philosophical topics in epic verse (cf. 7.523-25). Divine anger (*ira*) is a central epic theme, beginning with Apollo's rage in the *Iliad*.

7. *dire omens*: The belief in a reciprocal connection between the existence of the gods and the truth of divination through signs was, in Cicero's terms, the "citadel of the Stoics" (*De Div.* 1.6): if the gods exist then there must be signs; if there are signs then the gods must exist.

11. *obeying the law himself*: Stoics held that the universe was a living being endowed with supreme reason, mind, will, purpose, order, all of which were taken as god (or its fundamental attributes) and was in turn equated with Nature (cf. Cicero *Nat. Deo.* 2.30ff., 45-47). When Cicero discusses divine providence (*providentia*) he

seems to distinguish god (*deus*) and Nature (*natura*), making the former external to the latter's laws: "so god is not obedient or subject to any [part of] nature; therefore he himself rules the whole of nature" (2.77); but this is in fact the conclusion of a specific argument that "the nature of the gods" governs everything (and follows several unambiguous statements that Nature and the "whole world" are god). He then goes on to argue at length that "everything is subject to Nature" (2.81–87).

14. *chance rules mortals*: The apparently stark alternative between cosmic order and random chaos is itself thrown into confusion by the theory, also found in Stoic accounts, of a gradation of descending order from the heavens to the sublunary and terrestrial spheres (cf. Cicero, *Nat. Deo.* 2.56: "in the heavens there is no *fortuna* or accident or wandering ... everything is order, truth, reason, constancy. ... those things that lack these qualities ... are below the moon and on the earth").

17. *Leave them free to hope*: Cicero registers the same complaint against the gods who would terrorize mortals with omens: "It is a miserable thing to be tortured by one's impotence and to forfeit even our last common consolation of hope. ... So what use is it ... to know the future, if it cannot be altered?" (*Nat. Deo.* 3.14).

21–22. *signs of honor ... plebeian dress ... lictors' rods*: Roman plebeians were known for their drab, ordinary clothing, whereas Roman senators wore tunics with a red stripe and a white toga, and magistrates a red-striped toga as well (*toga praetexta*). High-ranking magistrates had a bodyguard called lictors, who carried before them the insignia of office, the fasces, a bundle of rods and an axe, symbolizing their power of corporal and capital punishment.

37. *lofty Thunderer*: The temple of Jupiter Tonans on the Capitoline Hill, an important site in imperial state religion built by Augustus in the 20s BC after narrowly escaping a lightning strike while campaigning in Spain; thus, strictly speaking, an anachronism, but most likely not an unconscious one (cf. Ovid, *Fasti* 2. 55–72; Martial, *Epig.* 7.60).

50. *Cannae and Trebia*: Sites of two infamous Roman defeats by Hannibal in the Second Punic War, in 216 and 218 BC, respectively.

51. *enrage foreigners*: For the preference for war with foreigners, cf. 1.21–25.

53–54. *Medes ... Susa ... Achaemenids*: Lucan blurs past and present empires in his reference to the Parthian East, which the Medes ruled before the Persians, whose Achaemenid dynasty ruled from

Susa. The Parthians, Rome's traditional eastern enemy, then succeeded the Persians.

55–59. *Massagetae . . . Suebi . . . Dacians and Getae*: The Massagetae lived east of the Caspian Sea; the Suebi were a German tribe, probably shorthand for Germans in general; the Dacians and Getae lived along the lower Danube. Together these peoples roughly delineate the northern and eastern boundaries of Roman power.

60–61. *Spaniards . . . arrows of the East*: Due to recent campaigns and the placement of legions it would be natural for Caesar to conduct wars in the West, Pompey in the East. The Parthians were known for their archers.

62–64. *strike the earth with lightning*: Cf. 1.80ff., and note to 1.73–87. Another hint of Phaethon, whose punishment by Jupiter will be recalled at 433–37.

72–247. *second civil wars*: The previous generation had been traumatized by the civil wars between Gaius Marius (157–86 BC) and Lucius Cornelius Sulla Felix (138–78 BC), which raged 88–81 BC, definitive years for the current leaders such as Caesar and Pompey, then in their youth. Pompey had been a protégé of Sulla; Caesar was a nephew by marriage of Marius, but also his second wife, Pompeia, was a granddaughter of Sulla. For the narrative device, Lucan might have had in mind Ovid's short conversation about Thapsus with one of Caesar's veterans at *Fasti* 4.377–86. Cf. also the admonitory speech of Nestor in the *Iliad* 1.245–84.

77–91. *marshlands . . . spare this one old man*: When Sulla marched on Rome in 88 BC Marius fled and ended up hiding in the swamps at Minturnae, near Formiae on the Italian coast, but was captured and sent to be executed. His barbarian executioner, said to be a Cimbrian, recognized him and let him go, according to Lucan's account, in order that Marius might later kill Romans and thus exact revenge for the Cimbrians, whom Marius had defeated ("Teutons' conqueror"). Marius was around seventy years old at the time. Cf. Plutarch, *Mar.* 36–40, for a prose version of the events.

99. *pardoned the gods*: An opaque idea, but Lucan seems to mean that each feels a certain justice in the situation: Carthage is pleased at the great Roman general's fall, and Marius feels, at the least, the tragic irony of being a desperate fugitive in the rubble of Carthage, Rome's most hated enemy. The American neoclassicist painter John Vanderlyn's *Marius amid the Ruins of Carthage* (1807) depicts this moment (now in the M. H. de Young Museum, San Francisco).

99–100. *wrath native to Libya*: Libya is metonymic for Carthage and Numidia, enemies of Rome, as well as a source of wrathful beasts

such as lions. Marius acquires strength from the Libyan ground
like the giant Antaeus, who derives his force from the Libyan soil
(cf. 4.622ff.).

101. *free droves of slaves*: Upon return to Italy Marius freed chain
gangs of slaves and conscripted them into his army.

105. *stormed the walls*: Of Rome. Marius marched on the city late in
87 BC and undertook a bloody purge of his enemies with the con-
sul Lucius Cornelius Cinna (cf. Plutarch, *Mar.* 41–45).

122. *death's new signals*: Those whose greetings Marius did not return
were understood to be marked for death (cf. Plutarch, *Mar.* 43).

126–36. *Baebius . . . Antony . . . Fimbria . . . Crassi . . . Scaevola*:   All
victims of Marius' retributions, except for Gaius Flavius Fimbria, a
partisan of Cinna and Marius who had been the latter's consular
colleague in 104 BC; he killed the son of Publius Licinius Crassus
(consul in 97 BC, father of M. Licinius Crassus the later triumvir),
who afterward committed suicide (though accounts differ). The sen-
ator Marcus Baebius (Tamphilus) is mentioned in Appian's victim
list; he may have been an old man and Sallust may have recounted
his savage dismemberment in his *Histories*. Marcus Antonius (con-
sul in 99 BC, grandfather of Mark Antony the triumvir) was a famed
orator often lauded by Cicero and is said to have predicted (proba-
bly in speeches, not as a prophet) the dangers of Marius (see Cicero,
Ep. ad Fam. 6.2.2). After he was found in hiding his head was cut
off and thrown on Marius' table (see Florus, *Ep.* 3.21.14; Plutarch,
Mar. 44). Marius had one or two tribunes of the people thrown
from the Tarpeian Rock, according to other accounts, a heinous vi-
olation of their sacrosanct status; the "stakes" (*robora*) may refer to
posts in prison to which prisoners were chained, but the reference is
uncertain. Quintus Mucius Scaevola, Pontifex Maximus (consul in
95 BC and authority on Roman law), was actually killed later in
82 BC by the Marian partisan Lucius Junius Brutus Damasippus,
either near or in the temple of Vesta: Cicero (*Ep. ad Fam.* 6.2.2)
mentions his death in the temple right after naming Crassus. The
death of the elderly priest at a god's altar recalls the death of King
Priam of Troy (cf. Virgil, *Aen.* 2.506–57; Ovid, *Met.* 13.409–11).

141–45. *Sacriportus . . . Colline Gate . . . Caudine Forks*: The first two
were civil-war battles in 82 BC. At Sacriportus, somewhere near
Praeneste but of uncertain location, Sulla defeated Marius' son in
battle. The Colline Gate is the northern entrance to the city, where
Sulla again defeated the Marians led by allied Samnites; their
leader, Pontius Telesinus, is said to have vowed to destroy Rome
and gain supremacy for themselves. Both were bloody battles, and

Sulla's dictatorship and bloody proscriptions followed. The Caudine Forks were the site of one of Rome's worst defeats, in 321 BC, to the Samnites.

159–60. *brothers fell upon brothers*: An ancient commentator claimed that these lines refer to Lucius Domitius Ahenobarbus (the character in the poem and ancestor of Nero) receiving the estates of his brother Gnaeus Domitius Ahenobarbus, who was proscribed by Sulla and killed, after being defeated in battle near Utica along with the Numidian king Iarbas, by Pompey in 81 BC.

172–75. *Thrace ... Bistonian tyrant ... Antaeus ... Pisa*: Thracians were notorious for savagery and violence; the legendary Bistonian king Diomedes fed his guests to his mares; for the man-killing Libyan giant Antaeus, see 4.623ff. In Greek myth, King Oenomaus of Pisa, in Elis, slew each of his daughter Hippodameia's suitors after defeating them in a chariot race.

185. *Catulus' ghost ... a Marius*: Quintus Lutatius Catulus (consul in 102 BC) committed suicide in 87 BC after being prosecuted by the tribune Marcus Marius Gratidianus, Marius' nephew, who in turn was brutally murdered at the tomb of Catulus, instigated by the latter's son and possibly carried out by Catiline, who was (possibly) Gratidianus' brother-in-law. Livy had narrated the murder in his history (*Per.* 88), Sallust likely had as well, and Lucan probably knew his uncle Seneca's reference at *De ira* 3.18. This brutal scene may also call to mind when Achilles' shade demanded the sacrifice of Polyxena at his tomb (cf. Ovid, *Met.* 13.439–82).

192. *tongue, cut out*: Cf. Ovid's Philomela, *Met.* 6.556–60 (compared with which Lucan is restrained).

205. *Fortuna of Praeneste*: At Praeneste (modern Palestrina), east of Rome, the goddess Fortuna Primigenia ("Firstborn") had an ancient and venerated oracle by lots (*sortes*). After the younger Marius committed suicide there in 82 BC, Sulla put its citizens to death, moved the city downhill, and settled a veteran colony. The sad fate of Fortune's own city is bitter irony, only enhanced by the fact that the temple's marvelous expansion was carried out by Sulla on the ruins of the old city.

208–9. *flower of Hesperia ... sheepfold*: After the battle of the Colline Gate, Sulla killed several thousand prisoners, mostly Samnites but very possibly including fellow Romans and/or Latins, in or near the "Sheepfold" (*Ovilia*) of the Campus Martius, an enclosure used for the annual polling (cf. Livy, *Per.* 88).

220. *he sat on high*: Sulla, who was said to have watched the slaughter of Samnites from the nearby temple of Bellona, goddess of war.

223. *Tiber's stream*: The common Roman practice of dumping the bodies of dead criminals into the Tiber also calls to mind Achilles' choking the Scamander with bodies in *Iliad* 21.218–38.

235–36. *'Blessed' and 'Savior' . . . Mars' Field*: Sulla considered himself lucky and added the titles Felix (Fortunate, Blessed) and Soter (Greek for Savior) to his name in 82 BC. Sulla died in 78, after settling and reorganizing the state as dictator, then stepping down. His burial in the Campus Martius (which Pompey supported) was an exceptional distinction and was the culmination of a state funeral of lavish pomp for him that divided the state over its due propriety: the consuls Lepidus and Catulus quarreled before and after the funeral, and their partisan armies quickly fell into open armed conflict (cf. Plutarch, *Sulla* 38; Appian, *BC* 1.105–7). Augustus raised his own mausoleum on the Campus Martius, setting the precedent for imperial burial there, for which Sulla can be taken as a pre-Caesarian precursor.

248–345. *his kinsman Cato*: Marcus Junius Brutus visits his uncle Marcus Porcius Cato (Uticensis)—great-grandson of Cato the Elder—by night to discuss the impending war. Both would fight on the "republican" side for Pompey. Cato, like his family before him, represented conservative republican values as well as a very public devotion to Stoicism. In 59 BC Cato had been temporarily imprisoned after strong opposition to Caesar, but was equally opposed to Pompey throughout the 50s. Lucan does not portray him as eager to take part in the civil war until after Pharsalus, and throughout the poem he acts as the moral compass of the Pompeians. He becomes the center of focus in Book Nine. Brutus, who does not much appear in the poem after this, would be forever revered or reviled as a chief conspirator in the assassination of Caesar. He was close to Caesar and had been an enemy of Pompey, who had killed his father, but he reconciled with him in 49 to join the ranks of the republican cause.

249. *lofty soul*: See note at 4.499 on *magnanima*.

251–2. *Helice of Arcady*: The constellation Ursa Major, from a Greek word meaning "to twist" (as in helix). She was a nymph of Arcadia in Greece (Parrhasis in the Latin text), named Callisto, who was raped by Jupiter, turned first into a bear by Juno, then by Jupiter into a constellation (cf. Ovid, *Met.* 2.401–530). The stars in Lucan also connote stability, orientation, and order, especially the unmoving polestar, which never sets: like Cato, sleepless and rolling the affairs of the world over in his mind and "not shaken by any storm [*turbine*] of Fortune" (258–59). That *Parrhasis* recalls the Greek word *parrhesia*, "free, candid, frank speech" (a concept

358   NOTES

often expressed in Latin by *libertas*, cf. 8.554), suits this context
where Brutus seeks frank and candid counsel from Cato about the
right course of action.

254. *turning public cares*: The sleepless Cato, preoccupied with public
affairs, repeats a standard epic image of the leader, as with
Agamemnon in *Il.* 2.50ff. and Aeneas in *Aen.* 8.19 (the latter a
more positive model than the former).

258. *Virtue's last refuge*: The driving of Virtue (*virtus*) out of the world
recalls the departure from the earth of Shame and Justice at the end
of the mythical Iron Age, traits embodied in the figure named As-
traea, a virgin goddess identified with the constellation Virgo (cf.
Hesiod, *WD* 197–200; Ovid, *Met.* 1.149–50); making Cato instead
of the heavens Virtue's last refuge again sets Cato up in opposition
or counterpoise to the gods (cf. 1.141). The theme of the fugitive in
exile points forward to Pompey's exile from Italy at the end of
Book Two (and eventually that of the entire republican faction).

281. *Better for you*: Caesar himself made the same argument in a letter
to Cicero: "what suits a good and peaceful man and a good citizen
better than to keep away from civil quarrels. . . . you will find
nothing safer nor more upright than to keep out of the whole con-
flict" (*Att.* 10.8b).

294. *a civilian*: Pompey at this time held no official magistracy.

302. *holy words*: This surprising line makes Cato sound like a prophet
or an oracle (cf. 9.708–34, when Cato bypasses, and his words of
truth replace, the oracle of Ammon).

314. *Dahae and Getae*: Two stereotypically distant barbarian tribes;
the Scythian Dahae lived beyond the Caspian Sea, the Getae on
the lower Danube.

326. *Decius self-sacrificed*: The rare Roman military practice of *devo-
tio* involved vowing one's own life to the gods of the underworld
and valiantly dying in battle to ensure victory and the safety of
others. Publius Decius Mus (d. 340 BC) and his son of the same
name were early Roman nobles famous for their acts of *devotio*.

344. *incentives for anger*: Or "goads"—the language here makes the ef-
fect of Cato's words seem like a maddening Fury of war, akin to
Virgil's Allecto (*Aen.* 7.419–62).

346–414. *Marcia remarries Cato*: In this strange scene, Cato's former
wife, Marcia, suddenly appears to ask Cato to remarry her after her
second husband, Quintus Hortensius Hortalus (consul in 69 BC), has
passed away (in 50 BC). Cato had given Marcia to a childless Horten-
sius after she had already had three children with him. Here she
comes straight from the tomb; in actual fact, Hortensius, a notorious

voluptuary, had died some months before, and it is unlikely that Marcia would have come to arrange the remarriage herself. From the Roman perspective, Cato's willingness to give his wife to a potential political ally who had no children would perhaps have displayed a certain kind of magnanimity and Stoic rectitude concerning the pro-creative purpose of marriage. The entire scene employs, often invert-ing by negation, stock conventions of elegiac poetry.

365. *CATO'S MARCIA*: Quotation of funeral inscriptions is common in Latin elegy. This epitaph would make it sound as though Mar-cia had only one husband, the Roman ideal of marriage.

372. *Cornelia*: The first mention of Pompey's wife, who will appear in Books Five, Eight, and Nine.

377–94. *The threshold . . . augur*: This negative description details nor-mal rituals and ceremonies of Roman marriage. Their absence in this "marriage" indicate Cato's Stoic austerity. A marriage proces-sion was led by torches, and the crowd would tease the groom with ribald songs called Fescinnine verses, believed to be of Sabine ori-gin, to ward off the evil eye. Religious custom required the pres-ence of someone with ritual knowledge to take the auspices.

395. *reverend face*: Latin *sanctus*, a striking term that continues the quasi deification of Cato and Stoic virtue.

409. *rough toga*: Cato is said to have worn the traditional woolen toga without a tunic underneath, which furthered his ascetic image.

410. *Quirites*: A traditional name for Roman citizens, its derivation is debated.

416. *walls a Dardan founded*: Capua; its legendary founder was Trojan Capys, a descendant of Dardanus and father of Anchises (cf. *Aen.* 10.145).

417. *makes his war base*: The consuls were to go to Capua and levy troops, along with Cicero, who reports in his letters on the sorry state of affairs and, to his reckoning, the complete lack of any plan (cf. *Ep. ad Att.* 7.20–22).

421. *nearer to Olympus*: A poetic exaggeration; the highest peaks of the Apennines are not higher than those in the Alps.

423. *Lower and Upper Seas*: Respectively, the Tyrrhenian Sea to the west of Italy and the Adriatic to the east.

424–45. *Pisa's shoals, east to Ancona*: The catalogue begins at the north end of the Apennines, with Pisa on the west coast, Ancona directly across the peninsula on the east coast; Dalmatia is the region opposite Italy on the Adriatic coast (in modern Croatia).

428–30. *Metaurus . . . Aufidus*: Rivers of eastern Italy. Metaurus = modern Metauro, Crustumium = Conca, Apis = Apsa, Pisaurus =

Foglia, Sena = Misa, and Aufidus = Ofanto, farthest south in the list at Cannae.

432. *Eridanus*: the Po, Italy's largest river, which the Romans also called Padus. Eridanus was a Greek name for a mythological river, which Romans poets had adopted for the Po.

433–37. *There is a legend . . .*: To enhance the river's poetic prestige, Lucan recalls the myth, told at length at Ovid, *Met.* 2.1–366, about how Phaethon crashed the Sun's chariot along the Eridanus and while mourning their brother his sisters turned into poplar trees.

438–40. *No smaller than the Nile . . . than the Hister*: Absurd hyperbole, even with the qualifications. The mention of the Nile here anticipates the discussion of the mystery of the Nile's source at 10.239ff. The Hister is the lower Danube, which enters the Black Sea in Scythia.

444–50. *Tiber . . . Luna*: Rivers of western Italy. The Tiber runs through Rome; the Rutuba is the modern Varo, far to the north in Liguria; Vulturnus is the Volturno in Samnium and Campania; the Sarnus is the Sarno near Pompeii; the Liris is the Liri in southern Latium; Marica is a sea nymph associated with the Liris, the mother of King Latinus. The Vescini (an emendation of the text's *Vestinis*) lived along or near the Liris, but by the Late Republic they had become a dimly remembered name. The Siler is the modern Sele, south of Salerno; the Macra is the Magra near Luna (modern Luni, near Sarzana) in the north.

453. *Umbrians and Marsians . . . Sabellan*: Native Italic tribes living in and around the Apennines; the Sabelli were the Oscan-speaking peoples of Italy including the Samnites.

456. *surf of Scylla*: The mythical monster that haunts the Strait of Messina, separating Sicily from mainland Italy, famous from *Odyssey* 10.

457. *Lacinia's temple*: The temple of Juno at Lacinium (modern Capo Colonna) near Croton, on Italy's southern coast.

458–61. *sea eroded . . . Pelorus*: Lucan describes the Strait of Messina; Pelorus is the promontory on the Sicilian side; the "double depths" are the two seas on either side. That the narrow strait had once been connected by land was a common idea by Lucan's time (cf. Ovid, *Met.* 15.290–92).

482. *Aeolus strikes*: In Greek myth, Aeolus was lord of the winds; in *Odyssey* 10 Aeolus gives Odysseus a bag of winds, which he is not supposed to open until nearing home. Behind Lucan's use here lies the famous storm of *Aen.* 1, which begins when Aeolus strikes his

mountain with his trident, freeing the winds. In the simile, the east
wind can be taken for Caesar, the south wind for Pompey.

488–500. *Libo . . . Luceria*: Republican commanders successively routed
from central Italy by Caesar's advancing armies. Caesar (*BC*
1.12–15) relates the withdrawals of Thermus, Varus, and Lentulus,
but not Libo, Sulla, or Scipio. Lucan portrays these as desertions
by cowardly commanders, wanting to maintain the Pompeian al-
legiance of the general populace, while Caesar boasts that several
cities received him by popular proclamation. Lucius Scribonius
Libo abandoned his post and joined up with Pompeian leadership
in Campania. Quintus Minucius Thermus was in charge of Um-
brian Iguvium and withdrew when the citizens took Caesar's side.
Faustus Cornelius Sulla, son of Sulla the dictator, was stationed at
and abandoned Capua. Attius Varus, according to Caesar, with-
drew from Auximon in Picenum when the people took his side;
Publius Cornelius Lentulus Spinther (*BC* 1.15) fled Asculum in
Picenum when most of his ten cohorts of troops deserted him; he
was later captured at Corfinium and pardoned. Quintus Caecilius
Metellus Pius Scipio Nasica left Luceria in Apulia, abandoning the
two legions that Pompey had given to Caesar for the Gallic wars
but then requisitioned for a possible Parthian campaign.

506. *aggressive Domitius*: Lucius Domitius Ahenobarbus, Cato's
brother-in-law, had been an enemy of Caesar for many years. Most
significant for Lucan, Gnaeus Domitius Ahenobarbus was the
birth name of the emperor Nero (then adopted by Claudius and
named Nero Claudius Caesar), and the poem's Domitius was his
great-great-grandfather. Lucan's treatment of him is complicated
by the broader question of the poem's attitude(s) to Nero himself.

508. *dishonored Milo*: Titus Annius Milo was tried and convicted in 52
BC for the murder of P. Clodius Pulcher; to maintain order during
the trial, Pompey, against all precedent, had armed troops sta-
tioned around the Forum.

524. *Ganges' tumid swell*: Mention of India's Ganges evokes Alexander
the Great, whose world-conquering march to the east ended there.

547. *Roman sense of shame*: Latin *pudor* ("shame" or "honor") is the
sense of dignified self-respect that comes with holding to the stan-
dards of behavior endorsed by one's social community; Caesar's
clemency violates the Roman aristocratic code of honorable death
in battle following defeat. Cf. 9.1310–14 for similar lines about the
death of Pompey.

550. *pardoned*: In a letter meant to be publicized, Caesar wrote at the
time: "Let this be the new way to be victorious, to secure ourselves

by mercy [*misericordia*] and generosity [*liberalitas*]" (Cicero, *Att.* 9.7c).

551. *How return to Rome*: Domitius' choice to escape shame by plunging into war recalls Hector's reasoning, based on his sense of honor, for why he cannot go into the city but must stand up to Achilles, even if it means death (cf. *Il.* 22.99–130).

558. *test beforehand*: Cf. Agamemnon's speech testing the courage of the Achaean army in *Iliad* 2.110–41. Like Agamemnon's, Pompey's speech falls flat and fails in its aim.

562. *private citizen*: Literally "called to not-private arms," i.e., public and legitimate, as opposed to Caesar, whose term of command had formally lapsed and who had been declared an enemy of the state. But nor was Pompey a magistrate; he was acting as general in a private capacity (a shadow that had lingered over his entire career; see note 294 above).

564. *Gallic madness*: See catalogue of Gallic tribes in 1.429ff.

570–72. *Catiline . . . Lentulus . . . Cethegus*: Lucius Sergius Catilina led the infamous conspiracy against the state that was forcibly suppressed in 63 BC (see Sallust, *Cat.*, and Cicero's Catiline orations). Publius Cornelius Lentulus Sura and Gaius Cornelius Cethegus were partners in the plot. The Cethegus family did not wear the usual tunic under their togas and hence were known as "bare-armed."

574. *Camillus or Metellus*: Early Republican heroes. Furius Camillus conquered Veii; the Caecilii Metelli had many famous members of consular rank in the early Republic, but Pompey is likely referring to the staunch *optimates* of his own times, especially Quintus Caecilius Metellus Pius, who raised private armies and fought the Marians in Italy for Sulla; Pompey shared consulship with him in 80 BC and then fought Sertorius in Spain. His adopted son was Q. Caecilius Metellus Pius Scipio, father of Pompey's wife, Cornelia.

575. *Cinna and Marius*: Lucius Cornelius Cinna, continuous consul in the turbulent years 87–84 BC and collaborator with both the older and younger Marius; both names were bywords for bloody sedition and civil discord, specifically from the partisan perspective of senatorial optimates.

576–78. *Catulus did Lepidus . . . Carbo . . . Sertorius*: Leading names from the losing side in the civil wars of the 80s–70s BC in which Pompey rose to prominence. Marcus Aemilius Lepidus, consul in 78 BC and strong opponent of Sulla's settlement after his death, had tried to bring his army into Italy like Caesar but was defeated by the army of his consular colleague Quintus Lutatius Catulus. Gnaeus Papirius Carbo was consul with Cinna in 85 and 84 BC, and again in 82 with the younger Gaius Marius; with Sulla's victory he was proscribed and fled, and Pompey had him executed in Sicily. Quintus Sertorius was a Marian and governor of Spain, but was proscribed; in 77 BC Pompey was sent to Spain to deal with him, but he continued to hold power and resist the Senate's armies until he was assassinated by an associate in 73 BC.

581–83. *Crassus . . . Scythia*: Third member of the first Triumvirate, Crassus had died in 53 BC on campaign in Parthia. "Scythia" is inaccurate, though such geographical fuzziness is common in Roman conceptions of lands on their margins, and it is probably used here due to metrical needs.

583. *Spartacus*: a Thracian gladiator who led a massive slave revolt in 73 BC that was finally and brutally subdued by armies under Crassus and Pompey in 71 BC. Associating Caesar, a proconsul of Rome and scion of an ancient patrician family, with the leader of a slave revolt is a blatantly propagandistic move.

585. *titles of honor*: Roman elites would habitually list all their offices and victories, on their tombs, for example, and often great achievements would become honorific names.

590. *my age*: fifty-six, six years older than Caesar.

594. *no private matter*: Since Pompey has said only kingship remains above him, anyone trying to surpass him would logically be aiming for a status that would call for public action in defense of republican liberty.

595. *Both consuls*: Lucius Cornelius Lentulus Crus and Gaius Claudius Marcellus. Caesar's grievance involved being denied the right to stand for the consular elections that year.

599. *several tours*: Caesar had been waging successful campaigns in Gaul since 58 BC.

601–602. *Rhine's cold current . . . 'Ocean'*: Caesar had bridged the Rhine in 55 BC and briefly entered Germany but retreated; in 55 and 54 BC Caesar crossed the English Channel and waged "exploratory" campaigns in Britain, but achieved no substantial successes and nearly met with disaster. Pompey belittles the size and nature of the North Sea.

609. *Cynthia*: The moon.

610. *pirates quit the sea*: In 67 BC Pompey was given command to quell the Cilician pirates, which he accomplished in less than two months. He resettled them on farmland in Cilicia.

612–14. *obstinate king . . . Sulla*: Mithridates VI, ambitious king of Pontus who menaced Rome in the 80s–60s BC; in 65–64

BC Pompey led campaigns against him in the Caucasus; he took refuge across the Bosporus in the Tauric Chersonnese (modern Crimea), where he committed suicide in 63 BC. Pompey calls to mind that Sulla had previously warred with Mithridates, and by defeating him he was "more fortunate" than Sulla Felix.

615–29. *No part of the world*: Pompey's lifelong achievements. Phasis is a river in Colchis on the eastern shores of the Black Sea, where Pompey campaigned and exerted Roman influence in 65 BC. It has a cold climate but is not particularly northern (Rome is at the same latitude). Syene is in Upper Egypt and in the tropics, thus casting small shadows at noon; though Pompey may have visited Syene— no other sources mention this—Lucan may simply be exaggerating the extent of Pompey's influence in East Africa. The Baetis River (modern Guadalquivir), in southern Spain, is apparently a reference to campaigns against Sertorius in 75 BC. Tethys is a mythical name for the outer Ocean River. (Lucan himself was from Corduba in the region of Baetica.) Pompey had made alliances with Arab groups during campaigns in 64 BC. The Heniochi were neighbors of the Colchi, east of the Black Sea. Pompey had maintained the Cappadocians as Roman clients, supporting Ariobarzanes as king. The cryptic god of the Judaeans is Jehovah, who was not to be named. Pompey took Jerusalem and reduced Judaea to Roman control in 63 BC. Sophene is a region in Armenia; Pompey had installed and removed kings there. The Cilician pirates, referred to again, had their strongholds in the Taurus mountains of Cilicia.

632. *Magnus sensed their fear*: In letters to Domitius, Pompey confessed that he did not trust the troops he had with him (see Cicero, *Att.* 8.12c–d).

636. *When a bull in his first challenge*: This simile echoes and contrasts with that in *Il.* 2.481–84, where Agamemnon is compared favorably to a successful bull. Cf. also *Aen.* 12.103–6. The second half of the simile is at best narrative misdirection, since Pompey never returns as victor.

646. *Cretan colonists*: Brundisium, at the end of the Via Appia; its foundation legend related it in some manner to the myth of Theseus, who on returning from defeating the Cretan Minotaur forgot to change his sails from black to white, the agreed-upon signal for his victory; on seeing the black sails, his father, King Aegeus of Athens, jumped into the sea that then took his name.

651. *within curving horns*: This description may allude to the connection of the name Brundisium with the Messapian word *brunda*, "stag's horn" (the Messapii were a native Calabrian tribe).

659–60. *Corcyra . . . Epidamnos*: In Greece across the Adriatic from Brundisium lay Corcyra (modern Corfu), and to the left up the Illyrian coast, Epidamnus (Lucan gives the Greek -*os* ending here), the older Greek name for Dyrrachium (see note at 6.16, and map).

662–63. *Ceraunia . . . Sason*: Ceraunia is a region of rocky headlands along the coast of Epirus north of Corcyra. Sason is a small rocky isle that serves as a landmark opposite Brundisium, midway between Dyrrachium and Corcyra.

665. *rugged Iberia*: Pompey had held supreme command (by proxy) in Spain since 55 BC and enjoyed active support there. The reason Lucan offers for him not going to Spain is not very convincing, as he could reach Spain by sea as easily as the East.

667. *eldest of his great offspring*: Gnaeus Pompeius, a military prefect; he would be executed after the disastrous Battle of Munda in 45 BC.

669. *Euphrates and Nile*: I.e., Parthia and Egypt.

672–77. *Egypt's kings . . . Scythian wagons*: Cleopatra and Ptolemy ruled Egypt as a client kingdom dependent on Pompey. Tigranes I was king of Armenia and son-in-law of Mithridates VI; Pharnaces II was son of Mithridates VI and received the Bosporan kingdom on the Black Sea from Pompey. The two Armenias are Greater and Lesser Armenia. The Riphaean Mountains were a mythical chain situated in northern Scythia. The Maeotian Lake is the Sea of Azov; that the natives drove their wagons across its frozen surface was a commonplace in Latin literature (see note at 5.465–70).

682. *the Latin year*: The consuls Lentulus and Marcellus, whom he sends to Epirus in Greece. The Romans designated their years by the names of the consuls.

703–706. *Eryx . . . Avernus*: A tall mountain in northwest Sicily; just north offshore are the Aeolian Islands (a plausible, though not entirely necessary, emendation of *Aegean* in the manuscripts). Gaurus is a mountain in Campania near Lake Avernus.

710. *pompous Xerxes*: The text says "the Persian." Caesar's ambitious earthworks recall (not for the last time) Xerxes' bridging of the Hellespont (Sestos and Abydos were cities on either side) and his digging of a canal through Athos in 480 BC (Herodotus, *Hist.* 7.22–24, 34–37). His cutting down of trees looks forward to his later forest desecration in Massilia (3.416ff). In the imperial period Xerxes occurs in contexts about engineering ambitions, especially in reference to projects planned and/or executed by Julio-Claudian emperors. Xerxes thus serves to sound the note of criticism of so-called imperial *megalourgia* ("grand work projects").

731–32. *Virgo . . . Claws*: The Claws of Scorpio actually indicated the
constellation Libra to the west of it. Lucan's astronomical reckon-
ing is loose and probably has poetic motivations; Virgo and Libra
setting at this time (March 17 = January 26, 49, Julian calendar)
would have been more accurate. Since the sun was in the Claws in
mid-November, Lucan may have thought Pompey left Brundisium
earlier than he did (e.g., much sooner after Caesar entered Italy),
or he might have doubly compensated for the difference between
the old and new calendars. Caesar says Pompey left at dusk (*BC*
1.28): on March 17 (pre-Julian) Virgo and the Claws were rising at
sunset. A poetic reason to mention Virgo exists: the myth of the
goddess Astraea (see note to 258).

750. *Chalcis*: The narrow, dangerous strait separating Euboea from the
Greek mainland.

753. *Nereus*: A Greek sea god, here metonymy for the sea.

755–58. *Pagasae . . . Clashing Rocks*: The *Argo* sailed from Pagasae to
the Phasis River in Colchis to fetch the Golden Fleece. The Sym-
plegades or Clashing Rocks, also called the Cyanean or Dark
Rocks, at the entrance of the Bosporus were fated to become fixed
forever if any ship made it through without being wrecked.

762–65. *Pleiades . . . Boötes . . . Venus*: Constellations, brought in
most likely simply to fill out the lovely image of dawn's slow rise.
Venus is the morning star (Lucifer).

770–73. *exile*: Cf. Aeneas and the Trojans fleeing fallen Troy into sad
exile at *Aen.* 2.801–3.

776. *Pharian*: After Pharos, the lighthouse island in Alexandria's
harbor.

BOOK THREE

3. *Ionian*: The sea south of the Adriatic, fanning out to southern
Italy and Sicily in the west and Greece in the east.

11. *Julia's sorrowful head*: Daughter of Caesar, b. 73 BC, married to
Pompey in 59 BC to seal a political alliance; she miscarried and
died in 54 BC. Behind her are other famous female ghosts in epic,
Creusa in *Aen.* 2.771–94 and Dido in *Aen.* 5.1–6; elegy also gave
models, Propertius' dead Cynthia (4.7).

13–20. *Elysian . . . Parcae*: A miniture atlas of underworld geography.
The Elysian Fields are the Fields of the Blessed, where the greatest
heroes go after death. The gods swore by the waters of the river
Styx. The Eumenides are the three Furies (by the euphemistic

NOTES 367

name "the Kindly Ones"), in charge of avenging bloodguilt, especially familial and so most appropriate to civil wars. The Acheron is the underworld river across which souls are first ferried by the boatman Charon. Tartarus is the pit where underworld punishments are meted out. The "three sisters" are the Parcae, the Fates (Clotho, "Spins"; Lachesis, "Apportions"; and Atropos, "the Unbending," cuts the threads of fate).

22. *triumphs*: Not true; Pompey's third triumph was in 62 BC, before they married.

24. *mistress Cornelia*: Julia jealously does not recognize Pompey's new wife. Cornelia was the daughter of Quintus Caecilius Metellus Scipio who married Publius Licinius Crassus (son of Crassus the triumvir) in 55 BC. When he was killed with his father at Carrhae in 53, she married Pompey in 52.

31. *Lethe's banks*: The underworld river of forgetfulness, of which souls drink before passing back into the world to be reincarnated.

39. *embrace*: Vain attempts to embrace the dead soul of a loved one are standard in epic: Odysseus' three attempts to embrace the soul of his mother, Anticleia (*Od.* 11.205–8); Aeneas' attempts to embrace Creusa (*Aen.* 2.792–3) and his father, Anchises (*Aen.* 6.700–702). The frustrated embrace also recalls Ovid's story of Ceyx and Alcyone, which this scene inverts. King Ceyx died in a shipwreck at sea and then appears to Alcyone in a dream (11.410ff.; cf. esp. lines 674–76); they turn into seabirds and give rise to the "halcyon days." The opposite outcome here will be the violence of civil war.

42–44. *empty image . . . death itself is nothing*: Epicurean reasonings about the emptiness of death, rendered into epic by Lucretius (cf. *De R. N.* 3). This opposition, slightly obscure for its succinctness, may be understood as leaving unstated the idea that death is nothing *if* the soul has feeling as it does in life. Discussion and treatment of the nature of death are as common to classical epic as to philosophy. The Gallic Druids' belief in reincarnation was mentioned at 1.478–95 (see note), and Cato will give reasons why death is not to be feared at 9.566ff.

64. *Curio*: Gaius Scribonius Curio, the tribune, is dispatched to secure the grain supplies from Sicily, Sardinia, and Libya (cf. Caesar, *BC* 1.30–1). He will reappear in Book Four.

74. *torrid zone*: The earth was divided into five zones: the frozen poles, two temperate and habitable zones between them, and the torrid equatorial zone, often associated with Africa as a whole.

81. *What chains*: The image suggests the representations, displayed in triumphs, of rivers and seas in chains to symbolize the conquest of

a region and its peoples, here the Rhine and Ocean for conquests in Germany and Britain.

89–92. *Anxur . . . Alba's heights*: Anxur or Tarracina is modern Terracina, at the southern end of the malarial Pomptine Marshes, 100 kilometers south of Rome on the Via Appia. Farther along the Via Appia was the famous grove of Diana Nemorensis at Aricia. Nearby were Alba Longa and the Alban Mount, where the consuls presided over the Latin Festival (referenced again at 5.400–402), about 20 kilometers from Rome.

99–100. *Sarmatians . . . Dacians*: Peoples living around the middle and lower Danube, whom the Romans fought and subdued throughout the first century AD.

110. *Palatine temple of Phoebus*: An anachronism, since the temple of Apollo on the Palatine was dedicated by Augustus in 28 BC. But it became a regular meeting place thereafter, a change indicative of the Caesars' broader realignment of political power.

114. *ivory chairs*: The *sella curulis*, special seats inlaid with ivory where certain magistrates sat in the Senate.

121. *Metellus*: Lucius Caecilius Metellus, a tribune in 49 BC who obstructed Caesar's designs in Rome, including his attempt to open the treasury (though Caesar doesn't mention this scene, saying only, "Caesar's enemies put L. Metellus up to impede . . . everything he tried to accomplish," *BC* 1.33). Later Caesar banished him from Italy. For the episode cf. also Plutarch, *Caes.* 35, *Pomp.* 62.

122. *Saturn's temple*: Used as the state treasury.

128. *incited a conflict*: Cf. 6.447–52.

133. *sacred blood*: Tribunes were protected from violence by strict legal and religious sanctions.

135. *Crassus*: When Crassus was leaving for Parthia in 55 BC, the tribune Gaius Ateius Capito cursed him, which was believed to have been effective when he died at Carrhae.

151. *manners of the toga*: In republican Rome citizens were not supposed to bear arms inside the walls, and the toga was the attire that symbolized this (ideal) urban peace and safety, often violated during the Late Republic.

152. *Cotta*: Lucius Aurelius Cotta (consul 64 BC), a relative of Caesar on his mother's side who remained neutral in the civil war but later was expected to propose that Caesar be called king outside Italy in accord with divine command in the sacred books.

158. *evil seeds of dreadful war*: The money in the treasury.

162. *Tarpeian rock*: Part of the Capitoline Hill from which convicted criminals were hurled, here, as often, metonymic for the whole Capitoline.

166. *the wealth of the Roman people*: The ultimate spendthrift heir, Caesar loots the long, glorious history of Rome.

167. *Perses . . . Philip*: In reverse chronological order. Perses, king of Macedon, was defeated in 168 BC; his father, Philip V, defeated in 197 BC, paid Rome 1,000 talents.

168. *Gauls left behind*: When the Gauls took Rome in 387–86 BC, they were bribed to leave, and when they did so, Camillus recovered the money.

169. *Fabricius . . . Pyrrhus*: In the early third century Gaius Fabricius Luscinus was given money by Pyrrhus, king of Epirus, to betray the state, but he refused and deposited it in the treasury.

171. *Asian peoples*: Attalus III, king of Pergamum in Asia Minor, bequeathed his kingdom to Rome in 133 BC.

172. *Minoan Crete*: Quintus Caecilius Metellus Creticus conquered Crete (island of the legendary King Minos) in 69–67 BC.

173. *Cato . . . Cyprus*: Marcus Porcius Cato was sent to annex Cyprus in 58 BC, and after selling off the royal treasures returned it to Rome (cf. Plutarch, *Cato Min.* 34–36).

174–75. *kings of the East*: In 61 BC Pompey brought back 20,000 talents of gold and coin from his eastern campaigns, including the defeats of Mithridates VI of Pontus, Tigranes II of Armenia, and Aristobulus of Judaea.

176. *all is carted off*: Pliny (*Nat. Hist.* 33.17.56) says that Caesar took 15,000 pounds of gold, 30,000 of silver, and 300,000 of coin, and "at no period was the republic wealthier." Failing to mention this in his commentary, he still snuck in the notice that his enemies had intended to take the state reserves as well (*BC* 1.14).

177. *Rome was poorer than Caesar*: But not for the last time; the imperial family was often wealthier than the public state treasuries (though after Augustus it also became harder to distinguish the public from the private imperial purse).

179. *around the world*: This extensive catalogue of forces parallels *Iliad* 2.484–77, drawing on Caesar's list at *BC* 3.3–5, embellishing details but not greatly its geographic expanse.

181–84. *Amphissa of Phocis . . . oracular waters*: Beginning in central Greece with Phocis and Boeotia; Cirrha is near Delphi, whose Mount Parnassos is always identified as twin-peaked. Dirce's spring flowed through the main Boeotian city of Thebes, founded

by Cadmus, and the Cephisus begins near Delphi—hence "oracu-
lar"—and flows through Phocis and Boeotia.

185–89. *Pisa . . . Chaonia*: First in the Peloponnese, then back to central
and up to northwestern Greece. The Alpheus, the main river in
Elis, flows through Pisa; Maenalus is a peak in Arcadia; Mount
Oeta is near Trachis in central Greece, where Hercules committed
himself to flames and became a god. Thesprotians, Dryopes, and
the Selloi of Chaonia all came from Epirus in northwestern Greece;
the Selloi were associated with the ancient oracular shrine of Zeus
at Dodona, which is silent because it was destroyed by the Aeto-
lians in 219 BC and ravaged again by the Romans in 167 BC. The
Dryopes are (semi-)mythical, but enter here naturally because of
the Greek root for oak tree, *dru-*.

190–92. *Athens . . . Salamis*: Apparently Athens was only able to send
very few ships, which seems to be supported by a fragment of Livy.
At the Battle of Salamis in 480 BC the Athenians proved their
naval might by defeating the Persians. By Apollo's dockyards
Lucan probably means Apollonia in Illyria, south of Dyrrachium,
where Pompey was gathering his forces.

193–95. *Crete . . . Gortyn*: Two of Crete's "hundred cities." Zeus (Roman
Jove) was born and nursed in Crete's Dictaean Cave. The Easterners
here are the Parthians.

196–98. *Oricos . . . Cadmus*: In Epirus, south of Apollonia, founded by
a Dardan (i.e., Trojan), perhaps Helenus (cf. *Aen.* 3.291–97, but
Buthrotum is named). Athamania in eastern Epirus was said to be
founded by the legendary King Athamas. The Encheliae were a
mountain Illyrian tribe; Cadmus, after he and his wife, Harmonia,
were turned into snakes, was said to have retired to Illyria (cf.
Ovid, *Met.* 4.568); Encheliae is related to the Greek word for eel.

199–206. *Colchian . . . new kind of death*: References to the *Argo*'s
voyage. Absyrtos is a small island in the northern Adriatic off the
Liburnian coast, which according to Apollonius of Rhodes was
where Medea's brother Absyrtos was dismembered and cast in the
sea (Medea is from Colchis). The Peneus is the large central river
of Thessaly (for which Haemonia is another name). Iolcus is the
Thessalian coastal city from which the Argonauts disembarked on
their quest for the Golden Fleece. The "original sin" of seafaring is
a common theme for the Argonaut myth, and Lucan exploits it in
connection with Thessaly as the ill-fated site for civil war (com-
pare 6.445–46).

206–11. *Mount Haemus . . . Peucë*: Moving north and east, the Hae-
mus Mountains are in northern Thrace, just south of the Danube;

Mount Pholoë, where Hercules fought with the centaurs, is actually on the border of Elis and Arcadia, and only Lucan (twice: see 6.432) locates it in Thessaly or Macedon; the Strymon River divides Macedon and Thrace; Bistonian = Thracian. The cranes' migration from the Strymon to Africa comes from *Il.* 3.3–6 and Virgil, *Geo.* 1.120, *Aen.* 6.309–12. In Homer they bring "death and doom" to the fabled Pygmies. Either their combativeness or their flight to Africa would make them appropriate in connection with the civil war and Pompey's eastern trajectory. Peucë, and perhaps Conë (not otherwise known), are islands off the mouth of the Danube in the Black Sea. Sarmatic refers to the region of the Sarmatians on the middle Danube.

212–25. *Mysia . . . Iulus*: Focus here is on Asia Minor. Ida is the mountain at the southern edge of the Troad; Mysia is south of it, between Phrygia and Lydia, through which the Caicus River flows. Pitane is a seaport city near its mouth. Arisbe is a small town in the Troad. Celaenae is a town in southern Phrygia. The Marsysas River of Caria flows into the Maeander, famous for its winding. Athena invented the aulos (double "oboe") but rejected it; when the satyr Marsyas took up the instrument and challenged Apollo to a music contest, upon losing he was flayed alive in punishment. The Pactolus and Hermus are rivers of Lydia, famed for their gold and associated with King Midas. Ilium is Troy; the Julian family claimed descent from Iulus, son of the Trojan prince Aeneas (a connection that underpins Virgil's *Aeneid*). Their presence is a bad omen because Troy had been sacked.

225–36. *Syria . . . magic utterances*: Moving south and east, to Palestine, Syria, and Egypt. The Orontes River runs along the coast in northern Syria; Ninos is either the city in Syria or else Lucan means Nineveh, the famous Mesopotamian city at this time in Parthian territory. Syrian Damascus lies on a windy plain; Gaza is on the southern, Tyre and Sidon on the northern, coast of Judaea. Tyre was "unsteady" from earthquakes; both it and Sidon produced purple dye for textiles from the murex, a mollusk. Idumea is a region southwest of the Dead Sea. The Phoenicians (who inhabited both Tyre and Sidon) were famous for their skill in navigation; the "Dog's Tail" (Cynosura) was a constellation name for our Little Dipper, which includes Polaris, the polestar. The Greeks, followed by the Romans, believed that the Phoenicians were the first to invent writing; in fact, Egypt preceded them, and the Phoenician alphabet is adapted from Egyptian hieroglyphs. Memphis is a city in Egypt; the reeds are the Nile's papyrus, the exclusive source of ancient paper.

236–40. *Taurus . . . Cilicians*: Moving back north into Asia Minor, the wooded Taurus Mountains are along the northern border of Cilicia. Tarsus is a city on the Cilician coast said to have been founded by Perseus. Corycus is west of Tarsus along the coast and had a famous cave where crocus was harvested (see note at 9.1004); Mallos and Aegae are also Cilician coast cities. Lucan reminds again about Pompey's earlier war with the Cilician pirates.

241–55. *distant East . . . rest to the gods*: Lucan exceeds credulity here by drawing distant India into the war, but it provides a convenient excuse to compare Pompey the Great with Alexander the Great. The Hydaspes was a tributary of the Indus, on India's western edges, the fabled Ganges to India's east. Alexander was from Pella in Macedon; his march to the east and decision to halt was a common debating topic in the rhetorical schools of Lucan's time. Sugarcane, saffron dye, flowing robes, and gemstones were stereotypical features of the fabled and poorly known India, as was the practice of self-immolation (suttee), which here rouses Lucan's Stoic apostrophe to heroic suicide.

255–59. *Cappadocians . . . touch the sky*: Cappadocia is in east-central Asia Minor, the Amanus Mountains in eastern Cilicia, and the Niphates Mountains are part of the Taurus chain in Armenia (east of Cappadocia). The obscure Choatrae are probably a mountain people of southeast Armenia.

259–67. *Arabs . . . front hoof*: South and east again, sweeping through Arabia and Mesopotamia. The Orestae of distant Asia are otherwise unknown. The Carmanians, known for their ferocity, lived in southern Iran along the Persian Gulf. Lucan refers to the fact that the constellations the Bear, which does not set in northern latitudes, and Boötes, which sets slowly, here in the south both set. Ethiopia, south of Egypt, is also referenced through (invalid) astronomy: Lucan says Ethiopia sees only one south-projecting leg of the Taurus out of the whole zodiac, which is untrue, but Virgil makes the same mistake (*Aen.* 6.795–97).

268–75. *Tigris . . . waves*: The Euphrates and Tigris are the two rivers defining Mesopotamia, which rise to the north in modern Turkey, which at that time formed the border between the Roman and Parthian ("Persian") empires. The Tigris was thought to flow underground for some distance before reemerging (Seneca, *Nat. Quaest.* 3.26.3–4). A rare three-line fragment of epic verse by the emperor Nero himself also describes this phenomenon.

276–78. *Parthians*: Rome's bitter enemies do not enter the war, but they are pleased that they have killed Crassus and reduced their Roman enemies to two fighting factions.

279–85. *Scythian . . . Croesus*: Back north and east one more time, to Scythia, central Asia, and the Black Sea regions. The Bactros River is in Bactria in central Asia; the Hyrcanian forests were southeast of the Caspian Sea. The Heniochi lived on the eastern shores of the Black Sea and claimed descent from Castor and Pollux of Sparta (Lacedaemon). The Sarmatians lived in northern Scythia. The Moschi lived near Colchis (with its river the Phasis) in the Caucasus. The Halys is a river in Cappadocia. Croesus of Lydia was told by the Delphic oracle that if he crossed the Halys to attack Cyrus he would destroy a great empire; he crossed it and was himself defeated (Herodotus, *Hist.* 1.53, 70–92).

286–93. *Don . . . Gades*: The Don (ancient Tanais) is actually west of the Riphaeus (modern Ural) Mountains, both of which formed notional northeastern geographical borders between Europe and Asia. Lake Maeotis enters the Black Sea at the Cimmerian Bosporus, which Lucan sets up as another entry to the outer Ocean parallel to the Pillars of Hercules at Gades (modern Cadiz) in the west. The Geloni lived along the Don.

294–98. *Issedonia . . . Geloni*: Poorly known and/or fictional peoples of central Asia. The fabulous Arimaspi were one-eyed people who lived in perpetual quest of a griffin's gold horde. The Massagetes were believed to eat their horses.

299–301. *Cyrus . . . spears thrown*: The catalogue ends with explicit comparisons with famous multiethnic hordes of the Persian kings Cyrus and Xerxes and to the Greek armies at Troy. Cyrus led a large expedition against the Massagetes (Herodotus, *Hist.* 1.205) and established an early model for a vast, geographically diverse empire. In Trojan War myth, Memnon is the son of the Dawn, thus his name indicates "Eastern." The Persian is Xerxes, whose army was so large and diverse that supposedly it was counted up by the number of weapons (Herodotus, *Hist.* 7.760).

302. *brother's lost love*: Agamemnon led the Greek expedition to recover his brother Menelaus' wife, Helen, stolen by Paris—the Homeric catalogue of Greek forces provides the model for Lucan here.

308–11. *Ammon . . . Syrtes*: The oracle in the Libyan oasis, "horned" because the god was in the form of a ram. Marmarica is the surrounding region, between Cyrene and Egypt. The Mauri (the Moors) inhabited the western coast of North Africa, and the Syrtes are shoals and shallows on the sea between Numidia and Cyrene. Paraetonia is a city on the coast in Egypt, here = African or Libyan.

317. *Phocaean men*: When the city of Massilia (modern Marseille) received Domitius and excluded Caesar, he laid siege to it (see *BC* 1.34–36, 56–58, 2.1–16, 22). Massilia was founded by Greek colonists from Phocaea on the north coast of Asia Minor. Lucan (along with other Roman authors) often confuses Phocaea and Phocis (around Delphi). The preceding catalogue had begun with Phocis; given the confusion with Phocaea, Lucan probably intended a neat ring-composition between the catalogue and the siege of Massilia.

322. *olive branch*: The olive was created/discovered by and sacred to Pallas Athena and symbolized peace.

324. *always sided with your people*: Massilia had supported Rome since the Second Punic War.

330. *accursed wounds*: The language of this strange line is medical. Perhaps a wound of divine origin and thus ominous, like that of Philoctetes, is meant; or perhaps the following lines suggest that *sacra* means "wounding the gods," committing sacrilege.

331–36. *gods who dwell in heaven*: The Gigantomachy, a favorite metaphor for the civil wars from at least as early as Horace and Virgil. The Massilians suggest that just as humans should not meddle in divine matters, non-Romans should not get involved in Roman affairs.

336. *Thunderer still reigns*: See note at 7.526.

347. *far from our city*: Like Rome, Massilia did not allow arms inside the city.

352. *Spain calls you*: Caesar was pursuing Vibullius Rufus, whom he had pardoned at Corfinium but whom Pompey had sent to Spain.

354. *lucky in war*: Not true; Massilia had a long history of successes against Gauls, Etruscans, and Carthaginians.

356. *Phocaea burned*: Like Rome founded by Trojan refugees; Phocaea (Lucan says Phocis) had been taken and burned by the Persians in 545 BC (Herodotus, *Hist.* 1.164–69), and ancient authors dated Massilia's founding to this event (incorrectly; it was earlier).

366. *Saguntum*: Spanish Saguntum, besieged for eight months in 219 BC and destroyed for its loyalty to Rome. The acts of cannibalism had become standard embellishments in rhetorical treatments of the siege.

391. *thick with warriors*: Lucan neglects to mention that the Massiliotes had vowed neutrality toward Caesar, but then had allowed Domitius in, thus siding with Pompey.

392. *heights of a hill*: The valley between it and the city is the valley of St. Martin.

399. *massive earthworks*: Like the Giants piling Pelion on Ossa to assault Olympus. The siege of Brundisium in Book Two used similar language, but this instance is larger, with more mythical and ethical charge throughout.

411. *forests wide are felled*: Felling trees is a common epic theme since the *Iliad* (23.108–26); cf. also *Aen.* 6.176–82, 11.133–38.

416. *There was a sacred grove*: 24 kilometers from Massilia. Caesar's violation of the sacred grove parallels the story of Erysichthon of Thessaly, who knowingly violated a grove of Demeter by cutting down a sacred tree, and was punished with insatiable hunger (cf. Ovid's version in *Met.* 8.738–878). Erysichthon's contempt for the Olympian gods is a fitting model for Caesar cast as a Giant assaulting Olympus.

419–32. *Pan ... Nymphs ... Silvanus ... shiver*: Rustic gods who inhabited wilds and especially sacred groves. That the grove is sacred not to Greek or Roman but to savage Gallic gods, described in lurid detail, is in keeping with Lucan's fascination with exotic ethnological lore.

432–34. *it adds to the terror*: The unknown gods of these woods and the fundamental fear of primitive religion recall the primitive Capitoline Hill in *Aeneid* 8.347–54, where the god is unknown and the quaking rustics tremble at the woods and rocks. Caesar, in effect, demolishes a surrogate for primitive Rome.

436. *yews*: The poisonous yew tree (*Taxus baccata*) was associated with the underworld.

458–60. *Ash trees ... common grief*: Oaks were sacred to Zeus at Dodona; alders were commonly used for shipbuilding; wealthy tombs were often planted with cypress trees (see Ovid, *Met.* 10.90–142 for a tree catalogue and the story of Cyparissus).

467. *nature's divine powers*: Latin *numina*, taking the point of the line to be a contrast between divine Fortune, who favors Caesar even in his wickedness, and the sort of minor nature deities presumably present in the violated woods (cf. Virgil, *Geo.* 1.10, *agrestum praesentia numina*, "deities present for rustics," a passage Lucan alludes to in the negative back at 3.419–20, "there were no rustic Pans . . ."). The wretches would presumably be the Massilians and/or Caesar's rank and file, who will suffer the pains of siege and battle: in other words, Caesar provokes the wrath of nature spirits, then skips off scot-free to Spain, leaving the divine wrath to those who will fight the battle.

473. *Mars*: Roman god of war.

474. *Spain*: Caesar departed for Spain and turned over the Massilian siege to Gaius Tribonius (who would later take part in Caesar's assassination).

481. *underground hollows*: Greco-Roman natural philosophy held that earthquakes were caused by the forceful movement of underground winds.

495. *shell formation*: Lucan describes what was called the *testudo*, or tortoise formation.

509. *siege shed*: These were built of light material such as wicker for ease of movement, and covered with dirt to resist fire.

532. *fortune on the sea*: This scene actually collapses two naval battles into one grand scene (and the burning of Caesar's siegeworks, related just above, happened *after* the second naval battle; first battle, *BC* 1.56–58; the second, *BC* 2.3–7).

536. *Brutus' turreted warship*: Decimus Junius Brutus Albinus was in charge of Caesar's fleet (not the famous Brutus, though he, too, took part in Caesar's assassination and was put to death by Antony).

538. *Stoechas isles*: The Stoechades, modern Îles d'Hyères, along the Gallic coast east of Massilia.

551–58. *triremes . . . six full tiers*: Ancient ships were designated by the vertical tiers of rowers they maintained. The early Greek trireme had three; later designs had four, five, or six levels of rowers; the fast two-level Liburnian was invented by the Liburni, an Illyrian people.

558. *massive flagship*: As admiral, Brutus commanded the *praetoria navis*.

567. *beak*: The prow or *rostrum* ("beak") of the ship was fitted out with metal and was used for ramming.

611. *Catus*: His name means sharp or clever. This and other later characters in this scene are invented. The epic convention of inventing characters for descriptions of unique, graphic, and pathos-ridden forms of death goes back to Homer.

615. *casts both spears out*: The hyperbolic image of blood expelling a weapon comes from Ovid, *Met.* 13.394.

629. *twin brothers*: Cf. the twin brothers in Virgil, *Aen.* 10.390ff.

663–73. *Lycidas . . . death got him all*: Probably a Massiliote, because of his Greek name. Some have suspected these lines were Lucan's dying words, according to the account of his suicide given by Tacitus (*Ann.* 15.70).

709. *pest most contrary to water*: Fire, the lightest of the four elements, and thus (in addition to obvious reasons) contrary to water, the heaviest.

712. *pitch . . . wax*: Both used to waterproof and seal the ship's seams.

737–39. *Tyrrhenus . . . Lygdamus . . . Balearic*: Tyrrhenus (the "Etruscan") is probably a Roman, Lygdamus a Greek; the Balearic Islands were famous for their slingshots.

789. *its first naval glory*: The siege had lasted for six months. Caesar relates that in the first naval battle the Massiliotes lost nine ships, and in the second, four ships were captured and five sunk. Lucan omits the prominent detail in Caesar that L. Domitius Ahenobarbus fled under cover of storm after learning that the Massiliotes were planning to surrender (*BC* 2.22).

BOOK FOUR

4. *Afranius and Petreius*: Lucius Afranius had served under Pompey against Sertorius in Spain and had governed Hither Spain since 53 BC (he will survive Pharsalus but die at Thapsus). Marcus Petreius was a seasoned officer governing in Spain and loyal to Pompey. Upon Caesar's approach he quickly joined his troops with those of Afranius and they prepared to meet Caesar at Ilerda on the Sicoris River in northeast Spain, just south of the Pyrenees (see map).

9–11. *Asturians . . . Iberian*: The Astures lived in Cantabria in northwest Spain, the Vettones in Lusitania; the Celtiberians—Celtic peoples of Iberia—lived in the middle Ebro valley.

13–15. *Ilerda . . . Sicoris*: Modern Lérida and Segre. Ilerda was founded in the late third century BC.

18. *Magnus' bivouac*: A partisan identification, since Pompey himself is not here. As at Massilia, the armies will fight from and between two hills; as with the Rubicon and the events at Brundisium, here, too, a body of water will separate Caesar from his goal.

22. *Cinga*: Modern Cinca, which runs into the Sicoris just south of Ilerda, after which their waters join the large Hiberus (modern Ebro), from which Iberia is named (see map). The Cinga and Sicoris bound a wedge of land between them.

62. *Ram . . . Helle*: Caesar arrived in Spain on May 1, 49, by the Julian calendar (June 22, pre–Julian). The Ram is the spring constellation Aries. Lucan identifies it with the flying ram that carried Helle and her brother Phrixus across the Hellespont (see note at 9.1185). The ram became the Golden Fleece in Colchis, and later turned into a constellation.

64–65. *Libra . . . Cynthia*: The constellation Libra, the scales of the goddess Justice; Cynthia is the moon. Basically, Lucan seems to say "it was on/around the vernal equinox" when the floods hit, though he's off by a few weeks.

69. *Nabataea*: The Nabataean kingdom is in Arabia; along with the references to Arabs, the Ganges, and Indians, here meaning out of the southeast.

73. *northwest wind*: Corus; an inconsistency, it seems, probably drawing on *Georgics* 3.356. Seneca (*Nat. Quaest.* 5.16.1–2), discussing winds, quotes Ovid, *Met.* 1.61–66, and Virgil, *Aen.* 1.85–86, as examples of poets packing all the winds into one storm, "which cannot in any way occur," he comments: Lucan, siding with the poets, disagrees.

79. *Gibraltar*: Latin *Calpe*, the monolithic limestone promontory of Gibraltar, which was one of the Pillars of Hercules.

79–81. *Zephyrs . . . Tethys*: West winds; the sea.

84. *pressed at the pole*: Imagining the Strait of Gibraltar as a true limit of the world, where the sky's moisture is insurpassably halted. The rainbow installed here at the world's end seems to act as the earth's circulatory system.

95. *Shipwrecked on the field*: Paradox; contrast with the land battle on the sea at 3.591.

104. *profit*: Caesar's account of the flooding, and the scarcity and massive price inflation it caused, is at *BC* 1.48–52. This recalls Virgil's "cursed hunger for gold" (*Aen.* 3.36–37); cf. Pliny, *Nat. Hist.* 33.3. 6, 33.14.48–49.

118–20. *supreme father . . . second lot*: I.e., Jupiter, whom Lucan rarely names; after defeating the Giants and Titans, the three sons of Kronos and Rhea, Zeus (Jove), Poseidon (Neptune), and Hades (Pluto), drew lots for their dominions. Jove got the first lot and the heavens, Poseidon the second and the sea, and Pluto the third and the underworld.

127. *Riphaeus*: A shifting geographic signifier for mountains off the northeast of the world map familiar to the Romans.

132–34. *the gods . . . forgiveness*: A fairly literal rendering of rather enigmatic lines.

145–46. *Venetians . . . Britons . . . Nile*: These boats are from Caesar, *BC* 1.54; the Nile boats (cf. Virgil, *Geo.* 4.287–88) and Venetian rafts (today's gondolas) are Lucan's addition.

154. *punish its haughty waters*: A motif that invariably evokes Xerxes lashing the waters of the Hellespont in Herodotus, *Hist.* 7.35.

158. *in love with death*: And presumed to be loyal to Pompey, as Caesar says (*BC* 1.61); they planned to move into southwestern Iberia, where Pompey had many old ties of allegience and extra forces could be recruited, so Caesar is eager to cut them off.

203. *Concord*: Concordia was a prominent part of Augustan religious ideology, in his attempts after Actium to ensure that civil war did not break out yet again.

260. *Fortune, in all her divine malice*: Taking this difficult phrase (*deorum invidia*) as a subjective genitive and making Fortune, who is characteristically invidious, the agent of the gods' collective or aggregate malice. (The alternative would be "in malice at the gods.")

276. *better cause*: Caesar's own comment here reveals the strategic character of his clemency: "all thought that Caesar reaped a great profit from his usual leniency, and his policy/tactics [*consilium*] was approved by all" (*BC* 1.74).

310. *sap his strength*: One model is Odysseus' wound in *Iliad* 11.474–80.

317. *Asturian*: A people in northwest Spain.

342. *aconite*: A lethally poisonous plant of the genus *Aconitum*, also called wolfsbane.

353–54. *Meroë . . . Garamantes*: City of the far southern Nile; Cancer is the sign of high summer; Garamantes live in arid North Africa.

361. *dignity*: Latin *maiestas*, cf. note at 8.780.

387. *terms of peace*: Afranius and Petreius surrended to Caesar on August 2, 49 (June 10 in the Julian calendar).

423. *spectators*: Caesar discharged those with property in Spain immediately; the others he marched to Gaul before discharging, providing them with food and making efforts to restore or compensate for lost property. Caesar swore not to harm them and that "no one would be forced to enlist against their will" (*BC* 1.86–87). We do not know how many of these "spectators" reenlisted and followed Caesar back into Italy and on to Greece to be closer to the action.

426–28. *Salonae . . . Iader . . . Curictae*: From south to north on the Illyrian coast, modern Solin, Zadar, and Krk in Croatia; the Roman colony of Iader received walls under Augustus.

430. *Antonius*: Mark Antony's younger brother Gaius, who had gone to help Dolabella off Dalmatia but found himself trapped on Curicta. The summary to the lost books of Livy (*per.* 110) informs us that this scene was in Livy's history; otherwise Lucan is our earliest and fullest account of these events, to which Caesar makes only the barest references (*BC* 3.10, 67).

438. *Basilus*: Lucius Minucius Basilus (who later participated in Caesar's assassination) had apparently come bringing help to Antonius and was on the mainland opposite.

456. *Octavius*: Marcus Octavius, one of Pompey's fleet commanders who caused Caesar's Illyrian forces difficulties all through the fall.

472. *old tricks*: They had been pirates.

484–85. *Charybdis ... Tauromenium*: The Greek city of modern Taormina, on the Sicilian side of the narrow Strait of Messina, was identified as the site of Homer's fabulous monstrous whirlpool Charybdis.

486. *Opitergium's farmers*: Modern Oderzo, north of Venice; Livy, from nearby Patavium (Padua), would for this reason have been attracted to this story of local interest (similar to the Euganean augur at 7.227–36, which derives from Livy).

489. *Vulteius*: Florus' account (*Epit.* 2.13.31–33), so similar to Lucan's that it probably leans on it, adds that Vulteius was a tribune in Caesar's army; critics have explored the significance of his name, from the Latin *vultus*, "face, looks," in relation to his spectacular death.

499. *high-minded*: Latin *magnanima* "great-spirited," a central Stoic virtue (translating the Greek *megalopsychia*) that Cicero regularly ascribed to Cato, defining it in one place as a mind that regards "all human affairs of slight concern and worth nothing" (*De orat.* 2.343), and which he came to connect with *fortitudo*, "courage," and *patientia*, "endurance," as well as *liberalitas*, "generosity" (*Part. or.* 77), but it also could come dangerously close to an arrogant desire to be first (*De off.* 1.61).

525. *Caesar*: Strangely reminiscent of the gladiators' salute, "Hail Commander, those who are about to die salute you!" (*Ave Imperator, morituri te salutant*), known from Suetonius's account of Claudius' mock naval battle (*Claud.* 21).

551–52. *beam of the Great Bear*: Conflated constellation figures, as though the Bear were drawing the Northern Wagon!

555–57. *Gemini ... Cancer ... Sagittarius*: The twins of Gemini were Castor and Pollux, sons of Leda; Sagittarius was the archer (*sagitta* = arrow), figured as a centaur—centaurs come from Thessaly—and as the sign opposite Cancer, would rise at sunset and be visible through the night. This would place the event in mid- to late August 49 BC (June 24 in Julian calendar), which is not impossible, but the chronology for events in Greece that summer is not clearly known.

559. *Histrian ... Liburni*: They were on the Liburnian coast; "Histrian" might be applied to any people living inland and north, in the watershed of the Hister (Danube).

562. *devoted*: See note at 2.326.

579–80. *Cadmus' seed ... Theban brothers*: A compressed reference to the entire Theban saga in Greek myth; Cadmus sowed dragon teeth from which the "Sown Men" (Spartoi) grew out of the ground and began to kill one another; five survived to found

Thebes (cf. Ovid, *Met.* 3.1–130). This beginning in civil strife is an omen for the end, when Eteocles and Polyneices wage fratricidal civil war (see note 1.592). Dirce was a spring in Thebes.

581–84. *Phasis ... Medea*: The same motif of the sown men occurs in the story of Jason, who had sailed the *Argo* to the Phasis River in Colchis. He had to kill the sleepless dragon, yoke fire-breathing bulls, and sow the dragon's teeth, and when men sprouted from the ground he threw a rock into their midst and they all fell to fighting—all accomplished with much help from Medea.

613. *Lilybaeum*: City on the west coast of Sicily. Curio perhaps reached Africa sometime in early August, since he learned of Caesar's successes in Spain during his campaigning (Caesar secured victory in Spain on August 2).

615–18. *Carthage ... Clipea ... famous beach ... Bagradas*: The Romans under Scipio Aemilianus destroyed, then rebuilt, their inveterate enemy Carthage in 146 BC. Clipea (or Aspis, modern Kelibia) was the site of the first fighting on land in the First Punic War in 255 BC. The "famous beach" is either Clipea or the Castra Corneliana mentioned at 689 (see note to 688). The Bagradas reaches the sea near Utica (see map). Caesar clarifies Lucan's terse and rather misleading verses: Curio first reached land at Aquillaria near Clipea, sent his ships around the headland to Utica, and marched there overland, camping at Castra Corneliana near Utica (*BC* 2.23–25).

620. *Antaeus*: A local monster defeated by the wandering Hercules (his name in Greek means simply "antagonist, enemy"). He was variously located: Strabo mentions a tomb of Antaeus at Phoenician Lixus on the far western shore of Mauretania (*Geog.* 17.3.8), and Petrarch relates how Sertorius opened his tomb in Tingis (modern Tangier), and that he was married to a native goddess, Tinga (*Sert.* 9). His defeat by Hercules is mentioned by Propertius (3.22.10) and Ovid (*Met.* 9.184), but Lucan's is the only extended narrative of it, which he models on the similar Hercules and Cacus story in *Aeneid* 8.185–305.

625–26. *Typhon, Tityos ... Briareus*: Giants of early Greek myth, born of Earth (Gaia); Briareus was one of the Hundred-Handers, born of Earth and Sky, who fought for Zeus in the Olympians' war against the Titans (Hesiod, *Theo.* 147–54, 617–735); Typhon/Typhaon was the overwhelming monster Earth bore for single-handed combat with Zeus (*Theo.* 820–80); Tityos was a giant whose liver was eternally eaten by vultures in Hades for having tried to rape Leto (*Od.* 11.576–81).

628. *Phlegra*: See note at 7.174.

634. *lie on the naked earth*: Compare with 9.1094–95.

640. *that great soul*: Hercules is called *magnanimum*—see note at 499 above.

643. *Nemean*: Hercules slew the lion of Nemea in Greece and wore its hide (the Latin actually refers to Cleonae, a town near Nemea).

645. *wrestlers*: One of the athletic competitions at the Olympian Games.

652. *Alcides*: Hercules, grandson of Alcaeus.

665–66. *Inachus . . . Hydra*: Hercules slew the many-headed Hydra in the lake at Lerna, which is on the Argolid shore just south of where the river Inachus meets the sea.

668. *cruel stepmother*: Hera (Juno in Latin), who harassed Hercules.

670. *hoisting Olympus*: When Hercules went west to fetch the apples of the Hesperides, he briefly held up the sky for Atlas while the god fetched the apples for him.

688–89. *Punic foe . . . Scipio's base*: When Scipio Africanus besieged Utica in 204–203 BC, his victories led to Hannibal's recall from Italy to face the threat; his campsite, called the Castra Corneliana, was near Utica, and Curio stationed himself there for his campaign.

692. *Roman conqueror*: Scipio Africanus soon roundly defeated the Carthaginians, ending the seventeen-year-long war at the Battle of Zama in 202 BC.

698. *outmatched*: Caesar's lengthy and careful account of Curio's disastrous campaign is a finely crafted study in how small (and large) mistakes of judgment by a commander can all too easily lead to tragedy. His first mistake: "from the start he had a poor opinion of the forces of Varus" and brought only two legions (*BC* 2.23–44).

700. *Varus*: Publius Attius Varus had governed the province of Africa in 52 BC; after fleeing Caesar at Auximon (2.492) he set out for Africa and took over the province, driving off Tubero, the newly appointed governor, when he arrived (see Caesar, *BC* 1.30–31).

701. *Juba*: King of Numidia just west and south of Rome's African province, which was centered on the coast around Carthage.

704. *his kingdom*: Greatly exaggerating the extent of Juba's sphere of control, but a convenient opportunity to muster an ethnographic catalogue of African peoples (most of whom will recur in Book Nine).

710. *Autolols . . . Numidians . . . Gaetuli*: Pliny places the Autolols to the far west of Mauretania, the Gaetuli also in Mauretania; our word "nomad" comes from the Greek name for Numidians (Lucan calls them *vagi*, "wandering").

711. *Moors*: The Mauri, for whom Mauretania was named.

712–13. *Nasamones . . . Marmarides . . . Garamantes*: All three peoples lived farther east, around the Syrtis Major and south of Cyrene.

714–16. *Mazax . . . Massylian*: Numidian peoples; for the latter, cf. *Aen.* 4.480–91.

718. *African hunters*: Passage emulates Virgil, *Geo.* 3.339–48; Pliny describes Gaetuli catching lions with cloaks in the Roman arena (*Nat. Hist.* 8.54).

724. *oust the king*: Caesar mentions Curio's proposal, as tribune, that the Romans annex Numidia (*BC* 2.25).

762. *ichneumon . . . asp*: The mongoose ("tracker" in Greek) and Egyptian cobra, its prey (he describes a spitting cobra).

768. *the ruse*: Caesar says Juba let spread the rumor that he had returned to his kingdom to deal with a border invasion, leaving Saburra behind with a small force, and Curio, "rashly believing this source of information," took the bait and gave battle (*BC* 2.38).

792. *mane flying*: A pun on Juba's name, which is Latin for "mane."

824. *spectacle*: Compare 2.221, 7.914–35.

839. *forced into valor*: Caesar's account, which probably drew on the report of Gnaeus Domitius Calvinus, an officer who tried to convince Curio to save himself, says, "Curio swore that after losing the army which Caesar had given him on trust he would never let Caesar see him again, and so died fighting" (*BC* 2.42).

849–50. *for her liberty as for its vindication*: that is, Curio's death is a belated divine vindication (*vindicta*) of the people's liberty, which they failed to protect to begin with.

856–61. *justice . . . Caesar's gold*: Curio had been a loyal optimate in the 50s, along with his father, but then to gain an ally in the city to serve his interests, Caesar bribed him in 50 BC, when he was a tribune, with a hefty sum to pay off his debts.

BOOK FIVE

2. *well matched*: Latin *pares*, like gladiators.

3. *Macedon*: Lucan's regular conflation of Thessaly and Macedon.

4. *Haemus . . . Pleiades*: Mountains in Thrace (and the name sounds like Greek for "blood"). The setting of the constellation Pleiades occurs in early November, traditionally marking the beginning of wintry weather and the end of safe sailing; this reference, in conjunction with the emphasis on January 1 that follows, may just indicate Lucan's awareness of pre-Julian calendar dates, which were two months later than Caesar's calendar (e.g., January 1, 48 = November 3, 49, Julian).

5. *new names*: Years were named for the two consuls, and the term of office for Lentulus and Marcellus was ending; Lucan does not

mention here that Caesar, after holding elections as dictator at the end of December 49, will be one of the new names (he buries this deep in the book and with sarcasm, at 409 below).

6. *Janus*: The two-faced god of doors and beginnings after whom January is named.

8. *Epirus*: In northwest Greece. Cassius Dio (41.18) locates a meeting of the senators siding with Pompey at Thessalonica in Macedon—called by the consuls *and* Pompey, with his authority as proconsul—featuring the same rhetoric: "they were the Senate and would maintain the government wherever they were."

10. *Curia*: The Senate house.

12–13. *strict law wields . . . axes and rods*: The axes and fasces were actual weapons and, hence, symbols of power granted to elected magistrates. In Latin there is a double or triple entendre hinging on the word *strictas*, which can mean (1) "unsheathe, brandish" a sword, (2) "dense, close-packed," and (3) "strict, rigorous" in legal contexts. A succinct image of the confounding of political and military spheres, varied and amplified for Caesar's political arrangements as dictator, is at 412–15.

26. *grow unequal*: At or near the equator.

29. *torched by Gauls . . . Camillus . . . Veii*: In 387–86 BC Gauls seized and occupied Rome, and the Roman army made its base at Etruscan Veii, deserted because recently sacked by Rome under the leadership of Marcus Furius Camillus, who afterward became a "second founder" of Rome. The traditional story was that the Capitoline Hill (Tarpeia) was saved from sack by heroic rearguard defenders. This rhetoric about the withdrawal rings true with other accounts, though Cicero thought it was madness (cf. *Att.* 7.11: "nothing more absurd"). The controversial historical example of Camillus threatens to get away from them in other ways (e.g., he was dictator five times).

37. *long peace*: Not a very accurate description for the Late Republic.

51–59. *worthy kings . . . Juba's scepter*: Cf. Caesar's account of Pompey's allied forces at *BC* 3.3–5; he mentions King Cotys of Thrace and his son Sadalas, who brought cavalry, and Rhascypolis from western Thrace. Taygetos is the mountain range west of Sparta. On Lucan's confusion of Phocaea and Phocis, see note at 3.317. In Rome, meanwhile, Caesar had Juba declared an enemy of the state and acknowledged other headmen as kings.

56. *Deiotarus*: King of Galatia (modern central and north-central Turkey), who had been well treated by Pompey in exchange for help

NOTES

385

against Mithridates VI of Pontus. Caesar notes that he brought six hundred Galatian cavalry to Pompey's allied forces in Greece.

62–65. *Pella . . . Lagus*: Pella = Alexandria (see note at 10.25); for Lagus see note at 1.730.

66. *sister's reign*: Cleopatra, whose claims to power are hereby denied, precipitating the civil-war crisis in which both Pompey (to his doom) and Caesar will become embroiled.

70. *Appius feared*: Valerius Maximus (1.8.10) also relates the story of Appius Claudius Pulcher visiting Delphi (possibly from Livy), with the prophecy put in much the same terms. Appius was consul in 54 with Domitius, and censor in 50 (his term had yet to expire when Pompey put him in charge of Greece); he was an augur as well as an avid expert and author on the lore of Roman augury and divination.

74. *just as far*: Delphi, believed to be the center of the world, displayed its "navel" stone (*omphalos*) to prove it. Zeus had set two eagles (or crows) loose at the extreme east and west, and they met at Delphi.

76. *Phoebus and Bromius*: Apollo and Dionysos, who shared the year at Delphi, each "ruling" for half of it.

77. *every third year*: A trieteric festival of Bacchus, common in Greece and especially associated with the god's birthplace, Thebes. (Greeks and Romans counted inclusively; we would normally say every other year.)

78. *flood*: For the flood myth cf. Ovid, *Met.* 1.253ff.

82–88. *avenge his mother . . . Python . . . Paean*: Apollo slew the monstrous Python, which inhabited the site of Delphi, and took over the oracle from the Titan Themis, who had possessed it, receiving his ritual name Paean from the victory shout of the inhabitants (so Strabo, *Geog.* 9.3.12). The deed avenges his mother, Leto, who had been driven to wander by an angry, jealous Hera, because the monster had ties to Hera, having received her child Typhaon to raise (according to the version in the *Homeric Hymn to Apollo*). Such a motive undercuts the strong traditional emphasis on Apollo's civilizing beneficence to humankind.

86. *exhaling*: A common physical theory for the oracle in antiquity; cf. Strabo, *Geog.* 9.3.5.

89. *Which higher power*: A rather sudden transition from mythic to natural-historical modes of explanation.

91–94. *suffers . . . human contact*: This is likely in contrast with Epicurean forms of divinity, which are distant, remote, untouched by human concerns.

97. *segment of Jupiter*: Conceived as the physical heavens.

99. *Cirrha*: The city on the coast below Delphi where visitors arrived by sea.

103-5. *Etna . . . Typhoeus . . . Inarime*: Mount Etna on Sicily and Campania's geologically active coast were explained by myths of earthborn Giants like Typhoeus buried underground in punishment. These lines are modeled on the very similar *Aen.* 9.715-16, where Virgil, in turn adapting *Iliad* 2.781-83 about Zeus' burial of Typhoeus, mistook Homer's "in Arima" as one word, *In-arime*, a name then given to Pithecoussai/Aenaria (modern Ischia) off the Bay of Naples.

107. *free one from the stain*: Those stained with the bloodguilt of murder or manslaughter could be ritually purified at Delphi, a common motif in Greek tragedy (e.g., Orestes in Aeschylus' *Eumenides*).

108. *curses*: I.e., Erictho's dark sort of magic (Book Six).

112. *Tyre*: The oracle was consulted for all sorts of large population movements, especially the sending out of colonies. Phoenician Tyre had been moved to send out colonies as a result of devastating earthquakes.

113. *Salamis*: For the story of Athens' consultation of the oracle before the Persian invasion and the subsequent abandonment of the city for ships, cf. Herodotus 7.140ff. The example of Themistocles, like that of Camillus, was used by the Pompeians (Cicero, *Att.* 7.11, 10.8.4).

117. *fell silent*: The latter-day decline and desuetude of the oracle was a common topic during the Empire (cf. Strabo 9.3.4, 8). A late story told how Nero consulted the oracle, and when rebuffed for his matricide he closed the oracle, but even if true the visit probably occurred after the Pisonian conspiracy and Lucan's death.

118. *Cirrha's priestesses*: The priestess of Apollo, known as the Pythia, delivered oracles in an inspired frenzy, seated on the tripod placed near or over an underground cleft.

129. *Phemonoë*: "Prophetic mind," also the name recorded for the first Pythia (Strabo, *Geog.* 9.3.5).

130. *Castalia*: The sacred spring at Delphi.

139. *barbarians torched*: A large army of Gauls invaded Greece in 280 BC, defeating Greek armies and reaching Delphi, where they were finally repulsed and driven back, their leader, Brennus, dying there (cf. Pausanias 10.23; Prop. 3.13.51-54 mentions Brennus torching Delphi). In 83 BC, Sulla also famously looted the temple to pay for his siege of Athens.

143. *Sibyl*: The oracular Sibyl of Cumae, in Campania, connected with the *Libri Sibyllini*, a collection of Greek oracles kept on the Capitoline and consulted by Roman priests in emergencies (Augustus took them into

his own private control), and made into a famous literary figure by Virgil in *Aeneid* 6, which Lucan uses as a model throughout this scene.

149. *Phocian laurel*: From Phocis, the region where Delphi was located; laurel (Greek *daphne*) was Apollo's plant, awarded to winners at the Pythian Games, and in myth deriving from the transformed nymph Daphne.

163. *Appius knew*: A self-proclaimed expert on divination, Appius can be expected to know the signs of "authentic" prophetic frenzy; Appius was known for disputing the common claim that augury was maintained as an expedient but false political tool.

176. *Bacchant*: The female worshippers of Dionysos known for being "inspired by the god" (*enthousiasmos*) and for their raving revels.

190. *Euboean*: Cumae in Italy was founded, in the eighth century BC, by Greeks from Euboea—where Appius soon will follow the oracle to his end.

215. *again . . . Brutus*: Caesar's assassin will follow the example of Lucius Junius Brutus, his illustrious ancestor, who drove out Tarquinius Superbus, the last king of Rome, then founded the Republic and served as a first consul.

230. *Stygian Lethe*: Waters of "forgetfulness" from the underworld, identified here by the Styx, another of its rivers.

235. *seize kingship*: Pompey had commissioned Appius to govern Greece, but he soon died on Euboea; from references by Cicero (who knew him well and corresponded with him), he seems to have been an arrogant, difficult man, and this reputation probably feeds into Lucan's treatment of him. The tone and theme of his end compares with Horace, *Carm.* 1.28.

240–46. *Carystos . . . Aulis*: The channel dividing the long, narrow island of Euboea, northeast of Attica and Boeotia, from the mainland narrows to the Euripus Strait roughly in the middle, where Aulis on the mainland faces, across choppy waters, Euboean Chalcis; "unkind to fleets" refers to the Greek armies bound for Troy, marooned at Aulis by unfavorable winds and deities; Rhamnus is farther down, on the northern headland of Attica, where the impressive ruins of the temple of Nemesis, goddess of divine retribution ("hates the proud"), can be seen today; Carystos is not opposite Rhamnus, as Lucan implies, but in a bay of southeastern Euboea, where marble had long been and continued to be quarried under the emperors.

247. *Meanwhile*: The chronology of events is as follows: Caesar says that he learned he had been named dictator, by Marcus Lepidus, upon reaching Massilia from Spain (approx. October 49, see *BC* 2.21); then he set out for Italy, where he faced and quelled a

mutiny at Placentia in Cisalpine Gaul. He will spend eleven days in Rome in December before crossing from Brundisium to Greece on January 4, 48 (*BC* 3.2, 6).

285. *pious paupers*: Other accounts also stress the men's economic motives (Appian, *BC* 2.47; Dio Cassius 41.26).

309. *disgruntled soldiers*: Arguments exposing disparity between hardships of the many and rewards reaped by the privileged few were common enough in Roman historiography and seem to have been staples of the *populares'* political rhetoric: cf. the speech of Licinius Macer, tribune and historian, in Sallust's *Histories*: "if they [the *optimates*] tenaciously retain those things, it will not be arms or secession that I propose but that you provide no more of your own blood. Let them exercise and hold their commands in their own way; let them seek their triumphs; let them and their ancestral images pursue Mithridates, Sertorius and the remnants of the exiles; but let the danger and toil escape those who are given no share in the fruits—unless perchance the compensation for your services is that sudden grain law, in which they reckoned everyone's freedom at five measures, which is of course no more than the sustenance in a prison [. . .] thus the fighting and conquering benefit only a few; the plebs, whatever happens, are like the conquered and will be more so every day, at least if those men are more concerned to retain their mastery than you are to reclaim your freedom" (3.48 = fr. 34, translation by A. J. Woodman 2007, pp. 160–61).

314. *discord*: Among Lucan's best paradoxical *sententiae*.

363. *Labienus*: Titus Labienus had been Caesar's second in command during the Gallic campaigns, but at the outbreak of war he took thousands of Caesar's cavalry and joined Pompey, to whom he had old, strong ties. In Caesar's own account Labienus is always presented with an undertone of angry contempt (e.g., *BC* 3.87, Labienus urges Pompey into battle at Pharsalus). He joined the fleets at Corcyra after Pharsalus and would die in the Battle of Munda in 45 BC, after which his head was brought to Caesar (so Appian, *BC* 2.105).

393. *throats came forward*: Appian says Caesar first said (almost bluffing) that he would decimate the ninth legion, which began the mutiny; then, relenting under entreaties, he identified 120 apparent ringleaders and drew twelve by lot for capital punishment.

399–404. *Hydrus . . . Calabria*: Calabria was the heel of Italy, Apulia just above it; Hydrus or Hydruntum is modern Otranto; Tarentum is modern Taranto; Leuca is on the very southern promontory of the heel. The Garganus forms a spur that faces north, across the

NOTES

389

Adriatic to Dalmatia, and south toward Calabria; both Sipus/Sipontum (modern Siponto) and Sal(a)pia (near modern Trinitapoli) are on the south side of the bay formed by Garganus.

410. *so long now*: A sardonic etiological account of the foundations of the Caesarian Principate, virtually dating the end of the Republic to this moment (later imperial annalists will also date the start of the Principate to Caesar's first dictatorship). See note to 247.

415. *imperium*: The all-important word from which we get "empire," it means "legally granted authority to command." Since, to Lucan, Caesar's consulship is illegitimate, it is an empty name.

423. *owl*: A proverbial bird of bad omen.

426. *consuls of the month*: Augustus began the practice, continued into the empire, of appointing consuls who often would serve for just a few weeks or months then be replaced (called "suffect consuls"), rendering the old practice of naming years by the consuls both more difficult and rather ludicrous (e.g., in AD 55, the year of Nero's first consulship, there were nine consuls, including Seneca).

430. *Latin Games*: See note at 1.590. Caesar is careful to mention his holding the Latin Festival before laying down the dictatorship and heading for Brundisium (*BC* 3.2); they had *not* been held (or held properly) the previous year amid the chaos.

449. *Phaeacia's shores*: The Romans identified Corcyra (modern Corfu) as the island of the Phaeacians visited by Odysseus.

465–70. *Bosporus ... Hister ... Maeotis*: Hister is the Danube; the Cimmerian Bosporus (modern Kerch Strait) joins the Black Sea to the Maeotis (modern Sea of Azov). The Bessi were a Thracian people; the name and the image come from Ovid, *Tristia* 3.10 (and before this, Virgil, *Geo.* 3.349–55).

492. *Palaeste*: On the shore below the Ceraunian Mountains; Lucan gets these details from Caesar (*BC* 3.6), who, however, only says of the crossing, "on the next day [he] made his landfall."

495. *Genusus ... Hapsus*: Parallel rivers along the Illyrian coast, north of the Ceraunians. Caesar says he took Oricum and Apollonia south of the Hapsus; north of the Genusus was Dyrrachium, where Pompey would make his base.

509. *not once*: Except at Pharsalus. Caesar was forced to stall for time while waiting for the rest of his forces to cross from Brundisium, and so he entered into negotiations with Pompey's side, the details of which he relates; during this time the opposing armies were divided only by the Hapsus River and often spoke, a flurry of hostilities once breaking out; Caesar takes the occasion to present Labienus as a hard-liner (*BC* 3.19).

513–15. *Antony . . . Actium*: Caesar says he waited several months until
the start of spring (probably around early April) for Mark Antony
to bring the other ships and men across from Brundisium, writing
stern letters to his officers to lose no chance to sail (*BC* 3.25). Curi-
ously, Mark Antony appears only here and a little further on in the
poem (except a mention at 10.86), Lucan making nothing of the
behavior of Antony in Italy as Caesar's chief deputy, which all ac-
counts describe as outrageous and heavy-handed. This under-
stated foreshadowing to Actium suggests Antony is already
gunning for supremacy—and/or rehearsing for failure.

541. *attempt the strait*: Caesar himself makes no mention of this esca-
pade, but its mention in Valerius Maximus (9.8.2), who wrote be-
fore Lucan, ensures that it is not his invention. The details there
include a small craft, Caesar concealing his identity, and his being
long tossed on contrary waves in a savage storm until finally giv-
ing up the attempt. Appian's account (*BC* 2.56–57) seems to rest
on good historiographical sources, and the scene likely appeared
in Asinius Pollio or Livy or both.

581. *a god*: This scene reworks much from Ovid's story of Jupiter and
Mercury visiting the poor happy couple Baucis and Philemon in
Met. 8.626ff.

585. *Amyclas*: Named after the town southwest of Sparta known for its
festival of Apollo and Hyacinthos, of unclear significance here, if
any, unless linked to the praise of "Spartan" living. His meteoro-
logical disquisition betrays his mastery of Virgil's *Georgics* 1.

619. *Zephyrs*: For wind names and directions, see list on p. 331.

669. *Aeolus*: The god of winds, who kept them locked in a cavernous
mountain prison (according to *Aen.* 1.50ff.).

674–75. *Tyrrhenian . . . Ionia*: Some storm! The Tyrrhenian is west of
Italy, the Adriatic on the east; the Aegean is east of Greece, while
the Ionian Sea is south of the Adriatic, off western Greece.

685. *second kingdom*: The seas, from the gods' original drawing of
lots.

691. *hell's house*: Hades, the third kingdom, is also pitching in.

700. *Night*: The original primordial goddess, child of Chaos, from He-
siod's *Theogony*.

703. *Leucas*: Large island off western Greece (modern Levkás).

716–18. *Sason . . . Ambracia*: Sason is a small island above the Cerau-
nian headland, near the Aous River, where other accounts place
Caesar's attempted crossing. Chaonia is the coastal region of
which the Ceraunians are a part; Ambracia is the region surround-
ing the large enclosed Ambracian Gulf farther south.

757–60. *so many people depend . . . to want to die*: A line of thought suspiciously similar to Cicero's sophisticated flattery of Caesar in his *pro Marcello*, responding to Caesar's statement that he had lived long enough: "Leave alone, I ask you, that wisdom of learned men about disregarding death. Don't become a wise man to our peril. . . . As it is, the welfare of every Roman citizen and the whole commonwealth has become interwoven with your deeds" (*pro Marc.* 25); a key text on the early postwar settlements that Lucan would have known well.

781. *cast off ships*: Lucan ignores Antony's breaking of the naval blockade at Brundisium that had contributed to their delay (Caesar, *BC* 3.23–4).

788. *Strymon*: See note to 3.206–11; also 9.971–73.

796–97. *Lissus . . . Nymphaeum*: On the bay north of Dyrrachium, Nymphaeum was 5 kilometers north of Lissus. Lucan breezes past with an epic simile an arrival that Caesar relates in some detail at *BC* 3.25–30: Pompeian ships chased the nearing fleet, which caught a lucky south wind and escaped north along the coast, reaching Nymphaeum when the wind changed again and apparently caused the wreckage of sixteen of Pompey's ships; two of Caesar's ships were caught off Lissus, the troops of one (Caesar says) being brutally put to death, the others defending themselves and escaping. Lucan reduces this episode to the emphasis on the winds found in Caesar's account.

798. *Aquilo*: The north wind.

803. *Cornelia*: It is possible that Lucan drew on a now lost historical account, like Livy, for this scene, but among Lucan's chief literary models is Ovid's tragic romance of Ceyx and Alcyone at *Met.* 11. 410–748.

817. *"Not now . . . sweeter"*: This stuttering slip, sounding at first the opposite of what he intends to say, appears as such in the Latin as well.

877. *Mytilene*: The chief city of Lesbos.

887. *their long love*: Not that long, actually: they married in 52 BC after the death of Julia in 54 and the younger Crassus in 53.

BOOK SIX

1. *had camped*: The events in Book Six occurred between April and July 48 (the Battle of Pharsalus took place on August 9; June 7, Julian).

16. *Dyrrachium*: When Romans took over the Greek port city of Epi-
damnus (modern Durrës in Albania) they renamed it Dyrrachium,
which according to Appian—who relates an involved, probably
mistaken, saga of the city and its name, 2.39—was the original
name. The Romans supposedly found the name Epi-*damn*-us
(Latin for "loss") unlucky, so they took the name of the rocky
coastal headland (meaning "bad spine" or perhaps "rough, ragged
beach"); Lucan focuses here on the topographic features. Since he
addresses Epidamnus in the closing lines of the poem, the city and
its name seem of some importance to him. Thucydides' history be-
gins with civil strife at Epidamnus (1.24ff.).

19. *Petra ... Taulantian*: "Rock" in Greek, on the bay southeast of
Dyrracchium; the Taulantii were the native people along this
stretch of Illyria between Oricum and Epidamnus.

20. *Ephyrean*: I.e., Corinthian—Homer once called Corinth, the city
of Sisyphos, Ephyra (*Il.* 6.152), and Epidamnus was a colony
founded by Corcyra and Corinth.

49. *encircling blockade*: Cf. Caesar, *BC* 3.43–47, on this "new and un-
precedented" blockade, by which he intended to embarass Pompey
by walling him in, cut off his large cavalry's access to grazing, and
protect his own foraging efforts to the rear.

55. *to the gods*: Apollo and Poseidon built the walls of Troy.

58. *a kingdom*: A small kingdom—obviously an exaggeration; the
area encircled was approximately 56 square kilometers.

61–62. *Sestos ... Phrixus*: See notes to 9.1184, 1185.

63–64. *Ephyra ... Pelops ... Malea*: I.e., Corinth, the city controlling
the isthmus between mainland Greece and the Peloponnese
(Pelops' Island); several plans and attempts to dig a canal across
the isthmus, saving ships the passage south around Cape Malea,
were made in antiquity, including Caesar's own projected canal,
cut short by his assassination; after Lucan's death, Nero himself is
said to have broken ground on a canal (Suetonius, *Jul.* 44, *Nero*
19); one was finally dug in the 1880s.

72. *Pelorus*: The northeastern promontory of Sicily (modern Punta del
Faro), here associated with the barking monster Scylla.

73–74. *Rutupiae ... Caledonia*: An early Roman settlement on the
shores of Britain (modern Richborough in Kent), possibly the land-
ing site of Claudius' invasion in AD 43; Caledonia was the name
for the land of the Picts in the far north, now Scotland.

81. *Aricia*: See note to 3.89–92; Diana of Aricia is "Mycenae's" perhaps
because of a tendency to associate her with Artemis of Tauris,

whose priestess in myth was Iphigeneia, daughter of Agamemnon, king of Mycenae.

85. *to the sea*: The ancient Tiber reached the sea at Ostia. Both Ostia and Aricia are approximately 25 kilometers from Rome: finally Lucan hits on a realistic comparison.

89. *exhausted*: Compare Caesar, *BC* 3.49, 58.

98–100. *Nesis . . . Typhon*: A small island, modern Nisida, near Naples, just offshore of the Phlegraean Fields, identified with the Giant Typhon.

104. *sacred fever*: Possibly what Greek medicine called *erysipelas*, or in Latin *ignis sacer*, but Lucan is probably drawing also on poetic sources (e.g., Lucr., *De R.N.* 5.660; Virgil, *Geo.* 3.566).

121. *unknown roots*: Caesar relates how his men made loaves from milk and a plentiful root called chara, and taunted the Pompeians with it (*BC* 3.48). Cf. also Suetonius, *Jul.* 68.

135. *Minucius*: Presumably the commander of the fort, mentioned also by Appian (2.60); several Minucii are known from the Pompeian side.

154. *Scaeva*: Caesar gives him high praise for his valor and hefty rewards: a promotion and 200,000 sesterces (*BC* 3.53). Lucan models him partly on Ajax in *Iliad* 12–15.

177–78. *prevailing . . . He will arrive . . . win back*: In one line, *vincimus . . . veniet . . . vindicet*—Lucan seems to play on Caesar's famous *veni, vidi, vici*, "I came, I saw, I conquered."

233–34. *Dictaean . . . Gortynian*: Cretan; Gortyn is a city on the north side of Crete.

239. *Pannonian*: Region south of the Danube, now Hungary and parts of other countries.

241. *Libyan*: The mixture of African hunter and European bear ensures that Lucan is describing an arena hunting spectacle (*venatio*).

257. *feigning words*: Appian relates this scene as well (2.60). Caesar mentions a similar ruse in Libya, where one of Curio's men got Varus' attention as though he wanted to speak with him, then, when he approached, tried unsuccessfully to kill the commander (*BC* 2.35).

278. *the shafts*: Caesar says his shield had 120 holes in it.

296. *spreading out the tents*: The next fifty lines draw on details from Caesar, *BC* 62–72.

314. *Torquatus*: Lucius Manlius Torquatus, a Pompeian commander (see note at 7.673–76.)

316. *Circe*: Virgil identified Cape Circeii, south of Rome, with Homer's isle of Circe.

322–23. *Henna . . . Enceladus*: Or Enna, in the center of Sicily, while the Giant Enceladus was imagined to be buried under Mount Etna on the island's east coast.

332. *restrained their raging swords*: Caesar knew he got lucky and had profited from some tactical mistake or other by his enemies (*BC* 3.70–72); Appian reports Caesar saying, "Today my enemies would have finished the war if they had a commander who knew how to win a victory" (2.62).

339–45. *Libya . . . Cato*: The later stages of civil war, defeats at Thapsus and Utica in 46 BC after which Scipio, Juba, and Cato committed suicide; and Munda in Spain, lost by Labienus and Pompey's sons in 45.

361. *banish wars*: Appian (2.65) reports their deliberations after Caesar's withdrawal: Pompey disregarded the advice to go back west, "which would have been best," because flight was disgraceful, Caesar seemed weakened, and Scipio, still in Thessaly, should not be exposed to disaster.

368. *Candavia*: Mountains just east of their current position; while Caesar stayed briefly in the region around Apollonia, making needed preparations, Pompey headed straight east across Candavia into Macedonia to meet up with Scipio (cf. Caesar, *BC* 3.78–79).

371. *Thessaly*: The best recent discussion of Lucan's long, learned excursus on Thessaly, including a map, is in J. Masters, 1992, pp. 150–78. Pliny describes Thessaly with the image Lucan implies: "all [these mountains] are curved inward *like an amphitheater*, with seventy-five cities hemmed in before them" (*Nat. Hist.* 4.8.30).

372–76. *Ossa . . . Pelion . . . Othrys*: Difficult lines containing one (arguably intentional) mix-up. The first two mountains, as always, evoke the Gigantomachy. In the winter the sun rises to the southeast, in summer to the northeast, whereas Ossa is to the northeast and Pelion and its chain to the east and southeast: Lucan reverses their correct placement. Mount Othrys is to the south, where the midday sun shines, and the direction toward which the morning sun verges in midsummer after rising in the northeast.

377. *Pindus*: The Pindus range bounds Thessaly on the west and southwest; Zephyr is the west wind, and Iapyx a southwest wind that favors the passage from Italy to Greece.

379. *Olympus*: North of Thessaly; Lucan means that the mountain protects those south of it from blasts of the north wind and that its

great height even blocks from view the circumpolar stars in the northern sky.

384. *Tempe*: The Vale of Tempe on the river Peneus as it nears the sea; Lucan relates the myth of Hercules severing Ossa and Olympus to drain a primordial flood that covered Thessaly (its name means "sea"). Herodotus' full description of Thessaly—as Xerxes is marching through—also mentions the notion that it was once a vast lake, and that Xerxes mused about damming the Peneus and flooding the whole land again (*Hist.* 7.129–30; Lucan's catalogue often links up with Herodotus here).

388. *Nereus*: A Titan god of the sea and father of the Nereids, among whom were Thetis, Achilles' mother.

389. *watery Achilles*: Because of his mother, Thetis. Achilles' kingdom was Phthia, in the south of Thessaly; Mount Pelion is connected with his father, Peleus.

391. *Phylace . . . Rhoetion*: Town near the gulf of Pagasae; the beach-head at Troy (see note at 9.1193), where Protesilaos, king of Phylace, was first of the Greeks to jump ashore, and first to die.

392. *Pteleos, and Dorion*: From the *Iliad*'s catalogue of ships (2.594), where they are located in the Peloponnese; there was a Thessalian Pteleos but not a Dorion; the Muses' wrath is against Thamyris the singer, who boasted he could sing better than they so they took away his power to sing. Pierus is a mountain north of Olympus associated with the Muses.

393–94. *Trachis . . . Meliboea*: South of Thessaly, Trachis has Mount Oeta, where Hercules mounted his own funeral pyre; he gave his bow to the one who would light the pyre, and this was Philoctetes of Meliboea, on the coast of Magnesia south of Mount Ossa (though the archaic location may have differed).

395. *Larisa*: The chief city of ancient Thessaly, on the Peneus.

396. *Argos*: Homer mentions a "Pelasgian Argos" (*Il.* 2.681), first in his list for the region, by classical times already forgotten, obscured by the more famous Argos of the northeast Peloponnese. Lucan mines Homer's whole catalogue for this region (*Il.* 2.681–759).

398. *old Thebes*: There was a Thebes in Thessaly/Phthia, near the gulf of Pagasae, but Lucan's reference draws in the more storied Boeotian Thebes; Echion was one of the five surviving Spartoi, father of Pentheus with Agave, who dismembered her son in a Bacchic frenzy and went into exile (though tying her exile to Thessalian Thebes may be Lucan's invention).

403. *Aeas*: Or Aous, rises in the northern Pindus range and flows north-west to Apollonia, where Caesar earlier had his base of operations.

404-5. *father . . . of Isis*: The river Inachus was the father of Io, who was raped by Zeus and turned into a cow, then wandered to Egypt and became Isis (cf. Ovid, *Met.* 1.568–747); but like Io, the Inachus has wandered out of the Argolid in the Peloponnese into Lucan's Thessalian catalogue (however, there is an Inachus in Oeta, and another that is a small tributary of the Achelous after which the modern town of Inachos is named).

406. *Oeneus . . . Echinad*: The Achelous River rises in the Pindus range, flows south, and reaches the sea in southern Acarnania, where the Echinades Islands lie offshore (Ovid tells the story of their poor relations with Achelous, *Met.* 8.575–610). Oeneus, king of Calydon, was the father of Deianeira, who promised his daughter to the river Achelous, but Hercules fought him for her and won (see Ovid, *Met.* 9.1–97).

407-8. *Nessus . . . Euhenos . . . Calydon*: When Hercules was taking Deianeira away, he came to the Euhenos (or Evenus) River, where the centaur Nessos offered to ferry her across; when he tried to steal off with her, Hercules shot him; the dying centaur tricked the girl into taking the blood that would end up killing Hercules (see *Met.* 9.101–33). Meleager was Deianeira's brother (see *Met.* 8.270–541).

409. *Spercheos . . . Amphrysos*: The first runs through Oeta into the Malian gulf, the second on the east side of Othrys in Phthia, where poets place Apollo as a shepherd (cf. Virgil, *Geo.* 3.2, *Aen.* 6.398; Ovid, *Met.* 1.579–80).

411-12. *Asopos . . . Anauros*: The Asopos, Phoenix, and Melas are small streams in Trachis near Thermopylae (in Herodotus 7.198–200, and Strabo 9.4.14); Housman moved this problematic line here, but based on the allusions we argue against deleting it. The Anauros was the stream in which Jason lost his sandal while crossing; Lucan explains its name as *an-auros*, "no breeze."

416-17. *Apidanos . . . Enipeus*: Main southern tributaries of the Peneus, also together in Ovid's list (*Met.* 1.579–80). Pharsalus lies along both these rivers, just to the south of the Enipeus, and most scholars today place the battle on the north side of the Enipeus. With "flood seized" Lucan may have in mind Herodotus, who says the Apidanos barely sufficed for the army of Xerxes (7.196).

418. *Titaresos*: The oily underworld waters of Titaresos, which glide on the top of Peneus' waters, comes from Homer's catalogue of ships, *Il.* 2.751–55 (which ends Homer's catalogue of Achaeans except for a final contingent of Magnesians from the Peneus and Pelion).

424. *fear of the gods*: The gods swore their oaths by the waters of the Styx, which had the power to put them in a deathlike coma for a year if they swore false oaths (cf. Hesiod, *Theo.* 775–806).

425. *Bebryces*: An obscure ethnic name for a people in Bithynia in Asia Minor, several of whom appear in the *Aeneid* (e.g., 5.373), and who were known mainly for their bully king Amycus, who challenged all visitors to a death match of boxing (cf. Apoll. Rhod., *Argo.* 2.1ff.); Lucan seems to cast them here as early settlers from Asia after the Trojan War (like Aeneas and his Phrygians in Italy).

427–29. *Leleges . . . Minyans*: The Leleges were a people associated since Homer with the Carians of Asia Minor and named by several authors as early settlers in Greece (Pliny names them and the Bebryces among extinct peoples). The seafaring Minyans were associated with the Argonaut tradition and were believed to have settled Thessaly from Boeotian Orchomenos; the Aeolidae—descendents of Aeolus—or Aeolians migrated from Thessaly early on and settled the islands and coasts of the north Aegean. Dolopians lived in the Pindus Mountains, and Magnesians along the Ossa and Pelion coastal range.

430–31. *Pelethronian . . . Centaurs*: Near Mount Pelion, always associated with Centaurs and their rivals the Lapiths, whose king, Ixion, the first murderer, lusted after Hera, so Zeus made a cloud image of her named Nephele and with her he had a son, Centauros, who coupled with the mares of Pelion to give birth to the Centaurs.

432–35. *Monychus . . . Alcides*: Two main roles of the Centaurs in myth were as antagonists of Thessaly's Lapiths and, at Mount Pholoë in Arcadia/Elis, of Hercules (Alcides). Ovid's Nestor narrates at length the war of the Lapiths and Centaurs (*Met.* 12.210–535). Lucan gets Monychus from there (12.499), but mixes in Hercules' battle on Pholoë. Virgil names Rhoecus and Pholus (*Geo.* 2.456, *Aen.* 8.294); the latter was a hospitable Centaur who hosted Hercules but then died accidentally in the battle (cf. Apollodorus, *Biblio.* 2.5). Lucan's conflation of Thessaly's and Pholoë's Centaurs may have been abetted by the fact that a Peneius River also flowed out of Pholoë (Strabo 8.3.5).

436. *ferryman*: Nessos, see note to 407–8.

437. *Chiron*: The wise old centaur of Mount Pelion known for training Achilles and other heroes, identified with the constellation Sagitarrius, who aims his bow at Scorpio (see note to 9.676–81). Haemonian = Thessalian.

441. *rocks were struck*: The horse was born when Poseidon (Neptune) struck the earth (cf. Virgil, *Geo.* 1.12–14), and some sources place this in Thessaly, famous for its horses.

444. *Lapith tamer*: The Lapiths were credited with inventing bit and bridle (Virgil, *Geo.* 3.115–22)—it was at the marriage of Pirithous, son of Ixion, to Hippodameia ("Horse-tamer") that war with the drunken Centaurs broke out.

445. *a ship*: The *Argo*, notorious as the first ship in which man set forth on the sea.

447. *Ionos*: A story not otherwise known, but money as a chief cause of warfare is a common motif in Latin poetry (cf. *Met.* 1.137–43, Prop. 3.7).

453. *Python*: Of extant sources only Lucan *derives* the Python from Thessaly, but the Valley of Tempe was closely tied with the Apollo vs. Python myth in relation to the Septerion festival at Delphi, when a sacred parade brought laurels from Thessaly.

456. *Aloeus*: Otus and Ephialtes, huge and powerful sons of Poseidon who threatened to pile Ossa on Olympus, and Pelion on Ossa to scale heaven, but Apollo killed them (the version of *Odyssey* 11.305–20).

467–69. *Sextus, unworthy son*: Pompey's youngest son, in his twenties during the wars, would lead the last doomed resistance to the Caesarians. History, written by those who defeated him, was not kind to Sextus, and his bold seizure of Sicily after the defeat of Brutus and Cassius at Philippi, which became a last desperate refuge for diehards and proscribed enemies of the state, continued to embitter the Caesarians against him as he stubbornly resisted defeat until 35 BC. Velleius Paterculus says, "Sextus was a young man crude in his pursuits, barbarous in his speech, vigorous in initiative, energetic and prompt in action and swift in his designs, in loyalty a marked contrast to his father, the freedman of his own freedmen and slave of his own slaves, envying those in high places only to obey those in the lowest" (2.73.1).

468. *Scylla's waves*: Sicily, whose Strait of Messina holds the monster Scylla.

472. *Delos' tripods*: One of Apollo's several oracular shrines was on Delos, his island of birth (see *Homeric Hymn to Apollo* 79–82), which Aeneas consults in *Aen.* 3.73–120.

473. *Dodona*: An ancient oracular shrine of Zeus at Dodona in Epirus, northwest Greece, which also saw significant rebuilding under Augustus. It was centered on a sacred oak grove, and acorns were considered to be the first food of primitive humanity.

477. *Assyrian worry*: Astrology, a stereotypically Eastern art, practiced by "Chaldaeans" (Babylonia) and "Syrians" (Syrio-Palestine).

479. *Magis*: The priestly class in Persia/Parthia, but the Greek *magos* had already long been used for a practitioner of strange and disreputable "magic" (used again with this broader sense at 501 and 641 below).

481. *Dis*: The Roman god of the underworld (Greek Hades/Pluto).

484. *Haemonian*: In this episode Lucan prefers the old and poetic name for Thessaly, which means "bloody." As Pliny says (*Nat. Hist.* 4.7.28), "Haemonia has often changed its names; the same land is Pelasgis, Pelasgian Argos, Hellas, Thessaly, and Dryopis."

486. *whose art is anything beyond belief*: Lucan's depiction of Erictho is designed to defy belief, and has repulsed many critics; Feeney dryly comments, "Those who find its horror too powerful should take every step they can to avoid living under a dictatorship" (1991, p. 289). Masters 1992, pp. 179–215, is an engaging study; Ahl 1976, pp. 130–49, and Johnson 1987, pp. 1–33, are also landmarks.

487. *Thessaly's ground*: As Ovid's Medean catalogue tells (*Met.* 7.220–31).

488. *rocks are affected*: Like those charmed by Orpheus' song (*Met.* 11.1–2, 18–19).

491. *stranger from Colchis*: Medea; see note to 487.

494–97. *deaf . . . never diverted*: These sound like Epicurean gods (cf. Lucr., *De R.N.* 3.18–24).

507. *foal's forehead*: This is so-called hippomanes ("horse madness"), an aphrodisiac obtained from the sweat of a pregnant mare or a patch of flesh from the head of a newborn foal (cf. Tibullus 2.4.58, Propertius 4.5.18, Pliny, *Nat. Hist.* 8.66.165).

513. *Nature's cycles*: The impossible feats (*adunata*) of witches have a rich pedigree in Hellenistic and Latin poetry, and Lucan draws on all available resources. A short list of the main Latin poetic sources for witches and magical arts includes Virgil, *Ecl.* 8, *Aen.* 4.480–521; Horace, *Ep.* 3, 5, 17, *Sat.* 1.8; Propertius 3.6.25–34, 4.5.1–20; Ovid, *Her.* 5, 6.83–94, 12 (Medea), *Am.* 1.8, 2.1, 3.7.27–35, *Met.* 7.1–424 (Medea).

529. *Maeander*: A river in Caria (modern Turkey) famous for its meandering (cf. Ovid, *Met.* 8.162–66).

530. *Arar*: A tributary of the Rhône in Gaul.

533. *at clouds*: Olympus, whether the mountain or the heavens, is conceived as so high that no clouds can normally touch it, so enjoying eternally serene weather (cf. 2.286).

540. *Olympus*: Here the heavens, not the mountain.

555. *tyrant songs*: In Latin *carmina imperiosa*, a suggestive phrase.

556–57. *compel . . . compelled*: Compare Delphi's mysterious mechanism (5.95–96).

559–62. *Phoebe dims . . . flames*: Describing eclipses.

601. *preserved in stone*: A sarcophagus ("flesh eater" in Greek).

637. *His faithful servants*: In the Latin these might be his or Erictho's servants, but since no servants of hers are mentioned again and Sextus has already been cast in strongly negative terms, this alternative seems preferable.

640. *Haemus*: Nowhere near Pharsalia. But Lucan seems to associate the Thracian Mount Haemus with Haemonia (see note to 484). Ovid's Orpheus sits grieving Eurydice on Haemus (*Met.* 10.77).

642. *crafting a spell*: Here as elsewhere, *carmen*, "song, poem, chant"— Erictho is very much a dark, devilish *poet*.

661. *illustrious child*: Cf. Aeneas' speech to the Sibyl before descending to the underworld (*Aen.* 6.103–23).

684. *Fortune is stronger*: Very nearly identifies Fortuna and Fata (contrast 2.1–17).

688. *Rhodope*: Mountain in western Thrace, regularly associated with Orpheus.

689. *fresh dead*: An apparent plot inconsistency, continuing through 708, since the Battle of Pharsalus is yet to come. But Lucan might easily defend himself against this criticism by pointing to the several days of standoff and minor skirmishing before the pitched battle that Caesar himself mentions (*BC* 3.84–85).

707. *Avernus*: A volcanic crater lake near Cumae in Campania believed to be the entrance to the underworld; here a general synonym for Hades/Dis.

714. *caverns of Dis*: Cf. Virgil, *Aen.* 6.236–336; Ovid, *Met.* 4.432–511.

720. *Taenarus*: Southern cape of Peloponnese, renowned as a gateway to Hades (cf. note to 9.40–42).

722. *Tartarus*: The murky depths of the underworld, where all the primordial Titans and Giants dwell (Hesiod, *Theog.* 721–819).

744. *poison from the moon*: Possibly the sort of moon dew mentioned at 564 (cf. Ovid, *Met.* 7.268), or some toxic mineral such as orpiment or realgar, which contain arsenic.

746. *froth of dogs*: Rabies, symptoms of which are hydrophobia and frothing at the mouth; a goose chase of folk magical and medicinal obscurities follows, rivaling Medea's potent brew at *Met.* 7.264–78.

747. *lynx . . . hyena*: Marvels of the lynx included its urine, which turned to stone, its possession of the clearest eyesight, and cures

for sexual desire and urinary disorders that could be obtained from it (Ovid, *Met.* 15.413–15; Pliny, *Nat. Hist.* 28.32–122). Pliny lists seventy-nine remedies obtained from the hyena; its first neck vertebra was known as the "Atlas knot," which if preserved with the genitalia—relevant to Lucan's theme—"will maintain the entire household in concord" (28.27.99).

748. *stag*: Stags/deer were believed to kill and eat serpents, inspiring numerous correlations between the two in magical lore (cf. Pliny, *Nat. Hist.* 8.50, 28.42.150).

749. *echenais*: A small fish that "holds back ships" (Greek *echein naus*); from this notion it was used in love magic and to cause delays in affairs, or here, probably to restrain the departing shade (cf. Pliny, *Nat. Hist.* 9.41.79).

750. *stones*: Eagle stones or *aetites* was the name given to rocks, some hollow inside and rattling, believed to derive from the nests of eagles (Pliny, *Nat. Hist.* 10.4.12, and 36.39.114, where he describes four types).

752. *flying serpent . . . viper*: Probably a relative of the *iaculus* and flying dragons of 9.899–914. The oyster-guarding viper is perhaps an eel (cf. 10.175).

754. *horned snake*: The *cerastes*, cf. note to 9.893–94.

755. *phoenix*: The legendary long-lived bird that burned itself on a pyre in the east and from the ashes was reborn (Ovid describes its eternal life cycle at *Met.* 15.392–407).

773. *Ruler*: Probably Dis/Hades.

774. *Elysium*: The Isles of the Blessed, where only the greatest heroes go after death; hence, no witches.

775. *Persephone*: Lucan uses her Greek name, fairly rare in Latin poetry, where her Latin name, Proserpina, is more common. She presumably loathes heaven because Zeus decided she had to stay with her husband, Hades, for part of the year since she had eaten pomegranate seeds, and her mother presumably because she acquiesced to Zeus' judgment (cf. Virgil, *Geo.* 1.39).

776–77. *third . . . Hecate*: Hecate was known as "triple" or "three-faced" because worshipped at crossroads (Latin *trivia*, "three paths"); Hecate was the archetypical goddess of witchcraft, regularly conflated into a composite chthonic goddess figure along with the Moon, Artemis/Diana, and Persephone/Demeter.

780. *dog, and sisters*: Cerberos, the three-headed dog, and the Fates (Moirai).

781. *ferryman*: Charon, cf. *Aen.* 6.298–304.

795. *Orcus*: The underworld or a god of the underworld.

797. *but once*: I.e., it hasn't yet crossed the Acheron into Hades so has not technically died.

798–99. *who is now our soldier*: These lines contain textual and interpretive problems, discussed in Ahl 1976, pp. 135–37, in part related to the problem noted at 689.

812–13. *Tisiphone . . . Megaera*: With Allecto, the names given by late Greek and Latin poets to the Furies (Erinyes/Eumenides).

825. *lady of Henna*: Proserpina, believed to have been carried off to the underworld by Dis at a lake near the central Sicilian city of Henna. That she has unspeakable secrets not to be revealed relates to the Eleusinian Mysteries, the sacred rites of which initiates were not allowed to reveal.

829. *worst*: Erictho abuses Dis with being the ruler of the third, last, lowest of the three realms (after Jupiter over sky and Neptune over seas).

832. *that one*: If Lucan had any specific god in mind here, it was probably one of the curious syncretistic gods of the magicians such as appear in the magical papyri from Hellenistic Egypt (such as Thoth/"Thrice-Great" Hermes); but after a Late Antique commentator identified a similarly unnamed god in Stat., *Theb.* 4.516, as "Demogorgon," Lucan's line was also glossed with this spurious deity who went on to have a long literary afterlife. Mention of the Gorgon here points forward to the Medusa story at 9.777ff.

867. *Parcae*: The Fates.

874. *blessed shades*: As Ahl notes of this underworld report, "Heaven and hell are populated along strictly party lines" (1976, p. 138); the first group, the sorrowful in Elysium, are historical *optimates* or aristocratic conservatives; Catiline and the following are historical *populares*, radicals and revolutionaries. Since Caesar is aligned with the *populares*, this group is thrilled at the looming victory of their party and a revolution of values and government in the underworld itself. The corpse's report draws on and subverts elements in *Aeneid* 6.756–886.

875. *I saw the Decii*: See note to 2.326.

876. *Camillus*: See notes at 1.184–85, 2.574, 5.29.

877. *Curii and Sulla, complaining*: See note at 1.184–85. The line hinges on Sulla's honorific name *Felix* ("Fortunate").

878. *Scipio*: Both Africanus the Elder, who defeated Hannibal in the Second Punic War, and the Younger, who defeated and razed Carthage.

880. *Cato*: Marcus Porcius Cato the Elder (or the Censor)—inspired to a life of rugged simplicity by the modest old house of Curius near his own estate—often ended speeches with *Carthago delenda est*

("Carthage must be destroyed"). His grandson Cato will commit suicide at Utica rather than live in a state dominated by Caesar.

881. *Brutus*: See note to 5.215.

884–85. *Catiline . . . Cethegi*: See note to 2.570–72.

887. *Drusi . . . Gracchi*: For the Gracchi see note to 1.288; Marcus Livius Drusus, as tribune in 91 BC, tried to carry through reforms in the manner of the Gracchi, but over the resisted move of granting Italian allies citizenship he was assassinated, which sparked the Social War (91–88 BC). Augustus' wife, Livia, was his granddaughter (though her father was adopted, born Appius Claudius Pulcher), and thus Nero's ancestor; his daughter Livia Drusa, on the other hand, was the mother of Cato of Utica.

900–901. *with pride, magnanimous*: Cf. note to 4.499 (the phrasing here is *magno superbi animo*, "proud/haughty with a mind great," perhaps suggesting the darker and dangerous side of greatness of spirit).

902. *shades of the gods*: The deified Caesars, and the phrasing "the Roman gods' *manes* [spirits of the dead]," seem designed to provoke. Augustus' ostentatious deification of Caesar after his death and the precedent it set for the ruling family was a scandal among the senatorial elite, and Lucan's own family had openly ridiculed the deification of Claudius upon his death (Seneca penned his satyric *Apocolocyntosis* for the occasion, venting spleen on the man who had exiled him).

908. *your father*: This is either a narrative foreshadowing of an episode Lucan planned for a later book but was not able to complete, or it refers to a well-known story involving Sextus later in Sicily (or both); cf. Ahl 1976, pp. 133–37, for the suspiciously similar story of a necromantic soldier delivering a prophecy of military success to Sextus in Sicily in the 30s; it seems likely Lucan was familiar with similar accounts that may have sourced the spirit of Pompey himself with the prophetic utterance.

912. *Europe, Libya, Asia*: For Pompey's triumphs, one on each continent, see note to 1.133–35; Pompey Magnus will die in "Libya" (i.e., Egypt), Gnaeus Pompey his older son in Europe (Spain), and Sextus in Asia (Miletus).

BOOK SEVEN

4. *backward course*: See note to 10.250; driving *faster* than normal against the eastward-turning sky, he *appears* to be going slower.

6. *feed his flames*: See note to 10.318–22.

10. *Theater*: See note to 1.146.

13. *roaring sections*: Theatrical imagery that continues through 213 with future ages cheering for Magnus as they read the poem.

16. *Hiberus*: Ebro River in Spain; his Spanish triumph.

19–21. *plain white toga . . . still a Roman knight*: Pompey had not yet been consul; instead, only nineteen when his father died and left him his loyal legions, Pompey rose to power as a victorious general in a time of civil war, demanded triumphs over opposition from Sulla and (once he was gone) other optimates, then secured a consulship in 70 BC after two triumphs that were quite contrary to constitutional traditions.

46. *Brutus' funeral*: Tradition held that the women of Rome mourned Brutus, the early regicide, for a whole year (cf. Livy, *A.U.C.* 2.7).

57. *day's end*: This book focuses on one day, August 9, 48 BC (and for effect toward the end, the night and following day), but Lucan will flash back at 180 to register the evil portents before the day of battle. From Caesar we know that the armies were in position for a few days before this, and Caesar was about to move camps entirely when he saw the Pompeians finally moving into battle formation, so he suddenly changed his mind and decided to engage them (cf. *BC* 3.84–85).

63. *indulging*: Caesar says the same, *BC* 3.82. Plutarch (*Pomp.* 67) says that Domitius dubbed him Agamemnon and King of Kings.

70. *add crime to our errors*: Ovid made famous the distinction between "crime" and "error" (cf. Ovid, *Met.* 3.141–42, *Tristia* 1.3.37–38).

74. *Tullius*: Marcus Tullius Cicero was with Pompey's armies, but had stayed behind at Dyrrachium because of illness and was thus not at Pharsalus; but his continual wit and sarcasm with others in camp, not always welcome, were remembered (so Plutarch, *Cic.* 38–9). After the defeat he rejected the command of the armies when offered by Cato, instead returning to Italy and reconciling with Caesar (Brutus did the same).

124. *delay*: Pompey invokes the example of Quintus Fabius Maximus (the "Greatest"), hero of the Second Punic War, five time consul and twice dictator, whose stalling tactics and war of attrition with Hannibal earned him the name Cunctator ("Delayer"). He earns high praise in Virgil, *Aen.* 6.845–46, and is placed on an ascending scale of greatness along with Pompey (Magnus, Caesar, Fabius Maximus, Augustus) by Ovid at *Fasti* 1.603–12.

151. *panic*: Plutarch mentions panic among the Pompeian armies (*Caes.* 43).

160–63. *Who . . . for himself*: Compare to Cato's words at 2.306–9.

174. *Phlegra*: The mythical birthplace of the Giants and site of their challenge to the Olympian gods, identified in Roman times with

Campania's scorched volcanic cape west of Naples, still called the Phlegrean Fields.

175. *Sicily's anvils*: Mount Etna, site of Vulcan's forge.

178. *Gorgon*: Pallas Athene had the severed head of Medusa the Gorgon on her shield, the aegis. See 9.783–875 with notes.

179. *Pallene*: The westernmost of Chalcidice's three peninsulas, which in early tradition was known as Phlegra, the (or one) site of the Olympians' battle with the Giants. The one-eyed Cyclopes forged for Zeus his lighting and thunder (Hesiod, *Theo.* 139–41).

181. *through various signs*: Valerius Maximus (1.6.2) relates many similar omens—probably taken from Livy, among others—warning Pompey against engaging in battle with Caesar. On the other side, Caesar relates some self-serving portents of his victory after the fact (*BC* 3.105).

200. *what gods*: Appian (*BC* 2.68) says Caesar sacrificed in the dead of night, making vows to Mars and Venus, promising to build the latter a temple for victory.

209. *Lake Boebeis*: A large lake that lies below and west of the Pelion and Ossa chain.

228–31. *augur . . . Antenor*: Plutarch (*Caes.* 47) also relates this story of the augur Gaius Cornelius, citing Livy—himself from Patavium (modern Padua), just south of which lie the Euganean Hills and the still-famous hot springs of Apanus (modern Abano)—as "most emphatic that this really happened." The Timavus (modern Timavo) is more distant, to the east across from Trieste, but famous for its founder, Trojan Antenor, recalled in both Virgil, *Aen.* 1.242–49, and Livy, *AUC* 1.1. Leigh 1997, pp. 6–40, discusses this scene and the intertexts.

236–37. *sad sky god . . . sun's pale darkness*: Or "the sad god of the sun in the sky." Lucan uses technical language of natural philosophy to say that the divine power (*numen*) gave signs of its sorrow that were visible in the appearance of the sun's physical body.

254–63. *took up position . . . Scipio*: Lucan seems to draw up Pompey's ranks according to his own designs. Caesar (*BC* 3.88) puts the First and *Third* on the left, where Pompey himself took position, Scipio in the center with *Syrian* legions, and the Cilician legion with Spanish cohorts on the *right*—Appian (2.76) adding that Lentulus commanded the *right*, and Domitius the *left*.

267. *horsemen*: Pompey's chief confidence lay in his 7,000, to Caesar's 1,000, cavalry. Caesar was far outmanned overall: Pompey's army numbered 45,000 to Caesar's 22,000.

271–72. *Cydonians . . . Ityraean*: Cydonea is a town on the north coast of Crete; the Ityraei were a people of northeast Palestine (Virgil, *Geo.* 2.448, also mentions their bows).

273. *usual foe*: I.e., Romans, and especially Caesar's legions. These are either Galatians under King Deiotarus, or Lucan refers here to the two high-ranking Allobroges brothers whose late defection along with some cavalry is made so much of by Caesar (*BC* 3.59–61).

278. *by chance*: Caesar says he had his troops ready to march out to a new camp when he noticed Pompey's army giving opportunity for battle (*BC* 3.85).

295. *hearten*: Caesar briefly summarizes his prebattle speech at *BC* 3.89–90.

312. *might be free*: Or "you might be a free mob [*libera turba*]," the rowdy, teeming populace despised and feared by most authors under the Principate (see 477–79).

318. *hatred*: Latin *invidia*, "envy, resentment."

360. *Saepta*: The "enclosure" in the Campus Martius where polling took place; see note to 2.208–9. Compare Caesar, *BC* 3.83.

374–87. *don't cut down . . . in that rampart*: The similarity of the speech's ending in Appian (*BC* 2.74) suggests a common historical source (presuming Appian is not using Lucan).

451. *such sad words*: Comparison with the shorter and less impassioned speech that Appian gives to Pompey (*BC* 2.72) suggests that Lucan has really warmed up to his theme here.

457. *no age can ever make up for*: A difficult line suspected of corruption, but this rendering represents the best attempt at it without resorting to Housman's less than fully convincing emendation.

463. *Gabii, Veii, Cora*: Ancient cities of Latium and Etruria, early conquered by Rome and hence bywords for vanished antiquity (cf. Virgil, *Aen.* 6.770–75; Propertius 4.1.34–36, 4.10.25–30).

464–65. *Alban . . . Laurentum*: Laurentum was the ancient city of legendary King Latinus, near the coast south of Ostia; ancient Alba Longa, in the hills southeast of Rome, where consuls presided at the annual Latin Festival upon taking office, presumably a religious institution going back to Numa Pompilius, Rome's second ruler.

468. *devouring time*: Cf. Ovid, *Met.* 15.234–36.

471–76. *empty cities . . . ready to fall*: Cf. 1.26–35; and after Lucan, Juvenal, *Sat.* 3.60–80.

482. *Cannae and Allia*: The disasters of Cannae (in the Second Punic War) and Allia (against the Gauls in 387–386) were "black days" on the calendar; Pharsalia was in fact marked on calendars, but for Caesar's victory, not the Senate's defeat.

501. *would be Roman*: Compare with Jupiter's prophecy of endless world empire in *Aeneid* 1.254–96.

505–7. *Dahae . . . Sarmatian*: Scythians beyond the Caspian Sea and along the Danube.

509. *fleeing civil horrors*: Horace, *Carm.* 3.24, sounds many of the same themes.

514. *Romulus*: After the competing auguries with Remus and the building of walls for their convict asylum, Romulus put his brother to death, the first instance of Roman civil strife (cf. 1.101–5).

519. *Brutus*: The original, Lucius Junius Brutus, who drove out Tarquin and founded the Republic.

526. *Jove reigns*: Recalls Horace, *Carm.* 3.5.1–2, "When heaven thunders we believe Jove reigns; Augustus will be considered a god among us once Britons and dread Persians have been added to the empire."

529. *Pholoë*: See note to 6.432–35.

530. *Mimas*: One of the blasted Giants (Horace, *Carm.* 3.4.52), as well as a mountain range on the north of Ionian Erythrae, mentioned with Rhodope at Ovid, *Met.* 2.222: when Jupiter's bolts blasted Phaethon and devastated the earth with fire.

531. *Cassius*: The sole mention in the poem of Gaius Cassius Longinus, the optimate who would capitulate to Caesar in 47, then later organize the plot to assassinate him. The historian Cremutius Cordus was tried for treason and took his own life in AD 25 for calling Cassius "the last of the Romans" in his histories (Tacitus, *Ann.* 4.34).

531–32. *stars . . . Argos*: See note to 1.583; Argos is the central city of the region dominated by the house of Atreus, which included its royal seat of Mycenae.

539. *swear by shades*: Latin *umbras*, "shadows, ghosts"—see note on 6.902 above.

551. *Crastinus*: Caesar's own text (*BC* 3.91) supplies Lucan with this foolhardy hero figure who storms first into battle and earns blame for it, like Protesilaus or Pandaros (*Iliad* 3.86–140) in the Trojan War tradition.

565. *Pangaea*: A mountain in southern Thrace, near the mouth of the Strymon.

607. *holds back cohorts*: Caesar attributes his victory to the third and fourth lines of reserve cohorts who took over midway in the fighting and who routed Pompey's cavalry (*BC* 3.93–94).

655–56. *Bellona . . . Bistones*: See note to 1.605; Bellona appears in Virgil's Battle of Actium description (*Aen.* 8.703); Bistones = Thracians, and Mars (Greek Ares) was associated with Thrace. In the *Iliad*, Ares and Pallas Athena are inveterate enemies among the gods, 5.30–35, 825–61 (Diomedes wounds him with Athena's aid); 21.391–415. Caesar here is like Turnus raving in battle, also compared with Mars (*Aeneid* 12.324–82).

671. *orders*: The social orders, of senators and knights (*equites*).

673–76. *Lepidi . . . best of men*: Names of Roman noble families, but it is not clear whom Lucan means specifically; Appian (*BC* 2.82) says ten senators and forty prominent *equites* fell in the fighting, but names only Domitius, as does Caesar (*BC* 3.99). Whether based in historical fact or not, it seems Lucan, to arouse pathos, has chosen old noble families whose names would still resonate into the Principate, when many old aristocratic lines had died out. The Aemilii Lepidi survived through the staunch Caesarean Marcus Lepidus, the triumvir with Antony and Octavian, but his son was executed by Augustus in a supposed conspiracy; the Lepidi intermarried with the ruling family and had close ties with the emperors (sometimes resulting in tragedy). Metellus Scipio was an adopted member of the old illustrious Caecilii Metelli, and also a member was the Metellus who opposed Caesar at Saturn's temple (3.120ff.); at least one Metellus (consul AD 7) was prominent under Augustus and Tiberius. Corvinus is conspicuous in its contemporary resonance: Marcus Valerius Messalla Corvinus (64 BC–AD 8) was son of a prominent Caesarean (M. Valerius Mess. Rufus, consul 53 BC) and was an Augustan literary patron with known republican principles; his great-grandson and namesake was consul with Nero in AD 58 and the brother of Emperor Claudius' third wife, Messalina. Lucius Manlius Torquatus, with illustrious ancestors in the early Republic, was a Pompeian commander who died after Thapsus in 46. But the name evoked even more another family, the Junii Silani Torquati, descendants of Augustus: M. Jun. Silanus Torquatus (consul AD 19) had three sons, all of whom met tragic ends from imperial family infighting under Claudius and Nero; the son of one of these, L. Jun. Silanus Torquatus, was accused by Nero of incest and treason in 65 and put to death.

683. *Thessaly*: Brutus will fall on his sword after defeat in battle at Philippi in 42 BC (not in Thessaly but in Macedonia).

691. *unmixed*: The point seems to be that *all* the dead were aristocrats, an incredible exaggeration; Caesar numbers the dead at 15,000.

696. *without him*: A good dig, but not true: Afranius and Petreius in Spain (4.357ff).

699. *Caesar saw him*: Not if Caesar is to be believed (*BC* 3.99); but Lucan fashions his prophetic dying words along Homeric lines (cf. *Iliad* 16.816–56, 22.355–63).

702. *successor*: He had been appointed governor of Gaul for 48 BC by the Senate before they left the city (see notes on 2.506, 3.317).

773. *he goes and calls back*: Lucan provides a rather nobler picture of Pompey at Pharsalus than the historical tradition paints. Caesar says (*BC* 3.94) that when the cavalry was routed, Pompey returned to camp, told the centurions that he would go around and hearten the men (as Lucan says he does), then disappeared into his tents and awaited the outcome. Both Appian (*BC* 2.81) and Plutarch (*Caes.* 45) portray Pompey as losing his wits—like Ajax at Troy—and remaining silent and dumbfounded in his tent until Caesar's troops stormed the camp, at which point he said, "So they are at the camp, too?" changed into simpler clothes, and fled to Larisa (so Caesar as well, *BC* 3.96).

785. *denied by fate*: Worried about the apparent contradiction of the later narrative, editors have sought to emend it away; but Pompey does not in fact die with Cornelia *by his side* (*praesente*) but alone in a boat of assassins, with her watching in vain from afar. Lucan may also mean that Pompey intends to die with her, i.e., commit suicide.

790. *dignity*: Loss in battle, civil or otherwise, was a massive disgrace to the commander's dignity or honor, hence the common expectation of going down fighting (like Curio) rather than facing one's peers alive but in disgrace. But Lucan's lines are somewhat strange; he may in fact be playing on the term *maiestas*, which in the Principate had become the regular legal term for treason ("lèse-majesté").

804. *woeful Africa*: Refers to the African war, in 47–46 BC, and the deadly battle of Thapsus, where Caesar defeated in pitched battle the armies under Scipio, Varus, Labienus, Petreius, Pompey's sons, and Juba, including a large cavalry of war elephants, which led to the suicide of several leaders including Scipio, Cato (at Utica), Petreius, and Juba; for Munda see glossary.

816. *What must he feel*: Caesar's official line was well publicized: "They drove me to it, they brought it on themselves" (cf. Plutarch, *Caes.* 46; Suetonius, *Jul.* 30).

828. *Larisa*: The principal city of Thessaly, north of the battle site.

836. *you could again arouse*: Caesar relates (*BC* 3.102) that after the battle, when he was pursuing Pompey, an edict in Pompey's name at Amphipolis called all military-age men to assemble, but Caesar did not know if it was a bluff or a serious attempt to regroup.

853. *press on*: So Caesar at *BC* 3.95–97, saying his men were "mentally ready for any effort." They stormed and took the camp, stocked with

massive wealth and lavish supplies, and also pursued and obstructed the fleeing enemy armies until they surrendered in exhaustion.

873. *plundered*: Caesar describes the luxurious camp to cast moral blame on the leaders for living lavish, dissolute lives even in wartime, and to rebut the charge of luxury cast on his own army; Lucan, usually an enemy of luxury, prefers to heap blame on the greed of Caesar's soldiers in taking possession of this bounty.

876. *Tagus*: Iberia's longest river (Spanish Tajo, Portuguese Tejo).

877. *Arimaspian*: Lucan is rationalizing the hoary old legend of the one-eyed Arimaspians who live far to the north and steal gold guarded by griffins (cf. Herodotus, *Hist.* 3.114); instead they are common pan miners.

903–5. *Orestes . . . Furies*: Agamemnon's son (and Pelops' descendant) avenged his father's murder by killing his mother, Clytemnestra, and her lover Aegisthus, then was hounded by his mother's Furies for bloodguilt. In one version he went as far as the Tauric Kingdom across the Black Sea, where he was purged at the altar of Scythian Artemis (Diana), where his sister Iphigeneia served as priestess (cf. Euripides, *Iph. in Taur.*).

906–7. *Pentheus . . . Agave*: Pentheus was driven mad by Dionysos for denying his divinity; then his mother Agave, went mad, too, and dismembered Pentheus before she came to her senses (cf. Euripides, *Bacchae*).

921. *reckons up the number*: Caesar estimates that of Pompey's 45,000 troops and 7,000 cavalry some 15,000 died and 24,000 surrendered, while 180 standards and 9 eagles were captured (Caesar, *BC* 3.130): Lucan is not outrageously hyperbolic. Appian, citing Asinius Pollio, says the dead numbered 6,000, though he also notes that no count of the allied dead was made (2.82).

932. *Hannibal*: After the Battle of Cannae, Hannibal was said to have given burial to the dead general Aemilius Paullus (cf. Livy, *AUC* 22.52). The denial of burial is probably Lucan's invention; Appius mentions a mass grave but nothing more specific (*BC* 2.82).

942. *Oeta*: Where Hercules mounted his own funeral pyre.

952. *with stars*: The Stoic world conflagration (*ekpyrosis*); see note to 1.73–87.

966–71. *wolves . . . birds*: Cf. *Iliad* 1.1–5, "[Achilles' rage] . . . made their bodies feasts for dogs and all the birds, and the will of Zeus was fulfilled."

967. *Pholoë*: See note to 3.206–11.

972. *You*: The cranes, delaying their migration for the feast; see notes to 3.206–11 and 5.788.

995.   *plowshare*: Cf. Virgil, *Geo.* 1.489–97.

996.   *new ranks*: For the Battle of Philippi, to the north in Macedonia.

1017. *Slaughters in the West*: Probably both the African and Spanish wars, with large-scale defeats at Thapsus and Munda.

1018. *Pachynum . . . Mutina and Leucas*: The southeastern promontory of Sicily, referring to the wars with Sextus Pompey ending with naval defeats in 37–36 BC; Mutina in north Italy (modern Modena) was besieged by Mark Antony in 44 BC after the assassination of Caesar; Leucas = Actium, where Octavian won his decisive naval battle against the combined forces of Antony and Cleopatra in 31 BC.

BOOK EIGHT

1.   *Hercules' gorges . . . Tempe*: Thessaly's major river, the Peneus, passes through a gorge between Olympus and Ossa called the Vale of Tempe just before it reaches the sea; in myth Hercules had formed the gorge (cf. 6.386–88).

4.   *wavering trail*: The Latin lines recall Ovid's description of the Cretan labyrinth at *Met.* 8.160.

30.   *Cilicia . . . Pontus*: See note to 1.363.

31.   *grieve . . . to recall*: Cf. *Aen.* 1.203.

44.   *Corcyra . . . Leucas*: The fleets had been left off western Greece, where Cato will soon rejoin them (cf. note to 9.35).

45.   *lands of Liburnians*: Region along the Illyrian coast opposite Italy, renowned for seafaring and its galleys, on which Rome's naval galleys were modeled.

84.   *intemperate sadness*: Pompey's speech to Cornelia recalls Seneca's literary letters *de consolatione* ("for consolation"), in which sympathy and reasonable argument, sometimes verging on hard love, are offered to the recipient to help him or, as often, her weather harsh blows of fortune.

107. *A Fury is my bridesmaid*: Latin *pronuba*, a married matron who conducted a bride to the bridal chamber; the image comes from an important passage in *Aeneid* 7.314–22, Juno plotting to unleash the Fury Allecto to drive the rest of the poem: "Let Lavinia be his bride. An iron fact of Fate. / But I can drag things out, delay the whole affair: / that I can do, and destroy them root and branch, / the people of either king. What a price they'll pay / for the father and son-in-law's alliance here! Yes, / Latin and Trojan blood will be your dowry, princess—/ Bellona, Goddess of War, your

maid-of-honor! So, / Hecuba's not the only one who spawned a firebrand, / who brought to birth a wedding torch of a son. / Venus' son will be the same—a Paris reborn, a funeral torch to consume a second Troy!" (trans. R. Fagles, Penguin, 2006).

148. *steal them*: Caesar's own account, not without its propaganda purposes, emphasizes the rapaciousness of Scipio (Cornelia's father) while proconsul in Asia during the wars, and after Pharsalus his own saving of temple treasures at Ephesus nearly plundered twice by his enemies (*BC* 3.31–33, 3.105).

156. *hostage*: Acknowledging the precarious situation of Cornelia: they might have used their possession of her against him, to curry favor with Caesar.

174. *enter their ports*: Cf. Caesar's account of Pompey's flight, including the refusal of several cities to grant entry to Pompey and the ships of other defeated leaders (*BC* 3.102).

193. *nor those, if any*: Imagining unknown peoples living beyond the sunset; compare the imagined equatorial peoples at 9.667.

203. *Wagon*: The Great Bear, or our Big Dipper.

211. *Little Bear climbs*: The pilot describes using the mast of the ship in front of him as a compass with Polaris the polestar as his guide; when Polaris is seen to be gradually rising up the mast, they are bearing north, toward Scythia and the Black Sea (Pontus). When these same northerly circumpolar stars are moving down toward the horizon, they are bearing south, toward Syria and Egypt.

214–15. *Bear Guard . . . Dog's Tail*: Arctophylax (also known as Boötes) and Cynosura, both northerly circumpolar constellations which will not set at high northern latitudes but will do so as one moves south.

216. *Canopus*: The second brightest star in the sky after Sirius, it is a far southern star and cannot be seen in latitudes north of the thirty-seventh parallel, but played a prominent role in Egyptian astronomy.

218. *on your left*: I.e., navigating westward from Egypt by keeping southerly Canopus on one's left.

228. *Fortune*: Similar language to Ovid, *Met.* 2.140–42, suggests that Lucan has the fall of Phaethon in mind as a model here.

232. *Psyria . . . Chios*: Chios is the large island south of Lesbos and Psyria is a small craggy isle just northwest of it. At *Odyssey* 3.165–72, Nestor relates how after leaving Troy the Greeks fell into dissension and split up; Menelaus caught up with his Nestor's ships at Lesbos and they pondered whether to sail homeward "above rocky Chios by Psyria island" or below it, and a divine sign told them to go straight west. On the strength of this intertext, which puts

Pompey in the position of Greeks fleeing Troy, we have emended the corrupt and dubious line to *Psyriae* over other weaker conjectures.

241. *his son*: Sextus Pompey.

245. *Deiotarus*: Galatian king; after Pompey's fall he supplicated Caesar and saved his kingdom, and lived until after the Battle of Philippi. See note on 5.56.

256. *Arsacides*: The king of Parthia, Orodes II, who had defeated and killed Crassus in 53 BC.

257. *treaty*: When the civil war broke out, the Parthians nominally sided with Pompey, but they did not participate in the war.

258. *Magi*: Greek and Roman authors used the term "Magi" correctly (when not using it as a disparaging term for fortune-tellers) to refer to a priestly class of the Iranian East.

262. *Alans*: Among the earliest references to the Alans or Alani tribe of the northern Pontus and, later, Eastern Europe; in the reign of Nero, Romans became aware of them when they began to attempt incursions south across the Caucasus.

264. *Achaemenids*: The Persian ruling dynasty that dominated Central Asia, the Middle East, and Asia Minor in the sixth to fourth centuries BC until being defeated by Alexander. Cyrus was an Achaemenid.

267. *Chaldean*: Babylonian.

268. *Hydaspes of Nysa*: A major tributary of the Indus River (modern Jhelum), along which Alexander fought his last major battle against the Indian king Porus; Nysa is a name of uncertain meaning long associated with the mythical eastern land where Dionysos was reared as a baby (and likely connected somehow with his name: Dio-nysos). Pompey never even saw the Hydaspes, but it connects him with Dionysos and Alexander.

269. *nearer to . . . Phoebus*: Gross hyperbole, but serving to present Pompey as another Alexander.

276. *restrained*: In fact, Pompey had ostensibly been preparing for an eastern campaign, but his long inaction is generally viewed as evidence of his refusal to leave Italy in fear of Caesar eclipsing him in Rome.

280. *Zeugma*: City on the upper Euphrates in Syria founded by Alexander's general Seleucus and conquered by Pompey in 64 BC, after which it remained the border outpost dividing the Roman East from the Parthian empire.

290–96. *Icaria . . . Telmessos*: A tour of Ionian isles and mainland cities; Icaria is an island west of Samos; Ephesus and Colophon are cities on the coast; Cos is an island and Cnidos a city on a narrow

jutting peninsula farther south, toward Rhodes. Telmessos was a
city on the west coast of Lycia, opposite Rhodes. In general, Pom-
pey's itinerary is that of someone on the run and avoiding the
coast.

297–300. *Pamphylia . . . Phaselis*: Between Lycia and Cilicia on the
southern coast of Asia Minor, and Phaselis was a town on its
western shore.

303–4. *Taurus . . . Dipsus*: The Taurus mountain range begins in Cili-
cia near the coast, and many spectacular waterfalls here still draw
tourists, among them the Duden Falls northeast of modern An-
talya.

310. *Syhedra . . . Selinus*: Towns on Cilicia's west coast.

322. *Marius*: See 2.70–140 and notes.

337. *Moor*: King Juba of Numidia. He may have had, or simply claimed
to have, a blood relationship to Hannibal, through a daughter of
Hasdrubal his brother, married to the Numidian chieftain Syphax.

343. *puffed him up*: Juba's arrogant pleasure at the Romans' discord
became a byword; cf. Plutarch, *Cato Min.* 57, for the story of Ca-
to's arrival in Numidia, where Juba was pleased that Scipio and
Varus were at odds.

352. *empire*: Most have accepted Housman's preferred emendation of
regnandi, "ruling," to *pugnandi*, "fighting," on grounds of sense;
but *regnandi sola voluptas* also here looks suspiciously like Virgil's
regnandi dira cupido at *Geo.* 1.37, instructing Octavian Caesar not
to feel "dread lust for ruling," which is precisely what drives Pom-
pey at this point to pursue his mad plan. (Compare also 7.284.)

357. *Macedon . . . Bactra*: Beginning in the mid–third century BC, Ar-
saces and his descendants succeeded the Seleucid rulers of Alexan-
der's empire in the east, beginning in Parthia and making conquests
eastward to Bactria and westward to the edge of Rome's sphere of
influence, easily filling the power vacuum as Seleucid kings in the
second century were forced to focus on wars with Rome. Mithri-
dates I took over Babylon and Media in the 140s BC. Bactra (mod-
ern Balkh, in northern Afghanistan) was not in fact the seat of the
Medes; the capital city of the Media region was at Ecbatana.

361. *Scythian*: See note to 2.581–83.

366. *Medes*: Used as a loose synonym for Parthians.

381. *Maeotis . . . Tanaïs*: The Sea of Azov and the Don River. The clos-
est Pompey came to matching this boast was during his war
against Mithridates VI of Pontus, who fled to his realms across the
Black Sea with Pompey pursuing him.

385. *Favor my endeavors, Rome*: The same words Caesar used at 1.217.

388. *with Parthian troops*: This mad and treasonous plan was actually carried out by Quintus Labienus, son of Titus Labienus, who after the defeat at Philippi joined the Parthians and proceeded to overrun most of the Roman possessions in the East until he was defeated by Antony's deputy Ventidius in 39 BC.

394. *Lentulus*: Lucius Lentulus Crus, consul the previous year (he spoke also at 5.17ff.).

412. *Hyrcania*: Region south of the Caspian Sea, which Pompey made a brief but abortive attempt to conquer after defeating Mithridates.

425. *Scythia*: See note to 2.581–83.

445. *Sarmatian plains*: The Sarmatians inhabited the relatively flat Pontic-Caspian steppe of south Russia and Kazakhstan.

464. *vigor . . . men*: In the Latin a macho pun on strength (*vires*) and men (*viri*), with the related value term *virtus* occurring two lines before.

508. *civil war first*: See note to 276.

515. *Dacians*: People living in modern Romania.

523. *old man*: Crassus the elder (sixty-three when he died), as opposed to his son who also died at Carrhae.

524. *Scythian*: See note to 2.581–83.

525. *these words*: A brief but effective instance of what was called *prosopopoeia* in classical rhetorical theory, when the speaker pretends to speak in the voice and character of another.

531. *Tigris*: See note to 3.259.

547. *shadow of a name*: Compare 1.148.

554. *resolution*: In Latin, *victa est sententia Magni*—Pompey's way of thinking and the rhetoric of its expression have failed to persuade his peers, a blow as decisive and heavy for a powerful Roman aristocrat as any defeat in battle.

556. *Cyprus*: See note on 8.878–84 for the story of the evil omen Pompey received when putting in at Cyprus; Lucan may have this story in mind, though he never makes it explicit.

558. *Paphos*: City in southwest Cyprus, connected with Venus (Aphrodite), who was born there, coming ashore after arising from the foam of Uranus' severed genitals (cf. Hesiod, *Theog.* 180–206).

563–67. *tower . . . lowest . . . Pelusium*: The lighthouse tower of Pharos in Alexandria, on the western edge of the Nile Delta; Pelusium is at the seventh mouth, in the east, near Mount Casius.

568. *Libra*: The autumnal equinox. Pompey died around September 28, 48 BC, but this date is from the pre-Julian calendar, which places his death in late July, in the constellation Leo. Even if aware of the discrepancy, Lucan was probably more attracted to the symbolism of the tipping balance.

571. *Casius Hill*: A sandy hill that formed a promontory east of Pelusium, where there was a temple of Zeus Casius.

577. *Acoreus*: Known only from Lucan and possibly fictional, but his name is a Latinized version of the Greek Ouchoreus, the name given to the founder of Memphis by Diodorus Siculus (*Bibl.* 1.50), which scholars suppose is a translation of the Egyptian *Mn*, "he who endures," *Min* in Herodotus (2.99), where he is remembered as the first to control the flood with dams and diversions at Memphis.

580. *Nile's cresting*: Cf. 10.409–10.

581–82. *Apis . . . Phoebe*: The Apis bull worshipped at Memphis as an incarnation of Ptah-Osiris, and the bull's mother, worshipped as Isis, here identified with Roman Phoebe, Diana as the moon. The bull was used for a religious year count (e.g., "X happened in the X year of X Apis-bull"), and according to Greek and Roman authors, the bulls were not allowed to live beyond twenty-five years, but local records indicate that most bulls died of natural causes after eighteen to twenty-two years (see Thomson, *Memphis under the Ptolemies*, 1988, pp. 190–211).

585. *his father*: Ptolemy XII Auletes, who had regained his throne with Roman muscle in 55 BC and on his death in 51 left his will with Pompey and the Romans to be its executors, a de facto acknowledgment of Roman supremacy. While in exile in Rome from 58 to 55, Ptolemy and his young daughter, Cleopatra, had stayed with Pompey.

587. *Pothinus*: The scheming eunuch advisor of young Ptolemy XIII, effectively ruling for the boy king.

611. *ousted sister*: Cleopatra.

613. *belong to Magnus*: In fact, the Romans had strong legitimate leverage over Alexandria, both from Auletes' will and the massive outstanding debts to Roman creditors. By deposing Cleopatra and violating their father's will, Ptolemy's court gave the Romans all the pretext they needed to intervene.

650. *neither side*: Not true, at least according to Caesar, *BC* 3.3–4.

659. *Achillas*: General in charge of Ptolemy's armies.

665. *Canopus*: An older port city just to the east of Alexandria; to Romans it was a byword for dissolute effeminacy.

676. *half-man*: Latin *semivir*, i.e., the eunuch Pothinus.

732. *Septimius*: Lucius Septimius, a military tribune and one of the thousands of Roman soldiers still in Egypt from Aulus Gabinius' mercenary expedition to restore Ptolemy Auletes to the throne in 55 BC. Caesar says Septimius had served Pompey as a centurion against the pirates (*BC* 3.104).

748. *will they*: A brilliant partisan jab against the official view of the conspirators.

754. *refusing in rage*: Latin, *indignatus*, also used of Turnus as he died, in the last line of the *Aeneid* (12.952).

779. *dignity*: Literally, "if they are amazed," meaning if his death is such as to merit wonder and awe.

803. *spectacle*: Latin *munus*, used for gladiatorial games.

847. *forbidden art*: Embalming.

854. *Macedonian*: Alexander the Great.

857. *mausoleums*: Named after the spectacular monumental tomb of Mausolus of Halicarnassus, erected in the fourth century BC, used in imperial period Latin as a general term for such monuments, especially after Augustus' own mausoleum, which rivaled the original.

871–74. *Beaten by sands . . . missing head*: Cf. *Aen.* 2.556–58.

872. *laughingstock*: A plaything or butt of jokes (*ludibrium*), used also of Alexander at 10.33.

878–84. *Cordus . . . under evil omens . . . Cyprus . . . up on the beach*: verbal echoes make it clear that the scene is modeled on Aeneas' burial of Misenus on the shores of Cumae in *Aen.* 6.149–235 (which in turn was modeled on Elpenor in the *Odyssey*), in the middle of which scene Aeneas finds the golden bough. Cordus is called "ill-starred" (*infaustus*), which may connect with his name, an agricultural term that means "born out of season." But the mention of Cyprus may also recall a story, related in Valerius Maximus (1.5.6), that when Pompey fled Pharsalus and was putting in at Paphos on Cyprus, noticing a grand building on the shore he asked his helmsman its name; when he heard it was called the "lower palace" he took this as an evil omen, turned away in sadness, and groaned. Cinyras was the legendary early king of Paphos, father of Myrrha and grandfather of Adonis.

885. *Cynthia*: The moon.

986–88. *Oeta . . . Nysa . . . Bromius*: The mountain south of Thessaly where Hercules climbed on his funeral pyre and ascended to become a god. Nysa was the fabled eastern land where the infant Dionysos (Bromius, "the roarer") was raised.

997–98. *Lepidus . . . Sertorius*: Marcus Aemilius Lepidus was consul in 78 BC, after the death of Sulla, and when he marched his army against Rome the next year, Pompey was on the other side, which proved victorious. Lepidus had been governing Cisalpine Gaul, and Pompey went to Mutina and defeated, without battle, his deputy Brutus (father of Caesar's assassin). His subsequent march overland through the Alps to Spain is also probably meant here. Pompey spent the next six years in Spain, helping the proconsul Metellus defeat the separatist Sertorius.

1008. *sorry gravestone*: Appian relates that the simple grave read, "Rich was this man in temples, but poor now is his tomb." In time hidden by sand, it and bronze statues erected by his relatives at Mount Casius were defaced and then put in storage in the temple, until Hadrian (AD 130–31) cleared the grave and restored the statues (*BC* 2.86).

1019. *Sibyl of Cumae*: Most likely a reference to an official consultation of the Sibylline Books that had warned against helping Ptolemy Auletes regain his throne in Egypt; the oracle was later used as evidence against Aulus Gabinius when he was tried in 54 BC on charges of treason for aiding Ptolemy (per Pompey's orders) without any commission from the Senate. Lucan is probably generalizing the oracle here, making it applicable to any Roman, not least Pompey.

1028. *sistra*: The ritual rattles used in Egyptian religious worship, especially that of Isis.

1031. *temples*: The first was that of the divine Julius that Augustus had built in the Forum; others followed.

1050. *highest priest*: The Pontifex Maximus (used ironically?), the priesthood held by Caesar and (upon the death of Lepidus in 13 BC) Augustus after him; on his precedent, Pontifex Maximus became one of the many titles and positions of authority regulary assumed by the emperors.

1051. *Syene*: Far southern city of the Nile.

1052. *Cancer*: I.e., midsummer.

1053. *Pleiades*: In Greece and Italy the setting of the Pleiades in early November was a traditional sign of the beginning of winter, which is rainy in those climates but dry along the desert Nile.

1060. *Jove of Casius*: At Casius was a temple of Zeus Casius as well as Pompey's tomb (cf. Strabo, *Geog.* 16.2.33).

1063. *Now it is FORTUNE*: A textual variant, changing "it is" (*est*) to "you are" (*es*), would complete the identification of Fortuna and Pompey clearly intended here: "Now you [Pompey] are Fortune lying in this mound."

1067–68. *Tarpeian . . . Tuscan*: A contrast between the religious worship of lofty gods such as Jupiter Tonans on the Capitol (connected with the imperial cult) and a humble patch of grass marked as sacred by Etruscan diviners after a lightning strike (cf. 1.650).

1076. *Cretans*: The proverbial mendacity of Cretans was connected with their religiously outrageous claim that the birthplace and the tomb of Zeus were found on their island. Epimenides the Cretan had called Cretans liars for this (his infamous paradox), and declared Zeus instead to be immortal.

BOOK NINE

1.   *spirit*: His *manes*; see note to 6.902.

5–6.   *black sky . . . lunar orbit*: The sublunary sphere had no stars, hence it was dark.

7.   *demigod spirits*: Latin *semidei*, translating the Greek *hemitheoi* or *daimones*. The ascent of Pompey's spirit recalls Cicero's *Dream of Scipio* (*Somnium Scipionis*), in which Scipio's grandfather tells him how "rulers and preservers of states" return to the heaven from which the divine fire of their souls derived.

35.   *Corcyra*: Island off western Greece (modern Corfu). Lucan does not make it explicit that Cato was not at Pharsalus, but had been left behind at Dyrrachium and after learning of the defeat crossed to the naval fleets in Corcyra (cf. Plutarch, *Cato Min.* 55).

40–42. *Malea . . . Taenaros . . . Cythera*: The two promontories at the south of the Peloponnese that form the Laconian Gulf, Malea on the east and opposite the island of Cythera, Taenaros on the west and a legendary entry into the underworld. The unpredictable winds in the strait between Malea and Cythera were already prominent in the *Odyssey* (cf. *Od.* 3.288, 4.15, 9.80: Odysseus blown off course to the Lotus Eaters, "as I turned the hook of Malea, the sea and current and north wind beat me off course and drove me on past Cythera").

44.   *Dicte's shores*: Crete's Mount Dicte.

46.   *Phycus*: City on North African coast near Cyrene.

49.   *Palinurus*: Aeneas' pilot who falls asleep at the helm ("Phrygian" = Trojan), falls overboard, and drowns before reaching Italy, but giving his name to a cape on the south Italian coast (*Aen.* 833–71); Lucan, for literary reasons, associates with him the Cyrenian city Paliurus, well to the east of Phycus.

60. *stepson*: Sextus Pompey, the son of Pompey's third wife (Cornelia was his fifth).

92. *Pelusium*: The eastern mouth of the Nile, where Pompey met Ptolemy's men and was killed.

96. *Magnus the Blessed*: In Latin, *felix Magnus*, an honorific adjective taken most notably by Sulla.

99. *Sextus*: Pompey's son, who visited Erictho in Book Six. He and his brother Gnaeus will lead a resistance to Caesar and Octavian that will persist into the 30s BC.

120–21. *Chaos . . . Tartarus*: The depths of the underworld.

139. *Cyprus*: Lucan refers to Pompey's ships fleeing after his death; they go to Cyprus then back south to Cyrene, where they meet up with Cato and the fleet from Greece.

144. *Magnus the younger*: Gnaeus Pompeius, Pompey's older son who was with Cato.

185–86. *Pellaean . . . Mareotis*: I.e., Alexandrian, and Lake Mareotis, south of the city.

188. *Amasis*: Pharaoh of the Twenty-Sixth Dynasty in the sixth century BC, who died just before the Persians invaded and conquered Egypt; Cambyses notoriously desecrated and burned Amasis' body, much as young Pompey proposes to do here (cf. Herodotus, *Hist.* 3.16).

192–94. *Isis . . . Osiris . . . Apis*: The dominant gods of late Egyptian religion; killing the Apis bull at Memphis had also been another of Cambyses' infamous sacrilegious crimes (cf. Herodotus, *Hist.* 3.27, and 3.16 on the sacrilegious nature of burning the dead in Egypt).

221. *Apulians*: Inhabitants of a region in southeast Italy (modern Puglia).

224–25. *Garganus . . . Vultur . . . Matinus*: Mountains in Apulia. Vultur is inland; Garganus forms the promontory spur that juts into the Adriatic, south of which was a small hill and/or town named Matinus.

258. *Juba*: King of Numidia; after the disastrous defeat at Thapsus, Cato, Scipio, Petreius, and Juba all committed suicide.

265. *Tarcondimotus*: A Cilician prince whom Cicero mentions once as a "very faithful" ally of Rome; he would die fighting for Antony in a naval battle before Actium, and his sons held power in Cilicia under Augustus.

331. *Parthian soldier*: Who killed Crassus, first of the triumvirs to die.

336. *Emathian Philippi*: Pharsalus (by Lucan's usual geographical conflations).

344. *Metellus*: Cornelia, daughter of Quintus Metellus Scipio.

353–64. *swarms . . . just war*: This bee simile reworks Virgil, *Geo.* 4.58–66, which directly precedes mention of discord and wars between rival bee kings. "Phrygian bronze" refers to the worship of Cybele, the Phrygian Great Mother. Hybla, on the southern slopes of Sicily's Mount Etna, was famed for its honey. Note that Cato's armed opposition to Caesar is now called "just war" as opposed to civil war, which even Cato had deemed "the highest crime" (2.303).

365–67. *constant work and labors of war . . .*: Cato's revival of his soldiers' morale through disciplined camp labors was a familiar topos of Roman historiography (cf. Metellus' reformation of the lazy army in Numidia in Sallust, *Jug.* 44–45, a passage Lucan may well have in mind). Cf. also Horace, *Carm* 3.2: "The boy must be toughened by hard campaigning and learn happily to endure constraints of poverty, riding against fierce Parthians, spreading terror with his sword, living in danger under the sky." For a good recent analysis of Roman military discipline in this period, see Phang 2008; as she says, "A basic aim of *disciplina* was the production and maintenance of *virtus*" (p. 287).

374–75. *Nature . . . Intrepid Virtue*: The Libyan march, framed as a showdown between *natura* and *virtus*, is a contest that would have strong Stoic resonances. But Nature in harsh, snake-infested Libya is far from the kindly, nourishing figure she often appears to be in Stoic texts. Cf. Sallust, *Jug.* 75.3, 76.1; also Horace, *Carm.* 3.2: "Virtue opens a way to heaven . . . she dares to take the forbidden path."

378–79. *Syrtes . . . land and sea*: Sallust, *Jug.* 78, also describes the ambiguous character of the Syrtes and explains the name, from the Greek for "to sweep," from the churning effect of the winds on its shallows.

390–91. *Titan . . . on ocean*: See note to 10.318–22.

434–43. *lake of Triton*: Lake Tritonis, a salt lake near the western bend of Syrtis Minor (modern Chott el Fedjedji in Tunisia), today a dry and passable salt flat except in the rainy season, though likely more of a regular lake in antiquity. Triton is the minor sea god whose symbol was his conch shell (cf. *Aeneid* 1.144–47, when he calms the storm on the Syrtis). His association with this lake, and its mythological ties to Pallas Athena, are already in Herodotus (4.188). There were also smaller lakes called Tritonis in Cyrenaica, one near Berenice (Strabo, *Geog.* 17.3.20) and another (?) near Cyrene (Callimachus, *Aitia* 1).

443–44. *Nearby . . . Lethon*: Local river associated with the river Lethe ("forgetfulness") in the underworld. It was nowhere nearby: as Pliny relates (*Nat. Hist.* 5.5), Lethon was a river near Hesperis in Cyrene, a city associated with the fabled Hesperides, but lying several hundred miles behind them at the other side of the Syrtes (see previous note).

455. *Alcides*: Hercules, who for one of his twelve labors fetched the golden apples of the Hesperides at the western edge of the world. This is the first of many indications to follow that Lucan is sketching his Cato-in-Africa sequence on the heroic models of Hercules, Perseus (see the Medusa narrative below), and Alexander the Great. Strabo relates of the latter's visit to Ammon's oracle, "Alexander was ambitious for the glory of visiting the oracle because he knew that Perseus and Hercules had made the journey there before" (*Geog.* 17.1.43).

460. *Garamantian*: From the Garamantes, a native people of North Africa.

462. *Cato*: Lucan's account makes it seem that Cato has been part of the abortive attempt to cross the Syrtes by sea. Other accounts make it clear that the fleet with the younger Pompey went by sea, while Cato set out from Cyrene overland with a large army.

488. *lovely and truly Roman*: Probably a twist on Horace's famous "Sweet and honorable it is to die for the fatherland" (*Carm.* 3.2.13).

493. *first to walk the sands*: Cf. Sallust, *Jug.* 85.47, for Marius' similar promise to lead by example and endure the same toils as all: "I will be with you personally in battle or in the column as both counselor and partner in danger, and in every situation I shall treat myself and you alike" (trans. Woodman).

511. *not return*: Foreshadowing of Cato's suicide at Utica in 46 BC.

517. *part of Europe*: In his similar account of Africa (probably a source here), Sallust also relates the alternative division of the world into two or three parts, but does not, like Lucan, lend more credence to the two-part division (cf. *Jug.* 17.3–6).

518. *Scythian Tanaïs*: The Don River in Russia, which enters the Black Sea eight degrees of longitude east of the Nile (the Ister/Danube would have been more accurate).

519–26. *Gades . . . sunrise*: I.e., Europe and Africa are equally wide, beginning from Cadiz in the west to the Nile and the Don, taken as the eastern borders with Asia; in the north, Asia is on the "left hand" side of Boreas, who points southward, and in the south, it is on the "right hand" side of Notus, who points northward. Eurus, the east wind, belongs wholly to Asia, while the western Zephyr winds derive from

Europe and Africa. Being utterly ignorant of sub-Saharan Africa, Greek and Roman geographers vastly underestimated the size of the continent, making a twofold division of the world into west and east seem more satisfactory to some (cf. Strabo, *Geog.* 17.3.1).

527. *in the west*: He means from Carthage westward, as the contrast with the Syrtes at 540 makes clear.

536. *citron*: Romans imported citron wood from Mauritania (modern Morocco); see note on 10.181–84.

546. *Jove*: Jupiter as god of rain and storms.

550. *Nasamonians*: Pastoral nomads dwelling inland from Cyreneica and along the Syrtis Major.

554. *wreckage*: The Roman historian Curtius Rufus also mentions the Nasamones' practice of plundering shipwrecks (*Hist. Alex.* 4.7.20).

570. *whipping all that sand up*: On Libyan sandstorms, cf. Sallust, *Jug.* 79.6.

571. *Aeolian*: Aeolus was the god in charge of the winds.

603. *our sacred shields*: The ancilia, which the Salii sacred brotherhood paraded through the city during a festival in March. In legend, one shield fell from heaven on Numa, Rome's second ruler, and he made eleven more to conceal and protect the original, which would give Rome strength as long as it was preserved. Lucan's rationalized reference turns Rome's symbol of divine right to power into the result of random violent weather.

620. *all the stars*: I.e., those familiar in more northerly Europe, since the celestial pole descends as one travels south.

625–38. *a stingy little stream . . .*: This example of virtue (*exemplum virtutis*) came from the traditions about Alexander the Great (cf. Frontinus, *Strategemata* 1.7, who locates it in Africa; Arrian, *Anab.* 6.26, admits that accounts differ on where it occurred; cf. also Plutarch, *Alex.* 42.7).

642. *Ammon*: The oracle of "Jupiter/Zeus" Ammon, represented with ram's horns, in vast, lush Siwa, west of the Nile. Pliny puts Siwa at 400 Roman miles southeast of Cyrene, so Lucan's Cato, supposedly heading west, is already *far* off track. The visit to Ammon is patently modeled on Alexander the Great's visit, when he was supposedly declared a child of Zeus (cf. Plutarch, *Alex.* 26–7).

647–48. *Ethiopia . . . Arabia . . . Indians*: An absurd lumping together of all "Eastern" peoples, though not unique to Lucan.

652. *grove of trees*: Siwa is several hundred square miles of lush green palm trees and olive groves.

655. *Berenicis . . . Leptis*: The region around Berenice, a city of Cyrenaica; two cities farther west, Leptis Magna (a Punic/Roman city

at modern Al Khums, Libya) and Leptis Minor in modern Tunisia (near Monastir), though which one Lucan intends is not clear.

665. *pauses high in summer*: The solstice, thus the Tropic of Cancer; actually, Siwa is about six degrees north of the tropic line.

667. *whoever you are*: The unknown peoples presumed to live south of the equator, beyond the torrid zone, which intense heat renders uninhabitable.

670–71. *Dog's Tail . . . Wagon*: Cynosura, our Little Dipper; the Wagon is the Big Dipper or Great Bear; instead of staying always above the horizon as in the north, they set and rise like other stars.

673. *Either axle*: Now describing the heavens from the equator, equidistant from the celestial poles. Inside the tropics, the apparent path of the sun, planets, and zodiac constellations, called the ecliptic, lies closer to directly overhead than it does either north or south of it, where it is never directly overhead.

676–81. *Taurus . . . same angle . . . Urn*: At the equator, since the ecliptic is perpendicular to the horizon, all twelve zodiac signs rise throughout the year at the same angle, taking roughly the same amount of time. All twelve signs are listed as pairs opposite each other: Taurus (second sign) and Scorpio (eighth), Aries (first) and Libra (seventh), Virgo (sixth) and Pisces (twelfth), Chiron = Sagittarius (ninth) and Gemini (third), Cancer (fourth) and Capricorn (tenth), Leo (fifth) and the Water Bearer = Aquarius (eleventh).

683. *Horned Jove*: Ammon.

690. *Labienus*: See note to 5.363.

710. *worthy of a god's*: Lucretius had called the teachings of Greek philosophers "oracles from the heart's temple," and holier than Delphic oracles (*De R.N.* 1.737–39).

713. *one's life is long*: This line, very compressed in the Latin, has caused editors problems, prompting many emendations; it may have a slightly different sense, something like "Whether the only thing that matters in life is whether you live a long time?" Both interpretations are recognizable versions of an important Stoic ethical concern, which put an honest and virtuous life far above mere longevity and survival.

721. *falls silent*: Strabo discusses the common theme of the obsolescence of oracles in relation to the temple of Ammon (*Geog.* 17.1. 43); here Cato's Stoic philosophical wisdom supplants and replaces any advice oracles can give.

731. *resort to diviners*: Cato was an outspoken skeptic of divinatory arts; Cicero records a saying of Cato, "he used to say that he marveled that one diviner [*haruspex*] did not laugh when he saw

another diviner. For how many things turn out according to their predictions?" (de Div. 2.24, repeated without naming Cato at de Nat. Deo. 1.71).

738. *carries his own javelins*: Sallust's Marius again warrants comparison (*Jug.* 100.3–5).

747–48. *strip success from virtue*: The contrasts here between virtue and fortune recall Sallust's opening praise of virtue and disparagement of the gifts of fortune at *Jug.* 1–4. Juvenal, *Sat.* 10.140–46, strikes the same theme, probably with Lucan's lines in mind.

754. *thrice . . . break Jugurtha's neck*: For Pompey's three triumphs see note to 1.133–35. Gaius Marius paraded Jugurtha, king of Numidia, in his triumph of 104 BC, after which he was executed. Sallust's *Jugurthine War* narrates the history of the war and Jugurtha's surrender, but stops short of the triumph.

764. *a mob of serpents*: Sallust had also emphasized the infestation of serpents in Libya's deserts (*Jug.* 89.5).

765. *asps*: Aspis was a common term for snakes, probably used for several species but definitely including African cobras, especially the Egyptian cobra (*Naja haje*), since Pliny says "the neck of asps puffs up, and there is no cure for its bite" and that the mongoose is its enemy (*Nat. Hist.* 8.35).

766. *dipsades*: The second-century AD Greek satirist Lucian wrote a short description of desert Libya and the *dipsas*, its worst and deadliest snake, which makes one die of thirst (*On the Dipsades*); in Greek *dips-* means "thirst." The soldier bitten by it later (920ff.) dies of heat and thirst; here Lucan makes the snakes themselves thirsty. Modern taxonomy uses *dipsas* for a group of New World tropical snakes and thus bears no relation to whatever species ancients called by this name.

773. *cupfuls*: Generally true: snake venom is harmful only if injected, not ingested.

782. *beguiling . . . true cause*: Lucan frames this mythic narration through the lens of contemporary scholarly debates about the relative value and uses of myth (e.g., compare Strabo, *Geog.* 2.7–18)—as Cato explores the world's limits the poet confronts the limits of knowledge.

785. *Phorcys*: A primordial Greek god of the sea, the father with Ceto of many early minor monsters and fabulous creatures that populate the world, including the Hesperides, who guard the golden apples; the Sirens; and the Gorgons, one of whom was Medusa (cf. Hesiod, *Theog.* 270–336).

803. *Eumenides*: The Furies.

804. *Cerberos*: The three-headed hound of Hades.

805. *Amphitryon's son*: Hercules (actually son of Zeus, but Amphitryon was his mortal father).

816. *Atlas*: Mount Atlas was regarded as the Titan son of Iapetos who (as punishment) held up the sky at the western edge of the world.

819–22. *Phlegra . . . breastplate . . . war of gods*: Pallas bore the severed head of the Gorgon on the front of her aegis, her cape-shield, and with it (in this version) turned the Giants to stone at Phlegra, ending the Gigantomachy. Cf. *Aen.* 8.435–38.

822–23. *Perseus . . . Danae*: Zeus poured gold into the lap of Danae and Perseus was born; her father, Acrisius, threw them in the sea and they washed up on Seriphos. The king of Seriphos sent him to fetch the head of Medusa the Gorgon. The full story of Perseus is one of Ovid's longer narratives in *Met.* 4.416–5.249.

824–29. *Parrhasian . . . cow*: Hermes (Mercury) aided Perseus by giving him winged sandals and a curved sword, with which he had already killed Argus, the many-eyed guardian of Io. Parrhasian = Arcadian; Cyllene is the Arcadian mountain where Hermes was born.

831. *from the bargain*: Athena (Minerva) will get the head of Medusa for her aegis.

853. *Tritonia*: Athena/Minerva; see 434–43.

870. *shadow*: Causing lunar eclipses.

884. *asp*: When not used as a generic term for snakes, *aspis* meant specifically the cobra (of which there are several species in Africa).

885–904. *haemorrhois . . . basilisk*: The sketchy, unsystematic nature of ancient natural history makes it hard to identify any of these snakes precisely (except the *cerastes*, which is almost certainly the horned viper that still bears that name). In fact, it is instructive that Lucan's account is among the handful of texts attesting to ancient herpetological lore. Lucan's treatment, as much literary as scientific, is based on such works as Nicander's poem *Theriaca*, about poisonous animals and their wounds, and its companion piece on cures, *Alexipharmaca*. The Greek names of the snakes are significant.

885. *haemorrhois*: Means "flowing blood," obviously named for the anticoagulant effect of its venom.

887–88. *chersydros . . . chelydros*: Names mean "land and water," i.e., amphibious, and "turtle-watersnake," if significant perhaps from its diet. Nicander says the *chelydros* looks like a *hydros*, has a dark, flat head, hunts locusts and frogs in marshes, and lives in trees and bushes; his *chersydros* looks like an *aspis*, hunts frogs in swamps, hisses, and (somehow) leaves withering devastation in its path. Both are perhaps species of cobra or viper.

889. *cenchris*: A snake whose skin looks like "millet" (Greek *cenchros*); Nicander locates it in Thrace and the Ionian islands, a long snake with horny scales also called the "speckled lion"; possibly one of the venomous viper species of Europe and Asia Minor (*Vipera xanthina*?).

892. *Theban serpentine*: A stone, of two varieties, *Thebanus ophites*, so called because it had snakelike markings (from the Greek *ophis*).

893–94. *ammodytes . . . cerastes*: The "sand-burrower" and the "horned" snake, probably the same or closely related, and matching the modern genus *Cerastes*; the horned desert viper (*Cerastes cerastes*) is sand-colored and horned. Nicander says the *cerastes* is like the *echis* (viper) but has horns, some two and some four. (The modern *Vipera ammodytes* of Europe is a false match.)

895. *scytale*: The "club, cudgel" snake; Nicander says it is like the *amphisbaena* but thick, with a flat and barbed (?) tail; possibly one or other species of puff adder (genus *Bitis*), which are stout with a notably smaller tail.

896. *dipsas*: "Thirsty." Aelian (*Hist. Anim.* 6.51) describes the *dipsas* as smaller than an *echis* (viper), white with two black lines on its tail; a species of saw-scaled viper (genus *Echis*) is not unlikely. See also notes on 766 above, 900 and 919 below.

897. *amphisbaena*: "Going in either direction"—in Nicander as elsewhere, it is "two-headed," also mottled and earth-toned.

898. *natrix*: "Swimmer," generic Latin for the equally generic Greek *hydros*, "water-snake."

899. *iaculus*: The "javelin" snake, possibly the *akontias*, "darter," in Greek; Pliny also says they dart out of trees.

899. *parias*: A "red-brown" snake (Greek *pareias*).

900. *prester*: "Scorcher, burner," hence Lucan's "fuming"; Aelian, credibly enough (*Hist. Anim.* 6.51), says that *prester* is one of the many names used for the *dipsas*, along with *kauon* ("burning"), *melanouros* ("black-tail"), *ammobates* ("sand-treader" = *ammodytes*), and *kentris* ("stabber").

902. *seps*: "Putrefaction," from the effect of its bite; necrosis is common with snakebites. Nicander calls the *seps* "thirsty" (*dipsios*, cf. *dipsas*), says it varies in coloration depending on the ground it inhabits, and that it lives in rocky outcrops and sandy places.

904. *basilisk*: "Little king," described variously by ancient authors, often including clearly fabulous elements. Nicander's "little king" is light

brown and has a sharp or pointed head, and that its shriek or hiss drives all other snakes away; no bird or beast will feed on its carcass on account of its terrible stench, and its bite causes the flesh to waste away (necrosis); accounts emphasize its small size. Pliny's basilisk, which moves upright and erect and is killed by "weasels," is probably a cobra; the hissing and the long-range effect of its venom suggest the spitting cobras (like the relatively short red spitting cobra, *Naja pallida*, which is most aggressive when young).

906. *dragons*: Latin *dracones*, from a generic Greek word for snakes, but here obviously the ancestor to our fabulous flying dragons; Africa's very large carnivorous monitor lizards (genus *Varanus*) may have contributed to these imaginary monsters. (Tree snakes of the genus *Chrysopelea* do "fly" or jump-glide, but these live in Southeast Asia.)

918. *Aulus*: The victim of Scaeva's ruse at 6.257 was also named Aulus.

919. *dipsas*: See note on 766 above. The deadly black mamba, found throughout Africa but not in the northern deserts, may at least be a contender for identifying the ancients' fearsome *dipsas*. Species of venomous vipers, of the genus *Echis*, which are aggressive and deadly, and range in North Africa, are also probable for one or another of Lucan's snakes.

967. *all there is to man*: Compare Juvenal, *Sat.* 10.172–73.

979. *Cinyps*: River of North Africa, near Leptis Magna.

1002. *great-hearted*: See note at 4.499 on *magnanimus*.

1004. *Corycian saffron*: The best saffron was harvested from crocus flowers in a cave near Corycus in Cilicia; ancient Mediterranean peoples used saffron extensively, as both a fabric dye and a perfume, and Romans in particular sprinkled saffron water at festivals, on stages, and in the arena (probably not least to cover foul odors). Lucan presumably describes the pressing of saffron (with an emendation of the confusing text), but interpretation of the lines remains doubtful.

1016–18. *Saïs . . . Sabaean*: Saïs was a city in the Nile Delta near Naucratis; the Sabaeans lived in Arabia, where the Romans obtained incenses such as myrrh and frankincense.

1020. *iaculus*: A fantastically improbable form of wounding no doubt inspired by its name, "javelin," and exaggerated tales of actual quick, long snake strikes.

1027. *venom raced*: Pliny (*Nat. Hist.* 8.33.78) also relates the common belief that the venom of a basilisk speared by a mounted rider will run through the spear and kill both rider and horse. Such lore may well reflect accounts of spitting cobras, as well as the great prominence of cobras in ancient Egyptian conceptions of royalty.

1032–35. *scorpion . . . Orion*: The hunter Orion, in one version of his death, boasted that he could kill any animal, and Earth then created the scorpion, which killed him. They both became constellations.

1036. *salpuga*: According to Pliny, the name in Baetica, Hispania (Lucan's birthplace: an authorial self-reference?), for a kind of venomous ant.

1071. *gates of the world*: Cf. Lucretius' praise of Epicurus, who with philosophical inquiry wanted to "break open the locked gates of nature" and with the power of his mind reached the "flaming walls of the world" to achieve a victory over heaven that left religion subjected underfoot (*De R.N.* 1.70–79).

1091. *endurance*: Latin *patientia*; see note to 4.499.

1105. *can be nothing*: Cf. note to 4.499.

1109. *Psylli of Marmarica*: The desert region south of Cyrene to Ammon; the Psylli were already shrouded with legends in Herodotus, who makes them the western neighbors of the Nasamones, but in a drought they decided to "declare war on the south wind," marched out to the desert, and, being buried in sand, were wiped out (*Hist.* 4.173). Pliny says some survived war with the Nasamones, and reports their natural resistance to snakes and their practice of exposing infants to snakes to test for adultery (*Nat. Hist.* 7.2.14–15). Plutarch also relates that Cato took Psylli with him on his march (though influence *from* Lucan is not impossible). Suetonius says Augustus summoned a Psylli man in hopes of saving Cleopatra from her fatal snakebite (*Aug.* 17.4).

1119. *too small*: So interpreting *parvus infans*; alternatively, they test all infants (which seems even more incredible, though one can imagine a ritual passing of a snake over a newborn).

1121. *bird of Jove*: The eagle.

1128. *played with serpents*: Recalls baby Hercules, whom Hera tested by putting snakes in his crib; they frightened his mortal twin, Iphicles, but Hercules faced and killed them.

1137–44. *dwarf elder . . . horns*: An impressive short catalogue of exotic-sounding woods found in other Greek and Latin poets when aromatic and medicinal plants are called for; long explanation would be beside their apparent main point of simply sounding good (*sonant flammis*, "resound in the flames")—and showing off his knowledge of other poets.

1167. *Twice had Phoebe*: Phoebe is the moon, thus two months. Leptis, near Thapsus, where Cato would commit suicide, is approximately 240 kilometers north of Lake Tritonis, where they seem to have started; Lucan's apparent itinerary makes them tour south and east for several hundreds of miles of detour. In fact, Cato marched from Cyrene, so Lucan's Tritonis must be one of the smaller ones there (see note on 434–43). Strabo says the march took thirty days (*Geog.* 17.3.20), but he may mean only the leg from Cyrene to Leptis Magna. Plutarch (probably incorrect) says the march took seven days (*Cato Min.* 56).

1183. *Thracian narrows*: This probably means the Hellespont or its vicinity, on the north side of which was Thrace.

1184. *swum for love . . . towers of Hero*: The story of Hero and Leander: Hero was a priestess of Aphrodite who lived in a tower in Sestos, on the north side of the Hellespont; her lover Leander, from Abydos on the south, would swim the strait to meet with her, until one stormy night he drowned (cf. Ovid, *Heroides* 18–19).

1185. *Helle*: Helle and her brother Phrixus fled their wicked stepmother, Ino, on the back of a golden ram sent by their mother, Nephele, and when going through the Hellespont she fell off and died, giving the strait her name, "Helle's Sea."

1186–90. *No thinner flow . . .*: The dividing line between Europe and Asia ran through the Hellespont, across the Propontis (modern Sea of Marmara), and through the also narrow Bosporus strait into the Euxine or Black Sea; Byzantium lay at the mouth of the Bosporus, on the north side and opposite Chalcedon.

1191. *Sigeum*: Headland on the coast northwest of Troy, where two ancient tumuli (still there) were believed to hold the remains of Achilles and Patroclus.

1192. *Simoïs*: River near Troy.

1193. *Greek at Rhoetion*: A coastal promontory north of Troy where Ajax was believed to be buried.

1196. *Phoebus' walls*: Poseidon and Apollo built the walls of Troy for King Laomedon.

1198. *Assaracus*: Son of Tros who founded Troy, great-grandfather of Aeneas.

1199. *Pergamum*: Another name for Troy/Ilium.

1201. *Hesione's crags*: Daughter of Laomedon, king of Troy, who (in a variant on the Perseus and Andromeda myth) was exposed on a rock for a sea monster and then saved by Hercules; she married Telamon and was mother of the Trojan War hero Teucer.

1202. *Anchises . . . secret marriage bed*: Venus (Greek Aphrodite) appeared as a mortal girl to Anchises on Mount Ida and seduced him, conceiving Aeneas.

1203. *a cave where a judge*: Where Paris rendered his famous judgment on the three goddesses Juno, Venus, and Minerva.

1203–4. *boy . . . snatched to heaven*: Ganymedes, the lovely son of Tros, first king of Troy, carried to heaven by Jupiter as an eagle to be his cupbearer.

1205. *Oenone*: In late mythological tradition, the first wife of Paris of Troy, a mountain nymph from Ida, whom he abandoned for Helen but who still mourned for him after his death near the end of the war (cf. Ovid, *Her.* 5).

1207. *Xanthus*: The river near Troy, also known as Scamander, which Achilles fights in *Iliad* 21.

1210–12. *Some stones . . . Zeus Herkeios*: Zeus (Latin Jupiter) as guardian of the "enclosure" (*herkos*) of a house, altars to whom were inside a house or courtyard; infamously, Achilles' son Neoptolemus killed King Priam at the altars of Zeus Herkeios.

1213–20. *O sacred mighty work*: In this passage critical to the whole poem, Lucan seems to have had in mind a similar passage defending poetry in Cicero, *Pro Archia* 24: "How many writers of his deeds is it said that Alexander the Great had with him! Yet when he stood at Sigeum at Achilles' tomb he said: 'Fortunate youth, who found Homer to herald your virtue!' Indeed. For if the *Iliad* did not exist, the tomb that covers his body would also obliterate his name. Our own Magnus [Pompey], who had matched his fortune with virtue, did he not reward Theophanes of Mytilene, the author of his deeds, with citizenship before his assembled soldiers?" Cf. also Arrian, *Anabasis* 1.11–12, which shows clearly that the entire visit of Caesar to Troy is modeled on the Alexander tradition.

1218. *Smyrna's singer*: Homer, claimed as native son by Smyrna in Asia Minor.

1225. *Phrygian*: Phrygia was the wider region of which the Troad was, loosely, a part.

1226–27. *my Aeneas . . . household gods Lavinia and Alba*: The household gods, Lares and Penates, of Troy were taken to Italy by Aeneas, who founded Lavinium near Rome, and Alba Longa reputedly preserved them.

1228. *Pallas*: The Palladium, statue of Pallas Athena on which the safety of Troy depended ("lasting pledge of safety" must be ironic).

1231. *Iulus' line*: Son of Aeneas, through whom the Julian clan—with the propaganda support of Virgil's *Aeneid*—claimed descent from Venus.

1236–37. *Ausonidae . . . Roman Pergamum*: A high-flown epic name meaning "Sons of Ausonia," i.e., Italians or Romans; ostensibly, Caesar is promising to rebuild Troy with a Roman colony, but also, viewed through Virgil, he seems to say he'll make Rome itself into a new Troy.

1240. *Iliadic breaks*: Not just delays at Ilium, but literary self-consciousness of the *Iliad*.

1245. *Pharos*: The lighthouse island in Alexandria's harbor.

1247. *full of turmoil*: Cf. Caesar, *BC* 3.106–7; of Pompey Caesar says only, "at Alexandria, he learned of Pompey's death."

1250. *king's attendant*: Pothinus.

1256. *king of Pella*: I.e., Ptolemy. Lucan freely uses Pella, the Macedonian city of Philip and of Alexander the Great, to refer to the Ptolemies and Alexandria, though the Ptolemies never actually ruled Macedon.

1309. *true devotion*: Latin *pietas*, the virtue of Caesar's future literary hero, Virgil's Aeneas.

1323. *did not despise his sister*: That is, if such a murder would simply please him.

1374. *what fine liberty*: An enigmatic exclamation; perhaps ironic, like the feigned happiness of his sorrowing companions, since *libertas* can mean specifically freedom of speech.

BOOK TEN

10. *just less than it loves you*: More literally, "love the Nile after you," presumably meaning if Caesar had died in Egypt, Romans would have reason to love, rather than hate, the country, an idea that recurs at 10.484–85.

25. *Philip of Pella*: Philip II of Macedon, whose capital was at Pella, father of "crazy" Alexander the Great.

35. *his own confines*: Juvenal, *Sat.* 10.168–73, draws on Lucan here for the same theme.

36. *spurning Athens*: Philip spent twenty years expanding his power, finally beating an allied army from Greece's chief cities, including Athens and Thebes, at Chaeronea in 338 BC, at which Alexander fought. Philip died in 336, and Alexander quickly turned his imperial ambitions toward the east.

45. *ocean's outer sea*: Alexander's irrepressible drive to continue east-ward, thwarted only by his mutinous men, was a prominent motif in his legends.

54. *left no heir*: On his deathbed Alexander reputedly said he left his empire "to the strongest" or "to the stronger." His generals be-came the heads of smaller "successor" (*diadochi*) states.

56. *his own Babylon*: Alexander died in 323 BC in Babylon, which he had conquered earlier. His sarcophagus was later taken to Alex-andria and became an important symbol of legitimacy for the Ptolemies.

58–59. *long pikes . . . legions' spears*: The long pike (*sarisa*) was a signature of the Macedonian phalanx just as the javelin (*pilum*) was of the Roman legion.

62. *Arsacidae's master*: Alexander; the Parthian Arsacidae were Ira-nian but Hellenized, using Greek on their coinage and styling themselves as Philhellenes. Lucan must be conceiving of them here as successors in some fashion to Alexander.

65. *Pelusian*: Pelusium on Egypt's eastern delta shore (see map).

70. *Pharos*: The small island in Alexandria's harbor that held the fa-mous lighthouse, linked by a causeway to the shore.

71. *Emathian halls*: I.e., Macedonian, since Ptolemy I had been from there.

74–75. *Spartan . . . Argos . . . Ilium*: Helen, queen of Sparta, whose ab-duction by Paris caused the Trojan War (Ilium = Troy); Argos, near Mycenae = Argives, Greeks.

77–80. *sistrum . . . Canopus . . . Caesar . . . Leucas*: The sistrum is the ritual rattle used in the worship of Isis; Canopus, west of Alexan-dria, was a byword for Alexandrian effeminacy and decadent lux-ury; Leucas is Actium, where Octavian beat Cleopatra and Antony in a naval battle in 31 BC. Caesar here is Octavian Augustus.

84–85. *our own generals . . . incestuous daughter*: First Julius Caesar, later Mark Antony. The Ptolemies practiced royal incest; Cleopa-tra was a daughter of Ptolemy XII and Cleopatra V, and was mar-ried to her younger brother and nominal co-ruler, Ptolemy XIII. Cf. the anti-Cleopatra rant of Propertius, 11.29–56.

93. *fathered offspring*: Caesarion (b. 47 BC), declared Caesar's true heir by Antony in 34 BC, executed by Octavian in 30.

95. *a brother*: Emending the text, which reads "brothers," poses no problems.

105. *Lagus*: Father of Ptolemy I (see note on 1.730).

106. *exiled*: Cleopatra and her brother were engaged in a civil war, the circumstances of which she goes on to explain.

131–33. *reaps . . . spent . . . born . . . bought*: In just two verses and twelve loaded words, Lucan unpacks Cleopatra's sexual politics: she exacts, completes, and spends (all *exigit*) a night that corrupts (*corrupto*) her judge, Caesar; thus their peace pact is "born," like Caesarion. The Latin leaves it ambiguous as to which party has bought the peace and with what gifts.

139. *more decadent*: Latin *corruptior*; in Roman moral thought, decay, corruption, and decline went not with impoverishment but over-abundance and extravagant luxury. Since Rome under the Caesars had largely incorporated such conspicuous Alexandrian luxury, this entire scene works as a satiric foundation narrative for Neronian Rome. Cf. Propertius 3.13 on this theme.

144. *royal porphyry*: "Imperial porphyry" came from a single quarry in Egypt, Mons Porphyrites, the discovery of which in AD 18 is mentioned by Pliny (*Nat. Hist.* 36.11); Nero had a large ornamental basin of this porphyry in his palace (now in the Vatican), and it was also used for his tomb (Suetonius, *Nero* 50).

146–47. *ebony from Meroë*: The capital of the Kushite kingdom south of Egypt in what the Greeks and Romans called Ethiopia (modern Sudan), it had long been the center through which trade in valuable ebony wood from tropical regions flowed north ("ebony" is an Egyptian word).

155–57. *Tyrian dye . . . crimson*: The Phoenicians at Tyre processed murex snails into "royal purple" dye, which could range in color from pink to a deep purple; Pliny says the highest-prized hue was dark and gleaming, the color of "clotted blood" (*Nat. Hist.* 9.62). Crimson (or scarlet) dye came from processing *coccum*, a scale insect that lives on the kermes oak (*Quercus coccifera*), of the Mediterranean, but often thought in antiquity to be a berry (cf. Pliny, *Nat. Hist.* 16.12).

165. *heads tortured into shape*: Previous translations interpreted *torta caput* as somehow referring to hairstyle; but Lucan may well be referring to head molding, which was practiced in ancient Egypt and other parts of Africa, especially in light of the emphasis here on bodily mutilation, as with the eunuchs that follow (see A. Favazza, *Bodies under Siege*, 1996, pp. 86–87).

175. *Red Sea's spoils*: Pearls.

178–81. *Sidonian . . . Chinese weave*: Lucan probably means that close-woven silk, imported from China, was dyed in Sidon, then loosened locally to give it a new, lacelike effect. Such complex reprocessing of products is a regular trope in Roman discourse on luxuries: on the same topic Pliny says, "By such complicated work and from such distant lands is [silk] sought, so that matrons may shine through it in public" (*Nat. Hist.* 6.54).

181–84. *tusks . . . wheels . . . Juba*: Tables made from sections of trunk from Mauretanian citron trees, supported on elephant tusks, were all the rage in the early Empire. Cf. Martial's epigram on a writing tablet made from citron (14.3): "If our wood had not been cut in slender tablets, we would have made a noble burden for a Libyan tusk." After Caesar's victory at Thapsus in 46 BC, King Juba committed suicide along with the Roman general Petreius.

184–85. *desire for favor . . . frenzy of ostentation*: Here and at 197 the key word is *ambitio*, which means both "currying favor" and "ostentatious display" (and in other contexts, "campaigning for office" or "political corruption"); hence our "ambition," but the meaning is much altered. The passage ponders the psychology of *ambitio*.

192–93. *Fabricius or grave Curius . . . that consul*: Standard examples of early republican morality, stern, simple, and incorruptible. The last refers to Quintius Cincinnatus, who in 458 BC was declared dictator by a Senate delegation that met him while he was plowing his fields. For Curius see note on 1.184, for Fabricius on 3.169.

199. *gods of Egypt*: A dig at Egypt's deified animals.

202–3. *Mareotis . . . Falernian . . . Meroë*: More extravagant processing: instead of local wine, grown in abundance on vineyards around Lake Mareotis south of Alexandria, Falernian wine is imported from Italy and aged in the hot, dry climate of Ethiopia.

205. *flowering nard*: True spikenard was imported from India, and comes from the plant's roots, not its flowers; but several species of valerian (or more exactly, plants known by the name *nardus*) were harvested around the Mediterranean (see Pliny, *Nat. Hist.* 12.26), and Pliny says that crowns woven with nard leaves were considered "most sumptuous of all" (*Nat. Hist.* 21.8); adding to the confusion, Greeks also called lavender by the name *nardos*.

224. *Pass down those gods*: Lucan seems to play on the word *prodere* here, and at 242 below, which means both "transmit, hand over, publish" and "give up, betray": the transmission of cultural knowledge becomes implicated in betrayal to foreign imperialistic ambitions.

226. *Plato*: Reputed to have traveled and studied in Egypt like Herodotus earlier, but solid evidence for this is lacking.

231. *for the powers above*: This line just hints at the theme of Gigantomachy.

233–34. *my year . . . Eudoxus*: Lucan imagines (not implausibly) Cae-
sar already designing his reformed Roman calendar, promulgated
in 46 BC. Eudoxus of Cnidus (fourth century BC), the Greek math-
ematician and astronomer, studied for some time in Egypt and
applied astronomy to develop an eight-year lunisolar calendar sys-
tem. Given that Caesar's calendar has, with only slight modifica-
tions, endured to become the worldwide secular calendar, his
boast here has proven true.

239. *head of the Nile*: The cause of the Nile's annual flood and the site of
the river's source, unknown until the late nineteenth century, were
subjects of perennial speculation and exploration in antiquity, as
Acoreus makes clear at 330ff. Connecting the theme of the Nile
with the civil war and Pompey's murder, Pliny relates that the Nile's
flood was lowest in the year of Pharsalus, "as though the river were
showing its opposition to Pompey's death with a certain prodigy"
(*Nat. Hist.* 5.10.58); Seneca instead relates an absence of flood for
two years under Cleopatra (42–41 BC), a sign of her and Antony's
eventual defeat (*Nat. Quaest.* 4.2.16).

248–61. *To those stars . . .*: Compare the similar synopsis of planetary
characteristics at Cicero, *Nat. Deo.* 2.119.

250. *run opposite round the pole*: The *annual* motion of the sun east-
ward and the same *monthly* motion of the moon, contrary to the
westward motion of the fixed stars; the planets "wandered" in
both directions along the ecliptic, generally eastward like the sun
and moon but other times mysteriously westward (retrograde).

260. *Cyllene's son*: Mercury (Greek Hermes), born on Mount Cyllene
in Arcadia. If Lucan means he is lord of the Nile's flood, there may
be mythological syncretism with Egyptian deities, such as Hapy,
the deified river god, or Khnum, god of the Nile's source, whose
cult was at Elephantine (though Hermes was also normally identi-
fied with Thoth); the focus again on a "lord of the waters" at 267–
68 would further support this possibility.

261–72. *When that one holds . . . summer days*: Translating it into
Greco-Roman astronomical terms, and with some mistakes and/
or looseness, Lucan describes here the Egyptian system for reckon-
ing the beginning of the annual flood, which also marked the
start of the Egyptian year. The first of Egypt's three seasons, the
Inundation, began when the Dog Star, Sirius, the brightest star in
the sky, rose in the morning, observed from sites in southern
Egypt, which occurred soon after the summer solstice. The phrase
"stars of Leo mix with those of Cancer" means, roughly, around
and after the solstice; "night recoups the hours" indicates the

autumnal equinox. Lucan says more or less the same thing twice
more in what follows: 280–82: the Nile floods after the Dog Star
rises until the equinox in Libra, "the Scales"; 289–94: the Nile
swells during Cancer and Leo and wanes at the equinox. This
whole passage is closest to a statement in Pliny that he attributes to
a Timaeus (cf. *Nat. Hist.* 5.10.55).

274. *Ethiopian snows*: Ironically, Acoreus rejects the explanation closest
to being correct: heavy summer rains in the Ethiopian highlands are
responsible for the river's rise. Other ancient discussions of the Nile
flood include Herodotus, *Hist.* 2; Seneca, *Nat. Quaest.* 4.1–2; and
Pliny, *Nat. Hist.* 5.10. Herodotus, followed by Seneca, rejects this
explanation for the same reasons as Lucan (calling it "the most plau-
sible but furthest from the truth"); Pliny takes it seriously.

275. *Great Bear*: Arctos, the northern constellations of the Bears
around the celestial pole.

280–82. *before the Dog Star shines*: See note to 261–72 above.

289–94. *Leo's burning jaws*: See note to 261–72 above.

290. *Syene*: City on the southern border of ancient Egypt (modern
Aswan), at the First Cataract, and one of the sites at which the
Nile's rise was first observed.

295. *Mother Nature*: In Latin *natura parens*, a common metaphor also
much used by Stoics.

297. *westerly winds*: The Etesian winds, which blow in the eastern
Mediterranean in the summer. Herodotus and Seneca reject this
explanation; Pliny includes it among the most probable.

307–17. *air vents . . . salty waters*: Compare variations on these ideas at
Seneca, *Nat. Qaest.* 4.2.26–30, 6.8.3–5.

318–22. *Nor do we doubt . . . the skies feed on the ocean*: Stoic natural
philosophy held that vapors of moisture from earth were drawn
up into the heavens and fed the living spheres of the sun and
planets. Cf. Cicero, *Nat. Deo.* 2.40, 2.118: "by nature the stars are
fiery; they are nourished by those vapors from the earth and sea
and other waters, which come forth from waters and fields when
heated by the sun; these nourish and refresh the stars and the
whole ether, which pour them back and draw them up yet again,
and nothing is destroyed, or just a little, which the fire of the stars
and the flame of the ether consume." (The Academics' skepticism
at the theory is expressed in the same work, *Nat. Deo.* 3.37.)

331. *Egypt, Persia, Macedon*: Caesar is hereby associated with the
great, and mad, conqueror-explorers of the past, native and for-
eign. Caesar's successors, from Augustus to Nero, sent several ex-
ploratory and military missions into southern Egypt and Ethiopia;

Nero's expedition, traveling south of Meroë, returned after find-
ing nothing but deserts and impassable swamps (Pliny, *Nat. Hist.*
6.35.181; Seneca, *Nat. Quaest.* 6.8.3–4).

334. *Alexander*: He toured northern Egypt as conqueror in 332–31 and
undertook an expedition west to the oracle of Ammon, but did not
himself pursue a southern expedition (hence "sent picked men");
Lucan includes him here surely more for the symbolic purpose of
linking Caesar once again with Alexander.

339. *Sesostris*: A legendary early king of Egypt, whose exploits of
worldwide conquest entered the Greek and then Roman historical
tradition through Herodotus' extended narrative (2.102–10). He is
now generally considered a late composite of great expansionist
pharaohs of the Middle and New Kingdoms, none of whom con-
quered as far north as was claimed for Sesostris.

343. *Mad Cambyses raved into the east . . . long-lived people*: Camby-
ses II of Persia (sixth century BC), son of Cyrus the Great, con-
quered Egypt and pushed southward in attempts to conquer
Ethiopia, but turned back for lack of provisions. The story, includ-
ing the cannibalism, is in Herodotus 3.21–26. (Herodotus often
describes the king as a raving madman, and also emphasizes the
Ethiopians' longevity.) Lucan's "into the east" is an instance of the
general tendency of the ancients to conflate the Upper Nile and
Ethiopia with India and the East (partly because they knew that
Indian trade came up through the Red Sea); another, more ex-
treme instance is at 360 below, when Lucan strangely says that the
Seres (the Chinese) were the first people to see the Nile.

351. *expose*: The same ambiguous term as at 224 (see note).

354. *At the equator*: A happy accident, since the Nile in fact begins at
Lake Victoria, right on the equator.

355. *Cancer*: The Tropic of Cancer; Lucan probably means that the Nile
rises south of the tropic line (inside of what we call the tropics).

356–57. *Boreas . . . Boötes*: The north wind and the "Herdsman," a
northern circumpolar constellation.

360. *Seres*: See note to 343.

375. *Meroë*: Royal city of Ethiopia (see note to 146–47); Lucan imag-
ines that the famed Ethiopian ebony is a local product, though
much if not all of it was harvested and imported from elsewhere
(in the nearest vicinity, from Punt, probably the modern Horn and
lush East Africa).

379. *line that strikes the Lion*: Leo, the constellation of high summer,
when the zodiac runs almost directly overhead and only the slight-
est shadows are cast at noon.

380. *regions of Phoebus*: Ethiopia and southern Egypt were associated with the sun, for obvious climatic as well as religious reasons (syncretism with Egyptian solar deities).

387–400. *Philae, the gates . . . Abatos*: Philae and Abatos ("unapproachable" in Greek) are both islands, and ancient sacred precincts, just above (south of) the First Cataract, which also marked the border of Ethiopia and gateway into Egypt; Syene and Elephantine lie just below it, also considered the opening of Egypt.

403. *river's 'veins'*: Something like these rocks is already mentioned in Herodotus (2.28), and Seneca (*Nat. Quaest.* 4.2.7–8) briefly describes the rituals focused here when the flood begins. Lucan's next few lines are also very similar to Seneca's description.

417. *goddesses of vengeance*: Furies or Eumenides, agents of divine vengeance for bloodshed.

421. *drench the . . . city fathers in*: The senatorial assassins of Caesar in 44 BC.

427. *the example*: Of glorious tyrannicide, connected with the provocative name of Brutus.

472. *a consul*: Pompey was not at the time a consul, but was of consular rank.

492. *Lagus boys*: I.e., Ptolemaic troops.

493. *Romans serve themselves*: As Lucan notes at 503, Ptolemy's armies included many Romans serving as mercenaries—but even so, they have an opportunity to serve patriotic interests by attacking Caesar (though this motive is undercut by the narrator at 515).

507. *adapted to foreign customs*: Caesar also mentions and disparages the Romans in the Alexandrian army (*BC* 3.110).

530. *their party will win*: Lucan's rhetoric throughout serves to justify from a cosmic perspective Caesar's continuing victory: the Fates must let him win lest the Egyptians gain a ghastly glory, and so that he can meet the tyrant's death he deserves.

548. *line of troops*: From here through to its sudden end, the poem follows closely the last sections of Caesar's narrative (*BC* 3.108–12).

564–65. *Mulciber . . . Etna*: Vulcan (Greek Hephaestus), god of fire and metallurgy, with Sicily's volcanic Mount Etna conceived as his forge.

573. *Alan*: See note to 8.262.

576. *world is not enough*: Compare 5.375.

577. *Tyrian Gades*: Modern Cadiz, outside the Strait of Gibraltar, Tyrian because originally a Phoenician settlement.

587. *barbarous woman*: Medea, who took hostage and eventually dismembered her younger brother Absyrtos to elude capture by her father.

600. *tally of your crimes*: Caesar's account makes it clear that the peace envoys were put to death; since Lucan's text is more elliptical and less explicit, editors have suspected that a line that made the murder clearer has fallen out. Respect for peace ambassadors was generally considered part of "international law" (*ius gentium*), a sort of minimum common code of ethics that Romans imagined all peoples could be expected to observe.

602–4. *Thessaly ... Pharnaces ... Hiberus*: In light of Lucan's repeated and persistent condemnation of Thessaly, this is harsh rebuke indeed. Pharnaces II of Pontus rose to power by disreputable treacheries, and was swiftly defeated (*veni, vidi, vici*) by Caesar at Zela in 47 BC. Hiberus is the Ebro River in Spain (from which Iberia), mentioned here, probably, in reference to the civil-war campaigns waged there.

631–32. *rooftops ... caught fire*: This is the fire that, in later tradition, was said to have destroyed Alexandria's library, though that part of the story is almost surely a later embellishment.

644. *Pharos*: See note to 70.

646. *Proteus*: The island of Pharos was joined in Hellenistic times by a causeway to the mainland, giving Alexandria its characteristic well-protected double harbor; in the *Odyssey* it is named as the site where Menelaus encounters the shape-shifting sea god Proteus (4.351ff.).

656. *the death of Magnus*: Beheading, an unworthy death for Magnus, was apparently too good for Pothinus.

657–58. *Ganymedes, Arsinoë*: Cleopatra's younger sister, Arsinoë, infiltrated the army and had Achillas killed, then placed her eunuch Ganymedes in charge of the army.

669. *will not be avenged*: One final forceful foreshadowing of Caesar's assassination that insists on a key element in the Pompeian interpretation of the event as vengeance due for Pompey (despite the fact that Caesar did not kill him).

675. *glory for the ages*: For killing Caesar and putting an end to civil war—despite the preceding rhetoric, which this contradicts.

688–89. *Scaeva ... Epidamnus*: See 6.127ff., and note at 6.16.

Notes on Petronius, *Satyricon* 118–24

118. *Mount Helicon*: A mountain in Boeotia sacred to the Muses.

    I hate the vulgar mob . . . : Eumolpus quotes Horace, *Odes* 3.1.1.

119.1. *By now the conquering Roman* . . .: Eumolpus begins with a lengthy passage decrying Roman luxury, a theme that seems somewhat more appropriate to satire than to epic.

10. *Corinthian bronze* . . .: A list of luxury items favored by the Romans. The Arab nations were the primary sources of frankincense.

16. *African Hammon*: Hammon, or Ammon, was an Egyptian god later conflated with Jupiter who had a shrine in the Libyan desert at the oasis of Siwa. The wild beast in question is the elephant.

24. *Persian style*: The Romans criticized the practice of castration and eunuchs, considered a stereotype of Persian decadence (cf. Lucan 10.166–70).

32. *citron-wood tables*: Pliny the Elder (*NH* 13.29) mentions the wood of the citron tree, highly prized for its ornately patterned grain (cf. Lucan 10.181–84 and note).

41. *Lucrine Lake*: A lagoon on the Bay of Naples famous for its oyster farms.

43. *the waters of Phasis*: A river in Colchis, at the far end of the Black Sea, known for its pheasants.

50. *fearless courage*: In Latin *libera virtus*, "free virtue," potent moral terms in Lucan.

52. *dignity*: In Latin *maiestas*; see note to Lucan 8.779.

53. *Conquered Cato*: Marcus Porcius Cato, the Republican hero in Lucan's poem, is here contrasted with Caesar.

74. *Now Crassus* . . . : Marcus Licinius Crassus, along with Pompey and Caesar, was part of the First Triumvirate and died in 53 BC at the Battle of Carrhae. Pompey died in Egypt in 48 BC, and Caesar was assassinated in Rome in 44 BC.

79. *There is a place* . . .: The Phlegraean Fields on the Bay of Naples, an area with much volcanic activity. Eumolpus likely refers to

Solfatara, where there is a crater with sulfurous emissions and mud pits.

80. *Dicarchis and Parthenope*: The original Greek names of Puteoli (Pozzuoli) and Neapolis (Naples).

89. *Dis*: A Roman name for Hades or Pluto, god of the underworld.

113. *Tisiphone*: Along with Allecto and Megaera, one of the Furies, Greek goddesses of revenge.

114. *the blade of Sulla*: When dictator during the civil war in 82 BC, Sulla slaughtered the followers of his opponent Marius. Compare Lucan 2.70ff.

121. *Cocytus*: One of the rivers in the underworld.

131. *Philippi*: Perhaps echoing the matron's prophecy at Lucan 1.740, Eumolpus seems to telescope all the battles of the civil war from 49 to 31 BC. At the Battle of Pharsalus (in 48), Caesar defeated Pompey; at Philippi (in 42), Octavian and Mark Antony defeated Brutus and Cassius. The Thessalian pyres refer to Pharsalus, which is in Thessaly. The Iberian race refers to Caesar's campaign in Spain. References to Libya and the Nile denote Caesar's campaigns in Egypt. "Apollo's army in the Actian gulf" refers to the Battle of Actium in 31 BC, where Octavian defeated Antony and Cleopatra, vowing a temple to Apollo in the process.

139. *The ferryman*: Charon, who ferried souls across the river Styx.

152. *the Titan Sun*: In some genealogies, the sun, Helios, is the son of Hyperion, one of the Titans.

155. *Cynthia*: The moon, often conflated with Artemis (Roman Diana), who together with her brother Apollo was born on Mount Cynthus on Delos.

171. *abandoned Gaul*: Caesar had been campaigning in Gallia (Gaul, or modern France) since 58 BC. By crossing into Italy (via the Rubicon River) with his army, he technically started the civil war, as commanders were prohibited from doing so.

173. *a Greek god broke crags*: Hercules, on his way back from Spain after having killed the monster Geryon in Spain, was famously the first to cross the Alps.

183. *Hesperian*: From the Greek word for "west," a poetic name for Italy.

185. *Saturn's land*: Italy is often called the land of Saturn, as the god Saturn is said to have ruled there during an early golden age.

190. *while I stain the Rhine*: A reference to Caesar's campaigns in Germany in 58 and 55 BC.

191. *driving Gauls away from our Capitol*: In ca. 387–86 BC Gallic tribes sacked Rome, and all but the Capitoline Hill was occupied; Caesar suggests that the Gauls are planning to do so again.

207. *let fall the die*: The infamous *alea iacta est*.

212. *a Delphic bird*: The raven, sacred to Apollo, god of prophecy.

215. *Phoebus*: Here the sun, often conflated with Apollo.

240. *the very son of Amphitryon*: Hercules, whose father was Jupiter, was raised by Amphitryon, husband of Hercules' mother, Alcmene. Hercules had scaled the Caucasus to free Prometheus from his chains.

244. *the dying Giants' darts*: The Giants, a monstrous race born from Earth, tried to scale Mount Olympus but were defeated by Jupiter.

247. *the lofty Palatine*: One of the hills of Rome, a residential area that under Augustus became the principal residence of the emperors.

273. *the mighty Auster*: The south wind.

279. *Together with both consuls*: C. Claudius Marcellus and L. Cornelius Lentulus.

280. *bane of Pontus*: The kingdom of Pontus, ruled by Mithridates VI, whom Pompey defeated in 63 BC.

281. *the wild river Hydaspes*: Actually reached by Alexander the Great, this is greatly exaggerated; Pompey reached only as far as the Euphrates River.

282. *broke up the pirates*: Pompey was given authority in 67 BC to defeat the Cilician pirates who had been plaguing the Mediterranean.

283. *triple triumphs*: Over Iarbas in Africa in 81 BC, over Sertorius in Spain in 71 BC, and over Mithridates VI in Asia in 61 BC.

284. *the Pontic Sea*: The Black Sea and the Bosporus were places where Pompey fought against Mithridates VI.

299. *Erebus*: Another name for the underworld.

300. *Erinys*: Greek name for Fury; the Fury Megaera is named in the following line along with Bellona, a Roman goddess of war.

312. *Dione*: Usually the mother of Aphrodite/Venus, here Venus herself, whom Caesar regarded as one of the ancestors of his family. Pallas is Pallas Athena, or Minerva.

315. *Cyllenian Mercury*: Mercury was born on Mount Cyllene in Arcadia.

316. *Tirynthian Hercules*: Hercules was born in Tiryns; Pompey is here compared to Hercules for his wide travels and many triumphs.

324. *Tartarus*: The deepest and gloomiest part of the underworld.

325. *the Apennines*: The tall mountain range that runs down the center of the Italian peninsula.

335–37. *Marcellus . . . Curio . . . Lentulus*: Marcellus and Lentulus are the two consuls of 49 BC (above, note on line 279) who refused to bargain with Caesar; Curio is Gaius Scribonius Curio, a partisan of Caesar who joined him after Caesar was declared an enemy by the Senate.

338. *godlike Caesar*: An allusion to Caesar's later deification, when he was given the cult title *Divus Iulius*, "the Divine Julius."

343. *Epidamnus' walls*: Pompey fled with his army for Dyrrachium (also known as Epidamnus) in Epirus when Caesar pursued him to Brundisium.

344. *Thessalian bays*: A reference to the Battle of Pharsalus in Thessaly, where Pompey was defeated.

Glossary

Roman given names are alphabetized by the name that occurs regularly in the poem rather than the standard practice of using the *gens* name (e.g., **Appius** Claudius Pulcher, listed under Appius, not Claudius; Marcus Porcius **Cato** rather than Porcius, etc.), or occasionally a cross-reference is used (e.g., **Sextus**, *see* Pompey). The glossary is not exhaustive, but any minor item not included here, such as names mentioned once in a catalogue, is normally explained in the notes. Entries on historical figures who appear as characters in the poem provide birth and death dates, when known, and highlight their relationships with other characters.

Pronunciation: Accented syllables are shown with an accent, and a diaresis (ë) indicates two syllables (e.g., Méroë is pronounced *MER-oh-ay*). The following vowel pairs are normally diphthongs, pronounced as one syllable, and are accented on the first vowel: áe = *eye* or *ee*, áu = *ow* or *aw*, éi = *ay*, óe = *oy* or *ee*, éu = *you*.

Abýdos A town on the south side of the Hellespont, opposite Sestos (2.712, 6.61).

Acháemenid The Persian kings, including Cambyses, Cyrus, and Xerxes, and their empire, conquered by Alexander the Great; used loosely to mean Parthian (2.54, 8.264).

Achíllas King Ptolemy XIII's general who murdered Pompey (8.659, 758, 830, 10.435, 499, 528, 662).

Acóreus A priest of Memphis who tells Caesar about the Nile (8.577, 10.217, 241).

Áctium Southern promontory of the strait leading into the Ambracian Gulf in western Greece, where M. Antonius had

his camp during the sea battle of that name, which he and
Cleopatra lost to Octavian in 31 BC (5.515).

Ádriátic The enclosed sea between Italy and Illyria/Dalmatia
(2.430, 651, 661, 3.199, 4.424, 429, 5.404, 675), also
known as the Upper Sea (2.423).

Áegae A town on the Cilician coast, east of Mallos (3.238).

Aegéan The sea between Greece and Asia Minor (1.112, 5.674).

Áegis The "storm shield" of Pallas Athena, displaying the
Gorgon's head (7.178, 658).

Áeolus/Aeólian In myth, the minor god in charge of the winds
(1.482, 2.704, 5.669, 9.571).

Lucius Afránius Consul in 60 BC, commander of Spanish le-
gions for Pompey, surrendered to Caesar, fought at Pharsa-
lus but escaped, was captured after Thapsus in 46 and
executed (4.4, 357).

Agáve In myth, mother of Pentheus, king of Thebes; driven
mad by Dionysos, she dismembered her son with other
Theban women in a Bacchic revel (1.616, 6.398, 7.907).

Álans A nomadic Scythian people living north of Pontus
(8.262, 10.573).

Álba(n) The ancient town of Alba Longa and the Alban
Mount, southeast of Rome, seat of the old Latin League
and site of annual Latin Games presided over by Roman
magistrates during the Republic (1.215, 574, 3.92, 5.427,
7.464, 9.1227).

Alcídes The mythic hero Hercules (see also), descended from
Alcaeus (4.652, 660, 676, 682, 6.435, 9.455).

Alexander (the Great) Son of Philip II of Macedon, conquered
the eastern Mediterranean, Mesopotamia, and Central
Asia, inaugurating the Hellenistic period and leaving an
ambivalent example of imperialism for those who followed
(8.280, 9.186, 10.334; see also 10.1–64).

Álps The high, extensive mountain range that forms the im-
posing natural boundary between the Italian peninsula and
continental Europe (1.200, 237, 328, 330, 593, 734, 2.452,
564, 666, 3.315, 8.997).

Ambrácia The region north of the gulf by that name, in west-
ern Greece (5.718).

Ámmon The horned oracular god of Libya's Siwa Oasis, equated with Zeus/Jupiter (3.308, 4.706, 9.642, 648, 658, 719, 737, 10.47).

Amýclas The humble sailor who takes Caesar out on stormy seas (5.564).

Antáeus Earth-born Giant of Libya, killed in a wrestling match with Hercules (2.174, 4.620, 627, 643, 672, 678).

Antónius/Ántony (1) Marcus Antonius (consul 99 BC), a famous orator, friend of Marius, who turned against him, and who was executed in the civil strife of 87 BC, grandfather of (2) and (3) (2.128). (2) Marcus Antonius (Mark Antony, 83–30 BC) served with Caesar in Gaul and in 49 BC as tribune of the people defended his interests, fleeing to his camp when the Senate passed its war resolution; always a right-hand man of Caesar, he rivaled Octavian as Caesar's heir, with whom he defeated Caesar's assassins and divided the empire as a triumvir; he ruled the Roman East with Cleopatra until their defeat at Actium in 31; afterward he committed suicide in Alexandria (5.513, 10.86). (3) Gaius Antonius, younger brother of (2), as a naval officer for Caesar in 49 BC he was blockaded and surrendered, and after Caesar's assassination he was captured in Apollonia, Greece, by Brutus and later executed (4.430).

Ápis (1) The god worshipped at Egyptian Memphis in the form of a live bull (8.581 see note, 9.194). (2) A river of eastern Italy (2.429).

Apóllo Greek god of healing (see Paean), prophecy (especially at Delphi), and, as Phoebus, identified with the sun god (3.191, 5.73, 87, 162, 181, 204).

Áppius Claudius Pulcher (d. 48 BC) Consul in 54 BC with Domitius, and censor in 50 despite scandal and prosecutions for corruption as a provincial governor; wrote a treatise on augural discipline, was father-in-law of Brutus and Gnaeus Pompeius (2), and died soon after going to Greece with Pompey (5.70, 126, 163, 194, 234).

Apúlia(n) Region in southeast Italy, loosely including Calabria (the "heel") and Brundisium (2.644, 5.401, 431, 9.221).

Aquílo The north wind, Latin name for the Greek Boreas (5.662, 798, and elsewhere as "the north wind[s]").

Aráxes A river of Armenia (1.22, 7.223, 8.523).

Árgo In Greek myth, the very first ship, sailed by Jason and the Argonauts, to fetch the Golden Fleece from Colchis (2.757, 3.202).

Árgos (1) Chief city of the Argolid region of Greece, a famous center of myths of the cursed ruling house of Atreus (7.532, 10.75); ruled by Eurystheus in the time of Hercules (9.457). (2) An early city of Thessaly, called "Pelasgian Argos" in Homer (6.396).

Arménia(n) Mountainous region southeast of the Black Sea, including the Araxes River plain, often in conflict, and alliance, with Rome in the Late Republic and early Empire (2.628, 674, 3.257, 7.223, 332, 627, 8.259, 9.291).

Ársaces/Arsácides/Arsácidae (pl.) The dynastic name for the Parthian ruling family, the king is called Arsacides, "descendant of Arsaces" (1.118, 8.256, 275, 365, 492, 10.62).

Arsínoë Sister of Cleopatra and Ptolemy XIII (10.658).

Áthens Capital of Attica and chief city of Greece (2.648, 3.190, 5.53, 10.36, 226).

Átlas Son of the Titan Iapetos who holds up the heavens, identified with the Atlas Mountains of western Mauretania (1.595, 4.705, 9.816, 10.182); gave name to Atlantic Ocean (4.656).

Áugury/Áugur Roman divination, especially concerned with bird omens; the official augural college informed the Senate and magistrates on divine matters relating to auspices (1.643, 2.394, 5.422, 7.228, 240).

Áulis The port opposite Chalcis where the Greek armies bound for Troy were stalled by adverse winds (5.246).

Ausónia(n) An old poetic name for Italy that tends to evoke Virgil's *Aeneid* (1.234, 6.354, 7.39, 513, 8.1043, 9.49); Ausonidae = Ausonians (9.1236).

Áuster The south wind (5.620, and elsewhere as "the south wind[s]").

Bábylon A principal city of Mesopotamia on the Euphrates, successively ruled by Babylonians, Persians, Alexander, and Parthians (1.11, 6.56, 500, 8.265, 358, 517, 10.56).

Bácchae/Bácchant Women worshippers of Dionysus who experience divine mania (1.721, 5.77, 176).

Bácchus Another name for Dionysos, god of wine, madness, and inspired poetry (1.71, 9.543, 10.215).

Báctra City of Bactria in central Asia, modern Balkh in northern Afghanistan (8.357, 513).

Bellóna Roman goddess of war (1.604, 7.665).

Béssian A Thracian tribe living near the Black Sea and Mount Haemus (5.470).

Bistónes/Bistónian Used as a synonym for Thrace (2.173, 3.208, 7.654, 964).

Boótes "The Herdsman," a northern circumpolar constellation (2.763, 3.264, 10.357).

Bóreas The north wind (1.422, 5.589, 659, 664, 6.380, 434, 9.42, 524, 10.356, and frequently elsewhere as "the north wind[s]").

Bósporus (1) The narrow strait that leads between Propontis and the Black Sea, described once at 9.1188–90, and possibly meant at 8.213. (2) The Cimmerian, or as Lucan calls it, Scythian Bosporus, between the Black Sea and Lake Maeotis (2.613, 5.465, possibly 8.213).

Brómius A cult name of Dionysos/Bacchus, means "the roarer" (5.76, 8.988).

Brundísium Chief port city of southeast Italy, where ships embark for Greece (2.645, 5.398, 434).

Brútus (1) Marcus Junius Brutus (ca. 85–42 BC), raised by his uncle Cato, whose daughter he later married (divorcing the daughter of Appius Claudius Pulcher); he was an enemy of Pompey, who killed his father, but fought with him against his friend Caesar, in whose assassination he would be a key conspirator, his name having symbolic weight for his relationship to (2) (2.248, 262, 299, 303, 394, 5.215, 7.678, 689, 8.748, 9.18, 10.425, 497). (2) Lucius Junius Brutus (late sixth century BC), first consul and founder of the Republic, after driving out the last Etruscan king, Tarquinius Superbus; his name stands for the justice of regicide and the glory of republican government (5.215, 6.881, 7.46, 519). (3) Decimus Junius Brutus Albinus (d. 43 BC)

served under Caesar in Gaul and commanded his fleet at
Massilia in 49 BC, but still took part in Caesar's assassina-
tion and died in the subsequent civil war (3.536, 557, 581,
587, 788).

Byzántium Greek city on the European side of the entrance to
the Bosporus (9.1188).

Gaius Julius **Cáesar** (100–44 BC) Nephew of Marius,
son-in-law of Cinna by his first marriage, became a ponti-
fex in 73, allied himself politically with Crassus in the 60s,
enriched himself in war in Spain and triumphed in 60, al-
lied with Crassus and Pompey to gain consulship in 59,
then spent 58–50 plundering Gaul and devastating its native
peoples with war; his wish to stand for consulate in 49, and
its opposition by his enemies, precipitated the civil wars of
49–45; after being declared dictator for life and enacting
sweeping reforms, including establishing an accurate solar
calendar, he was assassinated in Pompey's theater by a large
conspiracy of senators on March 15, 44 BC, after which he
was deified (*divus*) by his heir, Octavian, and received offi-
cial state religious worship in his temple in the Roman
Forum (occurs throughout).

Calábria The jutting "heel" of southeast Italy (2.663, 5.404,
646).

Cálpe The Rock of Gibraltar, the northern Pillar of Hercules
(1.595, 4.79).

Cambýses II (d. 522 BC) Persian king, son of Cyrus the Great,
infamous for the mad savagery he exhibited when conquer-
ing Egypt (10.343).

Marcus Furius **Camíllus** (ca. 446–365 BC) A Republican hero
at an early stage of Rome's expansion, five times appointed
dictator, conquered Etruscan Veii, helped save Rome from
the Gauls, and was hailed as a second founder of Rome
(1.184, 2.574, 5.29, 6.876, 7.421).

Campánia Region south of Latium and Rome, early settled by
Greeks (2.416, 5.105).

Cámpus Mártius The Field of Mars, on the west side of Rome
between the city walls and the Tiber River, originally where
soldiers trained and mustered, but by the Late Republic al-

ready much built up, including with Pompey's Theater (1.197, 622, 2.236, 5.418, 7.360, 8.843).

Cánnae Apulian town where Hannibal devastated the Roman army in 216 BC (2.50, 7.482).

Canópus (1) A very bright star of the southern sky visible only in lower latitudes and thus prominent in Egyptian astronomy (8.216). (2) A port city in the Nile Delta east of Alexandria, long the center of Greek trade, and notorious in Roman times for a luxurious and dissolute culture (8.674, 10.78).

Cápitol The Capitoline Hill to the west of and overlooking the Roman Forum, the sacred citadel of Rome, site of temples to Jupiter and the end point for triumphal processions (1.310, 8.679, 9.95, 753, 10.77).

Cárthage Phoenician (Punic) city of northeast Tunisia, home of Hannibal, whose long imperial competition with Rome ended in its destruction in 146 BC and its becoming a Roman colony (2.97, 3.366, 4.615, 828, 6.879, 8.339).

Carýstos City of southern Euboea and site of marble quarries (5.242).

Cásius A sand hill near the Pelusian mouth of the Nile where a temple of Jove stood, and the grave of Pompey the Great (8.571, 661, 1060, 10.546).

Castália The sacred spring at Delphi (5.130, 195).

Cátiline Lucius Sergius Catilina (d. 62 BC), patrician leader of a conspiracy that planned a violent revolution in 62, ending in failure when Cicero exposed the plot and marshaled its suppression; he was defeated and killed in battle by the M. Petreius who appears in Book Four (2.570, 6.884, 7.75).

Cáto (1) Marcus Porcius Cato the Elder (234–149 BC), also called the Censor, a stern moralist known for, among other things, his constant refrain that Carthage must be destroyed, great-grandfather of (2) (6.880). (2) Marcus Porcius Cato the Younger (95–46 BC), "of Utica," for the place of his death, also a stern moralist after his ancestor's example, and a Stoic; inveterate enemy of Caesar; his suicide after Thapsus made him into a glorious Republican martyr (1.141, 340, 2.253, 262, 292, 295, 301, 359, 365, 404, 413,

3.173, 6.345, 9.19, 59, 115, 142, 201, 228, 266, 269, 277, 308, 363, 372, 462, 513, 559, 685, 697, 915, 930, 946, 1002, 1169, 10.497).

Ceráunia Mountains on the northern coast of Epirus, opposite Brundisium (2.662, 5.489, 719).

Cérberus Three-headed dog of the underworld (6.737, 804).

Céres Roman goddess of grain = Greek Demeter (4.402, 6.827).

Cethégus/Cethégi (pl.) Gaius Cornelius Cethegus was a ringleader in Catiline's conspiracy, and planned to murder Cicero but was discovered, condemned, and executed; he had distinguished ancestors, but his recent family was known for dissolute and profligate living (2.572, 6.885).

Chalcédon Greek city opposite Byzantium on the Bosporus (9.1189).

Chálcis City of Euboea, opposite Aulis (2.750 5.235, 245).

Charýbdis In myth, monstrous raging whirlpool deadly to sailors, in a narrow strait opposite the monster Scylla, identified in Roman times with the Strait of Messina (1.587, 4.485).

Cilícia(n) Region on southeast coast of Asia Minor; had been center of piracy in the eastern Mediterranean, but Pompey defeated and then engaged its inhabitants as allies of Rome loyal to himself (1.653, 2.628, 671, 3.239, 4.472, 7.263, 627, 8.30, 45, 307, 315, 555, 1001, 9.270).

Címbri(an) A Germanic tribe that migrated south in the late second century BC and, entering Italy, was destroyed by the army of Gaius Marius in 101 BC (1.273, 2.91).

Lucius Cornelius **Cínna** (d. 84 BC) Consul in the years 87–84, cooperated with Marius and his party against the optimates, whom Sulla championed upon his return from the East; Caesar's first wife, Cornelia Cinna, mother of Julia, was his daughter (2.575, 4.863).

Círrha The city below, and used as a synonym for, Delphi (3.181, 5.100, 118, 141, 6.454).

Cléopátra VII (69–30 BC) Daughter of Ptolemy XII, ruler of Egypt from 51 BC; she and her siblings waged civil war against one another, and Caesar placed her in power in

48–47, during which time she had his son, Caesarion. After his death, she secured a marriage alliance with Mark Antony, having three children with him and ruling the Eastern Roman Empire, until their loss at Actium to Octavian in 31; the bite of an asp took her life, ending a three-hundred-year dynasty going back to Alexander the Great (9.1325, 10.69, 76, 99, 135, 176, 442, 449, 458).

Cónsul The chief civil and military magistrate of Republican Rome, two elected annually by assembly vote, traditionally held to have begun with Brutus' expulsion of the last king Tarquin, they gave their names to the calendar year; in the late Republic the electoral system succumbed to rampant rigging and outright violence, and this along with the disturbances of civil war led, under Augustus, to the consolidation of consular authority by the *princeps* ("emperor"), who thereafter selected consuls himself, often with several serving throughout the year (1.193, 522, 2.80, 294, 595, 3.92, 112, 4.400, 5.7, 409, 417, 426, 737, 6.883, 7.505, 520, 932, 8.396, 998, 9.309, 10.193, 472).

Corcýra Large island off Epirus where the Pompeians stationed their fleet (2.659, 8.44, 9.35).

Cornélia Daughter of Quintus Metellus Scipio, first married to Publius Licinius Crassus (2), but after he died at Carrhae with his father in 53 BC, she married Pompey, which signaled an alliance with Caesar's optimate enemies; she lived on in Italy after Pompey's death (2.372, 3.25, 5.803, 813, 8.49, 477, 707, 715, 776, 781, 809, 909, 947, 9.59, 207).

Córus The northwest wind (1.441, 2.654, 4.73, 5.623, 657, 666, 7.148, 9.994, 1239).

Corýcian Near the Cilician town of Corycus there was a large cave where the very best crocuses grew for the production of saffron; one ancient author says it was also the bed of the giant Typhon (3.247, 9.1004).

Cótys A Thracian king, allied with Pompey (5.56).

Crássus/Crássi (pl.) (1) Marcus Licinius Crassus (ca. 115–53 BC), who enriched himself in Sulla's proscriptions, was consul with Pompey in 70 BC (but on poor terms with him) and a patron of young Caesar; the three joined forces in 60 to divide power in ways advantageous to each; in 55 he and his son left for war against Parthia, but they met defeat and death across the Euphrates at Carrhae in 53. (2) Publius Licinius Crassus (ca. 85–53 BC), son of the former, was married to Cornelia before his death at Carrhae.

Cúmae An eighth-century BC Greek colony on Italy's Campanian coast, north of Naples, famous, and important in Augustan mythology, for its oracular Sibyl (1.604, 5.190, 8.1019).

Cúria The Senate House in Rome, and by extension the Senate (1.286, 520, 5.10).

Gaius Scribonius Cúrio (ca. 90–49 BC) A tribune of the people in 50 BC and a persuasive orator who allowed himself to be bribed by Caesar for his support; when civil war erupted the following year he served as a military officer for Caesar, going to Sicily then Africa, where he first beat Varus, but then died in battle with Juba (1.290, 2.64, 4.613, 693, 723, 728, 768, 834, 851, 860, 5.41).

Cúrius/Cúrii (pl.) (d. 270 BC) Early Republican hero of the Cúrii claw, consul four times in the early third century BC, he conquered the Sabines and defeated Pyrrhus, among other achievements, and became a model of frugality and incorruptible morals to those such as Cato the Elder who idealized him (1.185, 6.877, 7.421, 10.192).

Cýnthia The moon, identified with Artemis of Cynthos, the hill on Delos where she was born (1.236, 2.609, 4.65, 8.885).

Cyréne The chief city of the Greek-colonized coast of Libya, often also used to designate the whole area, otherwise called Cyrenaica (9.369, 1082).

Cýrus the Great (600 or 575?–530 BC) Achaemenid Persian king, father of Cambyses II, who forged through military conquest and skilled administration the extensive Persian Empire, and who by Greeks was most remembered for his defeat of Croesus, wealthy king of Lydia in Asia Minor (3.299, 8.266).

Dácians A people living on and near the lower Danube, who farmed, mined in the Carpathians, and traded and warred with the Greeks and later the Romans (2.59, 3.100, 8.515).

Dalmátia(n) Region of Illyria on the Adriatic coast north of Epirus, a Roman province since the mid–second century BC (2.425, 5.403).

Dánube *See* Hister.

Décius/Décii (pl.) Publius Decius Mus, father (d. 340 BC, year he was consul) and son (consul four times, d. 295 BC) of the same name, were the models for the rare practice of *devotio*, vowing the lives of the enemy and oneself to the gods of the underworld, then dying heroically in battle; a grandson of the same name also died in battle, but tradition does not attribute an act of *devotio* to him (2.326, 6.875, 7.422).

Deiótarus King of Galatia and strong ally of Pompey (5.56, 8.245).

Délphi(c) Oracular shrine of Pythian Apollo at Mount Parnassus, in Phocis (1.70, 5.73, 77, 116, 173).

Díctator A Roman magistracy with sweeping executive powers, appointed in times of emergency (5.408, 737).

Dis Roman god of the underworld, Greek Hades/Pluto (1.488, 618, 6.481, 574, 714, 889).

Lucius **Domítius** Ahenobarbus (d. 48 BC) Consul in 54 with Appius Claudius Pulcher, became pontifex in 50, married to Cato's sister Porcia; he had a long history of opposing Caesar, to whom he surrendered at Corfinium, then resisted his siege at Massilia, before going to Greece and dying at Pharsalus; his son was among Caesar's assassins, but joined Octavian before Actium, and *his* son married Augustus' niece Antonia; as a consequence of these political and marriage ties, his great-great-grandson and namesake became the emperor Nero (1.506, 7.260, 694, 701).

Don See **Tanaïs**.

Dyrráchium The chief port city of Roman Illyria, earlier the Greek Epidamnus (6.16).

Elýsium/Elýsian In myth, the Elysian Fields were originally a paradise for elect heroes at the ends of the world, but in Virgil it became an elite area of the single underworld beneath the earth (3.13, 6.668, 774, 872).

Emáthia(n) A Homeric name for Macedon, and used to designate both it and Thessaly to the south; see note to 1.1 (1.1,

734, 4.272, 6.349, 369, 389, 644, 690, 915, 7.198, 227, 503, 792, 925, 931, 988, 1004, 8.40, 51, 224, 239, 249, 318, 398, 434, 650, 9.16, 37, 302, 336, 1178, 1258, 1295, 10.71).

Enípeus A river in Thessaly, tributary of the Peneus, flows past Pharsalus (6.417, 7.136, 266).

Ephýra/Ephýrean Old epic name for Corinth (6.63); applied to Epidamnus because it was founded by Corinthian colonists (6.20).

Epidámnus The older Greek name for Dyrrachium (2.660, 10.689).

Epírus Large regional name for northwest Greece, subdivided into many smaller regions (2.683, 5.8, 536).

Érebus The underworld (1.486, 2.324, 6.572, 705, 815, 824).

Eríctho Fictional witch of Thessaly (6.566, 712, 807, 922).

Erínys A Fury, a feminine chthonic spirit who exacts retribution for bloodguilt or carries out curses against evildoers by driving them mad; *see* **Eumenides** (1.613, 4.201, 6.834, 8.107, 10.73); *civilis Erinys*, "civil (war) Fury" occurs at 4.201.

Ethiópia(n) A broad term used by Greeks and Romans to designate the region and peoples south of Egypt (3.265, 8.1026, 9.647, 812, 10.274, 336, 361).

Étna Or Aetna, active volcanic mountain in eastern Sicily, in myth considered the forge of Vulcan/Mulciber (1.46, 584, 5.103, 6.324, 10.565).

Eubóea(n) Large narrow island opposite Attica and Boeotia; *see* Chalcis, Euripus (2.750, 5.203, 235, 240); also in reference to Cumae, founded by Euboeans (5.190).

Euménides The Erinyes or Furies known by their euphemistic name "the Kindly Ones," given their iconic form in the Aeschylus play of that name, concerning the purging of Orestes' guilt for matricide (1.616, 3.16, 6.737, 771, 803).

Euphrátes The western of the two great rivers (the other being the Tigris) that run through Mesopotamia (2.669, 3.268, 271, 8.251, 346, 433, 530, 10.41).

Éuripus "The strait" between Boeotian Aulis and Euboean Chalcis (2.750, 5.244).

Éurus The east wind (5.668, 9.526, and elsewhere as "the east wind[s]").

Éuxine *See* **Pontus** (9.1189).

Fásces Bundled rods combined, outside the city, with an axe, which were carried by attendants of high magistrates called lictors, and symbolizing their power for corporal and capital punishment, for which the rods and axes could actually be used (translated as "rods" or "rods of office," 1.194, 2.22, 137, 5.13, 414, 732, 7.504, 8.93, 10.14).

Fórum Any open space in a Roman city where city business was conducted, and especially the central administrative forum of a city; when capitalized it indicates the Forum Romanum in the center of Rome, below the Capitoline and Palatine hills, where the Senate House and the Rostra were (1.256, 347, 2.170, 4.840, 5.33, 6.360, 7.77, 8.89, 901).

Fury Latin *furor*, used throughout the poem, beginning at 1.9, to indicate the state of mad frenzy that causes and/or results from civil war; rendered also in the mythic image of the Furies (Latin *furialis*, "like a Fury," at 3.12, 6.727; *see* **Erinys** and **Eumenides**).

Gádes Phoenician settlement in southern Spain beside the Rock of Gibraltar; figures as the western limit of the world (3.293, 4.705, 7.222, 9.519, 10.577).

Gánges The river in India, which the Romans knew only by vague report; it is used as an eastern geographical limit, and tends to evoke the imperial eastward march of Alexander and the mythical conquest of the East by the god Dionysus (2.524, 3.242, 4.71, 8.267, 10.41, 311).

Ganymédes The servant and general of Arsinoë of Alexandria (10.657, 672).

Garamántes/Garamántian A name that appears from Herodotus on for a people living inland from the Syrtes in North Africa (4.354, 713, 9.460, 577, 640).

Gargánus A mountainous promontory in Apulia on Italy's east coast (5.402, 9.224).

Genúsus A river in Illyria, south of Dyrrachium and north of the Hapsus (5.495, 497).

Gétae A Thracian people dwelling around the lower Danube (2.59, 314, 3.100, 8.260).

Giants *Gigantes* in Greek and Latin, Earth-born monsters who lost their war against the Olympian gods and were buried beneath mountains (1.39, 3.332, 4.623, 6.323, 739, 7.174, 9.818).

Górgon *See* **Medusa** (6.833, 7.178, 9.808, 815, 820, 835, 847, 855).

Grácchi Tiberius (168–133 BC) and Gaius (154–121 BC) Sempronius Gracchus, would-be reformers whose assassination by political opponents began the century of revolution and civil war that ended with Augustus and the Principate (1.288, 6.887).

Háemonia(n) An old poetic name for Thessaly, which Lucan loosely and inaccurately associates with Thracian Haemus (3.201, 6.439, 484, 491, 535, 542, 656, 770, 853, 7.965, 1002, 8.2).

Háemus A mountain range in eastern Thrace (1.726, 3.206, 5.4, 6.640, 7.206, 563, 10.566).

Hánnibal (247–183/82? BC) The Carthaginian general who began the Second Punic War and invaded Italy, waging war on Roman soil for fifteen years until compelled to return to Carthage, where his armies were finally defeated by Scipio the Elder at Zama in 202 (1.32, 42, 330, 4.830, 7.932, 8.340).

Hápsus A river of Illyria south of Dyrrachium, between the Genusus (north) and Aous/Aeas (south) (5.495, 497).

Hércules Greatest hero of Greek myth, son of Zeus, known for his strength and fearless determination, not necessarily his wits; accomplished twelve labors, including slaying the many-headed Hydra and fetching the golden apples of the Hesperides; slew the local giant Antaeus in Africa, briefly held up the sky for Atlas, battled the Centaurs, and mounted his own funeral pyre on Mount Oeta, rising to Olympus to become a god; Stoics often adopted him as a model for their moral ideal of *virtus* (1.440, 618, 3.187, 292, 4.640, 663, 6.386, 393, 8.1, 987; *see also* Alcides).

Hespéria(n) Traditional poetic name for Italy, meaning "Land of Evening (West)" (1.30, 243, 414, 586, 2.63, 208, 337, 433, 463, 563, 644, 776, 3.5, 52, 5.127, 210, 578, 625, 764, 779, 896, 6.357, 651, 7.336, 475, 849, 8.225, 340, 422, 936, 945, 1019, 10.76, 468, 481, 567).

Hibérus The longest river in Spain (modern Ebro), which gives the peninsula its name, Iberia (4.24, 355, 7.16, 10. 604).

Híster Danube (2.54, 440, 3.210, 5.466).

Quintus **Horténsius** Hortalus (114–50/49? BC) A famous Roman orator, lawyer, and wealthy voluptuary, Cicero wrote a (lost) dialogue named after him that exhorted to a life of philosophy (2.348).

Hydáspes A major river of northwest India (Punjab, in modern Pakistan), whose waters feed into the Indus, where Alexander fought a major battle against King Porus in 326 BC (3.248, 8.268).

Hýdra The many-headed serpent monster of Lerna's swamps, killed by Hercules (4.666, 6.437, 9.805).

Hyrcánia(n) Region south of the Caspian Sea, which was also called the Hyrcanian Sea by Romans, famous for its wild animals, especially its tigers (now extinct) (1.355, 3.280, 8.412).

Ibéria(n) Another name for Hispania or Spain, from its river the (H)iberus (2.665, 4.11, 6.281, 7.274, 626).

Inárime The mountain under which Typhoeus is buried, identified with Italy's Mount Vesuvius by Latin poets (5.104).

Índus/Índia(n) The modern river and country of that name, which for the Greeks and Romans was a source of exotic import items, fantastic ethnographic rumors, and endless fascination (3.247, 8.412).

Iónian The sea between western Greece and southern Italy (2.660, 3.3, 5.675, 6.30, 404), loosely, including the Corinthian Gulf (1.111).

Jánus The double-faced Roman god of doors and gateways, for whom January is named, and whose temple doors were closed only in the rare event that Rome was not at war (1.64, 5.6).

Jóve *See* **Jupiter** (3.193, 3.333, 5.321, 6.520, 7.179, 234, 526, 8.544, 1060, 9.215, 546, 734, 830, 1121, 10.258); identified with Ammon (9.682, 700).

Júba King of Numidia, fought on Pompey's side, committed suicide with Petreius after Thapsus (4.701, 721, 727, 752, 5.59, 6.342, 8.538, 9.258, 373, 1076, 10.184, 602).

Jugúrtha (ca. 160–104 BC) Numidian prince whose contests with rivals to kingship led to Roman intervention, then a long war with Rome after 112, which Marius prosecuted to success, with crucial help from Sulla; Marius triumphed over him in 104 and afterward had him executed (2.96, 9.754).

Júlia (ca. 83–54 BC) Daughter of Julius Caesar and Cornelia Cinna, she married Pompey the Great in 59 BC to seal her father's alliance with him, died in childbirth in 54, and was buried in the Campus Martius by popular will against opposition by the consul Lucius Domitius Ahenobarbus (1.124, 3.11, 30, 8.124, 10.94).

Júpiter Father (*Iov-pater*) of gods and ruler of Olympus and the heavens (*see* Jove), lord of rains and thunder (*see* Thunderer) and god of the Capitoline Hill in Rome (1.215, 677, 707, 5.97, 6.474, 516, 9.641, 648, 728); related to and identified with the Greek Zeus.

Titus **Labiénus** (ca. 100–45 BC) Caesar's chief officer in his Gallic campaigns, he joined Pompey's side at the outbreak of war, fought at Pharsalus and in Africa, and died at Munda (5.363, 9.690, 710).

Lágus The father of Ptolemy I, the general under Alexander who took his body to Egypt and established the Ptolemaic dynasty, which ruled Hellenistic Egypt until the death of Cleopatra VII (1.730, 5.65, 8.539, 851, 990, 10.4, 105, 492, 520, 660, 668).

Latin Games The *Feriae Latinae*, or Latin Festival, an ancient festival celebrated annually by the consuls at the temple of Jupiter Latiaris on the Alban Mount (1.590, 5.430).

Látium The name for the region around Rome, in early times inhabited by the Latin-speaking peoples (1.215, 272, 2.208, 3.99, 5.428, 6.11, 8.258, 10.73, 525).

Léntulus (1) Lucius Cornelius Len. Crus, consul in 49 BC, staunch enemy of Caesar, was killed with Pompey in Egypt (5.17, 7.256, 8.394). (2) Publius Cornelius Len. Spinther, consul in 57 BC, captured at Corfinium and pardoned by Caesar, escaped after Pharsalus and died soon after (2.495). (3) Publius Cornelius Len. Sura, consul in 71 BC, expelled by the Senate in 70, was a leader in Catiline's conspiracy, for which he was executed in 63 and buried by his stepson Mark Antony (2.272).

Léptis The name of two cities on the North African coast: Leptis Magna, at the eastern side of the Syrtis Minor (probably the one referred to at 9.655), and Leptis Minor, near Thapsus (likely referred to at 9.1175).

Lésbos Large Aegean island, famous especially for early lyric poets such as Sappho; its chief city was Mytilene (5.802, 822, 8.48, 129, 156, 161, 166, 172, 240, 721, 785).

Léthe The mythical river of "forgetfulness" in the underworld (3.31, 5.230, 6.761).

Léucas A large island off western Greece outside the Ambracian Gulf (8.45), used to refer to the Battle of Actium, conducted offshore (1.46, 7.1018, 10.80); also known for its high, sheer southern cliffs (5.703).

Libúrni(an) Coastal region of Illyricum, north of Dalmatia, known for its distinctive swift galleys (3.555, 5.559, 8.46).

Líbya Desert region west of the Nile and Egypt, used by Lucan for all of North Africa (1.223, 274, 399, 534, 733, 2.75, 100, 173, 439, 3.73, 310, 4.612, 624, 635, 642, 644, 690, 702, 725, 774, 831, 851, 5.40, 58, 522, 6.68, 227, 241, 339, 754, 879, 912, 7.264, 271, 827, 932, 8.204, 321, 331, 539, 1065, 9.51, 142, 373, 439, 462, 470, 481, 506, 512, 514, 520, 527, 564, 587, 620, 639, 644, 653, 668, 687, 752, 775, 777, 783, 834, 862, 883, 937, 979, 1000, 1170, 10.46, 97, 162, 359, 406).

Líssus Port town on Illyrian coast, north of Dyrrachium (5.796).

Lyáeus A cult name of Dionysos/Bacchus, means "loosener, liberator" (1.721).

Maeótis Modern Sea of Azov (3.291, 5.470, 8.381).

Mágnus *See* **Pompey.**

Málea The southeast cape of Greece's Peloponnese (6.64, 9. 40).

Mállos A city on the Cilician coast, east of Tarsus (3.238).

Márcia Daughter of Lucius Marcius Philippus (consul 56 BC, and stepfather of Octavian/Augustus), wife of Cato who, after giving him three children, was married away to Hortensius, then remarried to Cato after the former's death (2.347, 365).

Mareótis A large lake on the south side of Alexandria that connected the city to the Nile (9.186, 10.202).

Gaius **Márius/Márii** (pl.) (ca. 157–86 BC) Leading Roman political and military figure, Julius Caesar's uncle, consul in 107, conquering Jugurtha in 105, and then consul continuously between 104 and 100 while he exterminated several troublesome Germanic tribes; he enlarged the army by dropping property qualifications; the last several years of his life were dominated by civil strife between his supporters and those of Sulla; he died in the year of his seventh consulship, after which his son Gaius Marius continued his struggles until 82, when as consul he was defeated by Sulla's armies at Sacriportus and Praeneste (1.623, 2.76, 86, 97, 105, 138, 185, 202, 241, 575, 4.863, 6.885, 8.322, 9.247).

Marmárica The desert region of Libya south of Cyrene, also used loosely by Lucan for desert North Africa in general (3.309, 4.713, 6.343, 9.1110).

Mars Roman god of war and founding god of the city as father of Romulus and Remus (1.274, 325, 334, 706, 709, 3.473, 4.26, 410, 611, 810, 5.71, 324, 5.800, 829, 6.271, 279, 290, 440, 643, 7.129, 175, 459, 655, 708, 856, 8.173, 10.256).

Massília Greek city on the south coast of Gaul (modern Marseille), founded by Phocaean colonists (3.323, 376, 4.273, 5.54).

Matínus A small hill and/or town south of Garganus in Apulia (9.225).

Médes An Iranian people centered in Media, southwest of the Caspian Sea, whose large but relatively brief empire in the seventh to sixth centuries BC was conquered and succeeded by the Achaemenid Persians; Lucan uses Medes as a loose synonym for Parthians (2.53, 4.715, 7.521, 598, 8.254, 357, 364, 390, 465).

Medúsa The snake-haired Gorgon with a petrifying gaze whose head Perseus severed and gave to Pallas Athena for her aegis (9.785, 792, 795, 799, 837, 872).

Megáera The name of one of the Furies (1.617, 6.813).

Mémphis Egyptian royal city at the head of the Delta (1.685, 3.234, 4.147, 6.500, 8.579, 665, 10.5, 335, 409).

Méroë Capital city of the Kushite kingdom on the southern Nile (4.353, 10.147, 203, 294, 310, 375).

Minérva Roman maiden goddess, equated with Pallas Athena (1.640).

Moor(s) The Berber Mauri of Mauretania, the North African region stretching from Numidia in the east to the Atlantic coast, which became a Roman province under Octavian (1.228, 3.310, 4.711, 824, 8.347, 9.374, 10.574).

Múlciber Another name for Vulcan, god of fire and metallurgy (1.584, 10.564).

Múnda Site in southern Spain where Caesar's legions destroyed the Pompeian forces of Gnaeus and Sextus Pompeius in 46 BC, the last battle of resistance to Caesar, during which Labienus, Gnaeus Pompeius (afterward), and some 30,000 soldiers died (1.43, 6.340, 7.804).

Mytiléne Chief city on Lesbos (5.877, 8.130).

Nasamónians A North African people whom Herodotus locates southwest of Cyrene and to whom he attributes the annihilation of the Psylli, described by Lucan as poor, nomadic, and living off the wealth plundered from shipwrecks on the Syrtis (4.712, 9.550, 556, 575).

Néreus An old sea god, Old Man of the Sea (2.753, 6.388).

Níle The river whose flooding nourished Egyptian civilization and prompted endless amazed speculation as to its unknown sources (1.22, 730, 2.438, 669, 3.209, 272, 4.146, 5.510, 789, 6.340, 528, 904, 7.973, 8.335, 544, 567, 580, 611, 644, 664, 686, 787, 993, 1020, 1023, 1051, 9.97, 156, 164, 190, 197, 330, 517, 881, 936, 1011, 1266, 10.10, 50, 65,

112, 196, 200, 239, 266, 269, 273, 280, 288, 295, 303, 312, 316, 322, 330, 335, 338, 342, 346, 351, 352, 392, 406, 518).

Nótus The south wind (5.589, 622, 669, 9.407, 525, and elsewhere as "the south wind[s]").

Núma Pompilius Legendary second king of Rome, after Romulus, credited with founding most of Rome's oldest religious traditions (7.467, 9.600).

Numídia(n) Region between Mauretania and the area around Carthage (Roman Africa), ruled during Rome's civil wars by Juba I (4.710, 758, 786, 7.271, 8.342).

Nympháeum A port just north of Lissus on the Illyrian coast (5.797).

Nýsa Mythical place in the east where the god Dionysos was raised (1.71, 8.268, 987).

Ocean Oceanus, the world-encircling river of early Greek geography, used in Roman times for the outer ocean, still poorly known, and as a synonym for "sea" (1.400, 445, 450, 2.602, 3.82, 293, 4.23, 89, 110, 146, 4.708, 5.189, 656, 680, 7.1, 8.351, 983, 9.521, 784, 10.45, 270, 315, 319).

Óeta Mountain in Trachis, just south of Thessaly, where Hercules mounted his funeral pyre to be cremated and become a god (3.187, 6.434, 7.529, 565, 943, 8.986).

Olýmpic Relating to the Olympian Games, held every four years at Olympia, in Elis, Greece (1.319, 4.645).

Olýmpus/Olýmpian Greece's tallest mountain, in northern Thessaly, where the Olympian gods dwell (2.5, 421, 5.4, 683, 6.379, 387, 532, 7.206); also used to denote the heavens as home of the gods (1.579, 2.286, 3.44, 4.31, 80, 670, 6.540, 7.561, 8.205, 10.249).

Oríon In myth, a mighty hunter killed by a scorpion and turned into a constellation (1.711, 9.1035).

Oróntes A river of northern Syria (3.226, 6.57).

Óssa Mountain in eastern Thessaly, south of Olympus and north of Pelion, associated with the Gigantomachy (1.423, 6.372, 387, 458, 7.209).

Páean Apollo as the healer, and his victory shout after slaying Python, thus especially connected with the Delphic god (1.724, 5.83, 85, 5.145, 174, 206, 230, 7.176).

Pállas Athena (Roman Minerva), maiden goddess of war, wisdom, and handicraft (3.215, 322, 7.178, 658, 9.438, 821, 830, 846, 851, 858, 1228).

Pangáea A mountain in southern Thrace, near Philippi and the Strymon (1.725, 7.565).

Párcae The three goddesses of Fate, Clotho, Lachesis, and Atropos (3.20, 6.867, 906).

Parnássus The sacred mountain below which the oracular sanctuary of Delphi is situated (3.182, 5.75, 80, 136).

Párthia(n) The Iranian and Philhellenic ruling group that controlled central Asia from the Euphrates to the Indus beginning in the mid–third century BC, whom Romans regarded as their inveterate enemies (as the earlier Greeks did the Persians), especially after Crassus' defeat at Carrhae in 53 BC; their royal dynasty was the Arsacidae (1.116, 249, 503, 2.582, 3.276, 6.55, 7.508, 8.263, 273, 278, 281, 331, 359, 388, 401, 406, 421, 427, 444, 456, 493, 520, 9.331, 10.57, 63).

Pélion Mountain in eastern Thessaly, south of Mount Ossa, associated with the Gigantomachy (6.374, 457, 7.564).

Pélla/Pelláean The Macedonian royal city of Philip and his son Alexander, used by Lucan to refer to all things Alexandrian, including the city and its kings, the Ptolemies (3.245, 5.62, 8.577, 745, 9.185, 1256, 1329, 10.25, 64, 68, 647).

Pelúsium/Pelúsian The city at the easternmost mouth of the Nile Delta (8.567, 665, 1020, 9.92, 10.65).

Penéüs The principal river of Thessaly, which goes to the sea through the Vale of Tempe (3.200, 6.416, 419, 8.39).

Péntheus Mythical king of Thebes and enemy of Dionysus; see notes to 6.399, 7.906.

Pérgamum A Homeric name for the citadel of Troy that Virgil recycled and passed on to later poets (9.1199, 1237).

Marcus Petréius Seasoned military commander in charge of Spanish legions for Pompey; committed suicide with Juba after Thapsus (4.4, 155, 221, 227).

Phárnaces II King of Bosporus who invaded the Caucasus while the civil wars raged, defeating a Roman army, but then was swiftly beaten by Caesar at Zela in 47 BC, the occasion for which he declared *veni, vidi, vici*, "I came, I saw, I conquered" (2.674, 10.603).

Pháros/Phárian The lighthouse tower of Alexandria; the adjective is used to mean Alexandrian/Egyptian (2.776, 4.274, 6.342, 7.805, 819, 8.219, 331, 538, 611, 628, 669, 681, 692, 704, 732, 751, 765, 838, 875, 9.1, 62, 88, 162, 171, 1245, 1252, 1264, 1323, 1338, 1359, 10.70, 79, 98, 105, 112, 158, 213, 221, 229, 443, 510, 644).

Pharsálus/Pharsália Thessalian town on the Enipeus River, near which the pitched battled between Caesar and Pompey was fought on August 9, 48 BC (1.41, 3.313, 4.844, 5.417, 6.347, 389, 640, 7.72, 207, 242, 480, 620, 729, 868, 909, 916, 963, 8.16, 327, 631, 9.285, 1219).

Phásis The river of Colchis in the Caucasus, where the Argonauts sail (2.617, 755, 3.284, 4.581).

Phémonöé ("prophetic mind") Name of Lucan's Pythian priestess, as well as the recorded name of the first Pythia (5.129, 193).

Phílip (1) Philip II (382–336 BC), king of Macedon who expanded his kingdom and conquered Greece, bequeathing his legacy of military expansion to his energetic son Alexander (10.25). (2) Philip V (238–197 BC), king of Macedon, defeated by the Romans at Cynoscephalae in 197, beginning the era of Roman domination in Greece (3.167).

Philíppi City in eastern Macedon, where Octavian and Mark Antony defeated the armies of Brutus and Cassius, avenging the assassination of Julius Caesar, in 42 BC (1.726, 740, 6.645, 7.682, 1019, 9.336).

Phlégra The site of the devastating primordial war between the Olympian gods and the Earth-born Giants, located in Pallene in Macedon as well as in the scorched volcanic landscape on Italy's Campanian coast (4.628, 7.174, 9.819).

Phócis The region around Delphi (3.181, 5.55, 149), incorrectly identified by Lucan with the Ionian city of Phocaea (3.273, 5.55).

Phóebe The moon, as Artemis/Diana, sister of Phoebus (1.83, 577, 6.559, 8.582, 9.1167).

Phóebus Apollo, especially in his capacity as the sun god; *see* Titan (1.52, 701, 723, 727, 739, 2.346, 436, 732, 760, 3.110, 215, 243, 440, 543, 4.135, 5.52, 76, 133, 141, 157, 177, 193, 232, 454, 589, 794, 6.367, 373, 411, 519, 7.253, 8.269, 572, 9.393, 660, 863, 1125, 1196, 10.310, 318, 380, 545).

Phóloë A mountain on the border of Elis and Arcadia where Hercules battled with the Centaurs, but which Lucan believes, or would have his readers believe, is located in Thessaly (6.432, 7.529) or Thrace (3.207, 7.967).

Phrýgia(n) Region in central Asia Minor, used by Virgil to refer to the Trojans, and so, too, in Lucan it is a synonym for Trojan, usually referring to the myth of Aeneas (1.213, 3.225, 9.51, 1208, 1225, 1228, 1236), once of the Phrygian Magna Mater, Cybele (9.358).

Píndus Mountain range on the western side of Thessaly (1.720, 6.357, 7.206, 564, 941).

Pléiades The constellation near the horn of Taurus whose clustered stars were, in myth, the seven daughters of Atlas, and a prominent part of the poetic and agricultural calendar since archaic Greece and Hesiod (2.762, 5.4, 8.1053).

Po The major river of north Italy, named the Padus and Eridanus in antiquity (5.299, 306, 9.935, 10.341).

Pómpey/Pompéius (1) Gnaeus Pompeius Magnus (106–48 BC), served in his father's army during the Social War and took over his legions on his death in 87, amid the chaos of civil war, prosecuting missions for Sulla and earning an unconstitutional triumph in 81; brought the long war with Sertorius in Spain to conclusion in the 70s, triumphing again in 71, after mopping up Crassus' victory over Spartacus; he was consul in 70, younger than normal and without having moved through the standard course of magistracies; suppressed piracy in the Mediterranean in 67 and conducted wide-ranging wars in Asia until 62, triumphing again; allied with Crassus and Caesar throughout the 50s, he eventually turned against Caesar and joined his optimate enemies in the Senate, leading to the civil war that took his life and ended the Republic. (2) Gnaeus Pompeius Magnus

(79–45 BC), elder son of (1), son-in-law of Appius Claudius Pulcher, in 49–48 commanded a fleet that harassed Caesar's ships off western Greece, after Pharsalus went to Africa, then Spain, where he mounted a massive army that was defeated by Caesar at Munda, after which he was executed (9.144, 176; 9.460). (3) **Sextus** Pompeius Magnus Pius (ca. 67–35 BC), younger son of (1), in Lesbos with Cornelia during Pharsalus, after his father's murder went to Africa, fighting at Thapsus, then joined his brother in Spain; survived Munda and continued to stage resistance to Caesar; during the proscriptions of Antony and Octavian, he took control of Sicily and made it a base for opposition, gaining a shaky truce with the triumvirs in 39 BC; hostilities renewed between 38 and 36, with notable successes, but after a naval defeat at Naulochus he was captured in Asia and executed (6.467, 923, 9.99).

Póntus/Black Sea The large inland sea northeast of the Mediterranean, entered through the Hellespont and Bosporus, also called the Euxine Sea ("hospitable"); Pontus was also the name given to the kingdom on its southern shore (1.20, 2.675, 3.290, 7.267, 733, 8.30, 213, 10.602).

Pothínus The eunuch regent for young Ptolemy XIII, architect of Pompey's murder (8.587, 10.118, 127, 413, 544, 653).

Psýllus/Psýlli A semilegendary people of North Africa who are immune to, and versed in magic to counteract, snakebites (9.1109, 1126, 1131, 1148, 1164).

Ptólemy (1) The hereditary name for the kings of Hellenistic Egypt, descended from Alexander's general Ptolemy I (8.856). (2) Ptolemy XII Auletes (117–51 BC), father of Cleopatra, Arsinoë, and Ptolemy XIII (3), in exile in Rome in the mid-50s and restored through Roman intervention; he named the Roman Senate as executor to his will (10.85). (3) Ptolemy XIII (ca. 62–47 BC) co-regent with his older sister Cleopatra, whom he and his advisors ousted; responsible for the murder of Pompey after Pharsalus, and upon Caesar's arrival waged an unsuccessful war against the Roman general and his new favorite, Cleopatra (5.60, 8.545, 589, 627, 646, 675, 9.332, 345, 1332, 1346, 10.537, 587).

Pýrrhus (319–272 BC) King of Epirus in northwest Greece who warred with Rome and invaded Italy but was finally forced to retreat (1.32, 3.169).

Pýthia(n) The priestess of Pythian Apollo at Delphi who delivers the god's oracles in a divine trance; the adjective refers to Delphi in general (5.139, 174, 6.455, 472).

Pýthon The monstrous serpent slain by Apollo before he took over Delphi's oracle (5.184, 6.453, 7.177).

Rómulus The legendary founder of Rome, who gave it its name, he and his brother, Remus, were sons of Mars, suckled by a she-wolf, and founded Rome as a settlement for convicts and outlaws ("asylum"); he killed Remus for jumping over the new city walls, and he himself became the god Quirinus (7.514, see also 1.101–5).

Rhámnus Coastal city of northeast Attica, with a famous temple of Nemesis (5.242).

Rhascýpolis A Thracian prince, ally of Pompey (5.57).

Rhíne Major river dividing Gaul from greater Germania, ancient Rhenus (1.497, 514, 2.54, 2.328, 601, 3.82, 4.125, 730, 5.279, 303, 7.510, 8.515, 10.163).

Rhódes Large Greek island off Caria to the south, sacred to the god Helios, a major sea power and center of intellectual culture in the Roman period (5.52, 8.294, 9.1242).

Rhódope A mountain in southwestern Thrace (6.688, 7.530).

Rhône The major river of southern Gaul, ancient Rhodanus (1.468, 3.537, 4.125, 5.280, 6.154, 531, 9.935, 10.341).

Riphâeus/Riphâean A mountain chain in the northeast, beyond the Black Sea, that was the notional and barely known boundary between Europe and Asia. Lucan and others make it the origin of the Don (Tanaïs) River (2.676, 3.286, 4.127).

Rods and Axes *See* Fasces.

Róstrum/Róstra (pl.) The platform for public speaking in the Roman Forum, adorned with the ramming "beaks" of captured ships (1.297, 4.840, 7.77, 359, 8.843, 9.262).

Rúbicon A small river in northeast Italy, north of Ariminum, the border between Cisalpine Gaul and Italy (1.202, 232, 2.526, 7.301).

Sadálas Son of a Thracian king, Cotys, ally of Pompey
(5.56).

Sarmátian(s) A people related to the Scythians and living
around and east of the Don River (1.465, 3.99, 211, 283,
297, 7.507, 8.445).

Sáson A small rocky isle off Epirus, across from Brundisium
(2.663, 5.716).

Scípio (1) Quintus Caecilius Metellus Pius Scipio Nasica (ca.
100–46 BC), his long name resulting from adoption, often
Metellus Scipio for short, an optimate leader, father-in-law
of Pompey after Julia's death, instrumental in passing the
declaration of war in 49; he governed Syria and brought its
legions to Pharsalus, from which he escaped to Africa and
commanded the resistance there, committing suicide while
trying to escape after the disaster of Thapsus (2.499, 6.343,
7.263). (2) Publius Cornelius Scipio Africanus (236–183 BC),
heroic general of the Second Punic War, luring Hannibal
out of Italy by invading Africa, where he defeated the Car-
thaginians (4.689). (3) Publius Cornelius Scipio Aemilianus
Africanus (185–129 BC) captured and destroyed Carthage in
146 BC, probably meant along with (2) at (6.878).

Scýlla The mythical monster that devours men and ships, in-
habiting a narrow strait across from Charybdis, identified
with the Strait of Messina (1.588, 2.456, 6.468).

Scýthia(n) The name Greeks and Romans gave to people(s)
living beyond the Danube, around the north of the Black
Sea and in the Caucasus; Lucan also uses it, quite loosely,
for the Parthians (1.20, 397, 477, 2.54, 442, 583, 613, 677,
3.91, 279, 5.465, 662, 6.362, 534, 7.512, 904, 8.213, 255,
361, 425, 524, 9.291, 518, 1025, 10.573).

Selínus A Cilician port city (8.310).

Séres The name for the East Asian peoples from whom the
Romans imported silks, generally identified with the
Chinese (1.21, 10.180, 360).

Quintus **Sertórius** (ca. 126–73 BC) A Marian leader in the
bloody civil discord of the 80s BC who became disaffected
and ended up staging a hearty resistance to Rome in Spain,
setting up an alternate state on the Roman model among

natives and exiles, but who after eight years was assassinated by an associate (2.578, 7.17, 8.998).

Séstos A town on the north side of the Hellespont, opposite Abydos (2.712, 6.61).

Séxtus *See* **Pompey.**

Síbyl of Cúmae Legendary prophetess believed to be responsible for the ancient Sibylline Books, kept in the temple of Capitoline Jupiter and consulted by a priestly college in times of crisis; made famous in literature through her representation in book 6 of Virgil's *Aeneid* (1.604, 5.143, 190, 8.1019).

Sícily Large island southwest of Italy, separated only by the narrow Strait of Messina, rich in history and myth because of its mixed native, Phoenician, and Greek population, a Roman province since the mid–second century BC and the principal source of grain in Rome before the annexation of Egypt by Octavian (1.585, 2.461, 3.64, 186, 5.105, 6.72, 908, 7.175).

Sícoris A river in Spain, feeds into the Hiberus (4.15, 141, 152, 355).

Spártacus The leader of a large-scale slave revolt in Italy, in 73–71 BC, that took the Romans two years and the combined armies of Pompey and Crassus to suppress (2.583).

Strýmon A river in eastern Macedon that comes to the sea near Mount Pangaea (3.208, 5.788).

Styx/Stýgian The underworld river, eldest daughter of Ocean and Tethys, upon whose waters the gods swear their oaths (3.14, 5.230, 736, 6.99, 421, 573, 577, 633, 707, 725, 735, 771, 774, 817, 837, 854, 7.201, 708, 894, 914, 956, 9.1037).

Súlla (1) Lucius Cornelius Sulla Felix (ca. 138–78 BC), the optimate leader in the civil war of the 80s, rose to prominence as an effective military officer under Marius in Africa and Gaul; as consul in 88 he marched his army on the city amid violent unrest, expelled Marius, then went east to campaign; his enemies took control of the city and outlawed him; he returned in 82, defeated the Marian armies, and, as dictator, enacted devastating proscriptions of the opposition, executing thousands and seizing their property, with the support of young Pompey, and reorganized the state to strengthen the power of the Senate; he laid down his power before he died in 78, and was buried with pomp and splendor in the Campus Martius (1.353, 357, 362, 622, 2.125, 146, 182, 203, 224, 235, 242, 245, 614, 4.863, 6.334, 877, 7.361, 8.29, 9.247). (2) Faustus Cornelius Sulla (d. 46 BC), son of (1), served under Pompey in his eastern campaigns and naturally took the optimate side in the civil war, and fought at Pharsalus and Thapsus, after which he was captured and killed (2.490)

Súsa Capital city of the ancient Elamites (third to second millennium BC), and continuing as a major city under successive empires, including Assyrians, Persians, and Parthians, for whom it was the winter capital (2.53, 8.516).

Syéne City on the Nile in southern Egypt (modern Aswan), at the First Cataract (2.619, 8.1051, 10.290).

Syhédra A Cilician coastal town (8.310).

Sýrtis/Sýrtes (pl.) Two shallow gulfs, treacherous to ships, on the North African coast: Syrtis Major, the larger, is west of Cyrene; Syrtis Minor, the smaller, is in the bend of the east coast of modern Tunisia (1.398, 534, 732, 3.311, 4.706, 5.522, 8.219, 539, 662, 9.375, 378, 389, 395, 403, 458, 465, 540, 552, 562, 693, 751, 888, 940, 1068, 10.47, 605).

Táenarus The central cape at the south of Greece's Peloponnese, believed to be an entry to the underworld (6.720).

Tánaïs The Don River, which runs into Lake Maeotis beyond the Cimmerian Bosporus (3.286, 8.381, 9.518, 934).

Tarcóndimotus A Cilician prince who fought on Pompey's side (9.265).

Tarpéia(n) A sheer precipice on the Capitoline Hill from which criminals were thrown for execution, used also to indicate the Capitoline generally (1.213, 3.162, 5.28, 320, 7.880, 8.1067).

Társos or **Tarsus** A city of eastern Cilicia (3.237).

Tártarus The murky depths of the underworld, where the Titans lay imprisoned (3.18, 6.722, 770, 792, 830, 873, 7.914, 9.121).

Taulántian A native Illyrian people (6.19).

Táurus (1) A long mountain range that begins in Pamphylia and Cilicia and extends northeast through Cappadocia

(2.628, 3.236, 8.303–4). (2) The second zodiac constellation of the Bull (3.266, 9.676).

Taýgetos Mountains west of Sparta in Greece (5.53).

Témpe Also called Hercules' gorges, a deep vale through which Thessaly's Peneus River passes before it reaches the sea (8.1)

Téthys A Titan goddess of the sea (1.448, 4.594, 2.621, 3.246, 4.81, 5.686, 6.73, 534).

Téutons A Germanic tribe that migrated into southern Gaul in the late second century BC with the Cimbri and was largely annihilated by Roman armies under Marius in 102 BC (1.275, 2.75, 6.284).

Thémis The Greek goddess of established tradition or law, a Titan and the original holder of the oracular shrine at Delphi, supplanted by Apollo (5.84).

Théssaly Mountain-ringed valley of northeast Greece, location of Pharsalus (occurs throughout; see notes to 6.371ff.).

Thunderer Jupiter Tonans, to whom a temple was built by Augustus on the Capitoline Hill in the 20s BC after nearly being struck by lightning while on campaign in Spanish Cantabria (1.38, 213, 2.37, 3.336, 5.100, 6.285, 7.50, 8.258, 9.4).

Tígris The eastern of the two great rivers, along with the Euphrates, that run through Mesopotamia (3.268, 272, 6.57, 7.510, 8.251, 9.446, 531).

Tisíphone The name of one of the Furies (6.812).

Títan The generation of gods before the Olympians, used by Lucan to designate the Sun, which in early Greek myth had been Hyperion or Helios, a separate god, but was later fully identified with Phoebus Apollo (1.17, 98, 449, 579, 4.61, 91, 6.372, 636, 829, 7.2, 497, 8.191, 238, 9.390, 477, 816).

Tríton A salt marsh lake in Libya, connected with Pallas (9.434).

Tritónis/Tritónia Epithet of Pallas Athena, connected with the number three (*tri*) but given various explanations in antiquity (9.442, 853).

Typhóeus/Týphon In myth, the monstrous child of Earth (4.625, 5.105, 6.100).

Týre Major Phoenician port city, south of Sidon (3.228, 5.112).

Tyrrhénian The sea west of Italy (2.233, 424, 5.674).

Útica Old Phoenician port city at the mouth of the Bagradas, just northwest of Carthage, and capital of Roman Africa, chiefly known to the Romans as the site of M. Porcius Cato's suicide after the Pompeian defeat at Thapsus in 46 BC (6.340).

Publius Attius Várus Pompeian commander who, after Caesar's march into Italy, fled to and held Africa as governor; he fought at Thapsus and died at Munda in 45 BC (1.493, 4.700, 750, 752, 8.343).

Véii Ancient Etruscan city conquered by Rome in the fourth century BC (5.29, 7.463).

Vésta/Véstal The Roman goddess of the hearth whose eternal fires were tended by the Vestal Virgins (1.216, 589, 639, 2.133).

Vúltur A mountain in west-central Apulia (9.224).

Vultúrnus An Italian river in Samnium and Campania (2.445).

Xérxes I (reigned. 485–65 BC) Persian king who crossed the Hellespont and invaded Greece with a massive army, was beaten by Athens at Salamis in 480, and retreated (2.710, 3.300).

Zéphyr The west wind (4.79, 5.619, 6.377, 9.523, and elsewhere as "the west wind[s]").

THE STORY OF PENGUIN CLASSICS

Before 1946 . . . "Classics" are mainly the domain of academics and students; readable editions for everyone else are almost unheard of. This all changes when a little-known classicist, E. V. Rieu, presents Penguin founder Allen Lane with the translation of Homer's *Odyssey* that he has been working on in his spare time.

1946 Penguin Classics debuts with *The Odyssey*, which promptly sells three million copies. Suddenly, classics are no longer for the privileged few.

1950s Rieu, now series editor, turns to professional writers for the best modern, readable translations, including Dorothy L. Sayers's *Inferno* and Robert Graves's unexpurgated *Twelve Caesars*.

1960s The Classics are given the distinctive black covers that have remained a constant throughout the life of the series. Rieu retires in 1964, hailing the Penguin Classics list as "the greatest educative force of the twentieth century."

1970s A new generation of translators swells the Penguin Classics ranks, introducing readers of English to classics of world literature from more than twenty languages. The list grows to encompass more history, philosophy, science, religion, and politics.

1980s The Penguin American Library launches with titles such as *Uncle Tom's Cabin* and joins forces with Penguin Classics to provide the most comprehensive library of world literature available from any paperback publisher.

1990s The launch of Penguin Audiobooks brings the classics to a listening audience for the first time, and in 1999 the worldwide launch of the Penguin Classics Web site extends their reach to the global online community.

The 21st Century Penguin Classics are completely redesigned for the first time in nearly twenty years. This world-famous series now consists of more than 1,300 titles, making the widest range of the best books ever written available to millions—and constantly redefining what makes a "classic."

The Odyssey continues . . .

The best books ever written

PENGUIN CLASSICS

SINCE 1946

Find out more at www.penguinclassics.com

Visit www.vpbookclub.com